INSTANT
BOATBUILDING
WITH
DYNAMITE PAYSON

INSTANT BOAT

BUILDING

WITH
DYNAMITE PAYSON

The Fastest, Easiest Way to Build 15 Boats for Power, Sail, Oar, and Paddle

HAROLD H. "DYNAMITE" PAYSON

International Marine / McGraw-Hill
Camden, Maine • New York • Chicago • San Francisco • Lisbon • London • Madrid • Mexico City
Milan • New Delhi • San Juan • Seoul • Singapore • Sydney • Toronto

The McGraw·Hill Companies

10 9 8 7 6 5 4 3 2 1 CCW CCW 0 9 8 7

Library of Congress Cataloging-in-Publication Data

Payson, Harold H.
    Instant boatbuilding with Dynamite Payson : the fastest, easiest way
to build 15 boats for power, sail, oar, and paddle / Harold H. "Dynamite" Payson.
        p.   cm.
    Includes index.
    ISBN 978-0-07-183674-6
    1. Boatbuilding—Amateurs' manuals.   I. Title.
    VM321. P325   2007
    623.82'02—dc22

                                                          2007001133

Questions regarding the content of this book should be addressed to
International Marine
P.O. Box 220
Camden, ME 04843
internationalmarine.com

Questions regarding the ordering of this book should be addressed to
The McGraw-Hill Companies
Customer Service Department
P.O. Box 547
Blacklick, OH 43004
Retail customers: 1-800-262-4729
Bookstores: 1-800-722-4726

A portion of Chapter 3 previously appeared in *Ships in Scale*; Chapters 7, 8, and parts of Chapter 5 previously appeared in *WoodenBoat*; Chapter 12 appeared in *Small Boat Journal*; and Chapter 16 appeared in *National Fisherman*.

Photos courtesy the author unless otherwise noted. Boat plans by Philip C. Bolger, for H. H. Payson & Company, unless otherwise noted.

To all the builders of small boats.

CONTENTS

INTRODUCTION

Instant Boats are easy-to-build boats designed by marine architect Philip C. Bolger. Built of plywood, glue, and common lumber, they go together with easy carpentry methods and a greatly simplified method of laying out and cutting the parts when compared to traditional boatbuilding methods. In spite of their simplicity, however, they are fine boats—strong, seaworthy in their intended uses, and often very attractive.

It doesn't matter where you live, or if you don't have access to fine boatbuilding materials or exotic fittings. Plywood and construction lumber are available everywhere that houses are built, and glues can be bought at most hardware stores or by mail order. People have built these boats in Fiji and Philadelphia, South Africa and South Thomaston, Maine (where I live), and in garages, living rooms, high-rise apartments, and outdoors.

In other words, *you* can build a boat—one you'll be proud of—and I'm going to show you how.

PLYWOOD BOATS

People started building boats with plywood almost as soon as modern plywood was invented, around the middle of the twentieth century. What made it possible was the invention of waterproof glues that would hold the individual plies together reliably. The first plywood boats were identical to conventionally planked boats—the builders just ripped narrow planks out of wide plywood panels and substituted them for the real lumber planking.

Pretty soon, though, folks started designing boats specifically for plywood construction. Instead of having individual narrow planks, the sides and bottoms of the boats were covered with broad panels. This made them "slab-sided"—in other words, the sides and bottom were curved in only one direction, because that's how a wide plywood panel bends naturally. While this precluded some of the graceful curves and complex forms that are possible with narrower planks, it did make "planking" the boats quite easy.

Under the skin, however, these boats still had traditional construction, and they required traditional boatbuilding skills and procedures. You still had to loft the boat—draw it out full size in three dimensions, working from the plans and a table of offsets. You still had to construct a fairly elaborate jig to build it on, and you had to do some serious and exacting woodworking to build the backbone (keel, stem, and sternpost), transom, and frames.

The Next Evolution of Plywood Boats

The next step in the evolution of the plywood boat occurred when some designers realized that the biggest "limitation" of plywood—that it would bend in only one direction—was really an asset. Once a plywood panel is bent in one axis, it becomes immensely stiff in the opposite axis. Boats, therefore, could be engineered as structures of curved panels and joined at the edges with very little internal framing.

Phil Bolger, who designed all but two of the boats in this book (the exceptions are the 12' Fisherman's Skiff, designed by Axel Gronros, and the Chopping Tray, which was designed by Woodbury Snow and is shown in Chapter 10, page 104), was one of the innovators of this kind of boat. His Gloucester Light Dory, also known as the Gloucester Gull, was designed according to this method. With no backbone, few internal frames, and relatively thin plywood sides and bottom, the Gloucester Light Dory is indeed light in weight. The uncluttered interior is easy to keep clean and easy to sand and repaint when necessary. She has been built thousands of times by amateurs and professionals all over the world. I built 117 of them myself, and I think she's one of the prettiest and best rowing craft ever created.

As good as Bolger's early plywood boats were, however, they still retained characteristics that scared off some amateur builders. You still had to loft them full-size. You still had to build a jig. And you had to "spile" the shapes of the big plywood panels—in other words, after you set up the jig, you would use it to make a pattern of the sides, then lay the pattern out flat and transfer the shape to your plywood.

After I had made a pattern or two, I realized that I could just keep reusing it and I'd never have to spile that boat again. Then I started thinking, "Why not make the pattern part of the boat plans so that *no one* ever has to spile the boat again?" Once I got to thinking, I just kept going. If you had the shapes of the plywood panels to start with, you wouldn't need a jig—you could attach all those panels edge-to-edge, with just a few simple forms to hold them in place, and that would define the shape of the boat. And *that* would mean no lofting either.

I got in touch with Bolger, and he agreed that an entire series of boats could be designed this way. While he was at it, he figured that he could make many of the angles constant along the entire length of the boat. This would make beveling chine logs and stems a lot simpler; things would fit together better with less skillful woodworking; and it would make bending the panels in place easier than ever. All in all, this new series would be the easiest, quickest-to-build group of boats ever. The series would be perfect for the amateur who wanted to build a good boat but who didn't want to spend years developing the skills to learn how to do it.

Just one hitch: I would have to build every one of Phil's new designs to make sure that the plans were accurate and the curves were fair. I took on this job eagerly, and the results showed up in my book *Instant Boats*. That's what Phil and I decided to call his new series of boats.

Tack-and-Tape Construction

Tack-and-tape is a construction method used with many of the Instant Boats. All of the earlier Instant Boats have chine logs—long pieces of timber that reinforce the seam between the bottom panel and the next panel up, which is either a bilge panel or a side panel, depending upon the design. In some cases, the chine log is on the inside of the joint; in some cases, it's outside. Either way, you apply glue to the chine log and then nail it to one of the plywood panels. Then you apply glue to an adjacent edge of the log and nail the other panel down.

On some boats, that chine log was all you needed for a good strong joint. On others, you'd want to reinforce the joint on one or both sides with a strip of fiberglass tape and polyester resin—the same stuff that fiberglass boats were built from. (These days, most people who build tack-and-tape boats use epoxy resin instead. It's more expensive than polyester but is stronger.) The nails, or "tacks," don't provide much of the strength—it's really the glue and glass tape that hold the boat together.

If you want to get really precise about the terminology, any boat built according to this method can be called a tack-and-tape boat. But only Phil Bolger's can be called Instant Boats.

Stitch-and-Glue

In the interests of an even cleaner design, even easier building, and even lower weight, some later boat designs (both by Phil and some by other designers) eliminate the chine log. This leaves you with an edge-to-edge joint between two panels of plywood and nothing to nail into except the other piece of plywood. Because this joint is usually on an angle, it's a bit tough to get your nails straight through the face of one panel and into the edge of its partner. And if you haven't cut out your panels right on the money, there might be gaps along the joint, making straight nailing even harder.

Stitch-and-glue to the rescue. To temporarily hold the two panels in alignment with each other, drill small holes near the edges of both panels, then pass short lengths of thin wire through the holes and "twist-tie" the panel seams together. These are the "stitches," which are taken out before the seams are glass-taped. (You can also use electrical "zip" ties.)

Something also had to replace the chine log to reinforce the finished joint, and it turned out to be a clever invention called a fillet. This is a mass of thickened resin (again, either polyester or epoxy) that's filled with a bulking or thickening agent and spread along the entire length of the inside of the joint. Before it hardens, it's formed into a smooth "cove" or concave shape with a simple tool like a big tongue depressor, an auto body putty applicator, or even a stiff ball or a lightbulb. Then it's covered with a layer of fiberglass tape and unthickened resin, just as in tack-and-tape construction, and the whole thing hardens into a nice clean joint that's stronger than the plywood itself. (The outside of the joint also gets a layer of tape and resin.)

This method has some other advantages. The stitches do a great job of pulling the panels together, even if there's some twist in the design (or maybe you cut one of them inside the line). No longer do you have to bevel the edges of the panels to fit flush against one another, because the fillet will cover and fill any gaps that remain after you've drawn the panels together with the wire. In fact, epoxy joints are *stronger* when there's enough of a gap between the wood for a lot of epoxy. And almost any boat that was originally designed with a chine log for tack-and-tape construction can be modified easily and successfully for stitch-and-glue.

There's a lot of overlap and flexibility between the two methods, and the terminology gets pretty fuzzy. You might use nails and fillets together and skip the stitches. If a design is accurately drawn, cut out, and set up, you might be able to skip nails and stitches altogether and hold the panels together temporarily with duct tape, or even masking tape, while the fiberglass-and-resin joint cures. I've known people who use hot-melt glue for the temporary panel alignment, too. If it works, why not?

What do you call one of these boats, if you build it without tacks and without stitches? You could call the building method *taped-seam construction*, in general. But let's call the boats in this book Instant Boats and accept the fact that the construction method is usually flexible enough to permit the builder to use a large amount of discretion and ingenuity.

ABOUT THIS BOOK

Like my second book, *Build the New Instant Boats* (also published by International Marine), this book covers all the basics of the Instant Boat building method in its first few chapters. This includes what kind of plywood, glue, and other materials to use; what kinds of tools you'll need; how to read and interpret the plans; and how to measure, cut, and assemble the pieces into a boat.

Then I'll move on to four building projects that are described in detail. I strongly recommend building a model of any boat before you attack it full-size, because it will help you understand how all the parts go together, and any problems can be dealt with simply and cheaply before you commit to cutting up large, expensive pieces of plywood. That's why I've presented an eighth-scale model of the boat Cartopper as a project.

Next, I'll show you how to build three real boats, full-size. The first is Payson's Pirogue, one of the simplest boats in the book: a 13', canoe-like craft that will probably get more use than just about any other type of boat. The second is Cartopper, a lightweight, do-everything skiff that rows well, sails well, and takes a small motor. You can build it just for rowing or fit it out for all three types of propulsion. The third boat that I'll cover in detail is Sweet Pea, Phil Bolger's thoroughly modern plywood adaptation of the traditional Maine peapod. A superb sea boat under oars, she sports a full-length removable keel and a rudder, and she sails as sweet as her name. Sweet Pea is a more involved project than Cartopper and one of the more complex boats in this book, but she's still far easier to build than any traditional, plank-on-frame boat.

You'll find some overlap between the detailed building descriptions for Payson's Pirogue, Cartopper, and Sweet Pea, and the more general directions in the earlier chapters. *If this is your first Instant Boat project, I recommend that you read the general directions before you delve into detailed building descriptions, because there's a lot of information in them that isn't covered in the building chapters.*

Finally, you'll see a gallery of twelve more instant boat projects covering a variety of types for just about any need. There are three dinghies or prams, a few rough-and-ready workboats, a day sailer, a vest-pocket sailing cruiser, a couple of speedboats, and a sort of Gatsby-era rumrunner on a budget. Some of these include brief sets of instructions called "building keys," and some of them don't, but in general, they're presented in less detail than the previous three boats to avoid excessive repetition and to keep the book to a manageable size and price. Because the building method never changes much, all the information you'll need is contained in the previous chapters. So even if you're not building Payson's Pirogue, Cartopper, or Sweet Pea, read those chapters anyway—you'll learn plenty that you can apply directly to these other projects.

Finally, together we'll make a pair of oars and discuss a variety of moorings on which to keep your boat.

All of the boats can be built directly from the plans in this book, although I strongly recommend buying the full-size plans (see the Appendix for details). I'll discuss this further in a later chapter, so here I'll just say that full-size plans are easier to work with and they're not expensive.

Stitches or nails? Chine logs or fillets? Full-size plans or build from the book? Power, sail, oars, or paddles? You'll make these decisions as you go along, and no matter what you choose, your Instant Boat will turn out fine. Let's build one!

PART ONE

INSTANT
BOAT
BASICS

CHAPTER 1

QUESTIONS, ANSWERS, AND FIGURING THINGS OUT

When I first began selling boat plans and giving out my telephone number, I was dealing with the unknown. On the one hand, I didn't want to sell plans and then run and hide, because I remembered when I had first begun building boats and would dearly have liked to ask a few questions. On the other hand, I feared incessant interruptions from people who wouldn't take the time to try to figure things out for themselves. What I feared most was phone calls in the middle of the night.

As it turned out, there haven't been all that many, but just a couple of nights ago, a fellow called me up. He sounded sober, and he asked, "Do you remember me? I built your light dory twenty years ago." We chatted for awhile, and the conversation continued like this:

ME: "Where are you?"
HIM: "China; your books are here in the Hong Kong library."
ME: "That's nice; my books are also in the library in Cape Town, South Africa. I like that. By the way, what time is it in China now?"
HIM: "It's in the afternoon here, 1:00 P.M. What time is it there?"
ME: "It's exactly midnight."
HIM: "You must be going to bed?"
ME: "I am in bed."
HIM: "Sorry about that. I'll drop you a line."
Click

But except for a few callers who have trouble with time zones, over the years I have found that most people are considerate, courteous, and appreciative of any help they can get. And the nature of their questions ranges from practical details to the philosophical.

WHICH BOAT SHOULD I BUILD?

Probably one of the hardest questions I'm asked is, "Which boat should I build?" My reply is usually more questions, starting with: "What skills do you have? What are you going to use the boat for? Where are you going to use it? How much time and money do you want to invest?" This last question is critical, because it often affects not only the builder but the builder's spouse as well.

In fact, the marital implications of boatbuilding are a frequent theme of comments in the chatroom on my website (www.instantboats.com). One example: "I'm going to build a boat as soon as my wife gives me my boat allowance." She apparently did, because he later wrote, "Your book made building this boat possible and has given me the confidence to take on bigger projects. My wife now believes that I can build more than a very large and expensive flowerpot."

And another: "To make a long story short, while separated from my future former, she dragged my Bolger-designed Sweet Pea to the road and put a 'FREE' sign on it. At least now I can build in peace."

So if you're married, the answer to the "what boat should I build" question is: Don't ask me! Ask your spouse. If you're going to use the boat together, make it a joint decision, leave me out of it, and go for it!

(The chatroom, by the way, has greatly reduced the number of phone calls that I receive from builders, because people answer each other's questions, make suggestions, and have a chance to show off their successes. It's a great resource, especially considering that I'm not much into computers and my wife, Amy, only checks my e-mail once a week or so.)

I will give you one more tip, however, on the subject of what boat you should build. Think about how many people and how much gear you'll have aboard and about the conditions of wind and water in which you'll be boating. Most of the plans show the boat's displacement waterline at a specified number of pounds, but this doesn't mean you can load the boat to this weight under all conditions and expect to get away with it. Once you've built your boat, try the weight loading cautiously and under different conditions until you know your boat's capacity and your own capabilities. But in deciding whether a particular boat has the right capacity for your needs, you'll have to make an honest assessment of your seamanship skills and your tolerance for excitement. I can't do it for you.

I'm not a boat designer either. Sure, I've built hundreds of boats, but I've designed very few, none of them recently, and none of them Instant Boats or anything like them. So don't direct design-related questions to me (hull modifications, structural changes, sail rig choices, etc.), because I just don't know. I build what the designer calls for. That way, if it doesn't work, I can blame him.

Nevertheless, some builders do direct design questions to me. Like this one from C.F. in Rutland, Massachusetts:

HIM: I'm looking for a rather specialized boat design. This October I paddled my 396-pound pumpkin across a pond in Rutland, and next summer I'd like to sail my giant gourd. I'm not sure if this is feasible, as I don't like to believe it has ever been done, but that's why I'm writing to you. My preliminary thoughts are to use a low square sail with a plywood deck that a wooden dowel mast would be affixed to. I may use a paddle for a tiller, as I don't think I can affix a keel. I might use outriggers for stability. The idea is to keep it *simple*. My goal is not speed, but to just travel from Point A to Point B. I know I wouldn't be able to tack; I'd be happy to just follow the wind. Please reply with your thoughts on feasibility and possible cost of your design.

    P.S. I'm giving away seeds. "If I can grow it, I can row it."

ME: I'm not a designer. As for the feasibility part, sure, people row and sail by here every day in giant pumpkins and gourds. Good luck to you.

    P.S. How about an umbrella for a sail?

WHERE DO I START?

A little girl of about six years old came into my shop one day and, spying all the boat models, she asked, "Where do you start?" I told her you start with the plans and that she had already started simply by asking the question and thinking about it. Start with the plans and by understanding as much about them as you can before moving on.

Common Questions and Problems

Since I go into the details of reading plans in Chapter 4, I'll confine myself here to some of the common questions and problems. For example, when a builder questions whether a measurement is wrong, I pretty much doubt it, having worked with Bolger over many years and having honored his request to "wring the plans dry of mistakes." Before I build a boat, I spend a few nights in a rocking

And they said it couldn't be done. Not an Instant Boat, this shapely craft took all summer to grow! (Photo courtesy Craig Fitzgerald)

chair looking hard at the plans in every way with my architect's scale rule in hand, building the boat in my head. Then, when I build the boat, I take note of any discrepancies (darn few, if any, even on the first go-round), and report these to Phil. Then he corrects the plans before he publishes them. I'm not saying that there are absolutely no errors, but chances are, if things go wrong, it's not because of the plans.

Often, it's because the builder has made certain assumptions that, if he had studied the plans and the building key carefully, he would have seen were wrong. When a customer who bought plans for the fast 18' runabout Diablo Grande called me saying that two width measurements from the centerline were wrong on frame C, I had my doubts. I pulled out a set of plans (and he had his), and we went over them. He said, "I drew a straight line between the two chines, and my measurements sure didn't match the ones shown." A check with my scale rule showed Bolger's measurements to be accurate. Well then, how could his be different? He drew the line where it was supposed to be and at the right heights shown on the plans, and he checked his measurements a few times. He was sure he had done it right. With both of us looking at the plans, it took me a few minutes to see what was happening.

Picking up my set of plans and looking at them nearly on edge solved the mystery. The line between the two chines, which the builder had assumed was a straight line, was in fact slightly curved. It appeared straight when looking down on the plans, but the curve showed up when looking at the plans from a different view.

This was a legitimate mistake that I can sympathize with, and I was happy to help him. But the fact is, many of the questions and problems that confront boatbuilders can be answered simply by taking more time to go over the plans and understanding what they say.

For example, there was the first-time builder who called up with a problem.

"I put the ¾" thick rub rails and chines on the sides just like the plans called for, but the sides won't bend around and fasten to the bow and stern transoms like they are supposed to."

Since the instructions for this boat call for the rub rails and chines to be installed after the sides are in place, I asked him why he had attached them first.

"I thought it would be easier to put them on with the sides laying flat on the floor rather than on the boat," he replied.

It was easier, for sure, but what he ended up with was thick laminations that were too stiff to make the curve. Bolger had a good reason for telling the builder to install the pieces in a certain order after all!

Well, okay. Even Phil makes mistakes occasionally, as I said. But perhaps the biggest mistake of all is doing nothing for the fear of making one, never testing yourself, never giving yourself a challenge. Don't be afraid to improvise and try other approaches. But if it doesn't work out, go back to the plans and see if you can figure out why.

When I first began working on Instant Boats, my biggest hang-up occurred when I was trying to build the 31' Folding Schooner. This was one unusual boat, and I had a hard time figuring out what was going on in the plans. To make matters worse, at that time I had never sailed, and I had no idea what all the ropes were for.

After the shock of trying to absorb the whole thing and beating on myself because I couldn't absorb it, sanity and composure returned. Changing my attitude from negative to positive, I decided to concentrate on what I did understand.

Then I saw that the schooner was really just two big skiffs connected together, stern to stern, by a huge deck hinge, so that one hull could fold over the other. Okay, I could handle that.

But what about all those ropes running everywhere?—peak halyard, stays'l halyard, throat halyard, jib halyard, topping lifts, backstays. It turned out not to be a problem, because the answers were right there on the plans in a numbered sequence, along with the keyed instructions. The plans even showed where the holes went in the masts, and in what direction. Here was a designer who understood what the "first-time" small-boat builder was up against, and who did something about it so that even the dumbest of us with no previous experience could build a boat to be proud of and get out on the water fast. Who could ask for more?

I live in the boonies in Maine, where a dog sleeps in the middle of the road, and I seldom see how other people's Instant Boats turn out unless someone pulls in the yard with one. Richard Lombardi, one of my summer neighbors, built a Diablo as his first boatbuilding experience at his year-round home in Nebraska, where he works as a lobbyist in the state legislature. (The 15' Diablo is nearly identical to the 18' Diablo Grande included in this book, only it is smaller.) During the building, Richard received no help from me, not even through a phone call. But he did receive lots of help, as you'll see.

One day I received a call from Richard, who said he was coming out for his annual summer stay at the family cottage, and he was bringing the nearly completed Diablo. My ears pricked right up. I was going to see firsthand the hows, whats, and whys of a first-time builder. But let my friend Richard tell it in a letter I received many years later.

Dear Dynamite,

It has been over thirteen years since I completed, with a lot of help from friends, two 15' Diablos Mr. Bolger designed. I understand that you are in the midst of another book furthering the Instant Boat system of boat building, and I want to share with you some stories that I hope might be useful as you continue to encourage people to "Just Do It" . . . "Build a Boat" . . . "You Can Do It."

When you and Amy [*the author's wife—Ed*] started this Instant Boat thing, you gave a lot of people permission to do something that they would ordinarily never have thought they could do. I am that case in point. I couldn't tell you a six-penny from an eight-penny nail, a jig saw from a Sawzall, or a thwart from a stem. But somehow, with a lot of support, we built these two boats that still ply the Muscle Ridge Channel in Penobscot Bay. Since you opened the possibility that I could build a boat, the only thing I needed to supply was the want-to.

The want-to came together on New Year's Eve thirteen years ago when, in the fullness of the moment, I struck a bond with a woodworker named Michael Herres. Come spring, after the adjournment of the Nebraska's Unicameral Legislative Session in June, we would build not one but two boats. I was to become forty years old and I thought this would be a fine midlife rite of passage.

We started exciting a number of folks whom we would later engage to help us during the construction phase. For me, at least, this project "took a village." I estimate that by the time we finished these two boats, I had enlisted the help of over thirty folks. This was great fun. People were really empowered by being part of this effort. It was one of many lessons that I was to learn.

Well, let me start at the beginning.

As newlyweds, my lovely wife, Pat, and I took some of our wedding cash and used it to buy a boat and motor. The motor gave us lots of trouble, so we sold the whole deal and used the proceeds to purchase a brand new 9.9 Mariner long-shaft outboard. Now we needed a boat to fit it. It didn't lake long.

We go to Pleasant Beach, in South Thomaston, Maine, every summer. Following in the footsteps of parents and grandparents before us, we play in the water. When we find ourselves in trouble, we call on Neil Payson [*the author's son—Ed*] or, as the family calls him, the Commodore. The Commodore is a lobsterman by summer, a math teacher by school year, but always a special friend and annual rescuer of my family's minor (so far) mishaps. In our small protected anchorage, we share a small rowboat with Neil that his father, Dynamite, made for my grandmother over fifty years ago. My grandmother always said that *Tige* was a lot like her: "flat on the bottom and wide at the beam." Generations of our family have learned to row in that boat. This is the kind of boat I wanted for my engine, just bigger.

I would be less than honest if I didn't say that the price was right. Two 15' Diablos cost less than $800. I do not underestimate the very real force of economics in boatbuilding, and Instant Boats are a real inflation fighter. The tool requirements are light, and usually you can find a person with tools who will be intrigued with what you are doing and might even help. The best investment is the full-size patterns for the Instant Boats sold by Peter Spectre. These allow you to draw the pieces of the boat on the plywood so you can cut them out. If you are math-averse, as I am, this allows you to reduce your measuring by 75 percent. The time saved here can be used later to assemble the boat twice because you didn't build the model that Dynamite told you to build before you built the real boat.

LESSON: Get the patterns. Build the model. Find a carpenter friend with tools.

Underwood, Iowa, is a small speck of a town on the rolling hills of Iowa where Interstate 80 cuts through. It occupies a large area of my psyche, however, because of the events that unfolded there in late June 1992.

After spending countless logistical hours beer drinking, talking, and actually building the hull and thwarts of one Diablo—only the seats and the rails remained—it was time to get this Diablo from the cornfields of Nebraska to the coast of Maine. The Commodore would help.

We picked up a used trailer and easily lifted the Diablo onto it. We made it snug with clothesline. As the sun set west of Garland, Nebraska, we began the Diablo's journey with an overnight in Lincoln, Nebraska. We departed in the morning for the 1,653-mile journey to South Thomaston, Maine.

The Commodore and I were "hot to trot." We stopped at McDonald's on the way out of town and immediately spilled the coffee that was made famous by litigation all over our laps. It was to signal events to come.

We got onto I-80, the Eisenhower Highway, outside Lincoln, and were on our way. A few glances back and we could see the boat was riding well. The car was pulling the trailer fine. I settled back and let the Commodore do the driving. The Commodore did, by journey's end, do most of the driving. The only thing he likes better than driving is lobstering off Muscle Ridge.

We passed the rolling green hills of Nebraska that sweep to the Missouri River as we crossed over to Council Bluffs, Iowa, and began the long, luscious drive through Iowa. The corn and soybean crop was well on its way . . . WHAM!

The Commodore looked in the rearview mirror to see the boat of a hundred hours of work do a 360-degree flip in front of a passing semi. I think the Commodore could see the eyes of the trucker when the trucker saw a 15' long by 5' wide piece of blond wood coming at him. The Commodore let out an expletive. I looked back to see the Diablo's descent.

Miraculously, the Diablo landed on its bottom in the breakdown lane, facing back toward Nebraska. Hearts pumping, we pulled the car over and ran to the boat.

Seeing was believing. We had almost killed ourselves and a Teamster, and I was staring at a boat that had done two 360s over Interstate 80 and survived almost entirely intact. The landing seemed only to have cracked some epoxy around the tops of the thwarts. This was all the more miraculous when I found out, after I had gotten the boat to Maine, that I had "starved the joints" (in Amy's words). By this, she meant that I hadn't put enough epoxy between the various pieces of plywood that were taped together.

We found every rope and tie-down in a two-county area surrounding the Underwood, Iowa, exit off of I-80. The boat and boat trailer became one, as did the Commodore and I. We made it safely the rest of the way. This "stress test" on I-80 did have the effect of building Pat's confidence as to the safety of the boat.

LESSON: Clotheslines are for clothes, not boats. Do not tie your boat down, up, to, or by a clothesline. It will break. I know.

As my friend Lynn says, only I would be lucky enough to finish off my boat in back of Dynamite Payson's workshop. Thousands of people have built Instant Boats, but my friendship with the Paysons allowed me to watch the daily parade of visitors who come to the workshop to visit and consult with Dynamite and Amy. During that time, in the final phase of construction, I didn't ask for help, and Dynamite resisted the temptation to offer, except when I was putting the rails on.

When you are a beginner, you are always scared of doing something wrong. Being scared makes you cautious, which can be paralyzing. I had reached that point in the bending of the rails into position when I confided my fear to Dynamite. His response was, "Rich—sometimes you just got to whump it." With that said, and after giving the rails a smart whack from a rubber hammer, they were put into place.

LESSON: When I have fear, a specific action can usually conquer it. Fear immobilizes. Action liberates. When confronted with a challenge, I have a voice in the back of my head telling me I should "just whump it."

Design-wise, the rails became the ultimate tribute to the sleek design of the Diablos. Standing above and looking down, people would ask me, "Did you steam the wood to get that bend?" And I would say, "Nah, sometimes you just got to whump it."

You autographed my copy of *Build the New Instant Boats* with the salutation, "Happiness is building your own boat." You were right!

Thank you for believing in me and all us other folks who have the audacity to build their own boats.

—Richard Austin Lombardi, your student

CHAPTER 2
MATERIALS FOR INSTANT BOATBUILDING

Plywood boats can last a long time. While writing this, I'm looking out my shop window at the Thomaston Galley, a 15'6" V-bottom designed by Phil Bolger for oar, sail, or power. It's now more than forty years old. I sold it when it was new, then bought it back a few years later because it rowed as well as the Gloucester Light Dory (which is saying a lot), and it was the only boat my wife would row home when the wind went down and the motor quit at the same time.

Her bottom was built of ¼" marine-grade Douglas fir plywood, fastened to ⅝" mahogany plank sides. She was sheathed outside with six-ounce fiberglass cloth saturated with polyester resin. She's been stored outside, summer and winter, for her entire life, and she's had good air circulation. She's free from rot, and I wouldn't hesitate to launch her for a sail or row.

I don't believe there is an inherent practical limit to the life of a properly built, glass-sheathed plywood boat. It doesn't matter how long they are in the water or out, left outside in the hot sun or buried with snow: These boats stay tight.

PLYWOOD

Grades of Plywood

A/B and A/C
Selecting plywood for boats used to be easy, because there were only a few grades to choose from: marine grade and exterior grade, the latter available in two qualities—A/B and A/C. They were all made from Douglas fir, and all were glued together with a waterproof glue. Marine grade was advertised as having no voids and, at that time, no patches either. A/B ¼" three-ply exterior plywood had two good outside sanded panels with a poorer grade in the center, and lots of patches. A/C ¼" three-ply exterior plywood had one good outside panel with patches, an interior panel with knotholes and voids allowed, and an outer unsanded panel, with more patches, voids, and holes allowed.

Since all these uglies could be readily seen on the outside, they were easily filled with a putty that the boatbuilder would make up from Fillite powder and polyester resin. (Fillite consists of tiny, hollow, glass spheres. It's used to thicken polyester and epoxy resins and reduce the weight and amount of resin required.) I never liked to use auto-body filler (e.g., Bondo), because it's harder than plywood, and no matter how much you sand it, it will always stand higher than the surrounding wood. To fill edge voids in plywood, tongue depressors slathered with glue are just the right size.

Most of the smaller Instant Boats call for ¼" plywood. Although I usually used marine-grade, I built many boats from ¼" A/B and A/C exterior plywood and never lost a boat, regardless of grade. A/C ⅜" exterior plywood, however, is another story. This is made in both three-ply and five-ply versions. The three-ply sheets have a thick core ply that is very prone to soaking up water, and this will cause the outer veneers to ripple or—worse—delaminate. So I stayed away from that material and used five-ply marine-grade wherever ⅜" plywood was called for.

Lauan Plywood
As plywood prices increased over the years, I began looking for alternatives. Then one day in nearby Camden, Maine, I watched Captain Paul Wolter, skipper of the sailboat *Palawan*, build a Bolger Elegant Punt out of cheap, three-ply lauan plywood. (Lauan, also known as Philippine mahogany, vaguely resembles true mahogany, but it costs far less and is generally considered not nearly as good a boatbuilding wood.) *Palawan* was owned by Tom Watson, the former chairman of IBM, and Wolter had sailed that boat all around the world for his wealthy client. So I figured he must know a thing or two and that he wouldn't willingly embarrass himself by drowning in Camden Harbor by his own hand, if he could help it. Since the price for lauan plywood was right, I decided to investigate further.

After repeatedly boiling and drying pieces of lauan plywood on my shop stove, I decided that the glue strength was fine but that the wood veneers themselves were not. The thin outer veneers, no more than $\frac{1}{32}$" thick, absorbed water like a sponge, got soft, and started falling apart. In my estimation, this disqualified it for any kind of quality boatbuilding. I've never built a boat from it, but I have seen some and patched some, and I would just as soon build a boat out of shredded wheat. But I'd rather have a boat than not, so if nothing else was available, I'd use it double thickness and cover it with ten-ounce fiberglass cloth for greater strength and longer life.

B/C Grade

B/C grade plywood is a lower grade than A/C but is still perfectly okay to use. Sometimes and in some places, it's available in southern pine, and in others, in Douglas fir. The prices are about the same, but the southern pine is slightly heavier and tougher-grained, and nails driven into the darker growth-ring areas cannot be set with a hammer blow in the pine, as they can with the fir. In order to prevent the nail heads from remaining proud, and thus spoiling the bond between the plywood surface and the fiberglass sheathing, it's essential to predrill and slightly counterbore the nail holes first.

When my son Neil needed a new boat for lobstering, we decided to build Bolger's 18' Clamskiff. We ordered fourteen sheets of $\frac{1}{2}$" five-ply exterior plywood and spruce porch flooring from our local lumberyard. But when it arrived, the five-ply exterior sheets turned out to be four-ply underlayment plywood. I heard somewhere this was not to be used for boats. But since the wood was there, my two sons were there and ready to go, and no one wanted to load the fourteen sheets back on the truck and take them back, I said, "Okay, let's do it."

The boat is now in its thirteenth year of hard use (Neil hauls 300 traps by hand from his boat from early spring to late fall) with no signs of plywood delamination, so I'd say that $\frac{1}{2}$" underlayment did the job just fine.

Okoume

Okoume, also spelled okume, or ocoume, is an African mahogany. It's available in waterproof plywood, certified to be free of voids. Peter Spectre and I taught Instant Boatbuilding classes for ten years at WoodenBoat School at Brooklin, Maine, and we used plenty of it, never having any trouble or seeing any voids in it. This is top-quality stuff, and of course you have to be willing to pay the price.

Meranti

Finally, there is a plywood called meranti, which is another Philippine mahogany very similar to lauan. (Some distributors say they're the same thing.) It's made as a marine-grade plywood, certified to be without voids and laminated with waterproof glue, and, as such, it should be a lot better than your typical exterior lauan plywood. I've never used any of it, but I am told it is harder, heavier, and stiffer than okoume.

Prices for Plywood

Here's how the prices for $\frac{1}{2}$" thick, 4' x 8' sheets stack up as of 2007:

Four-ply underlayment	$28
Five-ply exterior grade Douglas fir, A/B	$59
Nine-ply waterproof meranti, A/B	$75
Nine-ply waterproof okoume, A/B	$89

All the prices above are from the same plywood distributor, except for the underlayment, which is from my local lumberyard. Most lumberyards don't stock the more exotic species or certified waterproof panels. For these, you need to go to a specialty distributor (see the Appendix for some suggestions). Conversely, many of the specialists don't stock the construction-grade stuff. Prices fluctuate rapidly, and they vary considerably from one source to another, as does the privilege of picking the pile yourself to look for the best quality panels. Should you be lucky enough to be allowed to pick the pile at a local lumberyard, be sure to restack it neatly so as not to be turned away the next time.

BOAT LUMBER

Softwoods and Hardwoods

Pine, spruce, and fir—the common lumberyard softwoods—are all good for framing and chine logs. Cypress, which is often found in Florida, is another good choice, as is mahogany, an imported hardwood. I used to use a lot of our native red oak for rub rails and chines, but I found that it rots more quickly than any of the softwoods, especially in fresh water. If your heart is set on using oak, use white oak, which is highly rot-resistant but very expensive.

Spruce porch flooring, which can be found in most lumberyards, is about an inch thick and 4" or 5" wide for the average board. It comes in 20' lengths and is available with or without pressure treatment for rot protection. Don't use the pressure-treated stuff—its sawdust and sanding dust are dangerous to breathe, and the chemical treatment might impair its gluing properties. I have used the untreated porch flooring for the chines and rub rails on the 18' Clamskiff, where the long lengths saved me the trouble of having to scarf shorter pieces together.

Grains and Knots

When buying lumber, look for the straightest grain and fewest knots you can find. Straight grain is usually found in bigger, old-growth trees, and you are likely to find the best wood in 8" and wider planks. In fact, the wider, the better.

Sometimes knots are hidden and don't show up until the piece is sawed out. When this happens, and the knot appears on an edge of a piece that will be bent around the boat, like a rub rail or a chine, keep the knot to the inside of the bend. Likewise with poor grain: Keep it to the inside of the bend, and keep the straightest grain to the outside. Rub rails and chines are prone to breakage during installation, because the outer surface is in tension, trying to pull apart. Add poor grain or knots, and you'll just encourage them.

Bending and Cupping Problems

Sometimes, a rub rail or chine will break *after* it's installed—usually after it's glued and nailed on for good. So give them a fighting chance. If you find that the part doesn't quite want to make the bend, bend it as far as it will go willingly, then clamp it and leave it overnight. It will develop a "memory" for that part of the curve and from there will usually take the rest of the bend without your having to resort to using hot water or steaming.

Another common problem that's easy to solve is a board that is cupped and will not lay flat. In the summer, when your lawn is moist and the sun is hot, just lay the board on the grass, cupped side down. The moisture from the ground will swell its underside, and the sun will shrink its top, pulling the cup out in a matter of minutes. If you allow the board to dry out again, it will go back to its former shape, so watch the board, then grab it and nail it as soon as it's ready. In winter, put the convex side near your stove, and moisten the concave side. This will do the trick, but it's slower than Mother Nature's method.

FASTENINGS

Nails

I never use screws when nails will do the job. Nails are faster to use and are cheaper, and screws have the advantage only when you might want to take something apart later.

I use #14 silicon bronze ring nails and have a tray with four lengths of them: ⁷⁄₈", 1", 1¹⁄₈", and 1¹⁄₄". It's often not necessary to prebore the holes for #14 nails in softwood, but if you use larger nails, you will need to prebore. For #12 or #13 nails, a ⁵⁄₆₄" drill bit is usually about right, but since every job is different, and the toughness and dryness of the wood vary, you'll have to use your own judgment when to bore.

At about eight dollars a pound, bronze ring nails are quite expensive, but when used along with a generous application of glue, they create a joint so strong that you shouldn't ever plan to take it apart. I have tried to and have found that the wood destructs around the nail, leaving the nail in place.

For "quick and dirty" builders who don't want to pay the price of bronze, steel drywall ring nails can be substituted. When these nails are used with good glue, the joints will hold together for many years—but, of course, steel is more subject to corrosion than bronze.

Bronze ring nails should not be used for nailing plywood butt straps, because they can't be clenched. (Clenching is the process of bending the point of the nail back into the surface of the wood after it passes through. It's a good, strong way to hold two pieces of wood together from both sides.) They're brittle, and they'll break off when you attempt to bend them over, leaving a mess. Use #15 gauge copper nails instead: 1" is usually the right length. These smooth wire nails bend and don't break and are easily cut off and clenched over.

Screws

When it comes to screws, silicon bronze with straight slots are my favorite. I've used many boxes of 1¹⁄₄" #10 screws, as they fit all the standard oarlock sockets and are the right size for many other uses. The #10 size is slim enough not to split what they are screwed into, and they have plenty of holding power. Screw holes must always be prebored. Rub the screw across a piece of soap or paraffin wax to lubricate it before driving it in—it'll go in a lot easier and will be much less likely to shear off. When driving screws into plywood, countersink the surface only slightly or not at all. You want the heads to compress the wood and wind up flush with the surface.

GLUES

Of all the materials that go into a plywood boat, the choice of glue causes the most controversy. No matter what you use, someone will say, "If you use that stuff your boat is going to leak or fall apart," and he'll be glad to recommend something that works better. If you follow his advice, he'll take that as a vote in his column and he'll feel much better about himself.

In reality, I'm not that much concerned about glue selection, since all of the usual choices seem to work just fine. The way I see it, you can use Weldwood plastic resin glue, resorcinol glue, epoxy, and a new polyurethane glue called Gorilla Glue. I don't recommend the use of glues that come in cartridges, such as Sika Corporation's Sikaflex and 3M 5200. They have adequate strength, but they get all over the place, making cleanup very difficult.

Weldwood Plastic Resin Glue

I was brought up on the old-fashioned Weldwood plastic resin, and I never had any glue failures. I've used hundreds of gallons of polyester to stick fiberglass cloth to Instant Boats, and it works great. The epoxy glues available today are better still, and I'm all for them, but how much strength do you need?

A useful perspective comes from an old friend, Brian Amato, from Traverse City, Michigan. Brian writes:

> I'm fifty-eight years old. Back in the late '50s, my brother Dave used to build boats all the time. I learned to water ski behind a plywood runabout he built from a kit. We had never heard of epoxy resin or fiberglass cloth, let alone painting resin on our boats or taping seams. We just

used good ol' Weldwood brown powder and brass screws—built that sucker and painted it up and threw it in the water. I don't remember that we ever had any leaks to speak of.

Brian also mentioned that the aeronautical club of which he was a member used the stuff to build airplane propellers, and that none of them had come apart in the air.

Weldwood plastic resin glue comes as a brown powder that you mix with water to the consistency of heavy cream. Mixing it too thin or spreading it too thin will make glue failure likely. How much glue is enough? When you clamp or fasten the joint, glue should be forced out of the seam. If it's not, you've likely "starved" the joint. The wood may have absorbed too much of the glue, and there's not enough left in between the pieces to do the job.

Weldwood plastic resin glue has very low toxicity, it's easy to work with, and cleanup is easy, requiring just water. There's no need to use fillers: If you want it thicker, just add less water. The only fault that I'm aware of is that it is somewhat brittle. But as long as you use enough of it, this isn't a problem for any of the small boats in this book. This applies to all glued joints. Use plenty of glue, drive fasteners when called for, and rest peacefully.

Resorcinal, Epoxy, and Polyester Resin

I was interested in Brian's comment about using plastic resin glue for airplane propellers. During World War I, props were glued with casein glue, made from milk protein. These props didn't last very long . . . and neither did the pilots. During World War II, resorcinol glue came in use. This is a two-part glue made of powder and a hardener. When mixed, its color is beet red, and is said to be non-gap-filling. But to this day,

Weldwood plastic resin glue, from DAP, is sold as a dry powder that is mixed with water.

props are made from it by certified prop makers. Why not epoxy? Because epoxy becomes soft when heated, and I suppose a wooden prop does become heated as fast as it turns and under some conditions. (Boatbuilders need not worry, since a boat is not likely to heat up that much.) Interestingly enough, wooden propellers are rotated to the horizontal position when a plane is left in the open uncovered. This is so any accumulated moisture is distributed the length of the prop, rather than at its tip, which might throw it out of balance.

Resorcinol

Resorcinol is a two-part glue, consisting of a liquid resin and a powdered catalyst that have to be mixed together. I've used a lot of it for scarfing plywood. It's not gap-filling, the way epoxy is when used with a filler, but it's always worked fine for me, even with my less-than-perfect joints. A few minutes after the components are mixed, a skin begins to form on the surface. I just stir this in, get the glue on the joint fast, and never worry about it. Sometimes I use the skinned portion to fill slight gaps.

Epoxy

Epoxy is another two-part glue, consisting of a liquid resin and a liquid hardener. There is no question in my mind that epoxy is excellent for gluing and that it's the best choice for sheathing your boat with fiberglass cloth. It's tougher and better for both uses than polyester resin, and it comes in many formulations for different curing times. Some brands use a 1:1 ratio between the resin and the hardener, while others use different proportions. My preference is for epoxy that uses a 1:1 ratio in which precise measuring is not absolutely critical. If you use anything but a 1:1 formulation, you pretty much have to buy the manufacturer's specially calibrated pumps to make sure you get it right. These pumps aren't expensive, but if they're used only sporadically, they may get clogged up and might not give accurate measures.

As of this writing, epoxy sells for ninety-three dollars per gallon with hardener.

Epoxy Fillers

Fillers reduce the amount, weight, and cost of epoxy required, make sanding easier, allow the epoxy to be used to fill gaps, and make it possible to apply epoxy in significant thickness. Although the epoxy manufacturers offer a wide variety of agents, my favorites are Fillite powder and Cab-o-Sil, both from Eager Plastics, Inc. Cab-o-Sil, a "fumed silica" that is 94 percent air by volume (you might call it a "bulking" agent rather than a "filler"), is extraordinarily light and, when mixed with the epoxy, it makes a very smooth mixture. Fillite is composed of tiny, hollow silicate spheres known as microballoons. It's a little coarser than Cab-o-Sil, but by no means too coarse to produce a nice finish, and it sands very easily.

Curing of Epoxy

Some epoxies, when cured, leave an "amine blush"—a waxy surface that will prevent paints from drying if they're applied over it. The blush has to be washed off before sanding. Some epoxies don't leave this blush, so if you want to avoid the trouble, shop around carefully.

Exposure to Epoxy

Excessive exposure to epoxy can result in a severe sensitivity, which is like a really bad allergic reaction. There's a good chance that you'll avoid this if you build only one or two boats, but once you become sensitized, you'll never be able to work with epoxy again. Therefore, use the stuff with care. Always wear rubber or plastic gloves when applying it. When sanding, make sure there is adequate ventilation and wear a good dust mask. If you do get some on you, don't wash with acetone or lacquer thinner, as this will drive the chemicals right into your skin. I use Boraxo powdered hand soap to wash up and lacquer thinner to clean my tools.

Polyester Resin

Polyester resin shouldn't be used for gluing wood together, but it works fine for applying fiberglass sheathing on small boats. I've also used it successfully for the fillets to join plywood panels together in stitch-and-glue construction, treating it just like epoxy and thickening it with the same fillers.

I use polyester resin because I'm used to it, it's far cheaper than epoxy, it's more than adequate for the job, and I've learned how to doctor it to suit my needs. If you'd prefer to use epoxy resin on your boat, go for it, but be sure to follow the product instructions carefully; it's a little more temperamental than polyester, but it will do a good job.

At this writing, polyester resin sells for about eighteen dollars per gallon with hardener.

Laminating Resin

When I use polyester as an adhesive for cloth, I use a thin "laminating" or layup resin, the waxless polyester resin found in most boatyards, because the absence of wax in the resin keeps the surface ready for more bonding without further prep work. I can stop work and even go off sailing for the rest of the day, then get back to work on the boat the next morning without having to sand everything first.

Finishing Resin

Thicker "finishing" or "surfacing" resin contains wax, and even a half-hour pause on a warm day will cause the wax to float to the surface as the resin cures. Thus, your bonding surface will be lost until the wax is removed by sanding. I always use this waxed finishing resin for my final coats on the boat so that I can sand everything smooth for painting. Laminating resin doesn't sand as well. Although you can smooth the selvedge edges of 'glass cloth with coarse 20-grit sandpaper in a slow-turning, variable-speed drill after the resin is cured, I've never had any luck sanding large areas of laminating resin-coated cloth with a high-speed vibrating or belt sander; the sandpaper loads up too quickly. If you need to smooth things up with some sanding, take the time to apply a coat of finishing resin first.

Surfacing resin is more readily available off the shelf in hardware stores than laminating resin, but it is more expensive. As a less costly alternative, you can add a liquid wax surfacing agent to the laminating resin, which improves its "sandability." I use about a tablespoon of agent to a pint of resin to provide the wax for the last coats. To help them blend, warm the resin and the surfacing agent slightly (if it is somewhat solid) until the solution is as clear as water. Let the resin cool before adding hardener, or it will set up too quickly.

Like epoxy, you'll need to add some kind of filler to bulk up the polyester for making fillets and filling gaps.

Gorilla Glue

Finally, there's Gorilla Glue. This urethane glue hasn't been on the market very long, but it is fast becoming popular with less-than-skilled builders because it expands, filling

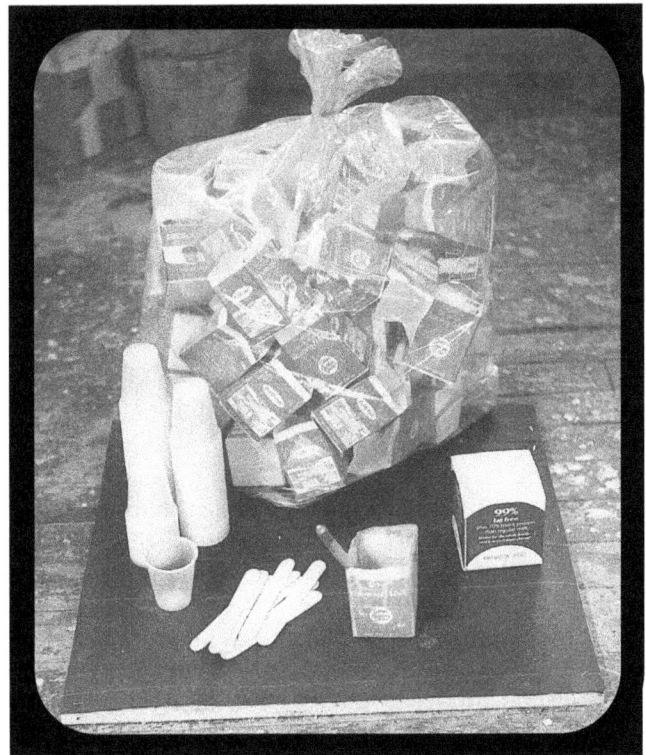

Working with most glues requires mixing containers and stirring sticks galore. Tongue depressors are good for applying fillets. An endless supply of mixing containers is available free from local public schools.

poor-fitting joints. It holds really well, and it's quite expensive, but if you're building just one or two small boats and you are in doubt about your joinery skills, then why not use it? Gorilla Glue has a short shelf life after it's opened and air gets to it. I've heard that turning the bottle upside down, so the air goes to the bottom of the bottle, greatly increases its shelf life.

PAINTS AND PAINTING

Varnish

In my opinion, Instant Boats should be painted, not varnished. Paint is easier to apply, and it protects wood better. Plywood doesn't have the beautiful grain of sawed lumber, so I feel it doesn't deserve the extra work that varnish requires. But I know I'm whistling in the wind here and that lots of builders like to varnish their Instant Boats. So if you're one of them, go ahead and have fun scraping, sanding, and reapplying six coats of the stuff every year.

Oil-Based and Water-Based Paints

For years, I used only expensive oil-based yacht paints, with all the solvents and driers that went with them, and I laid them on with top-quality badger hair brushes. But no matter how carefully I prepared the surface, these paints didn't work well on plywood. They would crack and peel in direct relation to how much exposure they received. (Most of my boats are left exposed throughout the year.)

When water-based paints became available, I dropped the yacht paints in a hurry. Water-based paints tend to wear off gradually without cracking or peeling. In addition, they don't smell, they're not loaded with harmful solvents, and they clean up with water. It doesn't seem to matter whether you use a high-priced paint or a run-of-the-mill house paint; they all remain on plywood equally well.

Wood Grains, Fiberglass, Sealers, Undercoaters, and Paint Adhesion

One day, however, I noticed that the quality and grain of the plywood can influence paint adhesion. Looking at my 20' lateen-rigged Bolger Zephyr, I noticed that the paint job looked fine right up to a line where a butt joint lay. On the panel on the other side of the joint, the paint was cracked and peeling. The boat's sides had been painted across their whole length without stopping, so it couldn't have been a difference in how the paint was applied. Close inspection of the panel showed wild, crazy grain going in all directions. I've seen this only rarely, and never on okume plywood, but it's something to watch out for on other types of plywood.

Fiberglass holds paint a lot better than plywood, and if you fiberglass the exterior of your boat (which I recommend), then either oil- or water-based paint will work.

Sealers are supposed to tame the grain of wood, penetrate the surface, and keep the grain from cracking. For years I used a thin, smelly sealer called Firzite. This worked well enough if the painting procedure was continuous. But when I built a stack of dories and stored them outdoors all winter, I was surprised to see them checked again. This turned me off from buying any special sealers, and in later years, I thinned either the epoxy or polyester I was using with a little lacquer thinner and used that.

Undercoaters are used to fill the grain of the wood, providing a thick, smooth surface for subsequent applications of thinner finish coats of paint. No one brand seems to be much better than another, but they are needed to produce a nice finish, so I use them.

Applying Paint

When applying paint, don't be a dabber. A dabber is someone who timidly sticks the tip of his brush in the can, gets just a little paint on his dry brush, and wipes most of it off on the lip of the can before applying it with short strokes. My advice is: Paint with the paint. Dip the brush in, get a good load on it, don't scrape your brush on the side of the can, and, all in one motion, get it on the boat. Brush it out so it won't sag. Take another dip, apply it ahead of the section you just applied, and brush back to the wetted edge. Keeping a wetted edge to blend each brushful into will result in a nice-looking, evenly applied paint job. Once you learn to "paint with the paint" and see the quality of the finish—not to mention the time saved—you'll never be a dabber again.

There are many reasons to pour paint out of a gallon can into another container: to mix colors; to prevent the full gallon from being exposed to air or contaminants during a lengthy painting session; or simply because you don't want to lug a gallon can when you only need a pint to do the job. But transferring paint from one container to another almost guarantees a mess, with some paint flowing down the outside of the can and some getting trapped in the groove of the lid. To avoid this, drive three or four holes in the groove with an 8-penny nail.

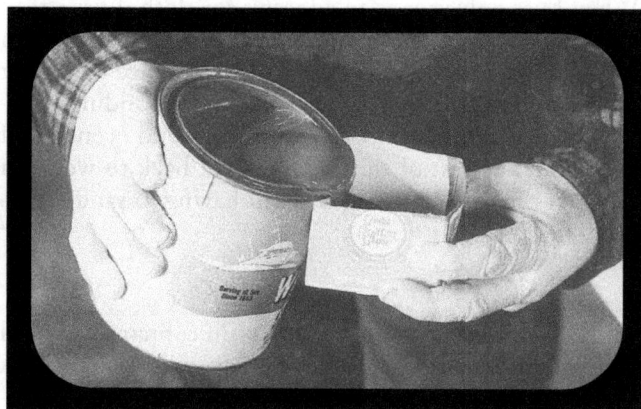

To transfer paint into a smaller container, jam a cut-down milk carton under the rim of the paint can, and you won't drip all over the outside of the can.

Dealing with Skin Forming on Top of the Paint

One hassle with paint is the skin that forms on top of it in the can during long storage periods. We've probably all tried dislodging the skin with a screwdriver or a stick, hoping that it would come out in one nice, clean piece, without leaving bits of dried paint in the can. And we've probably all failed and ended up having to strain the whole can or throw out the paint and buy more.

It's the air trapped inside the can, in contact with the liquid surface of the paint, that causes the problem. Get rid of the air, I figured, and you eliminate the problem. I tried blowing smoke into the can and jamming the cover down quickly, but this didn't work.

The solution came to me one day as I watched my wife, Amy, put waxed paper over a newly baked chocolate pie to keep it from skimming over. (I can relate to chocolate pie.) Since it worked for pie, why not paint? So I tried floating a piece of waxed paper right on the surface of the paint, and it worked!

You need the right size disc of waxed paper so that you can cover the paint right out to the sides of the can. Place the can on a sheet of waxed paper and use it as a template, trimming the paper with a knife. Make up a whole stack while you're at it, so that every time you're ready to close up a gallon or quart can, you have one handy. This method has saved me a lot of paint that otherwise would have been thrown out. It usually works with varnish, too, but occasionally the wax paper disc sinks to the bottom of the varnish.

Cutting waxed paper discs to float on the surface of the paint inside the can.

Next, cut the top off a plastic or paper milk carton (I use pint milk cartons) and jam this up tight under the rim of the can, molding its shape to the side of the can. Pour a little or a lot, and you won't spill a drop, and when you tip the can upright again, the excess paint will drip back through the holes you drove.

Paint Sickness

Many wooden boat owners think they should paint every year, whether the boat needs it or not. After a time, these boats become "paint sick": Water gets trapped between the multiple layers of paint—especially white paint, which reflects the sun—and because the boat never dries out, it starts to rot. I say paint a boat only when it needs it, even if it looks a bit shabby at times.

Of course, painting on layer after layer is the U.S Navy's way of maintenance. Their motto is, "If it ain't moving, paint it." I once asked a friend, Peter Karonis, who had been a destroyer captain during the Second World War, "What's all that black smoke I see boiling out of those ships that have been hit?" He replied, "That's paint burning."

That's about it in the paint department. I'm sure there are folks out there who will say, "I'd never do it that way. Dynamite's got it all wrong." To them, I say: To each his own. These methods work for me. Do whatever it takes to make you happy.

FLOTATION

I use Dow Chemical's Styrofoam extruded polystyrene house insulation for flotation. It is blue; it comes in 4' x 8' x 2" sheets; it has a fine-grained texture; it holds together; and it doesn't get waterlogged quickly. Stay away from white expanded polystyrene, which is coarse in texture, soaks water quickly, and has no strength. Use thickened epoxy for gluing pieces of rigid foam board to itself or to plywood. Don't use polyester resin—it causes the foam to dissolve.

As an alternative to rigid polystyrene, urethane foam is available in spray cans. Just spray it on, and it foams and expands until it fills whatever cavity it's in before it hardens. (In fact, if you use too much in an enclosed space, it might expand too much and break your wood joints.) It will save you from having to cut and fit rigid foam sheets, but it's more expensive.

CHAPTER 3

TOOLS

When working in my shop, I'm constantly amazed at how many tools it takes to complete what seems to be a small job. Just rounding off the top of a dory transom, for example, I use a hole saw in an electric drill, a circular saw, a hand saw, a hammer and chisel, a block plane, a spokeshave, a wood rasp, and a half-round mill file.

One way to determine what tools you need is just to start on the project and buy as you go. Sure, you could do the job with less, but *I* wouldn't want to. For me, the purpose in buying tools is to be able to do the job the best and easiest way in the least time possible.

Undoubtedly, my upbringing had a great deal to do with my style of working. My father, Herman Payson, was a first-class homebuilder with a deep appreciation of both hand and power tools and a good supply of both. He was of the old school; he took no coffee breaks and never wasted a moment. He got there fastest with the mostest, and if power was the way to go, he took it.

On the other hand, he delighted in using his old Stanley 45 combination plane with its battery of interchangeable knives that enabled him to do tongue-and-grooving, turn out sash work, and create an endless variety of moldings. Another of his prized possessions was an 11-point Disston hand saw which I was never allowed to use when I was a kid. It was bequeathed to me along with the rest of his tools, and it remains very special to me.

POWER TOOLS

It doesn't take a lot of tools to build an Instant Boat, and you can build a fine one indeed with just a few basic ones. But without question, the more tools you have of the right kind, the easier, faster, and more accurate the job will be.

Circular Saw

At the top of my list of handheld power tools is a circular saw, commonly referred to by the trade name Skilsaw. When used with a rip guide, you can saw all the long parts you want (like chines, rub rails, and gunwales) and bevel them at the same time. One of their greatest, and often overlooked, capabilities, however, is their ability to cut curves, including all the major panels for your boat.

Retract the blade so that it just breaks through the thickness of the wood, and you'll be surprised how tight a curve it'll cut. The smaller the saw blade, the more easily is it controlled, and the smaller its cutting radius. I use a saw with a $6\frac{1}{2}$" diameter blade; larger ones are too cumbersome.

Saber Saw

You can saw out plywood panels with a saber saw, but ever so slowly, and I wouldn't even attempt to use one to saw out chines from a plank. Nevertheless, a saber saw definitely has its place for sawing tight curves, such as limber holes and the individual pieces of plywood for laminated stems. With a saber saw, you can even start a cut in the middle of a panel without a starting hole. Just tilt the saw down on its nose, start the blade, and tip it back gradually, applying very light pressure as you go, and the blade will make its own hole. A saber saw will pretty much do what a band saw can do, as long as you stick to light work.

Drills

I suggest adding a $\frac{1}{4}$" or $\frac{3}{8}$" variable-speed reversible drill to your list, along with a bunch of twist drills from $\frac{1}{16}$" to $\frac{1}{2}$" for boring wood or metal. For larger holes in wood, use spade bits, which are a lot cheaper than the auger bits used with a bit brace.

Routers

The router is a great tool capable of doing a lot of work and a wide variety of it. I had been building boats for years when I decided that a router would be very effective in rounding the corners of gunwales. It was, but I splintered more gunwales than I care to remember before I learned to move the router along the wood in the direction opposite from which the cutter is turning. Gunwales love to break anyway, since their outside surfaces are in tension, and to start a running splinter in one is to invite disaster.

Hand Planes

I first bought an electric hand plane for cutting the edges of the $\frac{1}{2}$" marine plywood for dory bottoms. Trying to cut five layers of opposing grain with my old hand-powered plane, I'd get in a sweat quickly, even in midwinter, but

Most of the author's handheld power tools are older metal-bodied units. These are often available at yard sales and flea markets, and while they may need some refurbishing, they often give good value and performance.

when I finally bought an electric hand plane, I began to whiz through them, no sweat. Nothing works better than an electric hand plane for cutting scarfs and fairing down rudders and centerboards.

Owning one is nice, but owning two is better: If the cutters of one get dull, I can pick up the other and keep going. Both of mine are block planes that are good for short work but not so great for shaping long spars. Look for one with a comfortable grip and good balance. If it has spiral cutters, make sure that they're self-sharpening; otherwise, you'll have to find a specialist to sharpen them for you.

Stationary Power Tools

You can get by without owning any stationary power tools, but they sure can be nice to have. My first choice would be a table saw, and my preference would be a 9- or 10-inch Delta with at least a $\frac{3}{4}$- or 1-horsepower motor. I own an 8-inch Delta, which was all I could afford when I bought it new. With its $\frac{1}{2}$-horsepower motor, it is slightly underpowered for ripping 1" dry oak or twisty-grained 2" x 4"s, but I like the way it's made—so much so that, when I ran into its clone at a divorce settlement auction, I snapped it up. Its table is cast iron with a ground and polished surface. The miter gauge is well made and fits the table slots precisely. Its tilting table is a thing of the past, but its accuracy

and lightweight portability are a combination that would still attract me today. Granted, there are other good brands around, but I see more and more of them made of pressed steel. To my eye and touch, these don't measure up to what I have.

I have a 10" Delta band saw, and I wouldn't want to be without one for cutting breast hooks, quarter knees, and other tight curves that you can't do with a circular saw. My 10" Ryobi planer fulfills my surfacing needs, but I got along for years without a planer and you could too.

SANDING TOOLS

I own three power sanders: an old Stanley 3" x 21" belt sander, a Rockwell $4\frac{1}{2}$" x 9" orbital, and a Porter Cable 5" random orbital. I like the Porter Cable the best. It turns at 12,000 orbits per minute, has a hook-and-loop pad for quick changes of sanding discs and a built-in dust collector of reasonable effectiveness.

For sanding the long outside taped seams on my boats, I use a 30" x $2\frac{1}{2}$" sanding board with a handle at each end. Taking long sweeps with it fairs out any humps it encounters, leaving nice, smooth, pleasing lines. I like to use 3M "sticky-back" sandpaper, which is available in long rolls. Just stick a length of this on your long sanding board and go for it.

Sandpaper Grits

The 3M roll sandpaper is top-of-the-line quality. It is sharp toothed, and it hangs right in there, keeping its cutting power long after cheaper sandpapers give up. Three rolls of different grits were given me: 80, 150, and 320. I use 80 for fairing joints and for use with 5" "turtle-back" hand-held rubber block sanders. I seldom use the 150 grit, and the 320 grit is not needed at all for this fleet of small boats, although some builders will disagree.

Before I got this bonanza, I used 60 grit for everything—power sanders and all. This grit works well for sanding fiberglass or wood and leaves "tooth" enough for bonding on more fiberglass or for giving paint something to hold onto. I mention this because a friend of mine, who was somewhat of a perfectionist, sanded his boat "bottle smooth" with fine sandpaper, then laid on perfect coats of paint. Upon launching, sheets of paint came off right down to the bare hull.

Sixty grit paper in discs and 50 grit in sheets was about the coarsest paper hardware stores carried in this size, and they always had plenty. If I wanted a coarser grit, I made my own discs from floor-sanding paper. This was carried by the local tool rental store and was the toughest and best-cutting sandpaper I ever used. It comes in grits down to 12 grit, which is so coarse it looks like a truck backed up and spilled a load of crushed rock on it.

This was exactly what I use for repair jobs on old boats where I'm faced with removing umpteen layers of paint, with plenty of nails and bolt heads in the way. The 12 grit takes down everything in its path and looks for more, and the discs are easy to make. Just measure the radius of your sander's pad with a compass and swing whatever size circle is needed on the back of the sandpaper, then cut it out with a utility knife.

Cleaning Sanding Discs and Belts

When sanding discs and belts get warm with use, they clog up with paint or resin. You can clean some with a wire brush, but they are best cleaned with big crepe rubber

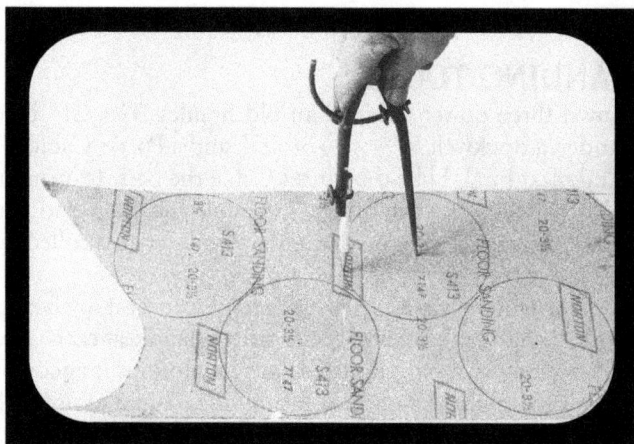

For really heavy grits, make your own sanding discs from floor-sanding paper.

sticks sold for the purpose. These sticks have saved a lot of sanding belts and discs from being thrown away before they're really used up. Clean the belts immediately when they become clogged.

BUYING GOOD POWER TOOLS

When you shop for a power tool, keep these questions in mind:

- How does it balance?
- Does it feel comfortable to your hand?
- Could you work with it for hours without tiring?
- And are the angle adjustments in actual degrees, or just guess marks?

Not all handheld power tools are well designed. Years ago, I resisted buying a funny-looking electric block plane that was priced at $150, but when I spied it at a sidewalk sale marked down to $50, I figured I could use it for my $50 worth and then dump it.

Instead of having a real grip like a saw handle, this plane had only a cow-horn-shaped projection sticking out from its body. Back home with the instruction book, I learned that you weren't supposed to hang onto the horn, but rather to curl your hand around it, letting your fingers flow around the body. Mine flowed directly over the air intake and very effectively blocked off the flow of cooling air. I bought this thing with my eyes wide open, so I couldn't feel cheated, but I am still wondering why any manufacturer ever let the design department put this one over. It is easily the most awkward tool I ever tried to use in my life, even when (or perhaps *especially when*) manipulating it as directed.

Think Small for a Circular Saw

If it's a circular saw you're looking for, think small. Unless you are building oceangoing commercial hulls, you don't need an 8¼" or a 10" blade. These are awkward and heavy for small-boat work and much more than you need for sawing plywood and standard boards. On my old Model #146, 6½" Porter Cable saw, the handle is directly over the blade, so it balances well. The knobs are black plastic of some kind, easy to see, and comfortably big to hold onto. The tilt indicator numbers are easy to read. Because of its design, I can clearly see where I'm cutting, and because of its small size, I can cut tight curves on boat stems that I wouldn't even try with a larger saw. Its size also makes it more controllable, which is not a bad idea with a handheld power saw of considerable RPM.

The Importance of Tilt Numbers

I mentioned tilt numbers above, and that's one of my pet peeves, due to a saber saw I own with only two numerals on its tilting action: 0 and 45. I wish I had noticed that before I bought it, because I've been paying for it in lost time ever since. If I want to cut a hole through a deck and allow for the rake of a mast, I take the angle of rake off the plan, using my sliding bevel gauge if it's not noted on the drawing. Then I adjust the pad of the saber saw and the blade to conform to the angle of the sliding bevel gauge. All that extra fiddling because I hadn't noticed the lack of numbers on that saber saw. Every time I use it, I think of the manufacturer who designed it that way, and I mutter, "Thank you. Thank you very much."

Avoid Sealed Bearings

Another thing to look for is sealed bearings. *If you see them, keep looking.* About fourteen years ago I bought a new 3" x 21" belt sander, and after twenty hours of use, the "sealed-for-life" bearings let go in the drive section. When I took it back to the store, the guarantee had run out, even though I hadn't used it up. I was told that it would cost nearly as much as the price of a new one to fix. So when I see power tools with sealed bearings guaranteed for life, I wonder, *whose life?*

I still remember with a great deal of satisfaction just how the sun reflected off its polished surface as it twisted and turned on its way to the bottom of one of the deepest quarries in the world, then in service as the Rockland city dump.

I went straight from the quarry to my local hardware store, and I asked the proprietor, who was also a house builder, what kind of belt sander he used. He passed a Stanley across the counter to me, and I bought it. Twelve years of continuous service from my Stanley sander convinces me that I made the right choice. (Unfortunately, Stanley no longer makes belt sanders.) Since then, I've had a strong tendency to believe a fellow craftsman's recommendations rather than those of any tool manufacturer. I'm convinced, too, that the fact that I can take it apart and grease any squeaking bearings myself has contributed to its longevity in hard service.

Pros and Cons of Plastic

One of the features I like about the newer tools is that more and more of the housings are being made of high-impact plastic, which would make even the dumbest of us have to work pretty hard at it to get electrocuted. But that's where my infatuation with plastic stops. When it comes to plastic power cords, I say no. When they get cold, they get stiff, and then they get in your way. Whoever had the idea of draping these congealed tentacles on power tools ought to be sentenced to have to work with one in the draftiest boat shop on the Maine coast in mid-January. I'm relieved to see that plain old flexible rubber cords are still used on the more expensive tools.

Even with the occasional design failure, I'm honestly impressed by all power tools—with what they can do and the ease with which they do it. I wouldn't want to give up any that I have, but my favorites are my circular saw, my saber saw, and—one of the best tools to come on the market in a long time—my variable speed reversible drill.

HAND TOOLS

I enjoy working with hand tools. While you can get by with few or no power tools, at least a small selection of hand tools is essential if you want to build a boat.

Hammers

I have five hammers: a small sledge, a ball-peen hammer, and three claw hammers (16 ounce, 13 ounce, and 8 ounce). The 16-ounce hammer is for heavier work, such as building shop steps or framing a house. I use the 13 ouncer for nothing much larger than 8-penny nails and the 8 ouncer for #18 wire nails, brads, and such. It's a simple pleasure, I suppose, but it helps keep me happy to own enough hammers so I can always reach for the right one for a particular job.

If you find you can't drive a nail straight with any of these hammers—and I've heard it said many times, "I'd like to build something, but I can't even drive a nail straight"—the problem may not be you. It may be the hammer itself. Look at your hammer's face. If it's smooth, it will slip off the nail head. Rub it sideways on 60-grit sandpaper and you will nail like a pro. A hammer's face should also be slightly rounded. This leaves a smooth dimple when the head of a nail is set more than flush, rather than crunching the wood and breaking the fibers, as a flat-faced hammer would do. A smooth dimple is easily filled.

While we're on this hammer and nail business, stagger the nails all you can when nailing a series of them down the length of a board. If you drive them all in a straight line, their cumulative wedging effect may split any wood that has straight grain.

Saws

For a hand saw, a 10-point crosscut will do. The "point" measurement is the number of teeth to the inch, so the higher the number, the closer the tooth spacing. A 10-point blade gives a relatively smooth cut without chattering, as an 8-point saw is likely to do. Stay away from stainless steel saws. Stainless steel is too soft to hold an edge, and you can't file a good edge on one in the first place. The only reason to own a stainless steel saw is to stow it onboard your boat. It can lie there, doing what it is best at—which is not rusting, period—until the time comes when having any saw is better than none at all.

You don't need a hand ripsaw, with 8 points to the inch. These poor saws are doomed to extinction for lack of use, except perhaps by the few users who delight in doing things the hard way.

. . . which reminds me of my late Uncle Harry. He was a house carpenter all his life, lived into his nineties, never had electricity in his shop, never owned or even drove a car, and did everything in moderation. I asked

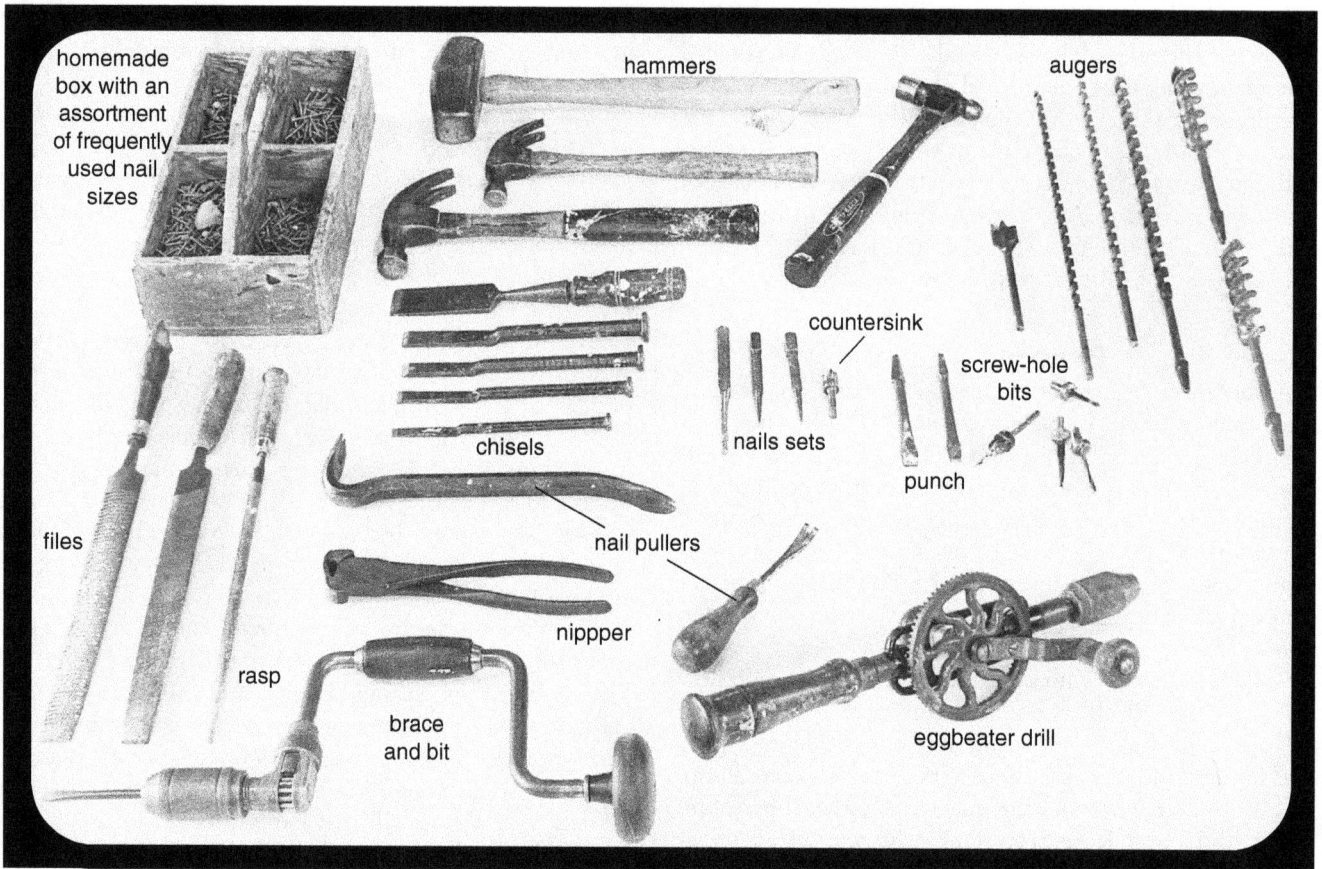

You may not need every one of these hand tools, but they'll all make your project go easier.

him once, "Uncle Harry, how do you stay so slim?" He replied, "I put all I want on my plate, then put half of it back." He used a hand ripsaw, but there aren't many like him anymore.

My father, of course was different. He never did anything by hand that he could do better or quicker with power. I'm all for that. I have an eggbeater-type hand drill, but when it comes to boring a series of holes, I reach for

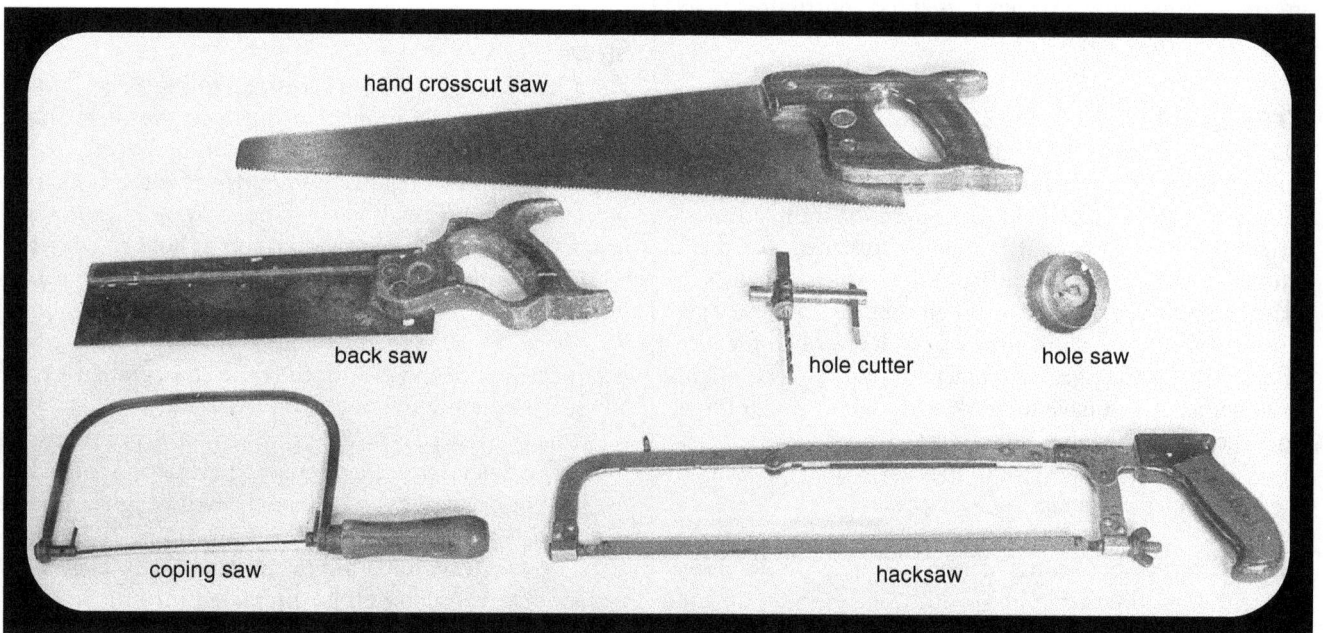

Even if you have a good selection of handheld power tools, a selection of hand saws will still come in handy.

You'll need lots of C-clamps but probably can get by without any pipe clamps (top) for these boats.

my electric drill, and when I want to rip a board, I use a circular saw or a table saw.

Clamps

You'll need a lot of C-clamps. When you're putting on gunwales or rub rails, or laminating a spar, you'll want enough clamps so that you can place them no more than one foot apart. My collection includes all sizes, from a ten-inch throat opening down to the two-inch size for model making. My favorites are the five-inch Jorgensons I bought years ago and have never seen on the market since. However, quality need not be top-notch to do the job, and four-inch openings are big enough for the boats in this book. If you can find them, buy some C-clamps with a V-shaped notch in the body pad. This allows you to hook the clamp on a sharp outside corner, which is impossible with ordinary clamps.

You won't need pipe clamps to build these boats. Use a Spanish windlass instead. This is nothing but a loop of rope tied around what you want to pull together. Put a stick in the loop and wind in the slack until the rope forces the pieces together. This is as simple as it gets, and it costs nothing.

Measuring Tools

Essential measuring tools include a steel tape measure (at least 12' long), a bubble level, a bevel gauge, and an adjustable combination square. A framing square, though nice to have, isn't essential. You need a level to set your boat's frames horizontally and vertically. Without it, you risk building a permanent twist in your boat. Also use your eyes. When you have one frame exactly where you want it, sight the other frames with it to check for accuracy.

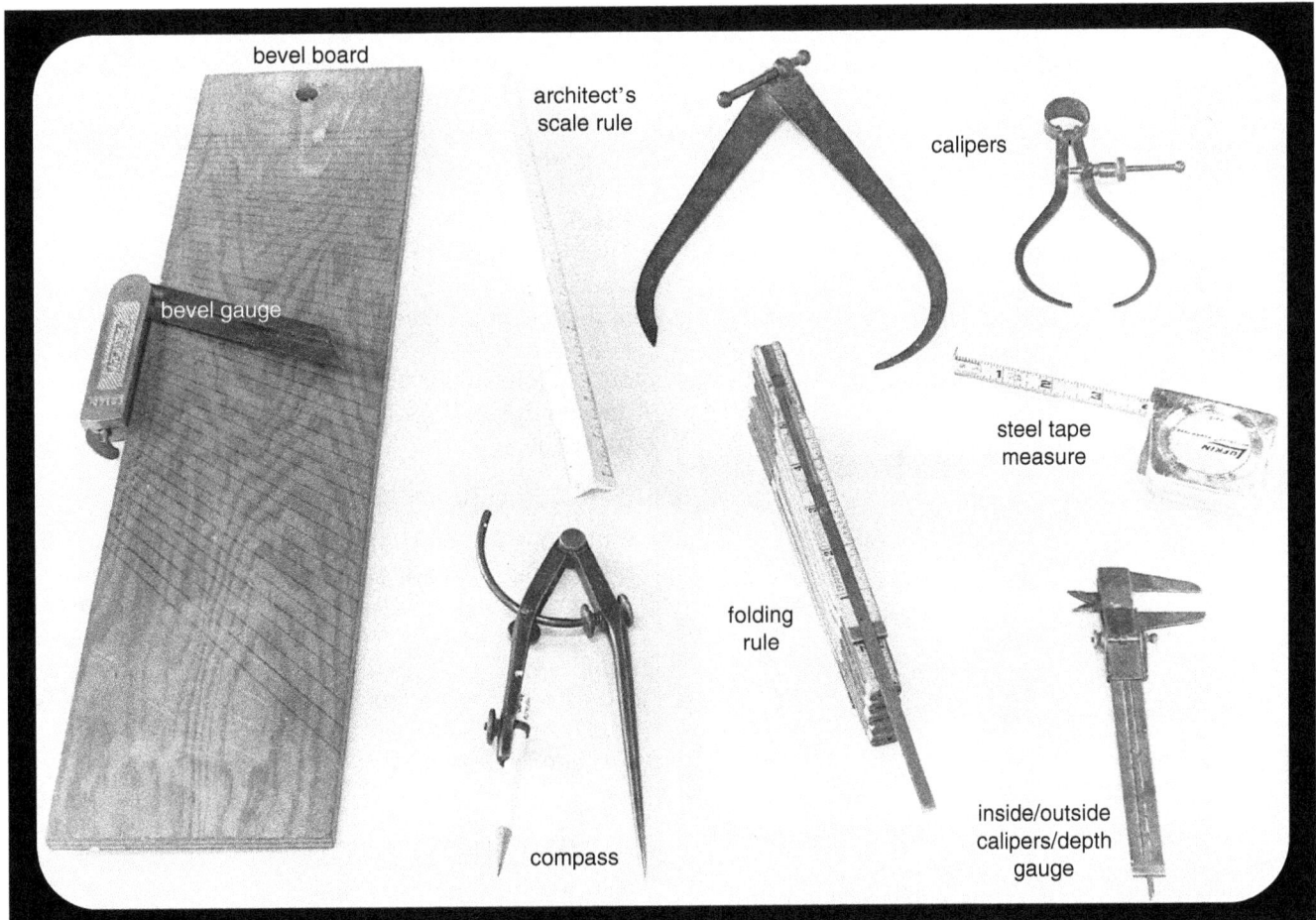

Measuring tools.

Planes

Buy the lowest low-angle block plane you can find, and it will do most of the hand planing you are likely to be faced with. The low blade angle gives a smooth cutting action even on end grain, where a plane with a higher angle blade would chatter.

I also have a smoothing plane, a long joiner plane, and a variety of others—some with metal bodies, some with wood bodies. The wooden ones slide easily, but their boxy shape makes them a mite clumsy.

You'll find a lot of these old clunkers at flea markets and lawn sales. They have wooden wedges to hold the plane irons in place and metal strike buttons to dislodge them. The irons have good steel and plenty of it, but they're apt to go out of adjustment when you strike the first knot. Then it's fiddle, fiddle, fiddle to get it set to the proper depth again. There's nothing precise about it.

Hammer adjustments are not for me. A whack on the end of the plane usually loosens both the wedge and the iron such that the blade can't cut at all. At this point, the carpenter says to hell with it and takes his hammer to both the wedge and the top of the iron—a popular approach, judging from all the brutalized iron tops I've seen (not to mention the ones I've been personally responsible for). If you're lucky, you might find an old wooden plane with a screw adjustment. I found one, and I'm still using it. My other old boxy wooden-bodied planes I've given away or sold to antique dealers, with the exception of one I made into a spar plane by hollowing out the sole and filing the blade into a deep, concave shape.

Chisels

Japanese chisels are the best I've ever used. Their steel has the right amount of hardness to achieve a superb cutting edge and hold it even with much use. Since they have a metal ferrule on their handles, you can beat on them. I used to use only all-metal chisels—handles and all—but

when I first got my hands on a Japanese chisel, it made me painfully aware of how many hours I had wasted waling away with inferior ones.

Gouges

A few gouges in different sizes are useful. To make shallow surface cuts, you'll want gouges with outside bevels. For cutting deep holes, you'll want inside bevels. You'll need different slips (appropriately shaped oilstones) to sharpen them.

Sharpening Tools

Edge tools need to be tip-top sharp for best performance, and they need to have the proper bevel and angle of attack. For chisels and plane irons, I find that a bevel that's twice as long as the thickness of the blade is a good compromise. This gives a sharp enough angle of attack to cut but not such a thin edge that the blade dulls quickly. After much use and much hand honing, the bevel becomes slightly rounded, and the flat angle of attack needs to be re-established on a grinding wheel. Do this carefully, with frequent baths of water, to avoid overheating the steel and ruining its temper.

I don't use any of the fancy sharpening jigs that are available—I just freehand it on a plain old whetstone. When I sharpen my block plane, I don't want the edge to be perfectly straight across. I want it curved ever so slightly so that when I plane the middle of a wide board, the corners of the blade don't dig in. And by sharpening by hand on a whetstone with no roller guide to precisely hold the blade, that's exactly what I get.

Files

Files are something I could never do without. Long ago I learned that a block plane, a mill file, and sandpaper, used in that order, gave me a nicely rounded end on a gunwale. I can control files but not sandpaper, so I keep a good array of them on hand for finishing work. Using a file first and then sandpaper, I get a clean, fair curve and save on sandpaper, too.

Other Tools

Other tools that are either nice to have or necessary include: side-cutting pliers, scissors, a countersink, a spokeshave (buy one with an adjustable blade, fine-tuned by two knobs on top of the body), a putty knife, a roller or squeegee, and paint brushes (1½" or 2" for most small gluing and fiberglass taping jobs, and a 3" for applying resin over large areas). And the list goes on—whatever you lack, you will find out quickly enough when you start the job.

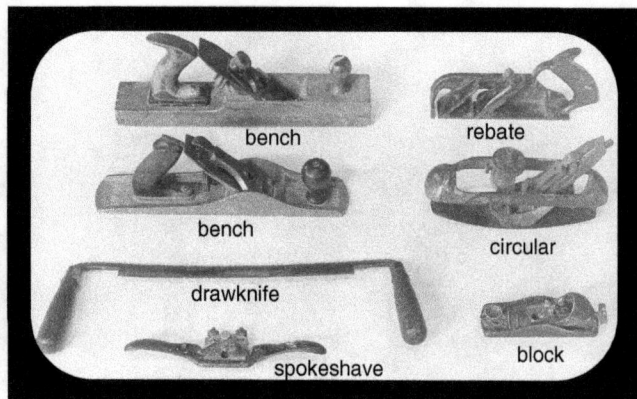

You'll need a low-angle block plane, like the one at the lower right. Some of these other tools are more appropriate for traditional boatbuilding, but a bench plane and a spokeshave are definitely nice to have for Instant Boats.

BUYING USED TOOLS

New tools are expensive, and if you want a well-outfitted shop, you might save some money by considering used ones. Come along with me on a tool hunt.

Start by answering a few basic questions, and you will quickly cut the problem down to size:

- How much should I expect to spend?
- What tools am I looking for?
- Where should I look for them?

I mention money first, because that's the name of the game. You'd like to know how much you would save by investing in a used tool instead of buying it new. The price you pay should depend on the condition of the tool, how badly you need it, and whether you are willing and able to do a little restoration work on tools that you buy at bargain prices.

Tool catalogs are useful for comparing the costs of the new tools with the used ones that you find for sale. When you have a specific tool in mind, check the catalog first and then do your shopping.

Thirty years ago I paid twenty-one dollars for a new Miller's Falls low-angle block plane. Four years ago, the catalog price for a comparable Stanley low-angle block plane was thirty-nine dollars. If I were to buy it today, I'd have to pay forty-five dollars.

It's easy to lay the blame on inflation, but inflation does not explain the fact that good-quality small hand tools—hammers, saws, eggbeater drills, spokeshaves, and that low-angle block plane—are rising much faster in price than power tools. I suspect the answer lies in less competition.

Go to a Home Depot or a Lowes and you'll see what a high-volume market power tools has become. There are so many manufacturers competing for this market that their prices are at a virtual standstill—and in some cases are even declining. Meanwhile, the few manufacturers of high-quality small hand tools can write their own ticket.

So take a good hard look at the price of a new tool first, and consider yourself lucky to pay between a third and a half of that for a used tool in good condition—or even up to three-quarters if it's in mint condition. I wouldn't pay more than three quarters of the new cost for the simple reason that sometime in the course of the year, a hardware store is likely to put some tools on sale.

For serious used-tool buying, I look for professionals who have just retired, private sales, and estate auctions. I'm especially interested if I personally know the individual or the boatyard and have reason to respect their work. Quality work and quality tools go hand in hand, and these are some of the best sources of quality tools. A shop's reputation is useful in judging the likelihood of finding good hand tools, but that reputation deserves extra attention if you're considering a major power-tool purchase, which can represent a considerable investment.

You will also meet up with used tools at most every lawn sale, flea market, and antique store. Availability, though, doesn't mean quality—not by a long shot. The most recent lawn sale I attended advertised tools and marine hardware, but after poking around the usual collection of bent and rusty screwdrivers, loose-jointed bit braces, and nondescript marine junk, I finally headed for home with a single purchase: a Pakistani taxi horn.

But I continue to watch the newspapers like a hawk for lawn-sale ads, and if they mention tools, I go, even though I have everything I need. I enjoy the browsing and the hunt and the faint anticipation that I still might find the one thing I really want and that the professional tool pickers have somehow overlooked.

There still are bargains to be found out there. Knowing what you are looking for will put you well ahead of the casual browser, and you might get lucky. If it's a hand saw you are after, you probably can find a good one, even at a lawn sale.

Hand Saws

Almost every household has a hand saw of some kind. Perhaps it belonged to a grandfather or a deceased uncle and has been hanging in a shed for years. Very likely its identity disappeared long ago under a coat of rust, and its handle is cracked and loose. But don't let its appearance fool you. You could be looking at a tool you will treasure all your life. Chances are the steel in that blade far excels anything you will find brand new in the average hardware store today.

If the handle screws say "Disston" on them, that saw is worth a close examination. Don't lightly put aside an Atkins, or a Winchester, either. But if you're holding a Disston, give it your full attention.

If the saw is pitted with rust, forget it—the teeth would break if you tried to set them. But if the rust is just a surface coat, take a look along the length of the blade. If it has sharp kinks, that saw has been badly abused. At one time or another, it probably didn't have enough set in its teeth, but that didn't bother the user: He just kept pushing harder until it buckled on him. Thumbs down again. If you ever succeeded in getting that kind of kink out, it would pop right back in again because the metal has been stretched.

On the other hand, a long, gradual curve or slight kink can usually be taken out if you overbend in the opposite direction and keep watching the curve pop back until at last it's straight.

Back in the days before handheld circular saws, carpenters had to rip their boards by hand using long, deep-bodied ripsaws with, on the average, five big teeth to the inch. When powered hand saws came along, the users of the old muscle machines weren't long in hanging them up or letting them lie where they were flung. Even professional tool pickers passed them by, not wanting to retooth them, or maybe not knowing how. That's why you can still find one from time to time, as I did.

I was about to toss it back on the pile with the rest of the junk until my eye caught the name "Disston" on it. I thought, *Well, maybe it's worth a try,* and I lugged the rusty relic home. I fixed that old Disston by cutting its blade down to size, retoothing it to a 10-point crosscut, and making a new handle for it. And was it ever worth it!

The hardest job that I had to attack with a hand saw on a regular basis at that time was cutting my dory sides flush with the transom. Those long, angled cuts, plus the glue in the plywood, took the edge off my other saws in a hurry. My rejuvenated old Disston did the same job twice as fast and still had plenty of cutting power left over for repeats. The reason is simple: That old blade has much harder steel. When Henry Disston stamped his product with "For beauty, finish, and utility, this saw cannot be excelled" right over his signature, he knew what he was talking about.

I've never seen a better saw, and I kicked myself because for years I had used a pair of Atkins finish saws, which I thought did a good job. And even though I had filed saws for years and was well acquainted with the quality steel of the old Disstons, I had waited twenty-five years to hunt one down.

Auger Bits

When it comes to looking for auger bits for use with bit braces, I search out Russell Jennings bits every time. They're so scarce that I'm immediately suspicious every time I find one, wondering how it ever got by the professional tool pickers, so I examine it carefully for straightness and the degree of wear.

C-Clamps

I'm equally particular about any C-clamps I find. Always try the adjustment screw: Does it meet the pad on the clamp body, or is it way out of alignment when you screw it in? If it's out of alignment, it is quite unlikely that you can straighten it properly.

Power Tools

Before you buy a used circular saw, electric plane, belt sander, or any other power tool, check the drive shaft for end play and up-and-down movement. Plug it in if you can, and if you see bright blue light arcing in its innards like a welder's torch, chances are the brushes are worn or sticking, or the commutator is worn, or it could even be a worn-out bearing throwing a load on the motor. Put it back.

Maintenance of Used Tools

Whether you're buying a new or a used tool, give some thought to maintenance. Will you maintain it yourself, or do you plan to have somebody else do it? Companies change hands so often these days, you can't be assured of getting service later.

My solution is to buy spares of the parts that I think might wear out, when I buy the tool. I'd rather float the expense of carrying a few extra parts, even if I never need them, than risk being held up on a job for lack of them. The cost is no worse than insurance and not half the trouble if you can just reach for a part you have squirreled away, make the repair, and keep going.

After decades of buying and using tools, and considering such things as guarantees and life expectancies, in most cases I prefer to buy new if I can, and used if I must. Please note that I say *most,* always remembering that in some cases older is better.

The end result of buying tools, whether new or used, depends on how sharp you are when you go looking. The hunt is fun, and it's a challenge, too. Win or lose, take or be taken—it all depends on you.

CHAPTER 4

BOAT PLANS AND BUILDING PROCEDURES

hil Bolger's boat plans pack a lot of information in a little space. It's not that they're complicated—they're ingenious. Since these are all fairly simple boats, it's possible to show all the information you need in a few views of the boat, plus a few detailed drawings. If a dimension is given in one view, Phil generally avoids giving that dimension again in another view. On the other hand, Phil is scrupulous about depicting details graphically. Wherever a detail is ambiguous when seen from one viewpoint, it is revealed clearly from another.

This approach not only makes the plans easier to read, but it also makes you study them carefully. Once you understand how a part is shaped in all three dimensions, you'll understand how it fits with other parts.

Before you cut your first board—before you even decide to build that particular boat—study the plans carefully, and you'll understand the entire building process. If it doesn't make sense to you on paper, it probably won't make sense to you in wood either. That's a hint that maybe you should choose a different, simpler design to start out with.

UNDERSTANDING INSTANT BOAT PLANS

The boat plans consist of some or all of the following views. The simpler the boat, the fewer the views.

Outboard Profile: This is a view of what the finished boat will look like, from the side.

Construction Profile: This is a cross-section. It shows all the construction details that you'd see if you took a chainsaw and split the boat down the middle lengthwise.

Construction Plan View: This is a bird's-eye view showing the construction details.

Section View: A section view is another cross section, but this time you're sawing across the boat's width. Often there are several section views to show construction details and dimensions at various points from front to back. The section views are always labeled so that you can "connect" them with the other construction views. Some of the boats

require simple building jigs. Details of the station molds (the temporary transverse frames around which the boat is built) are also shown in section view.

Detail View: Various construction details are shown at a larger scale for greater clarity. These often include stems, frames, gunwales, chines, transoms, seats, and rudders.

Body Plan: A body plan is a little trickier. It shows the shape of the boat but not the construction details, from dead ahead and dead astern at the same time. The drawing has a centerline, and the boat's port side is usually shown from the bow to the right of the centerline, and from the stern to the left of it. (Since almost all boats are symmetrical port and starboard, it's generally necessary to show only half the boat for you to understand the whole shape.) The parallel or sloped lines are what you'd see if you cut straight across the boat at regular intervals, so that you can visualize how the shape changes from front to back. These intervals are also shown either on the construction plan or the construction profile (or both), so that you can relate the boat's section shapes to the lengthwise views.

Expanded Panels: These are one of the best parts of Instant Boat plans—one of the factors that makes them so easy to build. Instant Boats are built from pieces of plywood that are cut out on the flat and then bent into curves. When you look at a construction plan or a construction profile, you're seeing the curved panels from straight above or straight from the side, so they're foreshortened. The expanded panel views show their true shape and dimensions when they're taken off of the boat and laid out flat on the floor. This allows you to easily measure and cut the panels on the flat without going through the procedure of lofting.

Nesting Diagrams: Nesting diagrams show how to lay out the major hull panels onto sheets of plywood for the most efficient use of stock. In many cases, the nesting diagram includes the expanded-panel views.

In addition, many of the plans are accompanied by a building key. These list the materials required and provide either general guidance or step-by-step advice on building procedures.

As I said, Bolger's plans have enough information to build the boat, but not too much. You won't find any advice of the put-the-screwdriver-in-the-slot variety, which I have seen from some other designers. Bolger treats you with respect and assumes that you have some common sense and enough patience to study the plans.

On the other hand, Bolger has the beginner very much in mind with his designs, and he's good at foreseeing trouble spots and warning the builder in advance. For example, he advises that side panels be marked and cut out of plywood as mirror images—like a pair of shoes, left and right—even though it might be a bit easier to mark them out identically on the plywood. This is because all the boats that are longer than eight feet call for butt straps to hold the fore and aft sections of the panels together. If you do this procedure without thinking "mirror image," you are going to find one butt strap on the outside of your hull and one on the inside—not pretty.

But don't get me wrong. You can and probably will make a few mistakes. That's part of the fun and challenge of boatbuilding, and at least with Instant Boats, the mistakes are never huge or expensive. Chalk it up as a learning experience, and see if you can beat Murphy next time.

BUILDING FROM PLANS

Take a look at the box in the lower right-hand corner of the plans (on page 45), and you'll see the number of the design. Phil Bolger has drawn more than 600 sets of boat plans over the years (more recently with the very capable help of his wife, Susanne Altenburger), and the number continues to grow.

Just above the box is noted the scale of the drawings. Most of the plans were drawn at 1½" = 1' on 17" x 22" or 22" x 34" paper. The plans were reduced to fit in this book; therefore, in spite of the scale notation, they are not reproduced here at any particular scale. (In fact, the scale boxes have been removed from many of the plans in this book.) Nevertheless, Bolger gives just about every dimension you'll need, allowing you to build the boats directly from the book if your eyesight is good and you want to save a few bucks. However, *I strongly recommend that you buy the full-size plans.* (See the Appendix for ordering information.) They're not expensive, they're easier to work from, and, because they're reproduced at the original scale, you can use an architect's scale rule on them to check any dimension (more on this later). You can even tack them up on your workshop wall for inspiration.

When I say "full-size plans," I mean the properly scaled, 17" x 22" or 22" x 34" sheets. When some builders ask for "full-size plans," however, what they mean is full-size *patterns*—true-size printouts that you can lay right on the plywood and trace around to get the actual size of the frame, stem, or whatever. These can save you the trouble of transferring dimensions from the plans to the plywood and springing battens to connect the points into fair curves—

Important Words to Understand When Using the Plans

Side Panels: These are the uppermost hull panels, the ones to which the gunwales are attached. In some cases (like Big Tortoise, Sneakeasy, and Clamskiff), they're vertical. In others (such as the Stretched Dory and Fisherman's Skiff), they are flared out at an angle. Occasionally, they're labeled the *topsides* panels.

Bilge Panels: Unlike all the boats mentioned above, which have only side and bottom panels, others—including Pirogue, Cartopper, and Ruben's Nymph—have a more complex shape with two panels per side (plus the bottom). The panel that fills the angle between the side and the bottom is the bilge panel.

Bottom: This is the bottom of the boat. But since all the boats are built upside down, the "bottom" is the uppermost surface while the hull is under construction.

Chine: The chine is the lengthwise joint between two hull panels. The designs that have bilge panels are referred to as "multi-chine" boats (two chines per side). Some of the single-chine boats have a long piece of wood called a chine *log* to reinforce the joint between the side and bottom panels, and sometimes this strength member is referred to simply as a "chine."

neither of which is at all difficult, by the way. (We'll go into the details below.)

As I said, Bolger's plans include all the information you need to transfer the shapes to the plywood, but if you'd rather save those steps, full-size patterns are available from my friend Peter Spectre at Compass Rose. (See the Appendix for ordering information.) Just remember that full-size patterns don't come with instructions, so unless you want to build directly from this book, you'll still need the full-size plans and the building key that goes with some of them.

For builders who prefer to draw out the pieces of their boats themselves, Bolger has made this easy by depicting the shape of the parts as they would be drawn on 4' x 8' sheets of plywood. (In some cases, the plywood rectangle isn't shown, but all the measurements on the parts are taken from a baseline, which represents the edge of the plywood. It amounts to the same thing.) Since the factory-cut edges of plywood sheets are precisely square, the builder can measure everything from the edges, squaring everything automatically. This is a better method than using a combination or framing square, which can easily throw you off if you hold it the least bit sloppily, or if the plywood has a ding, a splinter, or a glob of dried glue to keep the square from fitting against the edge nice and snug.

LAYING OUT THE SIDE PANELS

Lay your plywood flat on the floor. (If the boat calls for panels longer than 8', you'll need to join two pieces of plywood. See below.)

Take your steel tape measure and mark off the crosswise intervals shown on the drawing of the expanded panel. In most cases, you can make a mark every foot, but if there are intermediate measurements shown, mark them, too. Now, instead of using a square to draw these marks across the panel, measure the same intervals on the opposite edge of the plywood and use a straightedge to connect the marks. A sawed-off factory edge from a plywood panel makes a good, long straightedge.

Look again at the drawing and note the dimension in from the baseline (i.e., the edge of the plywood) for the first point at one end or the other of the panel. It'll be one of the upper corners of the side panel. Measure this dimension in from the edge of the plywood to the sheer line, right on the squared-across line, and mark it. Move to the next interval and mark both the sheer line and the lower edge of the panel. (On most of the plans, the sheer line is closest to the baseline, but on some of them, including Payson's Pirogue, the lower edge of the side panel is closest.) Do this without moving your rule or tape measure, because the dimensions for both edges are given from the baseline. Continue moving on until you've marked all the heights for both edges of the panel.

Some first-time builders have made the mistake of thinking that the dimension for the lower edge of the side panel is taken from the position of the sheer edge—in other words, they add the two dimensions—and the side panel ends up a lot deeper than it should be. It's a repairable error, but it wastes a lot of plywood.

You now have a lot of carefully measured points on your plywood. Now it's time to connect them into smooth curves for the outline of the panel. You'll need a batten—a long, narrow strip of wood that will take a fair curve. Battens can be made from pine, spruce, fir, or mahogany. For these small boats, cut them ½" square or so for the long curves and ¼" square for the short, sharper curves for the rounded stern ends on some of the boats. Battens should be cut at least a couple of feet longer than whatever they are going to be bent around. You need to allow them to overhang the last measured mark by a foot or so, so that the curve doesn't go flat near the ends.

Drive #18 wire nails into the plywood at every measured point, then bend your batten against the nails and see how many nails the batten touches. Sight along the batten to see that it forms a fair curve, one that is pleasing to the eye without quick humps or hollows. If the batten doesn't touch a nail or two by a small amount, just pull the nail and bend the batten until the line is fair. Remove the smallest number of nails you can to achieve that nice curve, while keeping in mind you are not building a piano here, only a boat. Also remember that the designer has drawn the boat on small sheets of paper, and you are drawing out the panels full size, so any small discrepancies on the drawing will be magnified. You will find, however, that Bolger's measurements are usually right on the money.

Measuring Plywood Panels for Layout and Dealing with Screwups

Phil Bolger's Instant Boat plans show the parts laid out on rectangular sheets of plywood. The plywood is lined off in intervals across the sheet, and to get the shape of a side panel, for example, all you have to do is hook your tape measure over the edge of the plywood right on that line and make a mark for the first measurement at the proper height.

This is about as easy as it gets, but don't underestimate the all-too-eager, unskilled, in-a-hurry, first-time builder: There hasn't been a set of plans drawn yet that he can't screw up.

After he makes the first mark, he unhooks his rule from the edge of the plywood, lays the tip on the previous measurement, and measures toward the opposite edge of the side panel—which increases the panel's overall depth considerably. He cuts the panels out right on the lines, but when the time comes to lay them on the (properly measured) station frames, he sees that they're not even close.

To recover, he can lay the side panel back on a fresh sheet of plywood and set the accurate edge of the side panel the correct distance from the edge of the plywood. He then can take correct measurements from the baseline for the panel's opposite edge, and cut off the excess. Or, he can just start over again.

Laying out the bilge and bottom panels follow the same procedures.

The reward of laying out these panels and other parts yourself rather than using full-size patterns is that you put more of yourself into building your boat, thus increasing your learning experience.

I know that these panels laying flat on the floor don't look like much, but what a transformation you'll see when you bend that preshaped side panel around the molds, step back, and spot that nicely lined sheer. Hey! It looks like a boat already!

BUTT-JOINING THE PANELS

Any hull panel longer than 8' has to be assembled from two or more pieces of plywood. Bolger's plans show the pieces joined together with butt straps. These are simply pieces of the same plywood from which the panels are made, laid over the inside of the joint and fastened down with glue and clenched nails. (Copper rivets work well, too.)

This is simple and effective, but I prefer a fiberglass-taped butt. This adds little or nothing to the thickness of the panel at the butt, so the panel takes a fairer bend than it might with a plywood butt strap. And I prefer the smoother look. If you sand the edges of the fiberglass tape well, you'll never see the butt joint after the paint is on.

Although you can join the individual pieces of a hull panel after they've been measured and cut, I prefer to butt-join

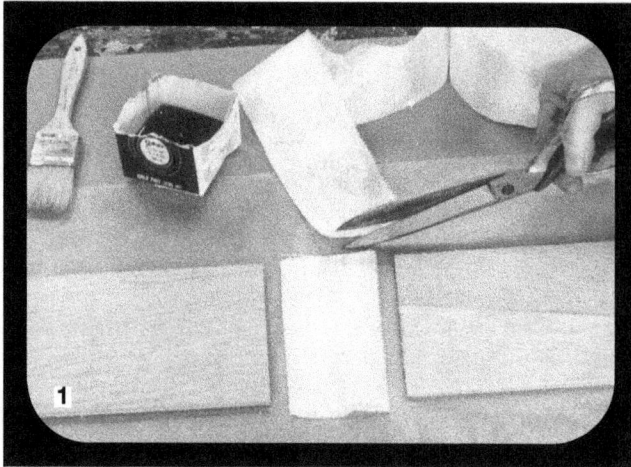

Lay a piece of waxed paper on a flat surface, and cut a length of fiberglass tape slightly longer than the joint.

The plywood has been turned over and the ends butted together on top of the resin-wetted tape. Now coat the top side of the butt with resin, and lay another piece of tape on top.

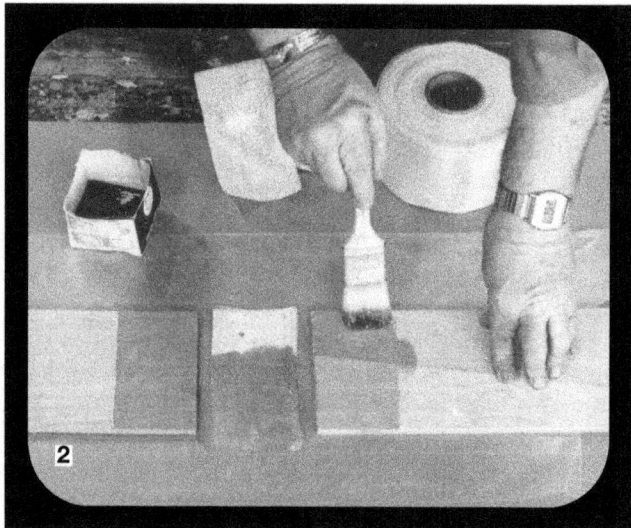

Saturate the fiberglass tape and the ends of the plywood with resin.

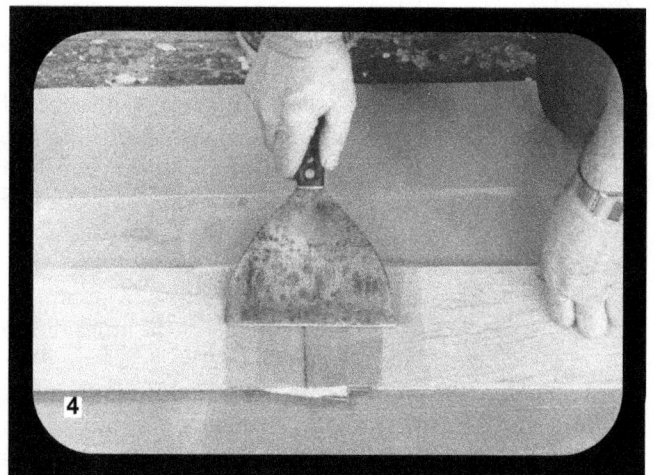

Saturate the top piece of tape with resin; place a piece of waxed paper over the joint; draw a wide taping knife across the joint to press the resin, glass, and wood together and force out any air bubbles.

The fiberglass butt joint can be used to join sections of individual hull panels or for complete sheets of plywood prior to cutting. For clarity in this small-scale example, I've omitted the small support sticks that go underneath the plywood pieces that are being joined.

two complete sheets of plywood first, then draw and cut out the panels in one piece. This eliminates the risk of edge-setting the individual pieces when joining them together. What's also nice about this fiberglass joint system is that you can do both sides of the plywood at the same time.

Lay out a series of 4' strips of wood at 2' intervals, all parallel to each other, with a wider board in the middle where the butt joint will fall. Lay a piece of waxed paper on the wider board. Coat the underside of both sheets of plywood with polyester or epoxy resin at the ends where they'll be butted, brushing the resin in a band wide enough

for the 3"-, 4"-, or 6"-wide fiberglass tape (your choice). Lay the tape on the waxed paper, give it a coat of resin, and plop the plywood down right on the center of the tape. Do the same for the top of the joint, and tack both ends of the plywood down snug to the board beneath.

That's it—both sides of the joint in one whack. After the resin cures, you can lay out your hull panels and saw them out right on the floor with a handheld circular saw with its blade extended just deep enough to cut through the plywood. This enables you to cut curves that are quite tight, and eliminates the risk of the saw kicking back.

Testing a Fiberglass Butt Joint for Strength

Before I was willing to trust my fiberglass butt joint in a boat on the water, I tested it for strength. Joining two pieces of $1/4$" plywood, I used only one layer of fiberglass tape on each side of the joint, and polyester resin, to make the weakest joint possible. In an over-the-knee test, the plywood itself broke well clear of the fiberglass joint, indicating that the joint was strong enough.

In practice, when installed in a boat, the joint is considerably stronger, because there are additional layers of tape on both the inside and the outside of the hull along the upper and lower edges. In addition, there is the boat's glass sheathing, making five layers in all.

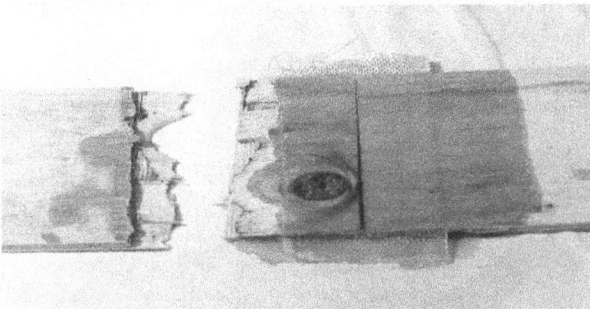

After it has cured, the joint is very strong. An over-the-knee break test fractured the plywood but left the joint intact.

If you want a stronger joint, take a disc sander and hollow out the joint slightly. Add a piece of fiberglass matting below the fiberglass tape, and use epoxy rather than polyester resin.

SCARFING PLYWOOD

Scarfing is a more elegant means of joining plywood panels together. It's more work than the fiberglass butt joint, and I haven't found it to be stronger, but if done properly, a scarf can be invisible when painted over, and there's a pride-of-workmanship factor that you may enjoy.

A scarf joint should be twelve times as long as the thickness of the plywood: $3\frac{3}{4}$" long for $5/16$" plywood, for example. Mark off that distance on each of the ends of both pieces that you will be joining. You don't have to draw the angle of the bevel on the side edges of the plywood.

Planing

I've tried all kinds of jigs and tricks and special tools, but I found that planing the bevel down with an electric block plane works best. You have to taper the bevel down to a feather edge; if the edges are a mere $1/16$" thick, they'll slip endwise when you clamp them together with glue in between. To make that feather edge, you have to support

the end of the plywood right to the very edge. After years of hard use, the edges on my workbench are quite rounded over, so I clamp a dead-flat piece of $3/8$" aluminum to the bench to support the edge of the plywood.

Support the very end of the plywood on a good rigid, square-edged surface, then plane it down, keeping the lines between the plies straight and parallel. I use an electric hand plane. Note the piece of railroad track holding things steady.

Sand the bevel smooth and dead-flat. *(Photo sequence continued on following page.)*

Check the flatness of the bevel with a straightedge. The back of a hand saw works.

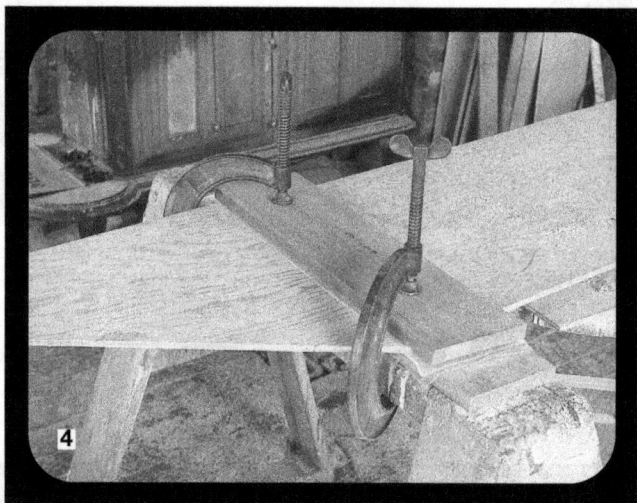

Apply glue to both sides of the bevel, place the pieces together, align them carefully, and tack them in place with brads to keep them from slipping. Then clamp the pieces with broad boards to distribute the pressure evenly; use waxed paper in between to prevent the work from sticking.

I cut the bevel with an electric block plane, but you can use a hand plane, too. Just start planing at the very end and watch the layers of the plywood as they're exposed. Keep them nice and straight and parallel as you work down toward the feather edge, and don't plane back further than your pencil mark. Don't try to achieve the feather edge with the plane, however, or you will tear out the edge and ruin the joint. You'll finish up with a belt sander, as I'll describe below.

If you wish, you can bevel more than one piece at a time. Lay the first piece down with the edge supported as described above. Lay the next piece on top of it, with its edge set back right to the line on the first piece that represents the top end of the bevel. Lay any additional pieces on top, staggering each one back the same amount. If you're

beveling four sheets of $\frac{1}{2}$" plywood at a 12:1 ratio, your stacked-up bevel will be 24" long. A long jointer plane would be nice for keeping that long bevel nice and flat. Don't just plane straight down the bevel: Work the plane at an angle.

Check, double-check, and check again to make sure that you're beveling the correct side of every piece, whether you do them all at once or one at a time. It's helpful if you label each piece as you cut it out (e.g., port side panel/ bow/inside, starboard bilge/aft/outside, etc.). Remember that for two panels to go together, one panel has to get beveled on the inside surface and the other on the outside surface.

I finish the taper down to the feather edge with an electric belt sander using 60-grit paper, checking my work frequently with a straightedge to make sure I keep the bevel flat. If the veneers that run with the direction of the cut seem too smooth, they can be roughened up a little with a wood rasp. I've tested trial panels for the across-the-knee break test with both smooth and roughened joints, and I couldn't detect any strength difference between them. Even so, I still roughen them before gluing.

Gluing

For the gluing procedure, find a clear area in which to work, and lay the matching pieces end to end, with the joint over a sawhorse. Lay a flat board, at least $\frac{3}{4}$" thick, between the panels and the sawhorse, and place a piece of waxed paper between the panels and the board. Once you spread the glue, things will get slippery, so you have to take special care to keep the panels in perfect alignment, which I'll discuss in a moment.

I use resorcinol glue for scarfs, and I mix it right to the letter of the instructions, even to the point of regulating my shop temperature. When you apply the glue, it will sink into the end grain of the plywood veneers but not into the flat surface of the wood. Before you close the joint permanently, leave it open for a few minutes. If the end grain has absorbed too much glue, add another dash. At seventy degrees, you won't have long to wait for the joint to cure. Cooler temperatures take longer. Keep the temperature steady throughout the curing process if you can.

Lay the glued surfaces together, lining up the feather edge of the top one exactly with the pencil line across the top of the bevel on the bottom one. Sight down the edges to make sure the curves are fair, and draw a pencil line on both edges of the joint, right across the angled line of the scarf. Drive a couple of brads through the joint, and double-check the pencil lines that you just drew to make sure they're still lined up.

Even with the brads and all the care you take, there is still some possibility of slippage when you apply pressure, so it is best to leave a little extra wood all around. When I cut out sixteen-foot hull panels, I leave about a half inch all around the cutting lines. After the glue is cured, I lay my pattern on again to check for accuracy of the layout before cutting out the final shape. (I work with patterns on some boats that I build in quantity.) If you don't use patterns, you can still check the measurements before you cut down to the line.

But I've jumped ahead a bit. First, you have to clamp the joint together before the glue cures. Lay another piece of waxed paper on top of the joint, and put another ¾" board over that. The boards above and below the scarf joint are necessary to get even pressure all the way across. Clamp the whole sandwich down to the sawhorse at both edges. Take up on both clamps as evenly as you can, and keep alert for slippage and misalignment. The next day, when the joint is thoroughly cured, remove the excess glue with your belt sander, and you'll have a joint to be proud of.

No joint that I've made in this manner has ever let go, but if this your first attempt, I recommend that you make up a few test panels before entrusting yourself and your loved ones to a boat built with these scarfs. If you break one over your knee and the joint stays intact but the wood on either side of the joint breaks, you're okay.

SETTING UP

Instant Boats are built upside down. This is the most sensible way to build them, because you will be working with gravity instead of against it. Build boats upside down, and the planks fall on the boat. Build them right side up, and they want to fall off. Simple, huh?

The boats are also set up plumb and square, but Bolger made this easy for you when he drew the plans. For instance, when the plans show the location of a frame on a side panel, you mark that location in pencil, right on the panel's inside surface. Then you just install the frame exactly on the line, and if your two side panels are identical, you have automatically squared and plumbed the frame. Marking and cutting the parts out as closely as your skill allows helps to ensure the accuracy of the boat.

This doesn't mean that you can't still screw it up. You can still get a twist in your boat if your sawhorses aren't all level, or if you allow a side panel to creep off the frame line when you're fastening it. Use your level, and take a good hard look at how things are aligned before you make any fastenings permanent and move on to the next step.

On most of the boats, the hull panels are bent around frames that you cut out of plywood, usually in one piece. On a few of the boats, however (including the Sea Hawk and the Fisherman's Skiff), you use simple jigs to establish their shapes. The difference is that the frames become a permanent part of the boat, while the jigs are just aids to building it. Bolger shows the station molds on the jigs built up from individual pieces of lumber. This is the economical way to go, but to save time, I usually cut the molds out of plywood in one piece, just like permanent frames. This also eliminates the possibility of assembling a mold cockeyed or having it go out of alignment.

On some of the boats, the frames or forms are held upright by clamping or nailing them to sawhorses. If that's too high to work at comfortably, make simple legs for the frames from 2" x 4"s, to hold them at whatever height suits you. For other boats, the frames are tacked directly to the panels. Mark the centerlines on bottom panels, transoms, stems, and frames or forms. (It's usually labeled "CL" on the plans.) When you lay the bottom down, make sure all the centerlines are aligned, and you'll guarantee yourself a straight boat. If your boat will have a skeg or drag strip on the bottom, make sure you mark the bottom's centerline on *both sides*. It'll save you a bit of grief later.

Frame-width dimensions are given to the inside chine lines. The plans show a little partial-circle cutout at the chine. This allows the glass tape to be fed through in one piece for the long joints. Mark this cutout on the frame, but cut it out only partially with a saber saw, leaving the cutout hanging by a tab. You want the corner of the frame to remain in place so that you can set the edge of your hull panel at the proper height. If you cut it out now, you'll have only thin air to align the panel to. It's easy enough to work around if you make this mistake, but it's easier if the chine corners are left intact. The reason to cut it out most of the way now is that it'll be difficult to get a saw in there later when the panels are glued in place.

Some of the boats are designed for tack-and-tape construction from the get-go, and others have chine logs at the bottom/bilge or bottom/side panel intersection. In most cases, you can leave out the chine log and build the boat stitch-and-glue style instead. This will save you some work fitting and beveling the chine logs. I've come to trust the glassed fillet joint, so I recommend this approach, but feel free to build to the chine-log designs as shown—they work just as well.

If you do build with the chine logs when using a building jig, you'll have to notch the frames to accept them. The logs go in after the side panels are in place, so cut the notches loose enough to give the logs some room for adjustment.

Although there are variations, the side panels go on first, then the bottom panels, and if there are bilge panels, they go on last. After cutting them to rough shape, mark and trim them until they fit just right between the side panels and the bottom panels. But don't put them on until you've given the whole setup a good looking over to make sure everything's fair. Not checking for twist almost always guarantees that there is some, and after the bilge panels are glued in place, you'll have to live with it. If the boat has no bilge panels, you can often forego laying out the bottom. After the side panels are set up, just plop a plywood sheet on top of them and trace the shape of their bottom edges right onto it. If the bottom has *rocker*—a curve in the fore-and-aft direction—make sure you hold the plywood down carefully all the way around when tracing around the sides for the shape.

Nailing through the side panels into the narrow frames (¼" plywood on most of the boats) calls for accurate aim. Bore tiny holes through the marked frame locations on the inside of the panels before putting them against the frames and you can't miss.

Use #18 wire nails to hold the panels to the frames. The tiny nails won't split the plywood edges, and you don't need much holding power, since the nails are only there to maintain temporary alignment between the parts. It's glue and fiberglass tape that will hold things together permanently.

If this calls for more accuracy than you want to deal with, and you would rather use screws than nails for this temporary fastening, screw wooden cleats to the sides of the frames, and screw the hull panels to them. (You still have to make sure that the hull panels are lined up properly against the frames.) This method has become popular, and when performed with an electric reversible drill-driver and the proper-sized screwdriver bit, it's fast.

PUTTING THE LONG SEAMS TOGETHER

If you marked and cut your panels accurately and tacked them in place right along the lines, they should fit together with fairly small gaps in between. You can pull most small gaps together with long strips of masking tape placed across the seams—that's right, masking tape. Because most of the designs call for little or no twist to the hull panels, and the panel expansions are very accurate, it usually takes very little to pull them into place.

Using Wire to Hold Panel Edges Together

Boats that do call for harder bends and twists in the planking may need wire to hold the panel edges together. I use #18 gauge mechanic's wire, which you can find in an automotive supply store in two-pound spools. It is strong but soft, pliable, and easy to use. Bore a series of pairs of tiny holes near the edges of the panels, one on each side of the gap. Crawl underneath the boat and poke a short length of wire through each pair of holes, then climb back out again and twist the ends together to bring the panel edges together. These little wire ties are the "stitches" in stitch-and-glue. Don't twist too hard, or you'll tear the holes right through to the edge of the plywood.

You don't need to be too careful about eliminating all the gaps, since the putty and glass will fill them in nicely. Gaps as wide as $1/4$" are okay. If the gap is so big that the putty will fall right through, however, back the seam lengthwise from underneath with a strip of masking tape. When I first tried this, I thought I was going to have a mess, with the putty sticking to the masking tape. But after the putty had hardened, the tape came off cleanly. (This is with a polyester resin putty mix. I haven't tried that with an epoxy joint.)

Using Resin and Putty

Once you're satisfied with the placement of the panel edges, mix up some unfilled resin (either polyester or epoxy), and brush the edges of the joint back to half the width of the fiberglass tape. Plywood edges soak up resin fast, and if not enough is applied, the edges will suck resin right out of the putty. So brush it on, let it soak in a bit, and if the wood begins to look dry, brush on some more. Let it dry a bit more, then fill the gaps with putty, applying it with a putty knife. Brushing on the unfilled resin first helps the putty bond much better.

The putty is made of the same resin, thickened with enough filler to make the consistency of peanut butter (smooth, not chunky). Most of the resin manufacturers offer a variety of fillers with different properties. I like Fillite because it expands when mixed, so the mix goes further. Fillite sands better than any filler I've used, and it's cheap.

Let the putty set up, then remove the masking tape and fill in the gaps. If you used wire stitches, cut them outside the hull, crawl under again, and pull them out with pliers. Some builders leave them in, but I always remove them, since they're not needed for strength and they get in the way of taping.

Let the putty harden overnight, then round the corners of the seams with a rasp and sand them smooth. Brush a fresh coat of unthickened resin along both sides of the seam, and lay a strip of fiberglass tape into it, taking care to lay it out smooth and fair. Brush another coat onto the glass, making sure there are no wrinkles. The glass tape should turn from white to clear when it's properly saturated with resin. Don't let any white areas remain, or the joint will be weakened. Using the resin manufacturer's guidelines to determine how much time to wait between coats, brush on some more resin to fill in the weave of the fabric.

After the resin cures, the boat will hold together. Flip it over and get ready to glass the inside seams.

Fillets

The insides and outsides of the joints are made in a similar manner, with one important difference. On the outside, you used just enough putty to fill the gap. On the inside, you're going to make a fillet—a nice, thick bead of filled resin that adds plenty of material to strengthen the joint. In a sense, you'll mold a fiberglass chine log in place. There are several steps, and ideally they are done in one operation without stopping so that the entire application cures as one solid joint.

Brush unthickened resin onto the inside of the seams, just as you did with the outside seams. Mix up enough resin for the joint and stir in the filler. A pint of thickened, catalyzed resin in a container will "kick" in about ten minutes, so you're going to have to work fast. If you can't use up that much in ten minutes, mix less.

Fill the seam with putty, really loading it in, then spread it evenly along the joint with a rounded applicator or an auto-body-type rubber squeegee that will change shape to accommodate the changing angles of the plywood joint. You should end up with the putty spread out to about $1^{1}/2$"

from the joint in both directions and smoothed to a nice, coved radius. Using a putty knife, quickly scrape up any excess putty that snowplowed off to the sides to minimize the sanding cleanup later. Then immediately roll the fiberglass tape into the fresh putty along the whole length of the joint. Smooth the tape into the putty with a 2" brush, giving the tape a gentle pull lengthwise if any wrinkles appear. When the tape is properly in place, immediately give it a coat of unthickened, catalyzed resin.

Let the joint set up a little and watch for the shiny, fresh color of the resin to fade to a duller look. This usually takes ten or fifteen minutes depending on temperature. Give the joint another coat of resin, and another, until you've filled the weave of the cloth and have achieved a nice, smooth surface.

It's important that the joint be done in one operation without stopping, and without allowing one application of resin to cure before the next one goes on. Temperature, humidity, and the quantity of resin mixed in the container all affect the cure rate. If you live where it's warm, give yourself as much time as possible by doing it early in the morning, when the temperature is as cool as the resin manufacturer's recommendations allow, and don't work in direct sunlight. On the other hand, if it is cold and damp, you may have to use twice the amount of hardener in polyester resin. More hardener will make the joint cure faster. Follow the manufacturer's guidelines.

If you see the resin starting to gel or harden, stop right there and give up on that batch. Trying to beat the hardening process by spreading lumpy resin on the job is futile . . . you are not going to win. Keep in mind that the thicker the mix, the quicker it hardens, so get it on there! When glassing a hull, a pint at a time is a safe mixture while you're still learning.

SHEATHING THE BOAT WITH FIBERGLASS

Remember my skeptical friend, Brian Amato, who questioned the value of epoxy back in Chapter 2? Brian also has some issues with fiberglass. He writes:

> Twenty years ago, I built a Glen-L "Eight Ball" sailing dinghy from plans. I did what I knew—1/4" plywood, Weldwood brown powder, brass screws and ring grip nails—and it floated, rowed, and sailed like a champ. It was still going strong after being stored outside for over ten years and NO GLASS!! Now, every time I read anything about building small boats, every Tom, Dick, and Harry says you have to sheathe the thing in cloth and resin, squeegee it out—more coats, more cloth—etc. How come none of the boats I've built in the past twenty-five years have ever come apart or leaked, and I've never used resin and cloth? Can't we just glue 'em and screw 'em, put some paint on 'em, and go enjoy them? I'm amazed Columbus ever made it without the *Santa Maria* falling apart. What's your take on all this glass stuff?

Testing the Strength of My First Stitch-and-Glue Boat

When I built the first stitch-and-glue boat, I wanted to see how strong this kind of construction was. I made an angled joint of two pieces of 1/2" plywood with a fillet of polyester-based putty, a layer of 3" fiberglass tape inside and out, and a layer of fiberglass cloth on the outside. I jacked up my pickup and put this joint beneath the tire, with the concave side down. I knew that something was going to give when the weight of my pickup was lowered on it, but *how* it broke was what I wanted to see. When the joint let go, it tore a layer of plywood cleanly across the board, leaving the fiberglass joint intact. This was proof enough for me that the joint is stronger than the plywood itself.

To test the strength of the stitch-and-glue building method, the author made a filleted, fiberglassed joint using polyester—not epoxy—resin, and lowered his pickup truck onto it.

The plywood itself failed, while the joint itself remained intact, proving that the method is strong enough to hold a boat together.

There are several good reasons for sheathing the boat in fiberglass. If your boatbuilding skills are not that good, any mistakes you make will be covered up in the fiberglassing process. This "covers" (so to speak) not only cosmetic errors, but also potential leaks and weak joints. Fiberglassing adds strength to the structure. It offers a lot of abrasion resistance. And it ends problems of paint adhesion, cracking, and peeling by sealing and covering the wood. It doesn't matter what you use for paint; fiberglass will take almost anything and keep it there. Yes, it adds weight, cost, and labor, but on balance, I'd say use it.

Flip the boat upside down again and give the entire exterior a coat of unthickened resin. Allow it to cure, then sand it down; I use 60-grit paper on a disc sander. The objective here is to provide a rough surface, with a lot of "tooth" to hold the next application of cloth and resin. Pay special attention to the edges of the fiberglass tape. Grind them down and feather them out, and get rid of any hardened bubbles and other imperfections.

Cut a piece of six-ounce fiberglass cloth large enough to cover the transom and overlap the sides and bottom by 3". Mix about a pint of resin and brush it on, including the overlap areas. Lay the cloth on the wet resin, and use a shop brush to smooth it out if necessary. Use masking tape to hold down any edges of the cloth that want to escape, then brush another coat of resin into the cloth. Start with a big glob in the middle and brush, roll, or squeegee it out to the edges. Doing it this way will force out any air under the cloth.

Roll out and cut a length of cloth to stretch from the transom to the stem. Don't cut it to shape at the gunwales—just let it hang for now. It's also too much trouble to try to fit the glass cloth in neat folds around the front of the stem, so just bring it over the sides of the stem and cut it off neatly, matching the profile curve of the stem. You'll cover the front face of the stem itself with several layers of fiberglass tape, and these will overlap the front edges of the glass on the sides of the stem.

Smooth out the cloth and brush on the resin. Don't mix more than a pint of resin at a time, and you should have no problems with it "going off" prematurely. When the resin is stiff and partially cured, you can trim the overhanging cloth at the gunwales with a sharp knife.

Throughout the entire boatbuilding process, pay attention to what you are doing, think ahead all you can, and if you are only just average-handy—or even less—you can build yourself a boat. Don't beat on yourself for not knowing how to do something; just ask someone who does. (If you don't know someone locally, the message board on my website, www.instantboats.com, is a good place to ask questions.) And don't be afraid to make mistakes. We're just talking about plywood and framing lumber here, not teak and walnut. If you blow it, you'll figure it out and you'll get it right the next time. Like the late, old-time boatbuilder Pete Culler once said, "Experience starts when you begin."

PART TWO

INSTANT BOATS
STEP BY
STEP

CHAPTER 5

BUILDING BOAT MODELS

Even though I build full-sized boats for a living, for years I wanted to build model boats—not full-rigged ships or anything like that, but down-to-earth models that matched my levels of skill and patience. I watched others try their hand at model making and learned a lot from their successes and failures. I saw the remains of a good friend's botched kit model go up in flames and decided then and there that stamped-out kits and working with balsa were not for me.

The type of model making that appealed to me the most was that described by the late Weston Farmer in an article in *National Fisherman*. His commonsense approach was to work with the plans of a full-sized boat—either a proven design that had already been built as a boat, or a new design, to proof-test it, if you will—and to use materials that he could find around the shop. So I started making construction models of my full-scale boats, building them from scratch exactly as shown on the plans. Some were built entirely for pleasure and are now on display on a shelf in my living room. Others were built so that I could examine the lines of the boat in three dimensions. Still others were built to test a set of plans; I wanted to check out the building procedure and discover where the difficult areas might be before I started on the real boat. No matter how experienced you are as a boatbuilder, building a construction model before tackling the full-scale boat is one of the best learning techniques around. The cost of materials is next to nothing, and cutting and shaping those small, flat pieces and transforming them into a model is bound to add to your abilities. The techniques for this type of model making are virtually the same as for full-sized boatbuilding, and the satisfactions are every bit as high. If you make a mistake . . . so what? Better to make your mistakes on the model while you improve your skills for the real thing.

So come along with me on a minimum-risk adventure in boatbuilding. We'll build a model of Cartopper as if we were building a boat (see plans on pages 50–54). Then, when we're done, we'll set it on the shop bench and use it as inspiration to build the real thing.

MODEL-MAKING TOOLS

Here are the hand tools I use for building models. You don't necessarily need every item on the list.

- Architect's scale rule. I consider this indispensable for model making. Like a good compass, you can trust; it lets you know where you are all of the time. Get one. Learn how to use it.
- Other measuring and marking tools: steel rule, small brass calipers, a centering rule, a plastic circle template
- Two-ounce jeweler's ball-peen hammer. Great for heading over brass wire or driving small pins
- Machinist's miniature vise
- Miniature hand drill, with a set of micro drill bits, from Nos. 54 to 80
- Set of tool-and-die maker's Swiss pattern files in twelve standard shapes: flat, round-tapered, three-cornered, and square, in different sizes
- Jeweler's saw: for fine cuts in any material
- Razor saw with replaceable blades. Get one that cuts on the pull stroke, like a Japanese saw.
- Miniature spokeshave: hard to find, but very handy. My set of three (with one flat and two different convex blades) was made by Aldon Products. I can't seem to find this company, but I do see the tools listed on various websites.
- Broken razor blades. In a variety of widths, these are in constant use as putty knives, chisels, scrapers, and more. I use a single-edge razor blade, take off the holder on top, and bury the blade in my vise to the width that I want. A quick hammer blow breaks the blade off because of its hard temper. (Wear safety goggles.) They don't always break exactly as you wish, so you might have to try a few times. When you're satisfied with the results, place it in a handle.
- Micro plane. Indispensable for delicate planing jobs.
- Extra-fine needle-nosed pliers
- Diagonal-cutting pliers
- Assorted production-grade sandpaper: 220 to 320 grit

- Emery boards
- Double-sided tape
- $\frac{1}{2}$" and $\frac{3}{4}$" brass dressmaker's pins. Common pins can be used, but they tend to be too large for delicate work.
- $\frac{1}{2}$" or $\frac{5}{8}$" paintbrush
- Clamps, small. For applying a lot of carefully regulated pressure, get a handful of micro C-clamps. Miniature clothespins about 2" long are also very helpful and fast. The ones I found in Wal-Mart's hobby section are inexpensive but need a little tailoring. The wire that holds them together has a tendency to come off and they fly apart. Glue the wire in place and they are great to work with.
- Clamps, large. I wouldn't want to be without a couple of "Quick Clamps" with rubber foot pads and quick release.
- Bellows-type glue applicator

. . . and the list goes on. How do you know when you have enough tools? It's when you have enough to match your talent, and perhaps a few more. By no means do you need all of what's listed here, but it's always fun to keep looking. Many of these tools can be found at a well-stocked hobby shop, and just about all of them, and more, are available from Micro-Mark. (See Appendix for contact information.)

The more power tools you have, the easier the job will be, and the less dependent you will be on hobby shops for wood of the proper size and thickness. I saw out all my planking on an 8" table saw fitted with a hollow-ground planer blade. This is a cross/rip combination with no set to the teeth, and with it, there's nothing to resawing wood down to $\frac{1}{16}$" thick; you can even go down to $\frac{1}{32}$".

A band saw is a great help, as is a scroll saw, which can be used for cutting small wood and metal parts in which the fineness of the cut is important. A Dremel tool is a great aid for cutting, drilling, and sanding small parts, and there's a huge selection of attachments and accessories available.

GLUES FOR MODEL MAKING

For most model-making projects, I get by nicely with Franklin's Titebond II Premium Wood Glue, which is a quick-grabbing glue that will bond a joint in only a few minutes. (It's fast enough to allow "clamping" the joints with your fingers.) Titebond is water resistant, not waterproof, but this is fine for a mantelpiece model.

Elmer's white glue, also not waterproof, is acceptable for model making. It is slower to grab than Titebond, but for a long seam that you have to fiddle with, the slow grab is a good feature. Both of them clean up with water.

I wondered if Titebond II could be thinned with water to slow down its quick-grabbing tendency a bit without sacrificing strength. The company puts its toll-free

number right on the bottle, so I called and a person answered—a real live person—no answering machine, no "press this" or "press that." When I recovered from my shock, I asked to speak with the glue technician. She said, "I am the glue technician." She told me that you can thin Titebond II, and to what percentage without a loss of strength. I couldn't believe it: Here was a real, live, courteous person who was reachable and had the answer—all in one call.

MODEL-MAKING WOOD

Most hobby shops sell model-maker's plywood—so-called aircraft plywood—in both 12" x 2' and 12" x 4' sheets. This is nicely made out of basswood or birch veneers, and it comes in various thicknesses starting as thin as $\frac{1}{64}$". In addition, many modeler's catalogs, including Micro-Mark, carry impressive inventories of solid wood veneers in varying thicknesses. You can purchase basswood, walnut, mahogany, cherry, and other species, usually in 2' lengths from $\frac{1}{32}$" to 2" thick. Buying a few sheets of this plywood or veneer can save you a lot of time, especially since it is usually milled to within a cat's whisker and can be depended on to produce accurate results.

But plywood and veneers are "peeled" from logs, and, if you are like me, you might find the flat grain boring to look at. For that reason, and for economy's sake, I mill most of my own model-making wood on my table saw. Most of the time I use white cedar, because it is native to my area and easy to find, and because it is so flexible that I can tie thin strips of it into knots without steaming, if I so desire. I also find basswood to be an excellent choice.

If you decide to mill your own, use whatever wood that is native to your area: pine, spruce, cypress . . . whatever. The qualities you are looking for are: no knots, straight grain, flexibility, workability, and easy bending without brittleness. Pick what you like to work with and go for it.

What about balsa? Bahh! It's about as interesting as oatmeal.

How thick should your stock be? Let's talk about scale for a moment. Most of Phil Bolger's plans are drawn to a scale of $1\frac{1}{2}$" = 1' (that's on the full-size plan sheets—not as reproduced in this book). If you build at the same size as the plans (in other words, $1\frac{1}{2}$" = $1\frac{1}{2}$"), then the model will be one-eighth the size of the real boat. In the case of the 11'6" Cartopper, your model will be $17\frac{1}{4}$" long. That's a nice size, so that's what you'll use: big enough to work on easily and to make an impressive display model.

Bolger specifies $\frac{1}{4}$" plywood for the hull panels. This translates to $\frac{1}{32}$" for the scale model. I wouldn't go that thin, because $\frac{1}{32}$" stock is tricky to mill on a table saw and too fragile for my liking. I use $\frac{1}{16}$" stock, which is safe to mill out and about right for bending, even though it is twice the scale thickness.

How much stock? Look at the plans, estimate the amount required, then mill out more than that to account for wastage and the inevitable ruined pieces. Once you have your saw operation set up, run a test strip through to get the exact thickness you want, then mill enough wood to do the job at this one setting. Nothing is more frustrating than to have to saw out another piece or two later and find you can't match the exact thickness you had before.

Of course, the width of your milled-out stock will depend on the maximum height you can raise the blade of your table saw. (The maximum cut of my 8" table saw, for example, is only 1¾".) If this isn't wide enough for your needs, it's easy to edge-glue pieces together. Lay waxed paper down on a flat surface: your saw table, a kitchen counter, whatever. Spread glue on the edges of the wood to be joined, lay the pieces on the waxed paper, make the joint, and wipe off as much excess glue as you can. If the pieces won't lie flat, cover them with another sheet of waxed paper and add weights. After the joint is dry—which takes only ten or fifteen minutes for Titebond II in a warm shop—sand the surfaces with 220-grit sandpaper to get rid of any excess glue.

If you don't want to buy small modeling tools and mess with small pieces of wood, you can build a model from cardboard, using scissors, glue, and Scotch tape. Making even a cardboard model is a definite help for the first-time builder, and the total investment is naught but time and effort.

THE PLANS

There are several ways to build a model of the Cartopper from plans. The easiest and most accurate is to use a set of builder's plans at the scale drawn by the designer, 1½" = 1'. (See the appendix for ordering information.) You can cut up the plans and use them as patterns, which will produce a fine model that is one-eighth the size of the real boat, or 17¼" long. There is no transferring of measurements, no lofting, no bending of battens—virtually no way to mismeasure and ruin the project. Everything is done one-to-one.

If you want to keep your plans intact, you can measure all the parts of the plans and transfer their shapes to wood, but this means using rules, battens, pins, and a lot more time. If you are looking at ten feet of snow out your shop window, you might want to consider this option. Or you can have the plans photocopied and cut them up to use them as patterns. Just trace around them and away you go!

The above two methods are viable if you have a set of builder's plans. *The plans in this book are exactly the same as the builder's plans, but they have been reduced to fit on the page and are therefore of no true scale.* That's no problem if you don't mind redrawing them to the scale you want, especially if you *are* looking at ten feet of snow out your window. . . .

But at the risk of sounding like a promoter, I'd recommend ordering a set of 1½" = 1' builder's plans and being done with it.

I might mention that building models this way—cutting up scale plans to produce patterns—will work for all of the boats in this book. If you already have a set of plans for any other Instant Boat and you would like to make a model of it, then you have no need to buy more plans. Cut up the plans and have a go.

THE SCALE OF THE MODEL

I included an architect's scale rule as one of the essentials in the list of hand tools on page 34. I can't give you every single dimension in this chapter, and the architect's scale is your key to pulling dimensions off the plans. The scale of 1½" = 1', which is the scale at which Cartopper is drawn in the full-size plans, is a comparatively large scale to work with and easy to read. Using the scale is simple—any school kid can do this—so just follow along.

Find the end of the rule marked 1½" for the scale that we'll be working with. Now find zero. It's not at the left end—it's set in a bit to the right. To the left of the 0, you can see the numbers 3, 6, and 9. These represent scale inches. The hash marks between the numbered marks represent intermediate inch quantities, or fractions of inches. Since there are twelve hash marks from the 0 to the 3, each mark represents ¼". There are also twelve hash marks from the 9 to the left end of the scale, giving us scale measurements in ¼" increments all the way from 0" to 12". Why is the 12" mark labeled with a big number 3 at the very left end of the scale? Hold onto that question. We'll come back to it soon.

Now look to the right of the 0, and you'll see whole numbers of different sizes going in both directions. That's because each edge of an architect's rule has two scales, one of which reads from left to right, and the other which reads from right to left. Since we just examined the inch marks at the very left-hand end of the rule, we now know how long a foot is, so we can see that the smaller 2, at the right of the photo, represents 2' from the 0. And the other numeral 2? That represents 2' from the 0 at the other end of the rule, on a different scale (3" = 1'). Not coincidentally, though, that

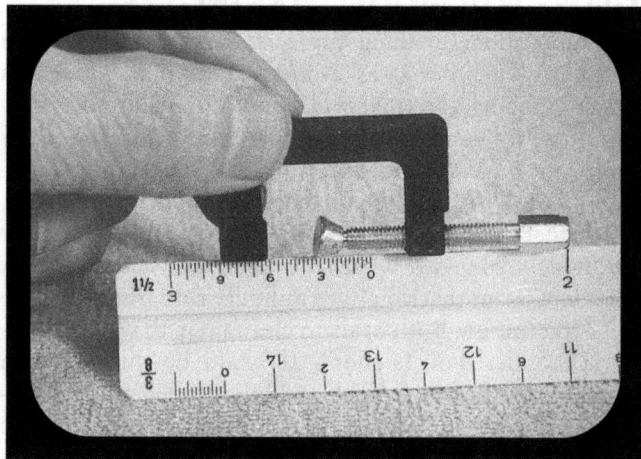

An architect's scale rule is an essential tool.

bigger numeral 2 falls right on the mark that represents 1' to the right of your 0. And the 3 at the very left-hand end? That's 3' on the 3" = 1' scale, but as you've already seen, it falls right on the 1'2" mark on the 1½" = 1' scale. The two scales that appear on the same edge of the rule are always in a 1:2 ratio *to each other*. So, as long as you pay attention to your 0, all of the *marks* are accurate, and you just have to decide if the *numerals* refer to the scale you're using, or to the one that starts at the opposite end of the rule.

So let me measure something. The C-clamp I'm holding in the photo is more than 1' long in scale, so I line one end of it up exactly on a foot mark. I'll pick whatever foot mark works so that the other end of the clamp falls on the inches part of the scale. I have 1' to the right of 0 and 9" to the left of 0: in other words, 1'9". Easy.

Follow the same procedure to take a measurement off the plans. Line the rule up so that one end of the feature is exactly on a foot mark and the other end falls somewhere on the inches part of the scale. No need to convert measurements from "real size" to the size of the model, multiply or divide by eight, or go through any other mathematics. Simply measure the part on the plans with the scale rule, then use the scale rule to transfer the measurement to the part layout.

If this seems like a lot of explaining for a simple process, you're right. But simple procedures can be the most difficult to explain. When my young son Timothy asked me what was so hard about writing, I answered, "Try writing about how to tie your shoes!"

In practice, the architect's scale is easy to use and very practical. Whether you are building a full-size boat or a model at 1½" or ⅜" scale or even less, this simple little tool is the key to understanding. It unlocks the door to plans drawn at any scale, and to what size wood to build them from. Get one and use it.

SIDE PANELS

You will start building the Cartopper model by making the side-, bottom-, and bilge-panel templates and laying them out on the planking wood. The exact shapes for all of these pieces are positioned together on Sheet 2 of the plans (page 51). Note that in the full-sized boat, each of

these pieces is made of two parts joined by a butt strap, but there is no need to build the model that way. You'll make each of the panels in one piece.

Start with the sides first. There are two identical side panels shown on the plans, but you only need to make one template. Therefore, you'll work with the panel at the top of the sheet. Cut along the lines representing the ends and the bottom of the panel, but for the time being, do not cut along the line representing the sheer; rather, cut along the straight line above the sheer. This is done to avoid edge set, or distortion, in the template while laying it on the wood.

Lay the side-panel template on the wood and trace around the bottom and the ends. Remove the template. Cut along the line representing the sheer on the template and lay it back down on the wood, aligning the bottom and the ends with the lines you have already traced onto the wood. Now trace along the sheer line.

Mark the locations of the three frames—A, B, and C—and label them. (Frame A is the one closest to the bow, C is closest to the stern, and B is between the two.) These are represented by dashed lines on the plans.

Cut out the side panel with a band saw or a scroll saw, being sure to leave the lines. Finish shaping the piece with a small plane and sandpaper. You can use the template to draw out the second side panel, or use the finished first side as a template for the second. If you do the latter, remember that you will have made the second side the width of a pencil point wider than the first. Therefore, after the second side has been cut out, put it next to the first side and trim it to match exactly. Be especially sure that the angles of the ends are exact. *Accuracy in later stages of the model depends on attention to accuracy here.*

This brings up an important point: At a scale of 1½" = 1', the width of a dull pencil point equals about ⅛". Unless you work with a sharp pencil at all times, you can accidentally add more than you might think to your model after you have traced around all sides of a template.

BILGE PANELS, BOTTOM, AND TRANSOM

Follow the same procedures for the bottom panel and the two bilge panels. Mark the locations of the frames and the longitudinal centerline on what will be the inside face of the bottom panel; the bilge panels needn't be so marked.

Make a template for the transom, trace it onto your wood, and cut it out. Then make the framing for the transom. Each piece of transom framing must be double-beveled (the same bevel on both the inner and outer edges), with the exception of the top transverse frame, the under edge of which should be left square. The bevel for the side frames is 18°; the bilge panel frames, 22°; and the bottom panel, 26°. Glue the framing to the inside face of the transom. Don't forget to install the motor board.

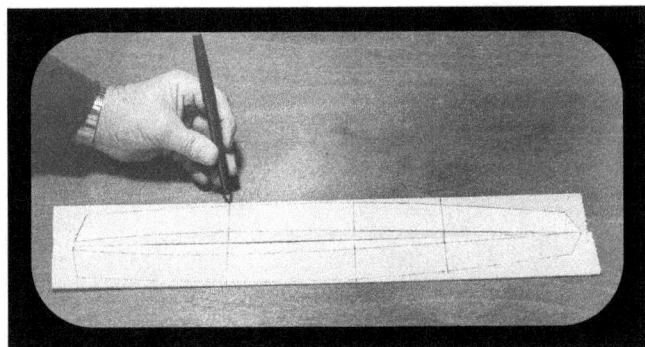

Using a template to mark the side panels.

STEM

Make a template for the stem, using the same procedure that you used for the side-panel template. In other words, cut along the outside face of the stem and along the bottom edge, but for the time being, do not cut along the inside of the stem. Rather, rough-cut up the line of the mast and along the sheer back to the stem head. Don't forget the notch in the stem at the forefoot to catch the forward end of the bottom panel.

Try to find wood with sweeping grain that approximates the curve of the stem. If you can't find any and must work with straight grain, position the template so that cross grain will be shared at both ends rather than concentrated in the middle. Alternatively, use aircraft plywood.

Lay down the stem template on the wood and trace along the forward and bottom edges. Remove the template, finish cutting the template along the inside face of the stem, reposition it, and trace along the inside face. Cut out the stem with a band saw or a scroll saw.

Sand the curved faces of the stem with an emery board, mark a centerline down the outside face, then mark two lines parallel to it to represent the forward edges of the stem bevels. Using a file, rough-cut the ever-changing bevels on each side of the stem right to these lines, following the rule that it is better to make a shorter bevel than a longer one. Later, when the frames are set up, a thin batten can be bent from the transom around the frames to the stem, and the bevel can be cut to its final, exact shape.

FRAMES

Make the templates for the three frames by cutting along the outside and straight across the tops. Do not cut along the inside edges yet. Following the same principles as for the

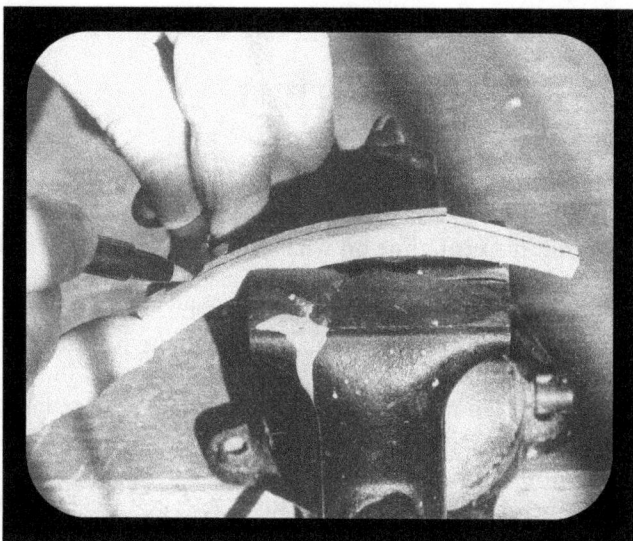

Shaping the stem bevels.

stem, lay out the frame templates on your wood to best utilize the pattern of the grain.

Trace around the frame templates onto the wood. Remove the templates, and cut the inside shapes of the frames. Then lay the template back on the wood and trace the inside shapes onto the wood. Mark the centerline of the frames.

Note that the edge of Frame A (nearest the bow) that adjoins the bilge panel is slightly curved. Do not make it straight. This frame is in two halves, which are butted and strapped together at the bottom; and at the top—above the cutout—there's a cleat.

I made Frames B and C in halves for better grain layout and tied them together with butt straps that face each other under the floorboard in the boat. The plans show these frames notched to support the ends of the floorboard, but they are hardly needed in a model, so I left them out.

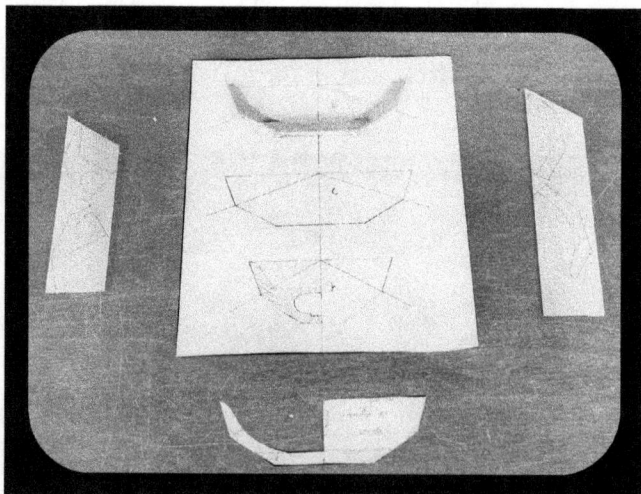

Marking the stem's centerline.

Marking and cutting the frames.

Frame A has a notch to take the after end of the mast-step. Since we are making the rowing model of the Cartopper, this notch need not be cut.

The plans also show limber holes in the bottom corners of the frames for the full-sized boat. I don't bother with these holes in the model. If you wish to put them in, make a tiny pattern for one hole and use it to mark all twelve. Don't completely cut out these holes at first. Leave tiny tabs ($\frac{1}{16}$" is fine) to hold the waste in place, since you need the corners for reference when assembling the hull. You can cut the tabs later.

ASSEMBLING THE HULL

Begin assembling the hull by gluing the after end of one of the side panels to the transom. Franklin Titebond glue grabs quickly, so if you use it, you can hold the parts together until the glue sets up. You could also use tiny clamps for this operation, hooking them on the transom frame. Then glue the other side panel to the opposite side of the transom.

Drop in Frame C, the one closest to the transom, aligning it with the frame position marks on the side panels. Do not glue it yet; use pins to hold it in place.

Pull in the bow ends of the side panels so they are touching, and hold them together temporarily with masking tape. Try Frames B and A in the positions marked on the side panels, beveling the edges of the frames so that the side panels bear evenly on them. The frames are positioned properly when their lower corners are aligned with the lower edges of the side panels. Don't worry about any discrepancy in the alignment of the top of the frames with the top of the side panels; this can be

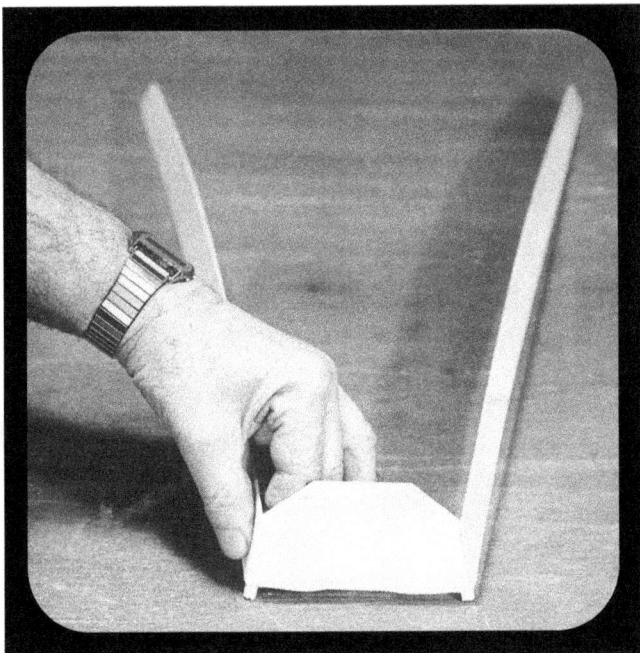

Inserting frames A, B, and C. Note that the side panels are held together temporarily at the bow with masking tape.

taken out later at the same time you fair the top of the transom into the sides.

FITTING THE BOTTOM PANEL AND STEM

Release the masking tape at the bow, and temporarily fasten the after end of the bottom panel to the bottom of the transom and to Frame A, skipping Frames B and C. Check both positions for centerline alignment. Do not glue down the bottom yet; use pins.

Clamp the stem to the forward end of the bottom, making sure the bottom fits into the notch in the stem.

Pull the sides in to the stem and check the bevels on each side of the stem. Trim as necessary so that the sides bear properly.

Take your time here. Adjust the assembly so that the stem, the bottom, and the side panels fair into each other properly. When you are satisfied that all is okay, first glue one side panel to the stem and then the other. Hold the pieces together until the glue sets, or pin them.

Remove the bottom and apply glue to the bottom of all the frames, the transom, and the stem. Lay the bottom back on and align the centerline of the frames with the centerline of the bottom. Hold or pin the bottom in place until the glue grabs.

FITTING THE BILGE PANELS

With the side panels and bottom in place, the model is really shaping up. Now it's time to close her in with the bilge panels.

Trial-fit the bilge panels, using pieces of masking tape to hold them in position as you work. As you fit them between the sides and the bottom panel, think of them as the skins of orange sections and try to achieve a fit that is as close as that. If the panels seem too stiff at their forward

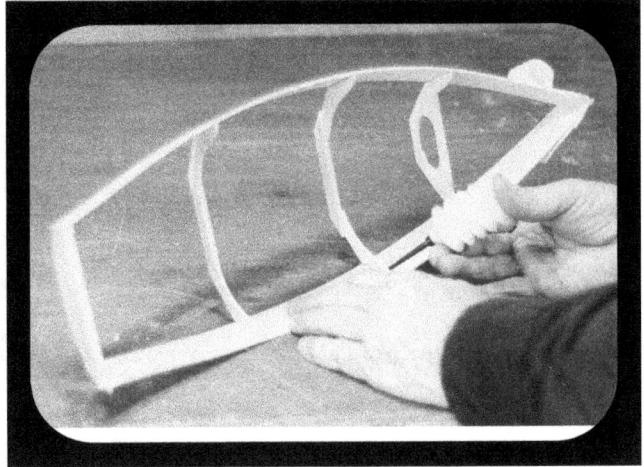

Fastening the side panels to the transom.

Installing the bottom.

ends to bend into place properly, sand them down a little thinner.

When you have each panel located properly in a fore-and-aft position, make a tick mark across the joint. This will allow you to reposition the panel exactly after you have taken it off for trimming.

To achieve a good fit, take a little off the inside edges of the bottom, side, and bilge panels with a file or sandpaper. Fit the middle of the panels first, then work toward the ends.

If you are in doubt about your skill here, the easy and safe way of doing this job is to cut the bilge panels wide enough to more than span the space they are to fill. Tape them in place on the outside of the hull, and from the inside, mark off their shapes using the edges of the sides and bottom as guides. Do not assume that because you have made one that fits you can use it as a pattern for the other. It's highly unlikely. Fit each one individually.

Sand and fit, sand and fit, until the panels slip into place like a hand into a glove. From experience, I can tell you that it pays to wait until both bilge panels are fitted before you spread glue on the frames.

Just as you must fit each bilge panel separately, glue them separately, too, but be certain that you are gluing the right panel to the right side of the boat. Apply glue to all the surfaces the panel will bear against. Rather than using Titebond, which grabs quickly, I suggest using regular Elmer's white glue along the edges of the frames and for the long joints between adjacent hull panels. Elmer's will give you time to adjust the panel before the glue sets. Save the Titebond for the ends of the panel, since they are the last points to be glued down and quick-grabbing will be an asset.

After the glue has been applied, lay the panel in place with your locating marks precisely aligned, and use a couple of pins to toenail the top edge of the bilge panel to the side panel. Then work from the middle toward the ends, checking for alignment as you go.

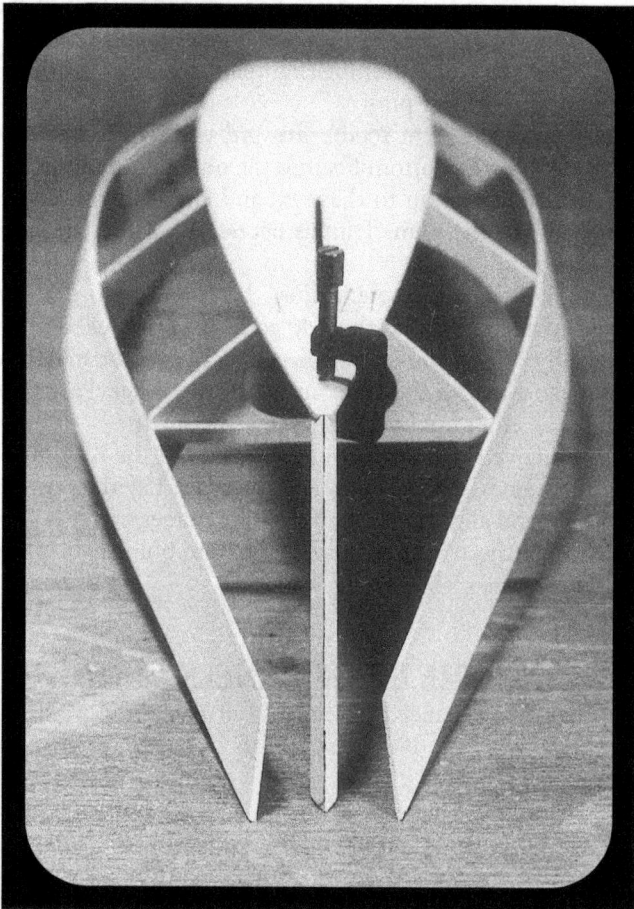

Clamping the bottom to the stem.

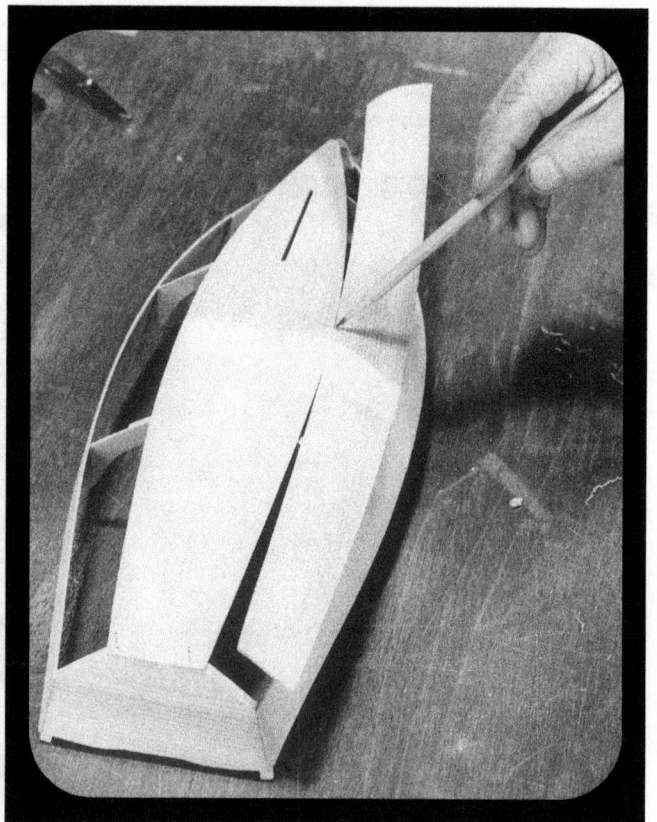

Aligning and fitting a bilge panel.

Follow the same procedure for the other bilge panel. At this stage, your model looks like a real boat, and everything added to it will bring it closer to mantelpiece status.

FLOOR PLATFORM AND SEATS

Cut the floor platform pattern from the plans and use it to make the platform from three pieces of wood, edge-glued together. Don't glue the platform down in the boat, because it is supposed to be removable. Even though the plans show reinforcement under the floor platform, there's no need for it in the model.

Cut the bow-seat pattern from the plans and make the seat from two pieces of edge-glued wood, or from one piece if your stock is wide enough. The projection of the after end of the seat misses its fit to the inboard edges of Frame A by quite a bit on each side, so make the template wider there to compensate. Note also that the sides of the seat to the stem look like straight lines, but in fact they are gently curved. Allow extra wood to fit and trim for this curve.

Fitting the bow seat is one of the trickiest operations in this model, much like fitting a breast hook in a full-size boat. Work carefully. If you can make this seat fit in place all at one crack without making any mistakes, chalk one up for yourself. If you bungle the job, don't worry. Throw the piece away, and try again. The great thing about model making is that the wood is small and expendable.

The movable 'midship seat is an easily built box. The parts for it can be cut with your table saw fitted with a planer blade and an accurate miter gauge for making square cuts. If you don't have a table saw, use a miniature miter box and a modeler's razor saw.

FALSE STEM

Using a sanding block, sand the forward ends of the planking straight across, flush with the outside of the stem. Avoid rocking the sanding block as you go, or you won't get a good joint for the false stem.

The stock for the false stem should be wide enough to go across the stem and beyond the outside edges of the planking, and long enough to extend from the stem head to the bottom panel with a little more to spare. Saw out this strip square-edged, making no attempt to taper it or shape it to the sides.

The false stem is bent over the stem itself. To do this, wet the outside of the false stem with your tongue, and pre-bend it with your fingers to the approximate curve of the stem. Then apply glue and hold the false stem in place with pins.

After the glue has set up, use your sanding block to fair the false stem into the side and bilge panels, and the bottom.

Installing the false stem.

GUNWALES

Rip the wood for the gunwales. On the real boat these are made from layers laminated together, but you can use a single piece of double thickness for the model. Make them a little longer than the length from the outside of the stem to the outside of the transom, taking into account the curve of the sides. For contrast, use fine-grained wood that is darker than the planking.

Actually, I made the gunwales from birch and soaked them in household ammonia to soften them up for bending. Ammonia stains light-colored wood a coffee color. You don't need a tank for soaking the gunwales. Simply wrap them in a paper towel, pour ammonia over them, then wrap the whole works in waxed paper and let it soak for a few hours or overnight. Maple also makes great gunwales. Save that old bureau or table that's headed for the dump and turn it into a model.

Cut and sand the hull panels so that they are flush with the outside face of the transom. Be sure to leave the corners sharp.

Fasten the gunwales in place one at a time. Spread glue as evenly as you can on the back of the gunwale, clamp it at the bow, and feed it along the side, pressing it against the

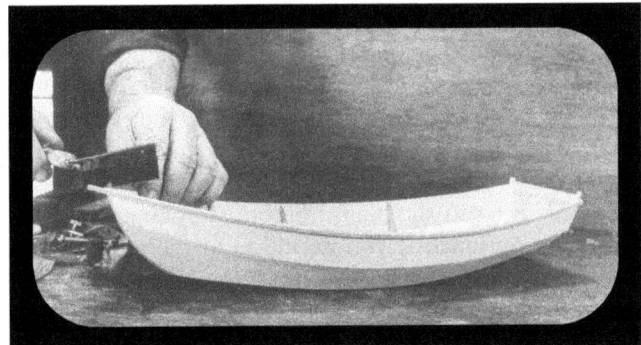
Trimming the gunwales.

Sanding the skeg to fit the shape of the bottom.

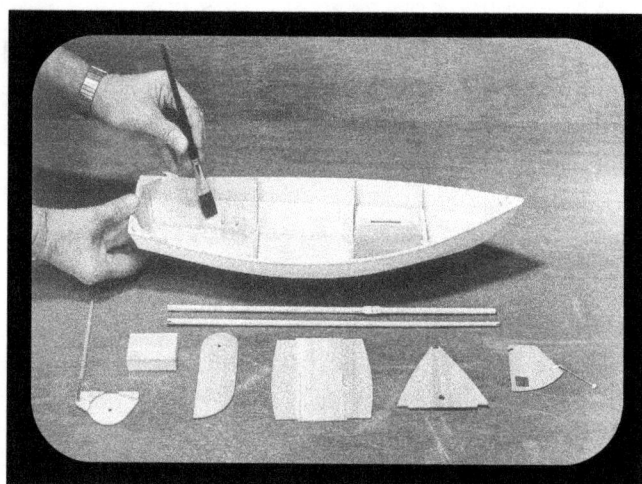

Sealing the hull. The breast hook, the quarter knees, the centerboard case, and the foot stretchers are in place, and all the other parts for the sailing version of Cartopper are ready.

planking with your fingers as you go. Use a couple of clamps near the transom to hold the quick hook in the sheer back aft.

Trim the ends of the gunwales, then lay the transom template on the inside of the transom. Align the top corners of the template with the corners of the model's transom, then mark the shape of the top of the transom and cut it to shape. Fair the ends of the transom framing down to the gunwales.

SKEG

Cut the skeg template from the plans along the edge that lies next to the hull, and leave extra paper underneath the skeg so that the template won't edge set. Lay the template on the wood and mark on the wood the edge of the skeg that is going to fit next to the hull. Finish cutting out the template, and mark the rest of the skeg.

Cut out the skeg. Then lay a piece of sandpaper, rough surface up, on the bottom of the boat where the skeg is to fit. Rub the bottom of the skeg fore and aft until it hunkers down for a tight fit. Glue the skeg in place.

FOOT STRETCHERS, BREAST HOOK, AND QUARTER KNEES

Make four foot stretchers. Determine their proper location in the boat from the plans, and put them in using spacers to regulate their position. You could measure their position, but by merely being off by a fraction, you can ruin the looks of the final result. Spacers regulate them quickly and easily.

According to the plans, the breast hook and quarter knees are optional. If you decide to fit them, follow the same procedures as for the bow seat, above. Make your templates from the plans, cut out your pieces, and trim with sandpaper until they fit like a glove.

FINISHING THE HULL

It's best to seal the hull before scribing the waterline. Will you use paint or varnish? It's your choice, of course, but I went with varnish for two reasons: It's easier to apply, and I feel that the wood grain of this model is worth looking at.

At this stage, avoid handling the model more than necessary to avoid staining it. Check the surface over carefully; any sanding from now on should be done using 320 or finer paper.

Use a good-quality brush. Nylon is best for water-based paints. One that is about ¾" at the ferrule and about 1" at the business end is okay for a model this size.

I thin my varnish almost in half with turpentine and add a dash of Japan drier to hasten the cure. This allows me to apply smooth, even coats, and the thinning cuts down on the gloss. I don't like high gloss on a model.

Don't forget to sand between coats, and clean up the surface with a tack rag.

SCRIBING THE WATERLINE

The waterline is scribed by setting the model on a flat surface and using as a guide the top of a piece of wood that is as thick as the waterline height. The plans show both a boot-top and a load waterline (LWL). You will mark the boot-top line first.

On the body plan, amidships, the top of the boot to the bottom of the boat measures 7", so cut a block of wood that is 7 scale inches high. Set the model on a flat surface, and raise the stern up or down until the top of the block of wood matches the extreme aft-end height of the boot top. Weight the model down so that it won't skitter around while you work. With the sharp point of an awl or a pencil, scribe the boot top all the way around the hull. Use a light touch.

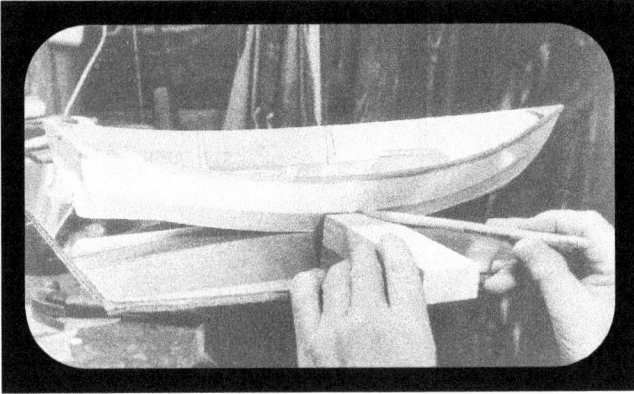

Scribing the waterline.

To define the bottom of the boot top, trim the height of your guide block by the scale thickness of the boot top and go around again. Then mask off the boot top and the waterline with masking tape to keep their edges sharp for painting.

So that's it—a construction model built to the plans of a full-sized boat.

The finished Cartopper model, complete with sprit rig.

CHAPTER 6
PAYSON'S PIROGUE

In his book *Boats with an Open Mind*, Phil Bolger honored me by calling this design Payson's Pirogue, because I had built the prototype from which he corrected his original drawings. Most modern plywood pirogues are flat-bottomed, single-chine designs, and these are popular in Mississippi and Louisiana. But since pirogues are pretty much unknown here in Maine (I'd never heard of them, myself), and this boat is multi-chined, I usually just call this a canoe. On the other hand, it's designed to be used with a double-bladed paddle, like a kayak, so you might want to refer to it as a *canoe-like boat*, or an *open kayak*, or whatever you will.

In any case, with her multiple chines giving her a somewhat more rounded cross section, Payson's Pirogue is a far cry from the flat-bottomed pirogues of the bayous, both in terms of looks and hydrodynamics, but she's only a bit more complicated to build. She's about as short as possible while still capable of handling two adults, and as you can see in the photo, those paddlers have to sit pretty close to each other and work in synch to avoid hitting each other's paddles. There's plenty of room for a single paddler, or an adult and a small child, however, and she's a wonderful boat for exploring creeks and ponds and other protected waters. It can be paddled kneeling, with a single-bladed paddle, but my guess is that the vast majority of builders and users will opt for the kayak-style, double-bladed paddle. The hull is a little deep for the comfortable use of a double-bladed paddle, but nothing you won't get used to. As long as you don't overload her so that the chine is submerged, her shape generates little drag, handling well and moving along nicely with little effort.

To save weight, Bolger made Payson's Pirogue completely open, and he says that plywood decks would make the center of gravity too high. However, you might be able to use fabric spray decks fore and aft for some protection. Given its lack of built-in flotation, though, I still wouldn't take it into rough water. One advantage of the lack of decks is that you can beach the boat, nose onto the sand, and step ashore with dry feet. Try *that* with a decked kayak! And, of course, whether there's built-in buoyancy or not, you should always wear a personal flotation device (PFD) in a boat of this sort.

The multi-chine design, plus the girder-like gunwale clamps, make the pirogue's structure so stiff that no internal frames are needed. With a thin foam pad laid right on the narrow bottom, your center of gravity will be low, and your hips will be nicely supported by the bilge panels, giving a comfortable seating position and the ability to use some "hip action" to heel the boat onto its sides. This will lift the ends out of the water, shortening the effective waterline and allowing the boat to turn a little more quickly—a handy feature when navigating small, twisty streams.

It's hard to estimate weight, because there are so many variables. The thickness and species of plywood that you use will have a big effect, as will the *scantlings* (the thickness of the structural members). In the upper left-hand corner of the plans, Bolger noted several areas where you can save some weight by reducing scantlings without seriously compromising strength. Probably the biggest weight variable is whether you sheathe her with fiberglass cloth on the outside, outside *and* inside, or not at all. Outside only will add about six pounds and lots of strength and abrasion resistance. Inside will make it easier to keep clean and, depending on how little care you intend to give her, may lengthen her

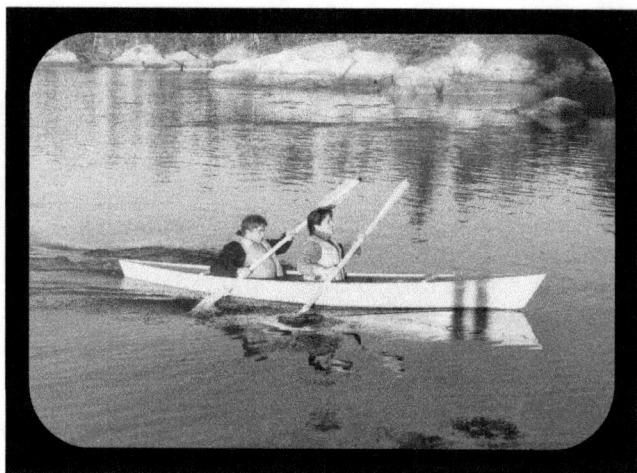

A Payson's Pirogue.

(continued on page 46)

Plans for Payson's Pirogue.

(continued from page 44)

life substantially. In my opinion, however, this isn't worth the extra weight. If you don't sheathe her at all, you'll have to pay more attention to keeping up her paint if you want her to be around for very long.

I built her with ¼" plywood, used a single strip of tape inside and out at each joint, and sheathed the exterior with fiberglass cloth. Built like this, it weighed thirty-four pounds.

Bolger has included plans for an unfeathered paddle, which is easier to store than a feathered one since it lies flat. A cute touch is the use of rubber furniture leg bumpers (or crutch bottoms) on the ends, which allow you to push off with your paddle without dinging the blades.

BUILDING THE PIROGUE

If you ever wanted to build a stitch-and-glue boat and didn't know where to start, this is the way to go. All of the plywood panels are easy bends and with no twist, so the first-time builder isn't confronted with wrestling hard-to-fit pieces in place. The only bevels appear on the stem and sternpost, and those are constant bevels, easily cut using a table saw. Add to this the investment of only two sheets of plywood, a roll of fiberglass tape, some fiberglass cloth, and resin, and you are in business.

There are no special techniques that have not already been covered, so the following description just covers the main steps in suggested order. Refer back to Chapter 4 if you need a reminder of how to accomplish any task.

Materials

2 sheets of ¼" x 4' x 8' plywood, AC or marine-grade
½ gallon polyester or epoxy resin if not sheathing exterior with fiberglass; 1 gallon if sheathing outside
3 pounds Fillite powder
1 roll 2" glass tape
4 yards of 38", 6-ounce fiberglass cloth for sheathing (optional)
1 pound of ¾", #15 wire copper nails for butt straps
Small amount of spruce, cedar, or similar plywood

Instructions

Start by placing the two sheets of plywood end to end, with the joint over a wide board. Tack the sheets down so that they won't move. Mark both of the long edges in 1' intervals, and draw straight lines to connect the marks across the panels. Starting with one of the side panels, measure the indicated distance from the edge at each of the 12" intervals, and drive a 1" or 1¼" #18 wire brad, until you've done the entire lower edge. Repeat for the top edge. Spring a batten around the brads, and draw in the top and bottom curves. Make sure you mark the location of the molds. Then repeat the process for the bilge panel and the bottom panel. Cut out the parts, and use them as templates to make mirror-image side and bilge panels.

(Make them mirror images, rather than duplicates, so that you have the same face of the plywood showing on both sides of the boat.)

Make butt straps with the grain running fore and aft. They should be 2" shorter than the width of the hull panels they will be used to join (as shown in the photos on the next page) so that they don't interfere with the long panel joints. Glue and fasten them in place with copper nails and let the joints set overnight. Pull them off the backing board the next morning, clip off the ends of the nails so that about ¼" remains sticking out, then hammer them down *with*, not across, the grain, to embed them into the surface of the plywood.

Lay out the molds as shown and mark the centerlines on both sides. Tack cleats on the forward face of the aft mold and on the aft face of the forward mold to catch nails that will be driven through the side panels during assembly.

Place the sides upside down on horses and fasten them to the molds, doing the middle mold first. Cut out the stem and sternpost on your table saw with the bevels as shown in the plans. If you don't have a table saw, you can cut the bevels with a circular saw, a band saw, or even by hand. The stem and sternpost are both straight, and the bevels are constant, so they couldn't be easier. But where the designer gives the lengths as "about 14¼" "and "about 9"," he means it. *Don't err on the side of going too short!* Cut them an inch or two too long, and plan to trim them down later. Fasten them to the side panels with glue and

Builder Job Sargeant uses a hot-melt glue to hold the bilge panels in place.

nails. When the glue is dry, round the edges with a file, followed by sandpaper.

Tack the bottom to the molds before you do the bilge panels. You'll do a lot of trim-and-try to get the bilge panels to slip into the space between the bottom and the sides with minimal gap. Lay one on, eyeball it carefully, maybe scribe the fit with a pencil from below, then take it off and trim it down with a plane, rasp, or whatever. When it slips into place, hold it down with thin wire brads, masking tape, duct tape, a hot-melt glue gun, or whatever you please. Don't worry if you trimmed a bit too much getting the bilge panel to fit—you'll soon fill the gap.

When you're sure the hull panels will hold together, draw lines parallel to and 1" away from the seams for the edges of the tape to follow. Give this area a liberal coat of resin, and fill the seams between the panels with putty made from a stiff mixture of resin and Fillite powder. If any of the gaps are so big that the putty would just fall through, back them with masking tape. When the seams are dry, round them off with a file and apply another coat of resin, fiberglass tape, and more resin to fill the weave of the cloth. When it's cured, turn the hull right side up and tape the interior seams. Here, the procedure is similar as for the exterior, except that you really load the putty into the joint, then smooth it with a round-headed tool, leaving a nice "coved" or convex-shaped bead of putty reinforcing the angle between the two panels. Scrape up any excess, then lay the tape into the fresh putty fillet. Brush over it with unthickened resin. Strive to have all the layers of the interior seam set up all at the same time.

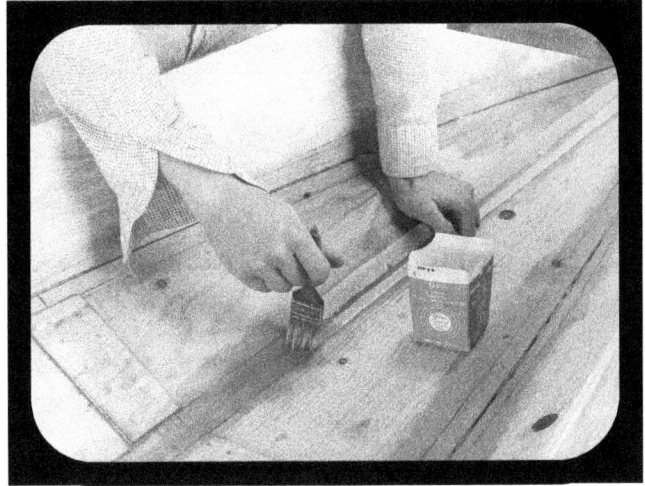

Taping the inside seams. Note the butt straps and the lines drawn parallel to the seams as an aid in placing the tape neatly.

Install the gunwale frames, the gunwales, and the thwarts, then flip the boat over again. If you wish to sheathe the boat, do it now. The 38" fiberglass cloth will nearly cover the hull's exterior in one application, leaving only part of one side panel uncovered. You can buy wider cloth that will cover her all in one job, though there should be plenty of scrap on the 38" cloth to do the job. Overlap the edges of fiberglass cloth by a couple of inches when you're fitting them, and lay on the resin.

Scribe the shape of the skeg against the bottom panel. To do this, clamp or support the $\frac{3}{4}$" stock firmly on the

After the outside seams are taped, the boat is turned right side up in preparation for taping the inside seams.

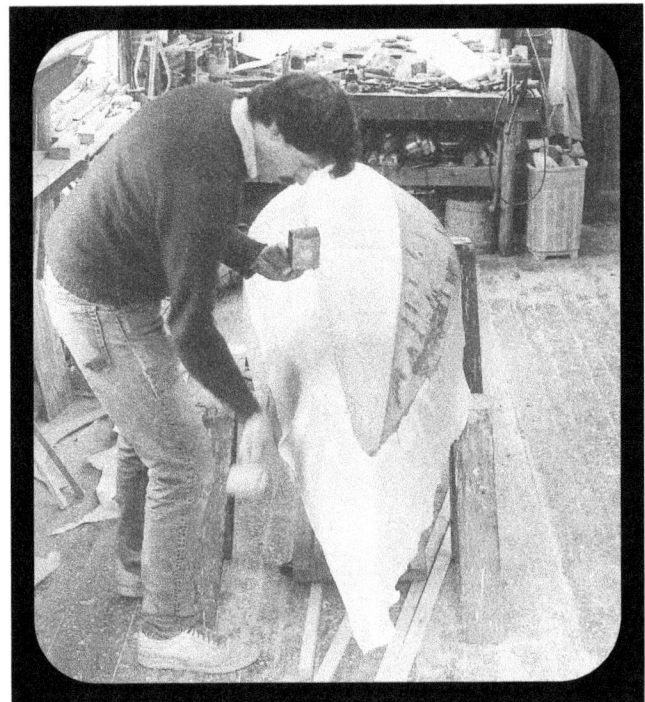

Using a roller to apply resin to the fiberglass sheathing.

outside of the bottom, take a block of wood that's thick enough to bridge the gap between the bottom and the skeg stock at both ends, hold a pencil firmly on top of the block, then drag the block along the bottom so that the pencil scribes the curve on the stock. Then measure the top and aft edges, cut out the skeg, and slather it with thickened epoxy or bedding compound. Bore holes through the bottom along the centerline and drive screws from the inside, through the plywood bottom and into the skeg.

If you don't wish to sheathe the exterior, you can seal it with unthickened epoxy for additional waterproofing. Even this isn't essential, however. You can get by just sealing the wood with a brush-on, paint-type wood sealer. Then either way, paint to the color of your choice.

BUILDING KEY FOR DESIGN No. 495, PAYSON'S PIROGUE

Materials
2 sheets of ¼" x 4' x 8' plywood AC or marine grade
Gallon of Polyester or Epoxy resin if outside of canoe is going to be 'glassed. (This will bring the weight to about 40 pounds. Or, with just the seams taped inside and out the weight will be about 30 pounds, and you will use half the resin.)
3 pounds of Fillite powder
1 roll of 2" glass tape
4 yards of 38" 6-ounce cloth if outside is to be 'glassed
1 pound of ¾" #15 wire copper nails for buttstraps

Construction Tips
Track two sheets of plywood to floor end to end (lay waxed paper under joint), and mark off at 1' intervals. Starting with the side panel measure in from the edge at each 12" interval and drive a 1" or 1¼" #18 wire brad. Spring a batten around the brads and draw in the top and bottom curves, and mark for molds. Repeat for bilge panel and bottom panel. Make duplicate side and bilge panels. Make buttstraps with grain running fore and aft, keep ends back 1" as shown, glue and fasten with copper nails, and let joints set overnight. Lay molds as shown and mark the centerline on both sides. Tack cleats on forward face of aft mold and aft face of forward mold to catch nails driven through the sides during assembly.

Assembly

1. Place sides upside down on horses and fasten to molds (middle mold first).

2. Install stem and sternpost, put bottom on then bilge panels. A hot-melt glue gun works great for sticking panel edges together, or you can use thin wire brads and tape—anything to hold the edges together until you can get the seams 'glassed.

3. When sure hull will hold together, scribe 1" parallel to seams for the edge of the tape to follow, give seams a liberal coat of resin and fill with stiff mixture of resin and Fillite powder.

4. When seams are dry, round off for taping, then turn hull right side up and tape the interior. The inside procedure is the same as the outside, except the tape is embedded in the putty *before* it hardens. The ideal taped joint is when all components set up together.

5. Install gunwale frames, gunwales and thwarts, seal and paint canoe to your color preference.

CHAPTER 7
CARTOPPER

Looks, lightness, and performance are built into the 11'6" x 4'0" Cartopper. Light enough to have earned her name (90 lbs), she's a do-anything boat for work or pleasure that can double as a tender. Her centerboard and kick-up rudder permit shallow-water sailing, and should the wind fail, she will take you home under oar or power.

You built a model of Cartopper in Chapter 5; now it's time to tackle the real thing. There isn't much difference between the two, except that in the full-sized boat, you will be working with larger pieces of wood. On the real boat, as in the model, the basic parts of the hull—the sides, the bilge panels, and the bottom panel—are cut square-edged and assembled that way. Beveling is required only for the stem and transom. But where accuracy was pretty important to getting a good-looking model, it's not so critical when working at full scale. Since the joints will all be filled with resin putty and covered with fiberglass tape, you'll be able to get by with some minor cutting errors. That's not to say you shouldn't work as neatly and accurately as you can, but you don't have to get nervous if your line wavers a little bit.

The author rowing a Cartopper.

BUILDING THE CARTOPPER

Materials
4 sheets of ¼" x 4' x 8' plywood
Waterproof glue
2 gallons of polyester resin (one with wax, one without), or epoxy
1 roll of 3" fiberglass tape
10 yards of 6-ounce, 38" wide fiberglass cloth
1 gallon of Fillite powder

Assembly of the Cartopper

Laying Out the Parts
Accuracy is important when laying out the parts of the boat on your plywood. Pay attention to your rule and straightedge, and by all means keep your architect's scale rule at hand for measuring any dimensions that you think you need but that haven't been provided on the plans.

Begin with Sheet 2 of plans, showing the sides, bottom, rudder-blade half, and centerboard trunk. These parts will be laid out on two sheets of ¼" plywood butted end to end. To make the job of sawing easy, and to protect your shop floor, lay 4' sticks under the plywood. Use a

(continued on page 55)

Grades of Plywood

Marine plywood, which has two good sides, is best if you are willing to pay the price. On the other hand, I've used much less expensive AC exterior plywood—good on one side, not so good on the other—and have never lost a boat. If you do use exterior plywood, be sure to lay out the parts carefully to avoid having the good side out on one side panel, for example, and the good side in on its mate. Some AC exterior plywood has a tendency to curl. If you run across curled plywood and decide to use it anyway, make sure that the sides, the bilge panels, and the bottom are laid out to curl in on the hull, not out.

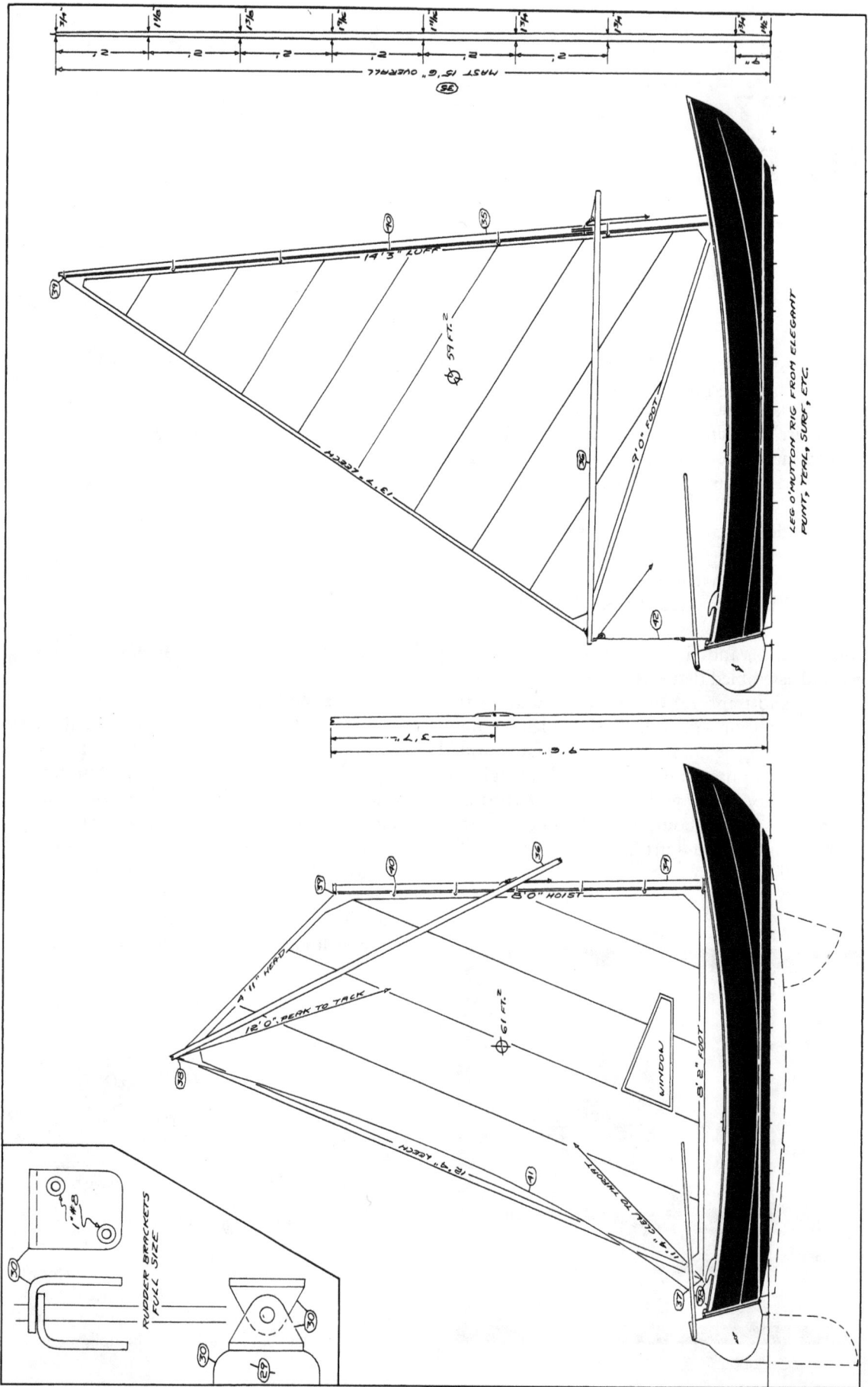

Cartopper, Sheet 1.

Cartopper, Sheet 2.

Cartopper, Sheet 3.

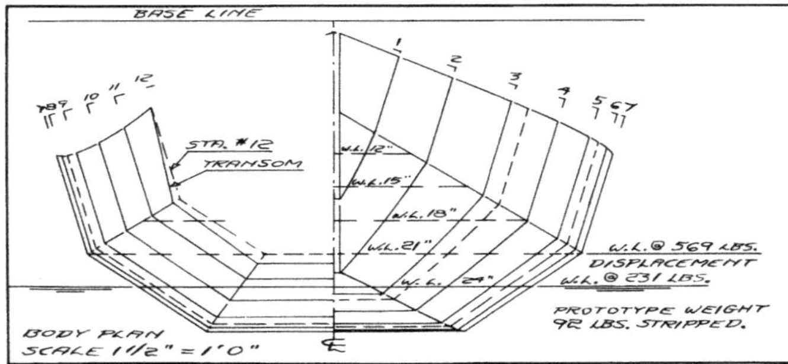

OFFSETS IN FEET, INCHES, & EIGHTHS TO OUTSIDE OF PLANK, FOR USE IF A JIG FOR MULTIPLE BOATS IS NEEDED, OR IF SUBSTANTIAL ALTERATIONS TO THE DETAILED DESIGN ARE INTENDED.

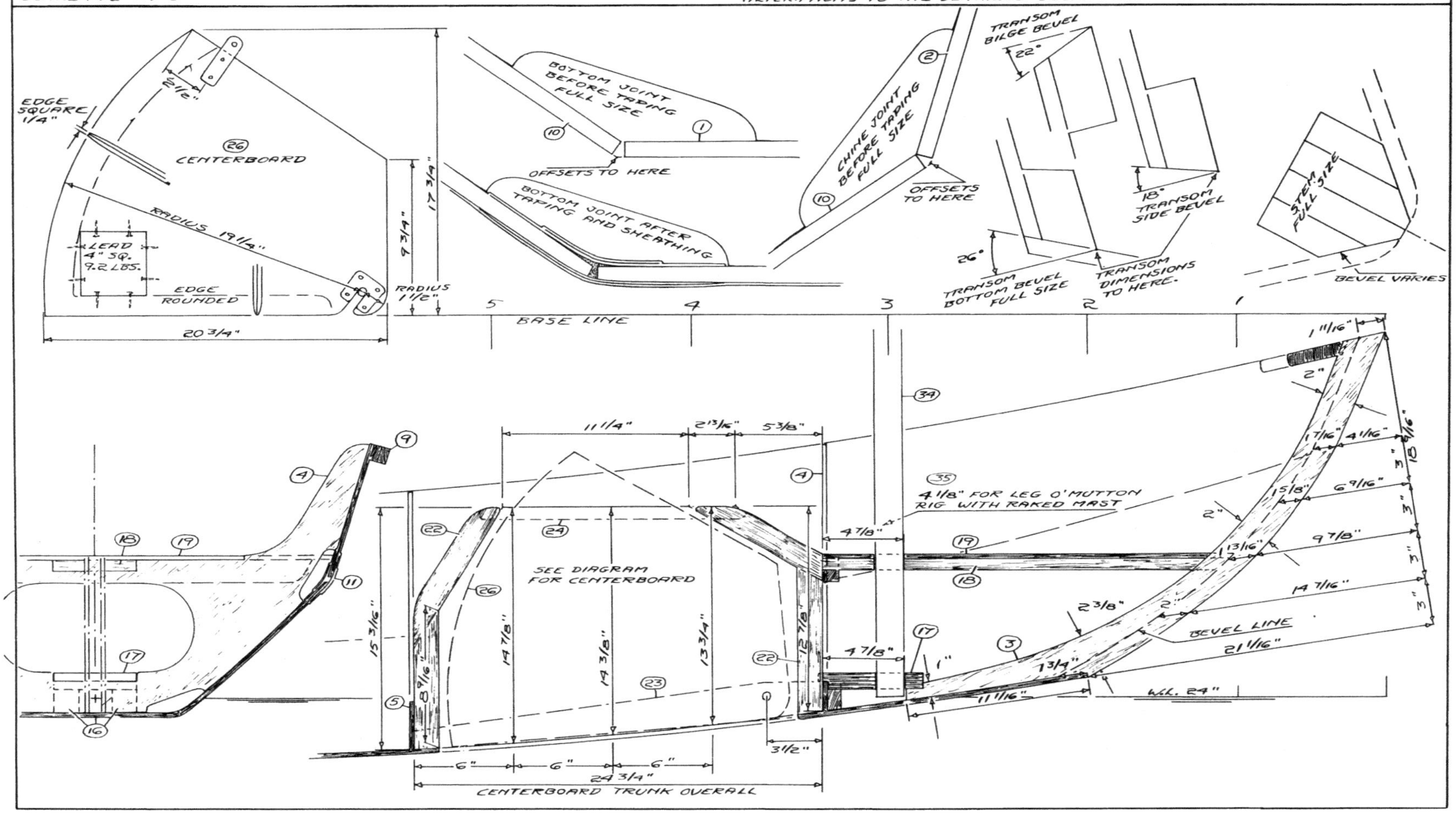

HEIGHTS FROM BASE LINE

	12	11	10	9	8	7	6	5	4	3	2	1
GUNWALE	0.7.6	0.9.4	0.7.6	0.1.6	1.0.1	1.0.1	0.11.4	0.10.4	0.9.1	0.7.3	0.5.1	0.3.2
CHINE	1.4.1	1.5.5	1.7.0	1.8.0	1.8.6	1.9.0	1.8.5	1.7.6	1.6.2	1.3.7	1.0.7	0.10.2
BOTTOM	1.9.0	1.11.2	2.1.2	2.2.6	2.3.5	2.4.0	2.3.7	2.3.2	2.2.1	2.0.5	1.10.6	1.4.2

HALF-BREADTHS

	12	11	10	9	8	7	6	5	4	3	2	1
GUNWALE	1.3.7	1.6.2	1.8.4	1.10.2	1.11.5	2.0.1	2.0.1	1.10.1	1.7.3	1.3.4	0.10.2	0.5.5
CHINE	1.1.3	1.3.6	1.6.0	1.7.7	1.9.0	1.9.4	1.9.0	1.8.5	1.7.3	1.4.6	0.8.0	0.3.5
W.L. 12"												0.2.6
15"												0.1.2
18"			0.8.4	1.3.2						0.14.7	0.4.3	
21"			0.11.0	1.3.1	1.6.4	1.8.5	1.8.4	1.5.6	1.1.3	0.8.0	0.2.0	
24"	0.1.4	0.6.4	0.9.6	1.2.1	1.4.3	1.5.0	1.4.1	1.1.6	0.9.7	0.4.7		
BOTTOM	0.6.0	0.7.5	0.9.0	0.10.2	0.10.7	0.11.2	0.10.5	0.9.2	0.7.0	0.2.4	0.0.4	0.0.4

BASE LINE

BODY PLAN
SCALE 1 1/2" = 1'0"

PROTOTYPE WEIGHT
92 LBS. STRIPPED.

DISPLACEMENT
W.L. 12" 431 LBS.
W.L. @ 369 LBS.

TRANSOM BEVEL
BOTTOM FULL SIZE

TRANSOM
SIDE BEVEL

TRANSOM
BILGE BEVEL

TRANSOM DIMENSIONS TO HERE.

OFFSETS TO HERE

CHINE JOINT
BEFORE TAPING
FULL SIZE

BOTTOM JOINT
BEFORE TAPING
FULL SIZE

BOTTOM JOINT AFTER
TAPING AND SHEATHING

OFFSETS TO HERE

BASE LINE

CENTERBOARD
EDGE SQUARE 1/4"
RADIUS 19 1/4"
EDGE ROUNDED
LEAD 4 SQ. 7.2 LBS.
20 3/4"

RADIUS 1 1/2"
9 3/4"
17 3/4"

SEE DIAGRAM FOR CENTERBOARD
CENTERBOARD TRUNK OVERALL
24 3/4"
13 3/4"
14 3/8"
14 7/8"
3 1/2"
6"
6"
6"

BEVEL VARIES
BEVEL LINE
4 1/8" FOR LEG O'MUTTON RIG WITH RAKED MAST
BASE LINE

Cartopper, Sheet 4.

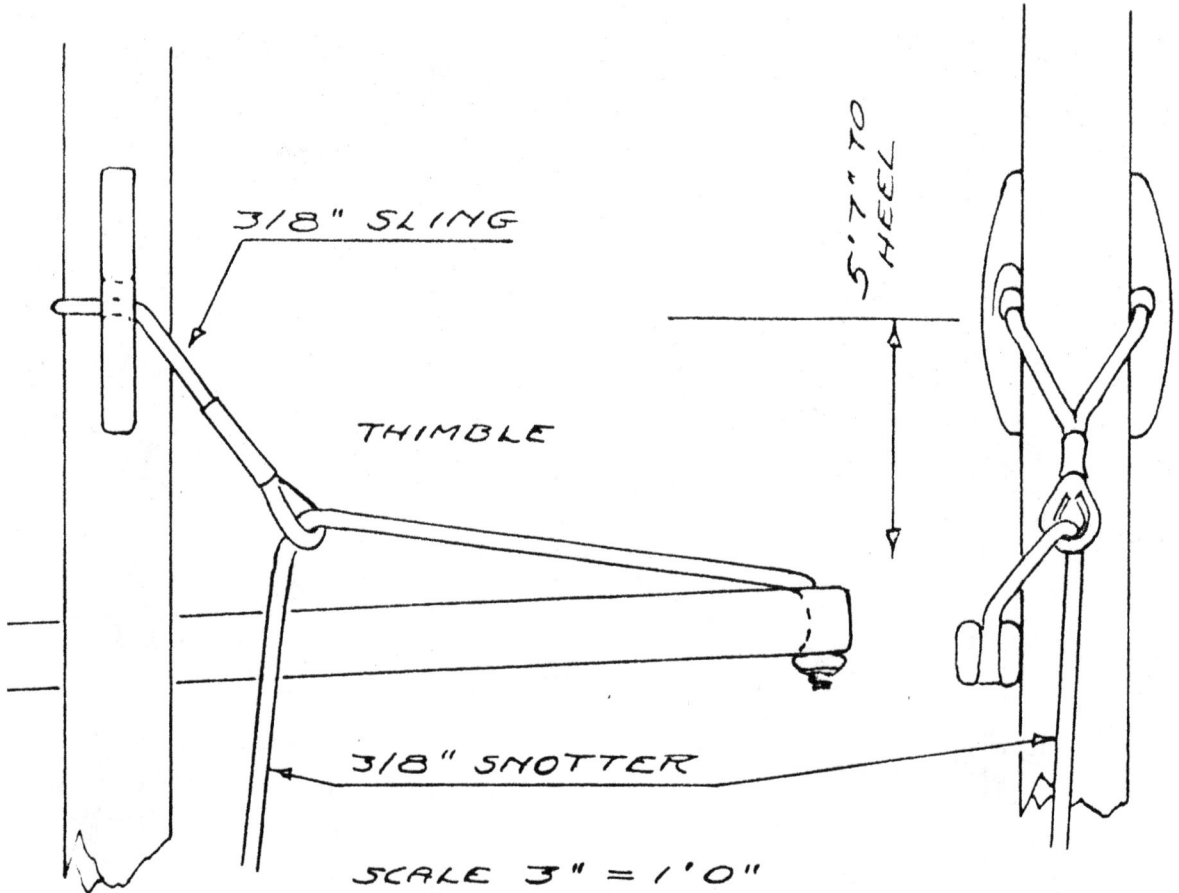

3/8" SLING

THIMBLE

3/8" SNOTTER

SCALE 3" = 1'0"
REVISED SNOTTER
FOR GYPSY #436

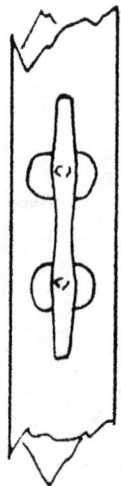

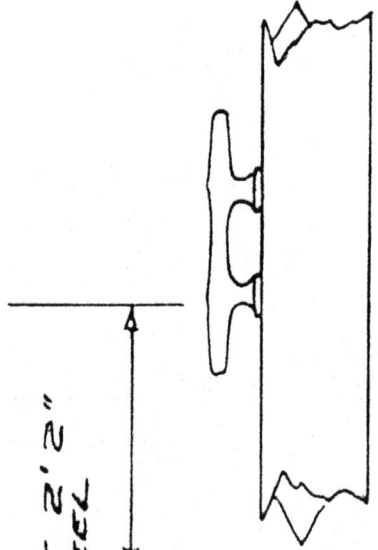

5'7" TO HEEL

ABOUT 2'2" TO HEEL

(continued from page 49)

wider stick at the butt joint, and cover this wide stick with waxed paper. Now lay down the plywood, and fasten the butted ends to the wide stick with 1" #18 wire brads so that the plywood can't move.

Mark off 1' intervals from one end of the butted sheets to the other on both of the long edges, then connect your marks with a straightedge and draw each line right across the sheets. Plywood sheets are manufactured to be square, so it is best to mark off your lines by measurement rather than using a framing square. Just a speck of glue or a small imperfection of any kind can throw a framing square out of whack without your being aware of it.

At each of the 1' intervals, measure in from the edge of the sheet to the sheer and the bottom of one side panel by the amounts indicated. For example, at the first interval, the dimension is $2\frac{7}{8}$" to the sheer and $11\frac{1}{8}$" to the bottom. Note that the same method is used to define the ends of the panel.

Drive small nails or brads (1" #18 will do fine) at each of the points you have defined, and lay a $\frac{5}{8}$" x 1" pine batten along the line formed by the nails. Don't panic if the batten doesn't hit every dimension right on the mark; the idea is to fair a line through the majority of these marks. Don't hesitate to pull a nail to fair the curve and avoid a "quick" place, but remember the goal: to pull as few nails as possible to achieve a fair curve that represents as closely as possible the designer's measurements. When you are satisfied that the curve is fair, mark along its length with your pencil.

Follow the same procedure in laying out the other side panels, the bilge panels, and the bottom panel. On the sides and bottom, mark the locations of the three frames—A, B, and C—for future reference. Frame A is the one nearest to the bow, Frame C is nearest to the stern, and Frame B lies between the two.

The frames and transom are measured and marked in a similar manner, except that the edge of the plywood is not used as a baseline. Start by simply drawing a straight line in the appropriate place shown on the nesting diagram and work from there. When laying out and making parts such as the bottom, the transom, and the frames, carefully mark the centerlines. These will be indispensable for proper alignment when you assemble the hull.

The nesting diagram has both bilge panels and both side panels facing the same direction. This will work fine if you're using marine plywood with identical faces. If you use exterior plywood, lay out these parts as mirror images instead. Otherwise, you'll end up with one good face and one rough face showing on the boat's exterior.

The Fiberglass Butts

Before cutting out the side, bilge, and bottom panels, the butts must be joined. The plans call for plywood butt straps, but I much prefer making a fiberglass joint, since I believe it to be simpler, stronger, and neater. I have found

that just one layer of tape on each side of the joint is ample for $\frac{1}{4}$" plywood, but you can make the butt stronger if you want by hollowing out the joint and using a layer of fiberglass mat followed by a layer of fiberglass tape or a strip of fiberglass cloth cut on a bias. I have had great success with polyester resin, but if you want to be extra-sure about the strength of the joint, use epoxy.

Tape the joints with 3" fiberglass tape. Run the tape right out to the edges of the panel instead of holding it back $1\frac{1}{2}$" from the edges, as the plans for the plywood butt show. You will be taping both sides of the panels, but do only one side now. Use plenty of resin; apply it out from the joint about $2\frac{1}{2}$" on each side. Place the tape in the fresh resin, spread more resin over the tape, and cover it with a strip of waxed paper wide enough to cover the entire area. Draw a wide putty knife over the waxed paper to smooth out the joint. Leave the paper in place until the resin cures.

With one side joined with fiberglass, now is the time to cut out the panels. A small portable circular saw does a great job. Even better is a special saw with a $4\frac{1}{2}$" blade, made by Makita for cutting plywood. But lacking these, you can also use a saber saw or even a hand saw, although I consider the last to be the least desirable option.

To avoid dulling your circular-saw blade, do not cut across the fiberglass butt unless your blade has carbide teeth. Rather, stop at the edge of the glass and use a saber saw with either a conventional blade or a diamond-toothed blade.

Once the panels have been cut out, turn them over, being very careful not to bend or break the joints, and tape the other side of the butts.

The Transom

The transom is made from a piece of $\frac{1}{4}$" plywood and framed on the sides and bottom with $\frac{3}{4}$" x $1\frac{1}{2}$" spruce,

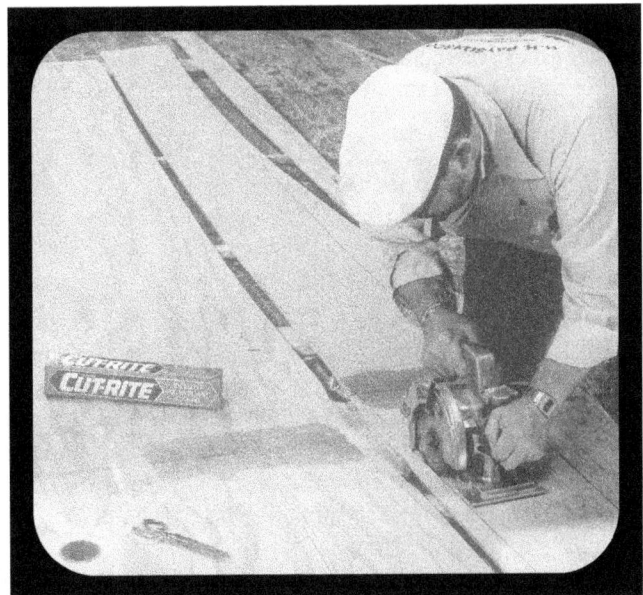

Cutting the hull panels from fiberglass-butt-jointed plywood sheets with a circular saw.

Assembling the motorboard inside the transom framing.

Use glue—no nails—to laminate the stem pieces.

pine, fir, or mahogany—almost anything, as long as it isn't oak, teak, or any other oily wood that doesn't glue well. The top framing must be wider to accommodate the crown of the transom and still bear against the side framing: a ¾" x 3" board will do the job.

Cut out the transom panel first according to the dimensions shown on the plans, and bevel its edges as shown on Sheet 4. (The bevel for the transom top is 21°.) Cut the framing and bevel it to match, then glue and nail everything together. Clean up the excess glue right on the spot rather than having to face hardened lumps later. Note that the bevel of the transom top goes in the reverse direction from the bottom bevel.

The appearance of the transom frame can be improved by beveling its inside edges to match the other side edges, rather than leaving them square. This also eliminates a water trap on the bottom piece of framing. It is worth the effort.

The transom motor board, No. 8 on the sheet showing the interior arrangement, should be made of two or more ¾" x 9"-wide vertical planks and fitted into the framing as shown.

The Stem

You can laminate the 2" stem from eight pieces of ¼" plywood if you want to take the trouble; I didn't and opted for four pieces of ½" plywood instead. Each piece is cut out separately with a band saw or a saber saw to the shape of the stem's profile, and then the pieces are glued together with waterproof glue and clamped. Don't use nails, because you have to bevel the stem.

Sheet 4 shows the layout of the stem in profile and also shows the stem head full size with the designer's notation: "Bevel varies." Well, it does, but not enough to worry

about. The bevel shown at the stem head is close enough to work with; it can be doctored, if need be, after the stem is set up on the hull, by running a batten around the molds onto the stem. Do this before the sides and bilge panels are sprung into place.

Lay out the stem according to the profile dimensions shown on Sheet 4, using a light batten to fair the line of the forward face of the stem, the bevel line ("bearding line" in boatbuilder's parlance), and the after face of the stem. Spring the batten around brads driven into the plywood at your reference marks. Note that the bottom of the stem is notched to accept the forward end of the bottom panel.

After the stem has been laminated, draw a centerline down the front face, then mark off the finished width of ⁵⁄₁₆" on the same face. The bearding line is where the inside face of the plywood planking touches the full width of the stem. The stem bevel changes from top to bottom, so pick up the measurements for the bearding line from the plans and use a flexible batten to draw these on both sides of the stem. You can saw out the stem bevel by cutting along the

Cutting the stem bevels with a band saw.

bearding line with either a band saw or a saber saw set at an angle of 21°. This will make a cut well clear of the final ⁵⁄₁₆" width of the outside stem face; the excess is then worked off to the ⁵⁄₁₆" width.

The Frames

The three frames are made from ¼" plywood to keep down the weight of the boat, but it is okay to make them heavier if you like. If you think that ¼" frames don't seem like much in the strength department, you are right; however, their lack of strength is overcome when the boat has been assembled. With the hull seams taped with fiberglass and the outside of the hull sheathed with fiberglass cloth, you essentially have a tough, one-piece structure. But until the frames are fiberglassed into the hull, they are pretty flimsy. Therefore, for the sake of rigidity when setting up the hull, cut only the outside shapes of the frames at this time, and you'll install them that way, like building forms. You'll cut their inner shapes later.

On the plans, the height of each frame at the sheer is given at the centerline, so lay out each frame to all the outside dimensions first, then cut it out across the top, full height, in one piece, square edged. The frame's inner shape is shown by curved, dashed lines; this shape must be taken off with an architect's scale rule, plotted on the frame, then drawn with a light batten or ship's curve. There's nothing fussy about this, but don't cut out the inner shape yet. Rather, bore ½" holes that are 5" or 6" apart just outside the line on the "waste" side, and with your saber saw, saw along the line between the holes, but not all the way: leave just a tab between the holes holding the pieces together. After the frames have been fiberglassed to the hull, you can finish cutting with a keyhole saw.

The same principle applies for the limber holes in the corners of the frames. Unlike the inside waste of the frames,

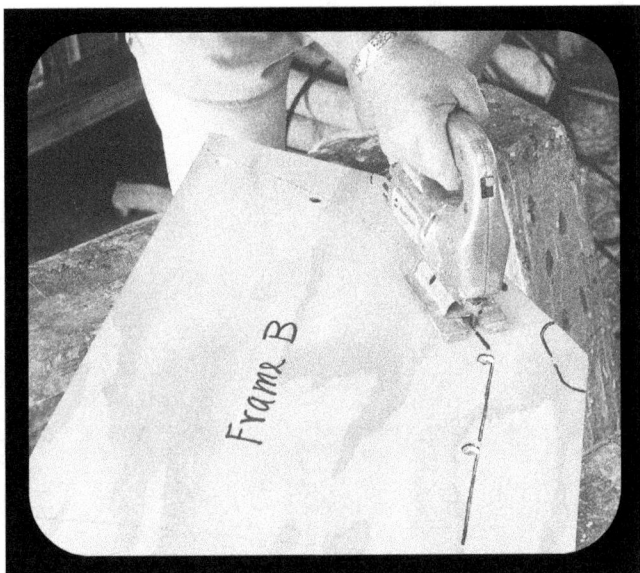

When cutting out the frames, leave the waste sections in place with small tabs of plywood.

Hull panels, frames, transom, and stem, all ready for assembly.

which must be left in place for strength until the frames are fiberglassed to the hull, the corners of the frames must be left intact so that you can use them to align the edges of the sides, the bilge panels, and the bottom when assembling the hull. Make a pattern of a limber hole and use it to mark off the others, and saw each limber hole almost out, leaving a tab to hold the waste in place until the hull has been assembled. Finish cutting the limber holes when you are ready to fiberglass-tape the inside seams.

Note that Frame A is curved in the area of the bilge panel. You can cut out the portion of Frame A that provides access to the under-the-seat compartment, but be sure to leave the top of the frame intact. Frames B and C are notched ¼" to accept the ends of the floor platform. The frames' ¼" thickness here doesn't seem to offer much support to the floor platform, so I added ¾" × 2" framing later, after taping the frames to the hull. I let the ends of this extra material extend out almost to the bilge panels.

Assembling the Hull

While construction to this point has taken a day or two, the actual assembly of the hull will only take a couple of hours—maybe less.

The hull is built upside down, just like the construction model, and it is supported on four legs to provide a comfortable height for working; mine are made from 2'-long 2" × 4"s. To provide a lip or ledge to temporarily support upside-down Frames B and C, I nailed an 18"-long 2" × 4" to the inside of each leg, which automatically set the tops of the frames 18" off the floor. (I'm on the short side, and this height works perfectly for me. If you are 6' or taller, you might want to make the legs 2'6", and make the supports 24" long.) Clamp the frames to the 2" × 4" legs, and fasten feet to the bottoms of the legs to keep them from toppling over.

Fasten temporary cleats made of scrap wood (¾" × 1", of various lengths) along the outside edges of the frames where

2" x 4" legs to hold the frames.

Fastening cleats to the frames.

Fastening the side panels to the transom.

need a couple of clamps to hold the side to the transom frame while you nail it.

Now for the bottom panel. Line up its centerline with the centerline of the transom, and tack it there. Then do the same thing at Frames C and B. It's useful to have a

the side and bottom panels will bear. The panels will be nailed to these cleats temporarily until you're ready to fiberglass the outside seams. To fasten the cleats to the frames, I drive plenty of 1" #18 wire nails through the frames into the cleats. These are easily pulled out later. You could use screws, however, if you're concerned about things holding together.

Fitting the sides, the Transom, and the Bottom

Position the sides against the frames, aligning the frame-positioning marks on the panels with the frames themselves, and the bottom edges with the corners of the frames where the limber holes will be. When everything is lined up correctly, tack them to the cleats (no glue yet).

Spread glue on one side of the transom framing, and nail it to one of the side panels with $7/8$" or 1" bronze ring nails. Apply glue to the other side of the transom and pull the end of the other side panel into it by hand. You will

Fastening the aft end of the bottom panel to the transom.

helper spot the centerline to the frames from underneath, while you tack from the outside.

Take care at this point that everything is lined up correctly. Sight down the centerline of the bottom and across the tops of the frames; check that the frames lie in the same plane. Although this type of construction is more or less self-aligning, it is still possible to put a slight twist in the hull if the floor you are working on is extremely crooked. A peek takes only a second but pays off big in the long run.

Fitting Frame A and the Stem

Tack temporary cleats to the after face of Frame A so that they won't interfere with the curve of the bottom panel. Tack a temporary cleat on the outside face of each side panel, near the forward end. These cleats should be positioned far enough back so that they don't interfere with nailing the sides to the stem. Slip a piece of rope around the side panels, behind the cleat, pull the panels together, and tie the ends of the rope together to hold the panels in approximately their final position.

Now ease in Frame A from below; clamp it to the bottom panel. Carefully match the centerline of the frame with the centerline of the bottom; make sure it is positioned properly in relation to the side panels; and tack it in place.

Fitting the Stem

Put the stem in place, with the notch in its bottom surface bearing against the end of the bottom panel. Align both centerlines, and clamp the two pieces in place—no glue and no fastenings yet. Apply glue to both surfaces of the stem where the sides are to bear, and bring the sides in together to land on the stem; adjust them so they are positioned correctly.

I emphasize that both sides must be brought in to the stem together. Do not bring in one side and nail it, then bring in the other; you will skew the hull. Hold both sides against the stem, and tack a 1" #18 nail at the top of each

Fitting the side panels to the stem.

panel into the stem. Adjust the stem slightly, if need be, and tack the bottom edges. When you are satisfied that everything is lined up correctly, permanently fasten the sides to the stem with 1" or $1\frac{1}{4}$" bronze ring nails.

Unclamp the stem from the bottom panel, spread glue on the bottom of the stem, push the bottom panel back

The side panels are sprung partly to shape at the bow in preparation for installing Frame A. The stem (left foreground) comes next.

Permanently fastening the stem to the bottom panel.

down to the stem, and fasten it in place with bronze ring nails.

Pull the temporary nails from the bottom at the transom, letting the bottom spring up. Spread glue along the bottom edge of the transom framing, push down the bottom, and fasten it with bronze ring nails.

FITTING THE BILGE PANELS

Fitting the bilge panels is the most difficult part of building the Cartopper, so take your time and work them in a little at a time. There is quite a bit of twist in these panels, and they don't mind giving you a hard time. Sooner or later as you go, you're likely to swear they'll never fit, but I assure you they will. They don't have to fit edge to edge. If the edges of the bilge panels are within 1/4" of their neighbors, you are still in good shape. Open seams can be dealt with by getting underneath the hull and running masking tape along the inside of the seams to keep fiberglass putty from oozing through.

There are two things to watch for when fitting the bilge panels. Be sure the middles of the panels are touching the frames before gluing and nailing their ends. And make sure the edges of the bilge panels don't sit proud of their neighbors. This is necessary for the panels to meet and flow in a fair curve.

You will discover tight and loose places when you put the bilge panels on. The loose places are no trouble, but the tight places must be freed so that the panel can be adjusted. Do this with a hand saw or a saber saw.

If the bilge panels take the curve smoothly and fit well, you can hold them in place with masking tape, duct tape, or hot-melt glue. If a bilge panel won't lie down

Use thin wire to pull the edges of the bilge panels to the bottom and side panels. Where things fit perfectly to begin with, you can get away with hot-melt glue or masking tape instead.

properly next to its neighbor, drill a series of small holes near the edges of both panels, and temporarily wire it in place. Soft, #18-gauge mechanic's wire, which is available at automotive supply stores, works best. After the seams are filled with fiberglass putty from the outside, the wire is pulled.

As with the side and bottom panels, spread glue along the transom edge and framing, and on the stem, then nail the bilge panels with bronze ring nails. Clamping the first bilge panel to the stem is easy, because you can hook the clamp to the stem. Your luck runs out on the second panel, as the first panel will interfere with clamping. I nail a stick on the side panel and use it as a button to hold the top end of the bilge panel while I nail it.

Puttying the Outside Seams and Stem

Now that Cartopper's hull is all tacked together and closed in, it's time to begin the "tape" part of this tack-and-tape construction method. The edges of Cartopper's plywood panels are going to be permanently joined with fiberglass tape over a putty of epoxy or polyester resin mixed with microballoon filler or Fillite powder. Begin by checking the hull seams once more to be sure they all lie together in fair curves that are pleasing to the eye. Then take a roll of 1" wide masking tape and tape all the seams from underneath. The masking tape will keep the putty from falling through the wider seams, and it pulls off easily when the job is done—one of the few lucky breaks for boatbuilders that Murphy missed.

With the masking tape in place, go back to the outside of the hull and mark each seam for the 3" wide fiberglass tape, using a 1 1/2" wide block of wood as a guide to make a line parallel to each seam. You only need to mark one side of each seam. Brush the seams with polyester or epoxy resin. The edges of the plywood will soak up resin, so coat them liberally now so that they don't pull resin out of the fiberglass putty that's going on next, weakening the bond.

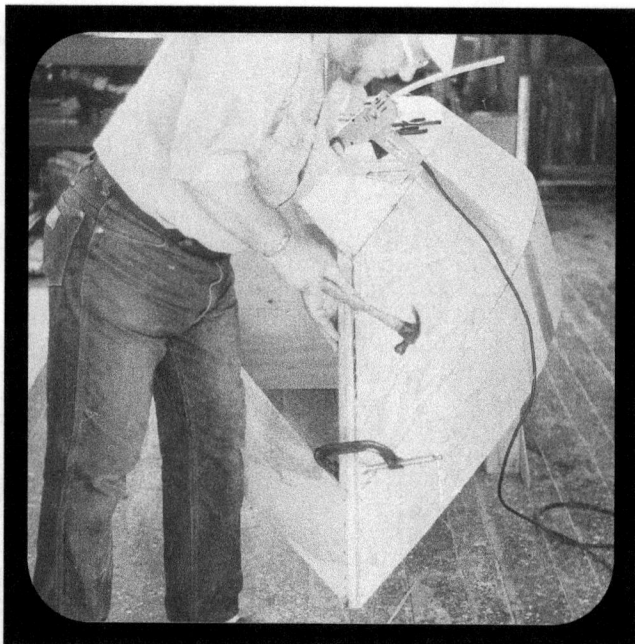

Fastening a bilge panel.

The Importance of Working Clean

When you're puttying or taping, you need to work with clean tools. The easiest way to keep them clean is to place them in a bath of acetone or lacquer thinner and clean them well between uses. If you get lumps of hardened resin on your smoothing tools, you have lost the whole show as far as neatness goes.

The same goes for yourself; learn to work clean. Use gloves to protect your skin, be sure there's plenty of ventilation, take extra precautions when you handle solvents, and wear a face mask when you mix fillers or sand surfaces. To give yourself more time, don't do fiberglass work in the sun; the resin sets up too quickly. If you are blessed with hot hands, remember to hold the containers at their edges, not in the palm of your hand.

To begin filling Cartopper's outside seams, pour about ¼" of resin into a pint milk carton, and mix in some hardener. A teaspoonful of hardener to a full pint of polyester resin is a good amount, with a little more in cold, damp weather and a little less in warm weather. If you're using epoxy, don't estimate—make sure you follow the manufacturer's instructions to the letter. In any case, mix the resin and hardener well before you add the Fillite or other filler. Use just enough filler to make a good putty about the consistency of peanut butter—not too drippy, not too stiff. Smooth the putty into the seam using a clean putty knife. You're trying to create a smooth, solid foundation for the

tape that comes later, and after the putty dries, you'll sand the panel edges smooth, too.

Mix more putty as you need it, but if a batch starts to stiffen up a little, move to the stem and quickly apply the putty there. The stem is going to need a lot of putty, because it's easier to fill out the stem area with putty and then round it with a rasp rather than round the plywood edges. As soon as the stem-filler putty hardens enough to shape, round it to shape with a rasp. The rasp will quickly fill up with putty, but a wire brush cleans it just as quickly.

Let the seams harden a few hours; overnight is better. Avoid bumping or disturbing the boat at this vulnerable stage, and don't remove any wire, tape, or glue. If you do, a bilge panel might part company from its neighbor. After the seams cure overnight, it's safe to take out the wires or "tacks," but don't move the hull around or turn it over until the outside seams are taped.

Sand the outer edges of the hull panels round to prepare them for the fiberglass tape. To do this, make up a special sanding board, long enough to accept long strips of sandpaper, with a hollow or concave base and handles at both ends. Staple very coarse 20-grit sandpaper to the hollowed side. If you can't find 20-grit paper at your hardware store (and chances are you won't), go to a tool-rental store and buy sheets of coarse sandpaper made for floor sanders. Lacking 20-grit paper, you can use 50- or 60-grit; it will just take longer to do the job.

Marking the seams before brushing on resin makes it easier to apply the fiberglass tape neatly.

Puttying the stem.

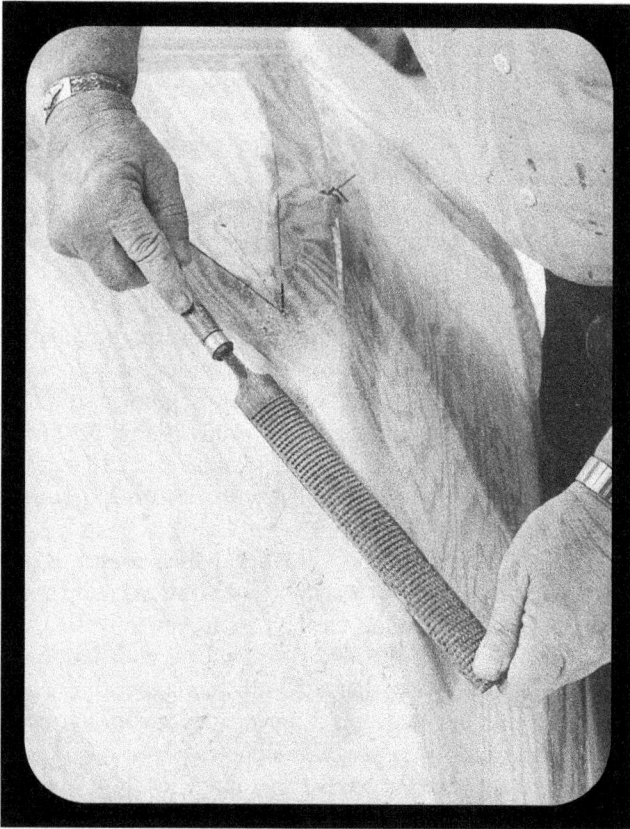

Use a rasp to round off the built-up putty around the stem.

Taping the Outside Seams

Do a little cleaning up first. Sweep off the hull, then the floor, because I can guarantee that if you drop a piece of wet cloth on a dirty floor, it will pick up everything there, and you might find yourself getting a little nervous as you pick out the bits while the catalyzed resin you so thoughtfully mixed up beforehand is hardening.

A 2-pound roll of 3" wide fiberglass tape is fine for the rest of the boat, but a strip of 4" wide tape does a better job on the stem. If you don't have it, a scrap of your 6-ounce cloth will do. You'll start at the stem, cover the whole transom next, then run 3" tape along the outside seams in between. The large pieces of hull sheathing will come later. Doing the sheathing in pieces this way is a lot easier than trying to get one piece of cloth to cover the entire length of the hull along with the transom and the stem. If you try to do it all with just one piece, you'll find yourself spending too much time trying to get sags and wrinkles out around the stem and transom, and you'll feel your composure slipping as time runs out. So don't tempt Murphy. Do the hardest places first: the stem, the transom, and the seams. Then fill in between with the larger pieces—no sweat.

Dry-fit the length of 4" tape or cloth to the stem, then use a brush to liberally coat the stem area with laminating resin. (If you're going to do the whole job in one day, you can use waxed, or finishing, resin.) Brush it out a little past where the tape will end. Lay the tape or cloth into the resin, and wet it thoroughly with more resin, using a 3"

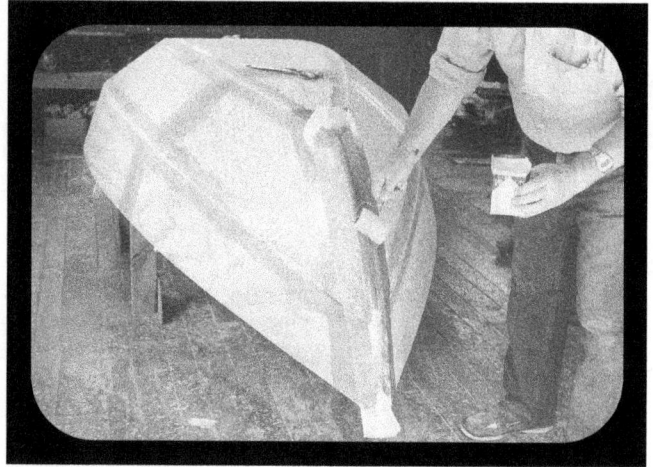

Taping the stem.

roller and a brush. The tape should smooth right out and take the shape of the stem. Use enough resin to wet the tape thoroughly and fill the weave of the cloth.

You're going to need about nine yards of 6-ounce, 38" fiberglass cloth. Measure out two 12' lengths of cloth for the hull sides' sheathing and set them aside. Then drape a piece of cloth over the transom and take it down as shown in the photo below. Let it flap over the transom corners onto the hull about 3" to 4", and let it hang down past the top of the transom about the same amount. Don't trim it any smaller yet.

Lift the cloth up onto the bottom of the hull, mix up some resin, and roll it on the transom and around onto the

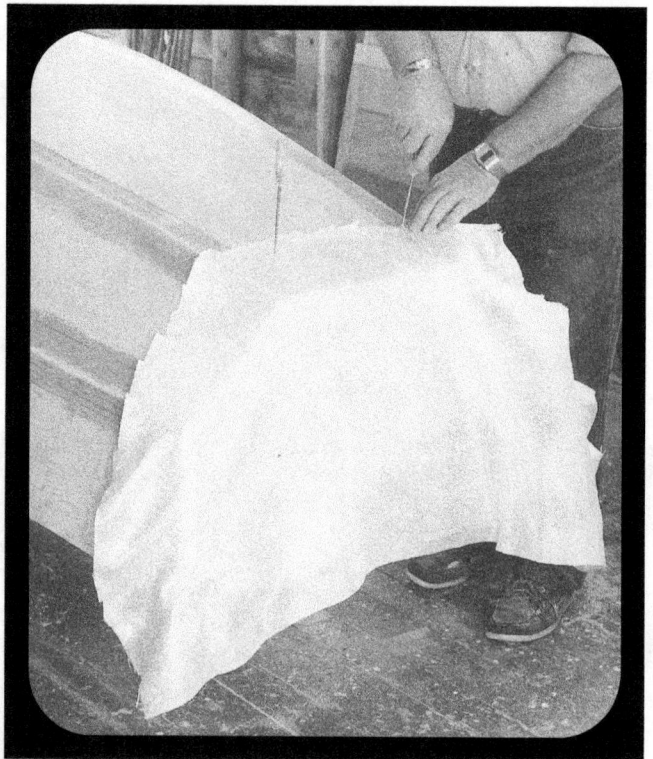

Drape the fiberglass cloth smoothly over the transom, with enough to overlap the sides.

With the cloth out of the way, roll or brush resin on the transom and overlap it onto the other hull panels.

Make sure that there are no white-looking places in the cloth; they indicate trapped air and not enough resin. When you're satisfied that the cloth is evenly saturated, wait a half hour to an hour until the resin hardens, then give it another coat with either a brush or roller to fill the weave of the cloth. A brush gets on more resin, but more resin means it will be hard to avoid sags on this nearly vertical surface. This, in turn, means extra sanding before you paint. Three coats of laminating resin do the basic job; then, when the whole hull is covered, you can add a finish coat of resin with wax in it.

Now for the long, outside seams. As you did with the stem, dry-fit a length of tape (3" this time), liberally coat the seam area with laminating resin extending out beyond your gauge marks, then lay the tape in the resin and wet it out thoroughly with more resin. Use enough resin to fill the weave of the cloth.

Why not go ahead now and cover the rest of the hull with cloth? Because the nails driven through the hull from the outside to hold the frames to the cleats were left sticking out for easy removal; remember, these cleats were nailed two ways. If you were to drive these nails in from the outside so you could fiberglass over them, you would be locking the cleats in and wouldn't be able to get them out when you got around to taping the frames to the hull. You can't pull them out now because the frames could shift, changing the boat's shape.

hull a few inches. Then put the cloth right in the fresh resin and, with either a paintbrush or a 3" roller, smooth and wet the cloth out. A roller does the best job of spreading resin evenly.

After the cloth is smoothed across the transom, concentrate on wetting out the corners and making the cloth lie around the corners smoothly. This is easier than it sounds, but the cloth must be well saturated with resin. After working the cloth around the corners, eyeball the length of lap you want for the cloth to run around onto the hull sides. Trim the cloth and roll it down snugly in place with more resin.

Lay the cloth back on the resin and roll on another coat.

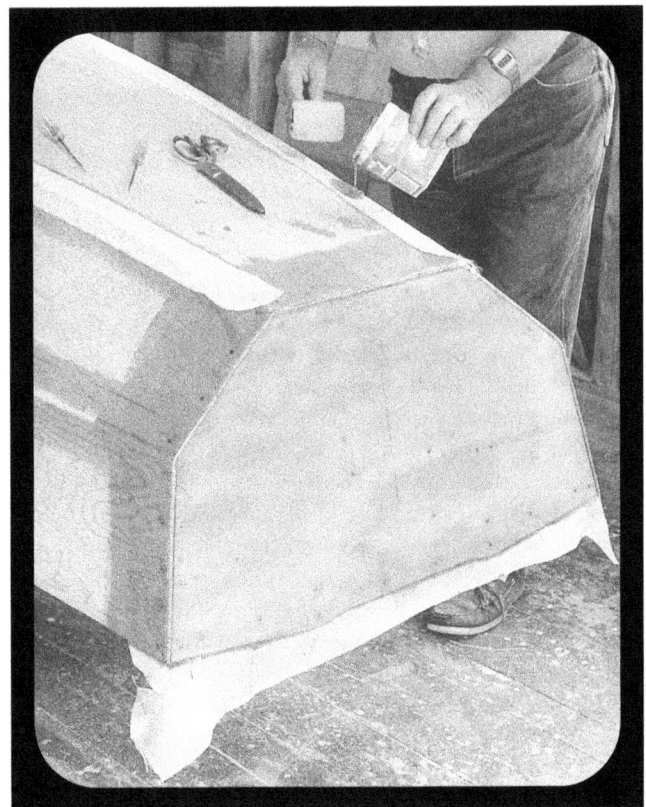

Taping the long exterior seams.

Filleting and Taping the Inside Seams

The long fore-and-aft inside seams are going to take the longest to tape and will be the trickiest to do because they take more putty. Here it pays to gain yourself some time by paying attention to temperature. I'd leave these seams until the coolest time of the day, or have a helper who knows what he or she is doing, so that these seams can be done in one smooth operation.

The procedure for puttying and taping the long inside seams is about the same as for the outside seams: mark your parallel tape guidelines with the 1½" guide block, apply resin to the seams, putty, and tape. You want to create a smooth fillet along these seams for the tape, and accommodating the ever-changing lay of the planks takes a little extra concentration. While you're thinking about this, you can work on taping the frames, even in the middle of a hot day.

The frames get taped on both sides to the hull panels, using short lengths of tape between the limber holes, so you're not likely to get into trouble here. Figure on about four hours, total, for this operation.

Start out by carefully turning Cartopper over, and place her on sawhorses, right side up. You can start taping the frames to the panels anywhere you want, but only remove cleats from the area where you're working; don't take all the cleats off any one frame all at once.

Take the cleats off the side panels, and fiberglass tape the side panels to both sides of the frames. Do the same for the bilge panels and bottom panel. Measure the distance from the edge of the top limber hole to the sheer, and cut four pieces of 3" fiberglass tape, enough for each side of the frame on both sides of the boat. In fact, you could cut lengths of tape for all three frames at once—twelve pieces in all. It makes sense to cut these pieces beforehand, instead of while your resin is hardening up. Think ahead all you can.

Mark the tape line with the 1½" parallel guide, coat the seam with resin, then mix up a small amount of putty—about a quarter pint will do. Lay Cartopper over on her bilge to make spreading the fillet along the seam easier. Use a tongue depressor to spread the putty; it makes a neat, coved application. If the putty is mixed a little on the stiff side, you can shape the fillet and it will stay put.

When each fillet is smoothed to your satisfaction, coat the area with resin, position the tape, and wet it out thoroughly with more resin. As each frame is taped to the side panel, the frame is locked in place enough so that the rest of its cleats can be taken out. One of the nice things about "tacking" with small #18 wire nails is that if your claw hammer won't pull them out, a pair of pliers will do the job.

Tape each frame and bilge panel with the boat heeled over, then heel her the other way to work on the other side.

The day after all my frames were taped, it was 65°F in my shop at seven in the morning—exactly right for taping the long seams. You're going to need a 1½" putty knife to

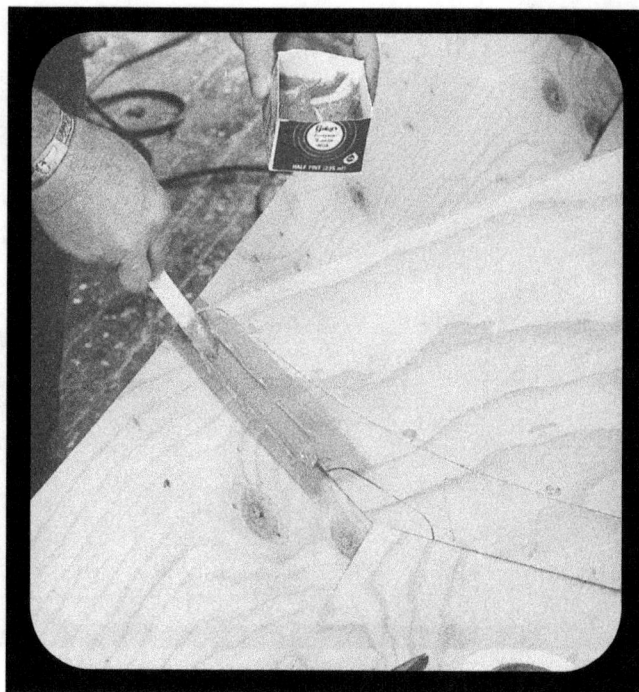
Forming a fillet between a frame and a side panel.

spread the putty on the seam, then a couple of shaped wooden blades that you make yourself, to shape the fillet. One should be rounded more than the other for the sharper angles from amidships to the after end of the boat. Better yet, if you can get hold of one, is an auto-body

Glassing the frame fillets.

Use an auto-body putty spreader to make a smooth fillet on the long inside seams.

repairman's putty spreader made from flexible rubber; this easily accommodates its shape to any change of angle.

Begin by cutting out the limber holes; they're just hanging from their tabs and can be easily sawn out with a narrow, tapered, keyhole saw. Cut the 3" tape to length and use the 1½" parallel guide to mark the tape line on one side of the seam. Saturate the seam with resin, then mix up a batch of putty. You want to mix enough putty to do each seam with one batch, so mix a half pint or more per seam. Get the putty in the seam fast, smooth the fillet, lay the tape in the fresh putty, coat it with more resin, and wet it all out so that the whole job sets up together.

Work quickly but carefully. Working alone, it's going to take about four hours to do all four long inside seams. With the inside seams and frames taped and cured, you can finish cutting out the inside of the frame panels.

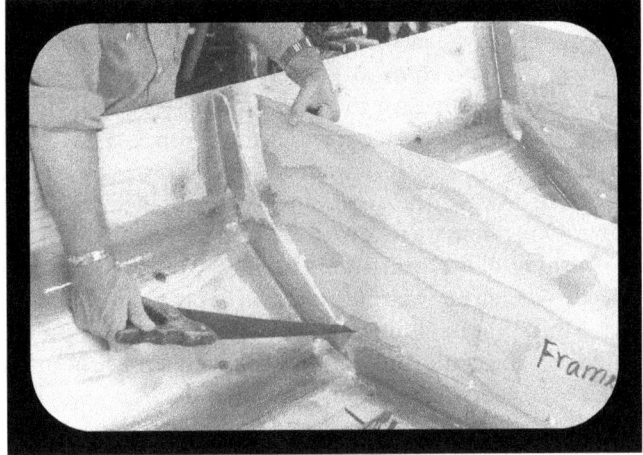

Brushing resin to fiberglass the fillets.

Cut out the frame waste after the inside seams have cured.

Now is a good time to put in the foot stretchers. These are the cleats that are fastened to the bilge panels that allow you to brace your feet as you row. Be sure they're positioned to suit your height. Now turn the Cartopper upside down to prepare for sheathing the hull.

If the outside tape needs to be sanded before the hull sheathing goes on, give the areas a coat of finishing resin or resin that's been doctored with a "surfacing agent." I sometimes use a surfacing agent made by Advance Coatings Company (see Appendix for contact information). I add a heaping tablespoon to a pint of resin. This makes sanding a lot easier.

Put a coarse, 20-grit disc in your variable-speed electric drill, and grind off any fiberglass bubbles in the tape or hull in preparation for laying the cloth. When you've finished sanding, give the rest of the hull a coat of laminating resin and let it sink into the plywood and set up.

Sheathing the Hull

To sheathe the hull, take the two 12' lengths of your 38" 6-ounce cloth, and lay one of the pieces on one side of

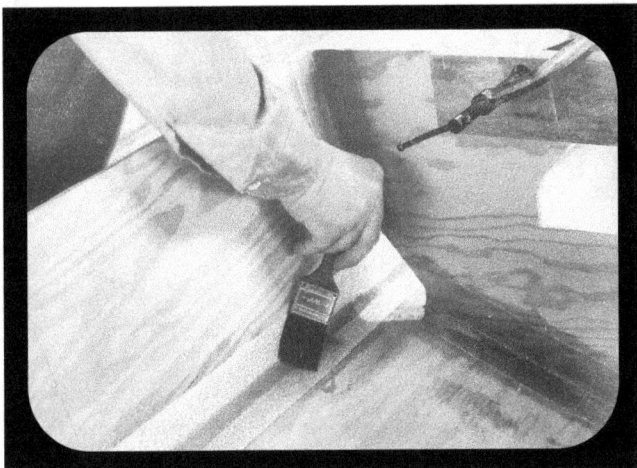

Smooth the fiberglass cloth over the hull with a brush.

your dry hull, with an overhang at the sheer. Trim the selvedge edge (the factory binding) at the sheer, leaving an overhang of an inch or so. Getting rid of the selvedge will allow the cloth's weave to move more freely in all directions. Smooth the cloth out with a dry brush, getting rid of wrinkles. Brush the cloth from amidships toward the bow, and then toward the stern, and the cloth will fit like a glove. Don't hesitate to give the cloth a tug with your hand if brushing alone won't do. The idea is to get the cloth exactly where you want it before you apply the resin.

Mix a pint of laminating resin, pour some right in the middle of the cloth, and start to work with a roller. Work it in an ever-widening pattern, starting in the middle so that the air is forced out to the edges. Cloth stretches when it is saturated with resin, and you want to avoid creating bubbles. Don't hesitate to give the cloth a pull when bubbles or wrinkles appear.

When everything's smooth, roll on a second coat of resin to fill the weave, and let it all set up before you start on the second piece of cloth. This is safer than trying to cram on the last piece of cloth and finding you can't brush it out because it's sticking to the first piece. Of course, if you're a pro, you can cover the whole outside without hesitation.

When you're ready to position the second piece of cloth, look for the selvedge edge on the first piece. You can match the two selvedge edges with an overlap of a couple of inches, or simply butt them. Smooth the cloth out carefully, wet it out as you did with the first piece, then treat it to a second coat of resin.

Use resin with wax in it for the finishing coat, and put it on lavishly with a 4" brush. If the temperature is up around 70° or 80°, you can start sanding within an hour if the resin looks dull and feels hard to your thumbnail. To hasten drying even more, take the boat out in the sun; you'll want to do your sanding outdoors anyway, if you have a small shop like mine.

Temperature and Handling Large Pieces of Cloth

I picked a 60°F morning for sheathing Cartopper, and it couldn't have been better for handling those larger pieces of cloth. Some manufacturers used to recommend laying cloth in fresh resin, then smoothing it out. But they never said how much cloth was easy to handle at one time or at what temperature. Sure, you can put a yard of cloth into fresh resin and get it laid down fast enough to stay out of trouble, even in warm weather. And that technique can be useful on a vertical surface. But there's no way I would try it on a hot day with a piece of cloth 38" wide and 12' long, like you're going to use on Cartopper. Imagine getting a piece of cloth that size half stuck, full of wrinkles, and find you're powerless to do anything more about it!

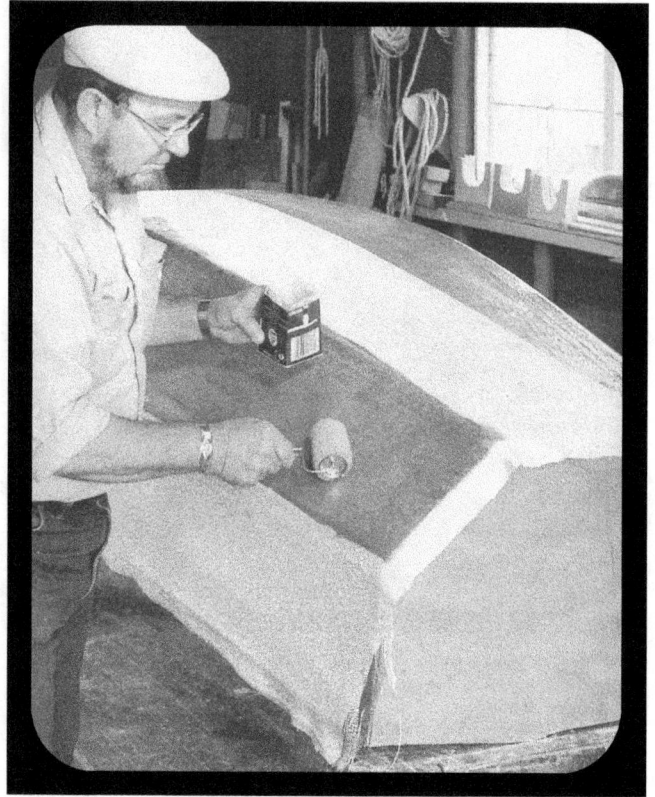

Rolling resin on the hull sheathing.

Get at this sanding as quickly as you can—when the resin is cured enough so that it doesn't clog your sandpaper, but before it sets up rock hard. It will save you a lot of time and makes it much easier to do a good job. If you use

Trim the edges while the resin is still "green," or just partially cured.

epoxy, remember to wash the boat to get rid of the amine blush before you begin sanding.

Trim any excess cloth away and then start sanding the bottom of the hull first, because it's always the first to set up. I use a belt sander with a 50- or 60-grit belt to sand the whole outside of the hull, except for the taped seam corners. (Don't hit them with a belt sander or you will be through the glass and into the plywood in one pass.) Then I switch to a half-sheet vibratory sander with 60-grit paper for final smoothing of the taped-seam corners. Wear a face mask! Don't bother going to a finer grit: you want to leave a fairly coarse surface to provide some "tooth" for the paint to grab onto.

You don't really have to sheathe the whole outside of Cartopper with cloth, but you should at least double up on the taped seams. I'd use 4" tape for the first layer and 3" for the second. By skipping the sheathing, you will save some weight and expense, but you'll lose abrasion protection and a good base for paint. Paint seems to last forever, without cracking or peeling, on the fiberglassed hull. For me, that alone is worth it.

The Skeg

Make the skeg from $\frac{3}{4}$" pine, spruce, fir, mahogany, or even oak, if you want. Scribe-fit it to the hull, bore through the hull from the outside along the centerline, bed the skeg in a marine bedding compound or in epoxy thickened with Cab-O-Sil or talcum, and fasten it from inside using 2" #14 stainless-steel pan-head screws with washers. Use shorter screws at the skeg's thinner end. Later, after painting, you might want to add a piece of $\frac{5}{8}$" half-oval brass to the skeg for protection.

If you don't have a helper to hold the skeg in place while you fasten it, clamp a couple of 2" x 4"s together side by side to the skeg and weigh them down to hold the skeg in place. I use a couple of pieces of railroad track for weights.

Gunwales

You're going to need four gunwales, two to a side, made from $\frac{1}{2}$" x 1" x 12'6" stock. Mine were made from slices

Drilling on the centerline of the bottom for the skeg. I'll use the chunk of railroad track later to hold the skeg in place while I drive the fastenings from inside the hull.

off a clear (as clear as I could get) 14'-long 2" x 4". Fir or spruce—it doesn't matter.

Why are the gunwales cut 12'6" when the boat's length is only 11'6"? That 11'6" is the measurement down the centerline, but it's about 12'1" around the sheer. Add another 5" for trimming, and 12'6" is the size to start with. Usually the outside edge of a 2" x 4" or plank has the best grain and is freer of knots, so keep the best slices for the outside course.

Pick a pair of gunwales—outside and inside—and spread glue on their inside faces. Position them along the sheer, and start clamping them in place, working from the bow aft, or from amidships. Fasten them from inside the hull with $1\frac{1}{8}$" bronze ring nails, spaced about 6" to 7"

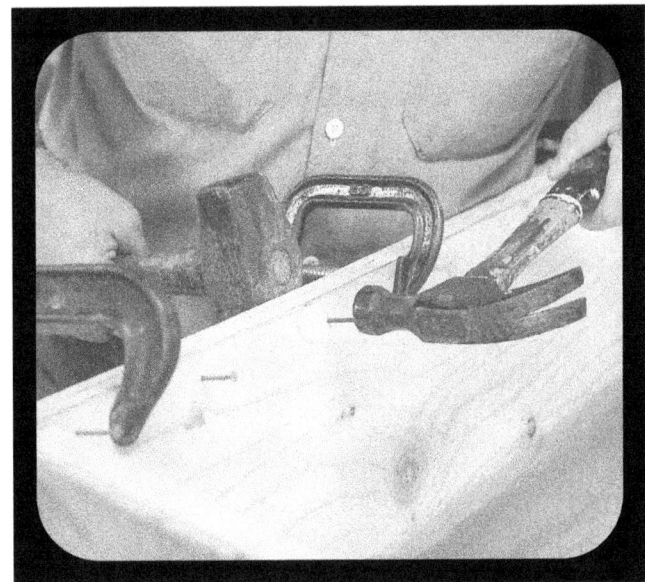

Fastening a gunwale with ring nails. A sledgehammer held on the outside of the hull provides some mass to hammer against.

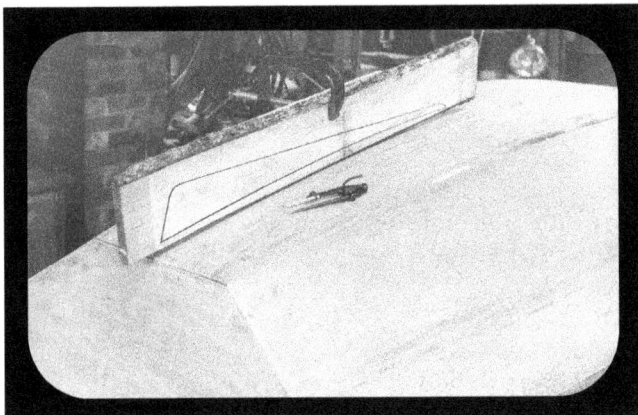

Scribe the skeg to the curve of the bottom.

apart. Wipe off any excess glue immediately, and trim their ends when the fastening is completed.

Finishing

Give Cartopper's interior a coat or two of sealer, and worry later about painting her. Since I'm already using polyester resin for the taping process, I generally thin some waxed resin about 30 percent with acetone or lacquer thinner and keep on going with it to seal the rest of the hull.

While you're waiting for the sealing coat of resin to set up, you can add a touch of class to Cartopper by striking her waterline and marking her boot top. If it weren't easy to do, I'd never bother.

You already struck the waterline on the Cartopper model in Chapter 5. Putting the waterline on the full-sized boat is done the same way. I put Cartopper on a sheet of 14' plywood resting on boards across sawhorses, but a garage floor, a paved driveway, or any good, flat level surface will do. After leveling the hull, make a sort of T-square that's the height of the top of the boot top. Mark the height around the hull, then cut the depth of the boot top off the T-square and mark the lower edge. You'll be finished in about an hour and sipping a cool one, while anyone using the string-and-level method will still be hard at work. You can skip the boot top and just put the waterline on using this method. It's so easy, it's fun.

Tape the waterline and boot top with masking tape, give her a coat of primer, then paint. My experience tells me that the base that's under the paint makes the biggest difference in a paint job that lasts and lasts—more so than the paint itself. Sheathing Cartopper's outside, as I mentioned before, provides that good base.

The Seats and the Floor

While the sanding primer dries, you can finish building Cartopper's interior. You have a bow seat to install, and you should put the mast partner support under it if you want to

Striking the waterline.

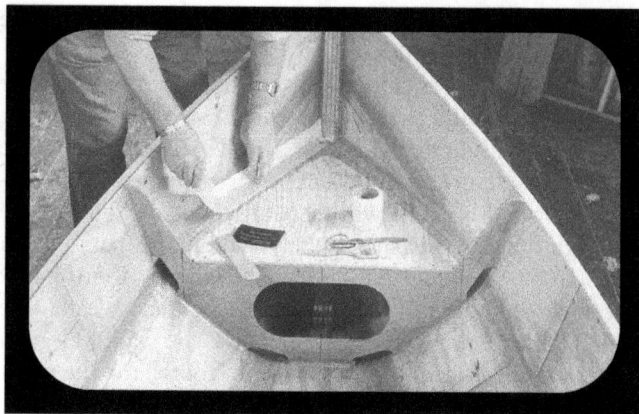

Installing the bow seat.

Framing the floor platform.

rig her for sail. The mast partner support is made from pine or spruce, 3/4" x 5" x 24½", shown on Cartopper's profile plan, Sheet 3.

The floor platform is shown as No. 14 and is built in three pieces. This seemed like more work to me, so I built it in one piece, since I had a piece of plywood large enough to do it. To fit it in one piece, measure its overall length (3'1") and its greatest width (2'9") with your scale rule, cut it a little larger, and scribe-fit it all around. Three pieces work pretty much the same way. Frame it as shown in the drawings, and give it a coat of sealer.

The movable box seat shown as No. 28 (Sheet 3) is as easy as anything you will ever make that is part of a boat, so I'll spare you the how-to, other than mention that instead of making its top flat, I curved it for a little more comfort.

A pair of edge-mount oarlocks, placed about 3" farther aft than shown in the plans, suited me, along with a pair of 6½' or 7' Shaw & Tenney spruce oars and a 3/8" Dacron painter.

Rudder and Centerboard

The rowing version of Cartopper is now complete. If you want to sail her, she needs a rudder, a centerboard, and a sail rig of your choice: the spritsail or the leg-o-mutton sail.

The real rudder is built the same as the rudder on the Cartopper model, shown here. Assemble one of the rudder cheeks and the filler blocks, then clamp the rudder in place and bore the pivot hole through the rudder and cheek at the same time.

Start with the kick-up rudder, which, along with the centerboard, is nice to have for shallow-water sailing. No. 31 on the keyed instructions says that the rudder is made of two layers of $1/4$" plywood to achieve its $1/2$" thickness— one piece of $1/2$" plywood is also OK. It also says "edges faired off where exposed clear of bearing," which means the edges must be tapered for a smooth flow of water over the rudder. Also, the trailing edge should be a longer and thinner

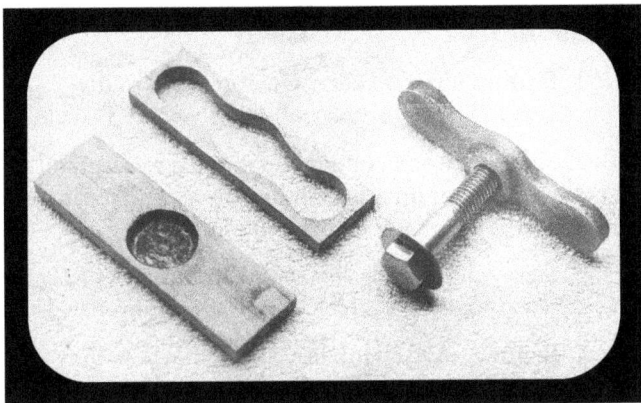

To make your own big wing nut, make a two-piece mold (left); $3^{1}/2$" long is about right. A completed wing nut with pivot bolt inserted is shown at right.

Place a locknut in the central recess and fill the cavity with epoxy, reinforced with chopped glass strands. Although it's not shown in the photo, you should insert the bolt into the nut before pouring to keep epoxy off of the threads.

taper or the rudder will chatter. Make sure you don't taper the area that will be covered by the rudder cheeks.

The top of the rudder blade has a radius of 6" and is bored for a $1/2$" pivot bolt with a wing nut set up to keep the rudder from floating up. This wing nut has to be about $3^{1}/2$" long to give good grip. I couldn't find one in a hardware store, so I made my own out of fiberglass and resin. No. 29 of the keyed instructions shows rudder filler blocks made to the diagram; No. 30 shows rudder cheeks made from $1/2$" or double $1/4$" plywood.

There is no need to repeat the keyed instructions at full length, so we will shift to making the centerboard. Note that on the plans there are different views of the centerboard

The centerboard and case for the Cartopper model show exactly how the real things go together as well. Note the lead ballast and the pivot *slot*, as opposed to a hole.

and centerboard case layouts and their construction. What you don't see in one view, you will see in another. As I have mentioned before, a numbered part matched with keyed instructions is about as good as it gets, so I won't go into the details of making the centerboard case, other than to mention that the dashed line (No. 23) is the outside framing.

The centerboard itself is made from $\frac{1}{2}$" plywood or double $\frac{1}{4}$" plywood and is tapered as shown. Don't let the pouring of the 9.2 pounds of lead scare you, but be careful. Wear eye protection and a dust mask. Lead melts at a low temperature—impurities will flow to the top. Skim these off and the lead is ready to pour. Drive nails as shown into the cavity, and lay the centerboard on a piece of asbestos board. Level the centerboard, make ABSOLUTELY CERTAIN there is no moisture present, and pour without stopping. After the lead has cooled, the excess (if there is any) can be trimmed off with ordinary hand tools, such as a block plane or a spokeshave, and then sanded flush.

The Sprit Rig

You have two choices here, a powerful and nicely shaped spritsail or the popular leg-o-mutton sail that fits a fleet of Instant Boats. The advantage of the spritsail is that both the mast and sprit, at 9'6", can be stowed inside the boat. The mast is made from a closet pole bought at your local hardware store, so it is easily replaceable. Since it is round, it is free to rotate, allowing the snotter attachment to turn freely with the mast. The sprit has a little more class, with taper at its ends, which are slotted to catch the pigtail (or loop) at the peak of the sail and the knotted end of the snotter. To peak the sail taut, just pull down on the snotter, which travels through the eye of the sling. This pushes the sprit up and puts tension on the peak. When you are satisfied with the set of the sail, belay the end of the snotter to a cleat on the lower part of the mast.

The $\frac{3}{8}$" sheet attaches to the clew grommet and slips around the thumb cleat, which is about as foolproof as it gets. And that's why Bolger designed it that way. Therefore, there is no way to tie the sheet down. To get around this safety measure by using a standard cleat and tying the sheet down guarantees a knockdown along with a bath, so don't attempt to improve on Bolger's foolproof thumb cleat.

The only disadvantage I can see for the spritsail is that you have to keep peeking around it to see where you are headed. Other than that, I like the looks of it, and yes, you can have a window put in it if you wish.

The Leg-O-Mutton Rig

This triangular-shaped sail has only two square feet less than the spritsail and calls for a $1\frac{3}{4}$" square mast that is 15'6" long. The 9'6" long sprit—which can be made with a little class, or made square with "little penalty," as Bolger puts it—is slotted at both ends and works exactly the same as for the spritsail. Key No. 42 shows the $\frac{3}{8}$" x 26' nylon sheet passing through a block attached to the clew grommet.

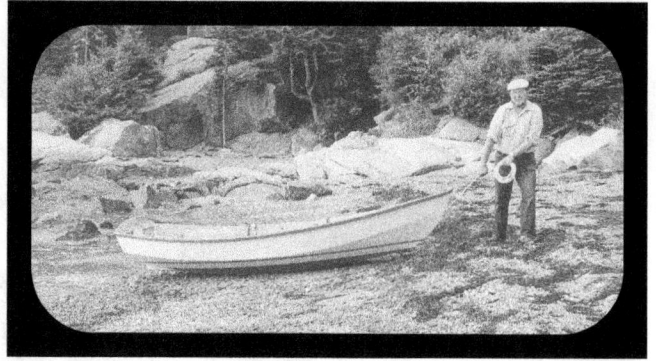

The author with a finished Cartopper.

The slot of the sprit catches in between, and, with a snap hook, leads to the $\frac{3}{8}$" nylon traveler.

Sailing is nice, but Cartopper also makes a nice tender under power. She's not a high-speed planing boat, though. Don't use an engine greater than 2 horsepower, or she will bury her stern while her bow reaches for the moon.

Cartopper is a very popular choice for hundreds of builders. At a weight of ninety pounds, she is easily cartoppable and will slide in the back of a station wagon or a pickup truck.

BUILDING KEY FOR DESIGN No. 519, CARTOPPER

Materials
All plywood is or can be $\frac{1}{4}$" thick, and all plywood components except the centerboard, No. 26, will fit on four 4' x 8' sheets as diagrammed.

Fiberglass materials:
$2\frac{1}{2}$ pounds of 3" glass tape
2 gallons of resin
10 yards of 38", 6-ounce cloth
5 pounds of Fillite powder

Assembly

1. Bottom plywood cut out and marked to diagram. Butt straps throughout, plywood 3" wide.

2. Sides, plywood cut out and marked to diagram; note mirror images with butt straps and locating marks for frames on opposite sides.

3. Stem built up to given profile from layers of plywood totaling 2" thick; attach to bottom panel.

4. Frame A to diagram; leave straight across the top with marks and drilled holes outlining cutdown to foresheets level after joint taping is complete; edges beveled toward the bow, $21\frac{1}{2}°$

on sides, 18° on bilge, 7½° on bottom; ¾" x 1½" backing cleats to take fastenings of foresheets and maststep.

5. Frame B to diagram; leave straight across top to be cut down later as with Frame A; bevel toward the bow 9½° on sides, 7° on bilge, 3½° on bottom.

6. Frame C similar to B; bevel toward the stern, 7° on sides, 6° on bilge, 4½° on bottom.

7. Transom plywood with ¾" thick fastening frame; dimensions on diagram are the inside (i.e., largest) face of frame; in beveling, the maximum dimensions of the plywood will be reduced about ¼" on the sides, a scant 5/16" on the bilges, and slightly less than 3/8" on the bottom; bevels are shown full size on detail construction sheet.

8. Motor board ¾" x 9" in two or more vertical planks. (Secure sides to transom; bend around frames and fasten to stem; bend on bottom, lining up centerline marks to align the assembly.)

9. Gunwale clamp in two courses to finish 1" square.

10. Bilge panels to diagram; mirror images as with sides. Fit in place as described in the book.

11. Joints filled and covered with epoxy putty; tape insides and outsides with fiberglass tape that is 3" wide.

12. Midships floor frame, ¾" x 3½" x about 32".

13. Fore-and-aft stringers of floor platform, ¾" x 3½" x 37".

14. Floor platform plywood cut into three sections and secured with exposed-head screws to be readily removable.

15. Skeg from ¾" x 3½" x 39", glued on and screwed from inside.

16. Supporting feet of maststep from 1⅜" x 1½" x 7", glued down and screwed from outside.

17. Maststep plywood built up to total of 1" thick, 5" x 6¼", including ½" lip over Frame A.

18. Center stiffener of foresheets serves as mast partner and as butt strap if foresheets are divided as diagrammed, ¾" x 5" x 24½".

19. Foresheets plywood; seam on centerline allows most economical use of plywood sheets.

20. Foot braces, ¾" square x 7", glued to bilge and screwed from outside; vary location to taste.

21. Sides of centerboard, trunk plywood to diagram (but check against frame location in assembled hull).

22. Head blocks of centerboard trunk, ¾" x 1½".

23. Bottom frames of centerboard trunk, sawn to profile from ¾" x 2¼" x about 25".

24. Top stiffeners of centerboard trunk, ¾" square x 1'6".

25. Centerboard pivot pin, ½" x 3½" carriage bolt.

26. Centerboard, ½" or double ¼" plywood to diagram (won't fit on the four sheets; try for scrap plywood the right size). Slot for pivot pin to allow board to be lifted off, reinforced with a 1/16" x about 2" square stainless plate on each side of board.

27. Centerboard pendant, ¼" Dacron, 14" long to allow board to drop to marked position; wooden toggle on upper end at least 1" diameter to stop without dropping into trunk. 1/16" x ¾" x about 3" stainless straps riveted flush with board to take ¼" pendant pin. Drill holes in board (not shown) and provide fid pin to hold board all the way up and in two or three intermediate positions.

28. Rowing seat, ¼" x 12" x 16" plywood with ¾" x 4½" sides and ends; loose on floor platform to put aside for sailing.

29. Rudder filler blocks, ¾" thick to diagram.

30. Rudder cheeks, ½" or double ¼" plywood to diagram. Brackets bent from ⅛" x 1¼" x 2" stainless screwed to rudder and transom, four in all (screw eyes will do in a pinch); ¼" pivot rod about 18" long, including bend or upset at the top.

31. Rudder blade, double ¼" plywood to diagram; edges faired off where exposed clear of bearing; pivot bolt, ½" x 2½" with wing nut set up to keep board from floating up.

32. Tiller tapered from 1" x 1¾" x 44"; ⅛" x 1" x 10" straps engaging rudder head make length to pivot 49" (long tiller is needed because in this boat the rudder carries a large proportion of the lateral plane load and will pull hard even when centered; also, she will sail best with crew weight concentrated amidships). Tiller swings over to stow along back of raised blade.

33. Sockets for ½" oarlocks; block up flanges to bring lock axis near vertical, not canted out with

sides. A second set of sockets, 10" abaft Frame A, may be worthwhile to trim the boat with two people. Oars, 7' spruce, or spruce shafts with plywood or fiberglass blades.

34. Spritsail mast, $1\frac{5}{8}$" diameter fir closet pole, 9'6" long (minimum and not intended to stand up to heavy hiking). Mast can also be aluminum or PVC pipe at least $1\frac{1}{2}$" outside diameter, or a 2" x 2" with corners rounded. The snotter will work best if the mast is free to revolve. Note $\frac{3}{4}$" square chocks at partners to prevent the heel of the mast from bearing on the thin hull bottom, with fore-and-aft cleats on the sides to belay snotter and tack downhaul.

35. Leg-o-mutton mast to diagram; thicknesses specified are for a square stick; if round, should be thicker up to 2" diameter at partners. Partner chocks and cleats as in spritsail rig. Snotter block slung about 48" above heel.

36. Sprit, 9'6" long with a $\frac{5}{16}$" x $\frac{3}{4}$" slot at each end; in prototype it was round, $1\frac{1}{2}$" diameter in the middle, tapered to $1\frac{1}{4}$" at heel and to 1" at the peak. A square stick without taper will work with little penalty. The sprit boom of the leg-o-mutton rig is identical. Snotter, $\frac{1}{4}$" rope with knotted end caught in heel slot; lead-through thimble, bull's-eye, or block slung 43" below masthead in spritsail rig, to cleat above foresheets.

37. Sheet for spritsail, $\frac{3}{8}$" x about 18' nylon on clew grommet of sail.

38. Sheet hooks on gunwales from about 1" x $1\frac{1}{2}$" x $5\frac{1}{2}$", well rounded off and screwed and glued to clamps. The sheet is hooked under the leeside hook and shifted across in tacking.

39. Throat of sail (head in the leg-o-mutton sail) lashed to masthead with part of the lashing passing over a $\frac{1}{2}$" deep slot in the masthead to hold the sail as high as possible. Furl sail by rolling it up to the mast from the clew with the leech inside the roll.

40. Separate luff ties; not a lacing.

41. Peak vang, $\frac{1}{4}$" x 17" nylon; standing end fast to peak of sprit; fall brought down to a hole in the transom near the centerline. This line should normally be slack, with length adjusted to stop the peak of the sprit from going forward of the mast when running before the wind, to allow the sheet to be slacked further without producing a rhythmic roll.

42. Sheet of leg-o-mutton sail, $\frac{3}{8}$" x 26' nylon; standing end snaps to $\frac{3}{8}$" traveler bridle knotted through holes in the transom, or the quarter knees if she has them, as far outboard as possible. Sheet goes to a block slung on the tail of the clew pendant, thence in to hand.

43. Make wing-nut mold in two pieces as shown. Wax both parts; car wax will do. Score the nut ridges (see profile) to keep nut from slipping out. Put masking tape on bottom of nut to prevent resin from creeping in. Set nut in cavity and pour mixture of polyester or epoxy resin strengthened with glass fibers. Nut should be stainless-steel hex locknut. (Bore $\frac{1}{2}$" hole in mold—do same with bolt.)

CHAPTER 8
SWEET PEA

When I asked Phil Bolger to design this peapod for me, I imagined myself striking out in the calm of the morning toward Spruce Head Island and then sailing back when the wind came up from the southwest in the late morning or early afternoon.

The boat didn't have to be that efficient for sailing, because I wanted her mostly for exercise: Stand-up rowing was what I had in mind. This kind of rowing uses back, leg, and arm muscles—while I'm facing forward, enjoying the scenery. It saves me from constantly trying to crane a neck that doesn't want to crane anymore. Years ago, when lobstering in a pea pod off Metinic Island, I found out that this was the way to go. You could row standing for untiring hours with far better control facing a steep chop than was ever possible sitting down.

As usual, Bolger came through with more than I expected. I was not very demanding in the Sweet Pea's design, specifying just that she should be mostly for stand-up rowing (she can be rowed sitting down, too) and be of tack-and-tape construction so that she'd be within the capabilities of builders who thrive on poor joints filled with sticky stuff. And, I wanted her to be pretty—not look like a banana. So, rather than have her ends exactly alike, Phil gave her a higher sheer at the bow and made her after sections fuller for more bearing. Her fine stern will keep me from being pushed ashore by a wave while exploring gunkholes. In general, Phil gave her looks that

knock my eyes out—and those of just about everyone who sees her.

And, of course, it wouldn't be Phil if he didn't throw in something different. We talked about the rudder in the first few exchanges of letters, with neither of us happy with what we could see in the way of conventional rudders. So when the plans arrived, there was a rudder stock mounted in a well inside the hull, and there was a "slipping keel" that could also be unshipped.

I must say that it took me a while to weigh the advantages of the slipping keel against the amount of work involved, but the more I looked, the more intrigued I became. Phil wrote:

> They used to use these [a long, removable skeg] in sizable sailing barges in Norfolk, England. I thought it would be nice if the thing could be removed, the for'd well plugged, and a short skeg shipped in the after well, for straight rowing.

This all made sense to me—here was a choice of keels according to how I wanted to use the boat. For sure, this was something different, but any reluctance for change was gradually won over by the sense of what I would gain. I knew

(continued on page 79)

The author demonstrating stand-up rowing. (Photo by Mark Abb)

The "slipping keel" ships and unships easily, making for a quick conversion from rowboat to sailboat and back. (Photo by Mark Abb)

Sweet Pea, Sheet 1.

Sweet Pea, Sheet 2.

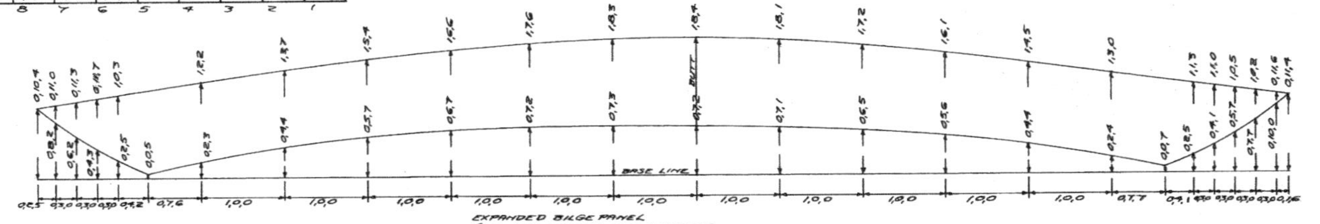

EXPANDED BILGE PANEL.
(USE WITH CAUTION, NOT ASSUMING
THAT ALL BOATS ARE EXACTLY THE
SAME SHAPE AS THE PROTOTYPE,
OR THAT BOTH SIDES OF ANY BOAT
ARE EXACTLY ALIKE.)

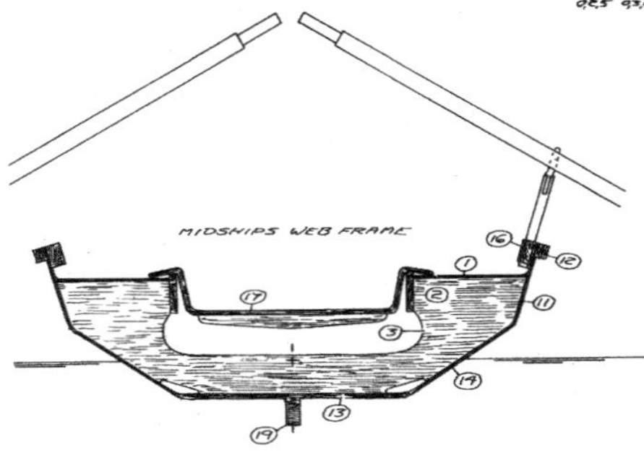

MIDSHIPS WEB FRAME

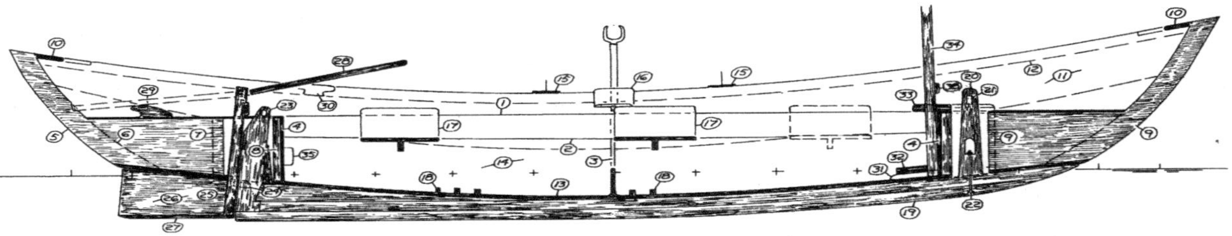

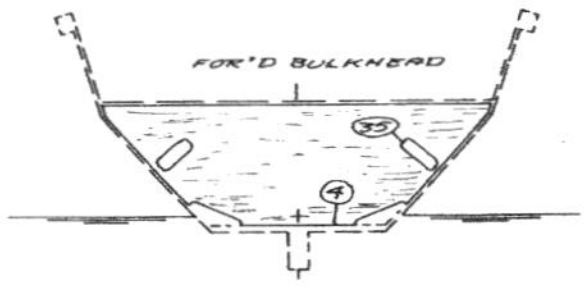

FOR'D BULKHEAD

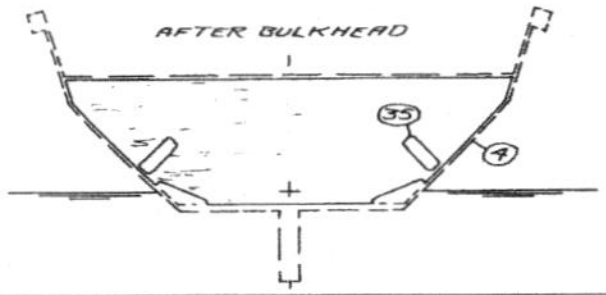

AFTER BULKHEAD

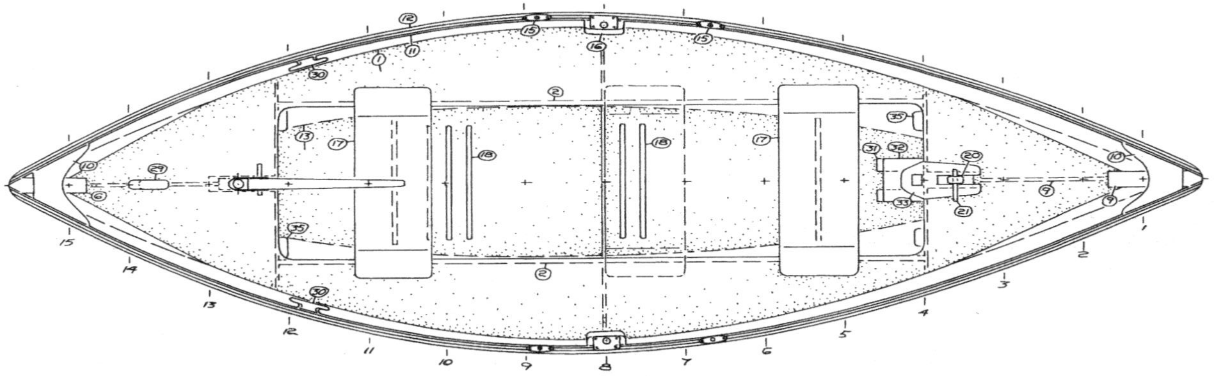

OFFSETS IN FEET, INCHES, & EIGHTHS
TO OUTSIDE OF PLANK, FOR CONVENTIONAL
PLANKING. FOR CONVENIENT STRIP PLANK, CORRECT
FOND TO INSIDE-OF-PLANK DIMEN-
SIONS.

BASE LINE

Sweet Pea, Sheet 3.

Sweet Pea, Sheet 4.

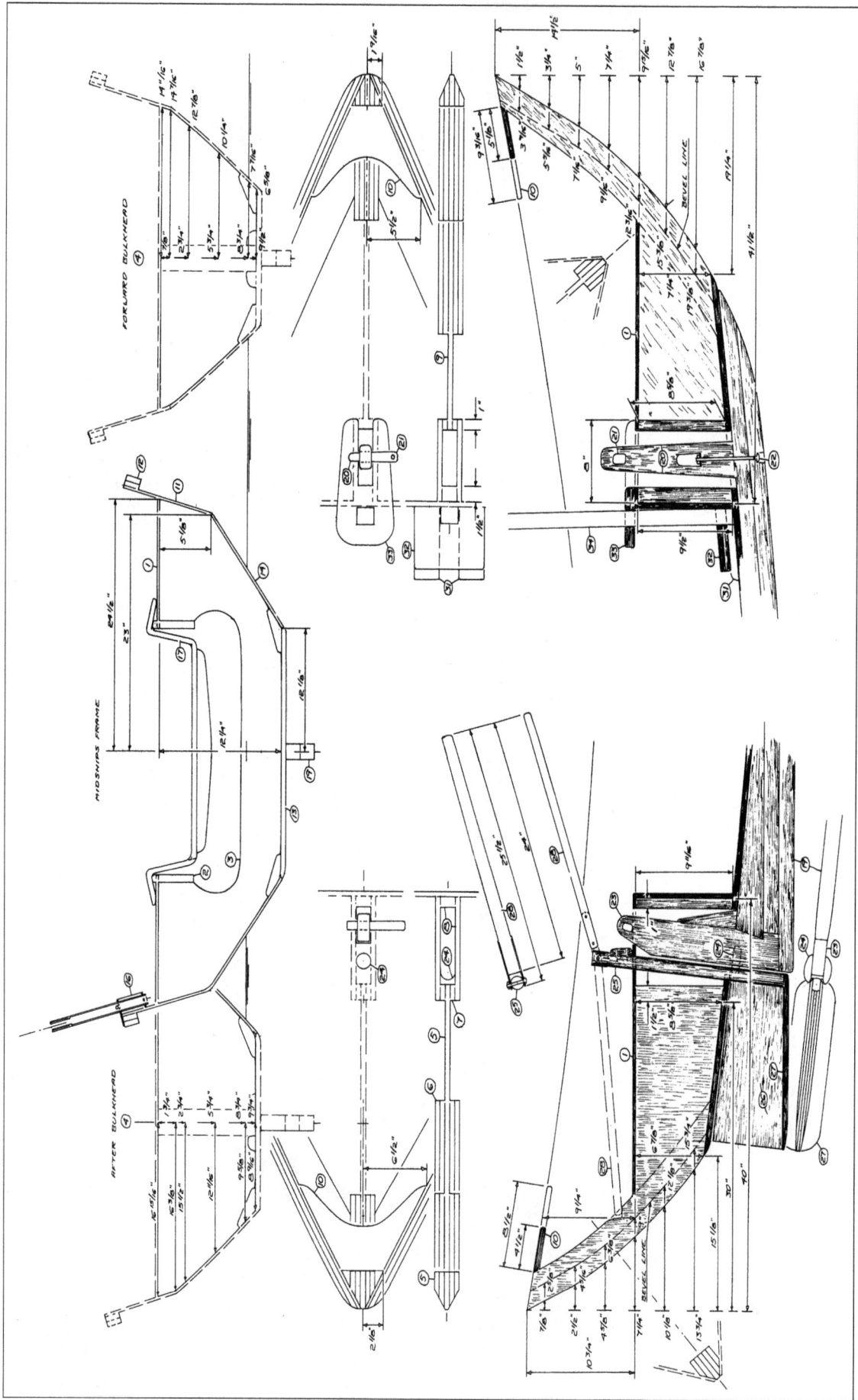

Sweet Pea, Sheet 5.

(continued from page 73)

from past experience that it's no easy job to mount a rudder on a fine-ended hull—except at the dock. I didn't like yoke steering, the excessively long tiller you'd need to keep your weight toward her middle, or the arched swinging of the tiller if the rudder was mounted on a raked sternpost.

So, the inside vertical rudderpost caught my eye. But perhaps most ingenious of all—and it's very simple but extremely clever—the tiller folds back with its end resting in a notch in the sternpost. When you want to row, you just drop the end of the tiller in the slot, and she will track straight ahead. Want to sail? Take it out, and instantly you're steering.

For sailing, I'll use the small forty-three-square-foot sprit-sail rig to start with, since its spars stow well inside the hull, out from underfoot on the chocks provided for them. Later on, I'm sure I'll want to try the fifty-nine-square-foot leg-o-mutton sail—the same as Cartopper's—to see what she will do with that. And, of course, the builder is free to experiment with a deeper keel and a deeper rudder. If you're just going to row the boat, you could dispense with the wells and put on a 1½" square keel or a short skeg and let it go at that.

So there you have it—this is one pretty boat! What's she going to cost? About $200 for fiberglass, polyester resin, and fillers, and $80 for exterior plywood, or roughly $300 for the rowing version. Add the $170 cost of either a leg-o-mutton or a sprit rig, and you have the whole package for around $500. Prices will be higher if you use marine plywood and epoxy resin.

BUILDING THE SWEET PEA

Materials
(See the building key on page 91.)

Assembly

Making a Butt Joint and Cutting the Side Panels
Start by laying seven slip sticks under two sheets of ¼" plywood that have been placed end to end for butt-joining. The center stick for a butt-joint support should be 7" or 8" wide. Lay a piece of waxed paper on the center stick, and place a piece of 3" fiberglass tape on it. You can make your own tape from cloth cut on the bias for even more strength. Study the weave of the cloth, and you will see how to make the 45° bias cut.

You are going to place glass butt straps on both sides of the 4' x 8' sheets of plywood at the same time, so mix up a half-pint of resin according to the manufacturer's directions, and saturate the adjacent underside of both pieces of plywood for about 3" in from their edges. Then, saturate the strip of tape on the waxed paper with resin, brushing it out beyond each side of the tape onto the waxed paper about 2".

Lay the first piece of plywood down so that its edge is at the center of the tape. If the plywood is wavy, tack it

Place waxed paper on the central support board. Lay down a piece of fiberglass tape and wet it out with resin.

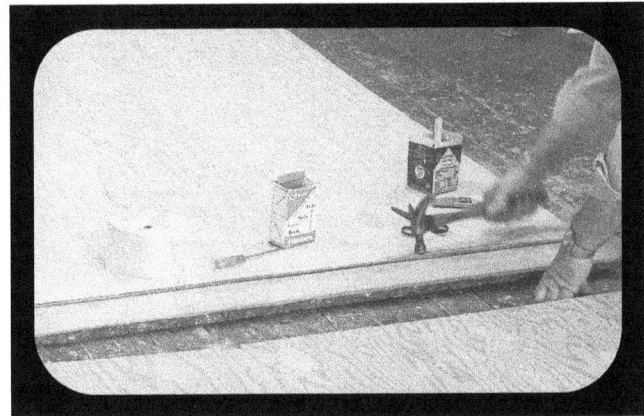
Brush resin on the bottom of one sheet of plywood, place it right down along the middle of the glass tape, and tack the plywood to the board.

Do the same for the other board, then apply resin and tape on top of the joint, followed by a sheet of waxed paper. Then draw a putty knife flat across the joint.

Fiberglass butt-joining plywood sheets.

down with #18 flat-head brads or escutcheon pins driven home so that the edges lie flush.

Butt the second piece of plywood against the first, and tack it down the same way. Saturate the upper surface of the joint with resin, and place a piece of 3" tape over it, wetting it out completely beyond the tape to a couple of inches on each side. Then place a piece of waxed paper down the length of the joint and draw a wide putty knife over it, smoothing the joint. Hold the putty knife at a very low angle, almost flat.

After both sides of the joint have been taped and the resin has cured, mark the long edges of the butted sheets in 1' intervals and lay out the side panels (called "topside" panels on the plans). Be sure to mark the locations of the forward and after bulkheads, the amidship frame, and the location of the sunken deck (a curved, dashed line on the plans).

Pry the butted sheets away from the slip stick to which they were nailed, cut the nails off as close as you can to the plywood, and grind them flush. Cut the first side panel out and use it as the template for the second panel by turning it over and placing it exactly on the 1' interval lines on the opposite edge of the sheet for a mirror image.

Laying Out the Deck and Bottom

There is room to lay out the deck between the two side panels if it's done in pieces; this saves two sheets of plywood. Make a full-sized paper template of the deck and lay out the bow and stern decks at each end of the sheet, and the side decks in between, as shown on the drawings (Sheet 3). All the pieces that make up the deck are joined by fore-and-aft butt straps made from 3" tape. Note that the outboard edges of the stern deck are straight between the bulkhead and the sternpost. This might look strange, but it allows the edges of

Using a flexible batten to draw a fair curve for the bottom panel.

the bilge panels that you'll put on later to lie fair with the edges of the bottom and topside panels in these areas.

The bottom panel is made from one 4' x 8' sheet of ½" plywood, cut lengthwise and placed end to end. However, the plywood needs to be wider at one end than at the other in order to accommodate the maximum width of the bottom. On your 4' x 8' sheet, measure 24½" up each 4' edge, draw a line, and cut. Draw a centerline lengthwise on that piece, and on the off-cut piece (which should measure 23½" x 8'). Butt the two pieces together end to end, using the centerlines for alignment. (Note that this differs from the layout instructions on the drawings, but it is much simpler and it works!) With a disc or belt sander, hollow out the joint by about the thickness of one veneer. Make the joint with a piece of fiberglass matting 6" wide and a 5" wide piece of cloth, following the technique you used for the side panels. You can hollow and fiberglass both sides at one go if you want.

Stem and Sternpost

While waiting for the butt straps to cure, lay out the stem and sternpost and the bulkheads. All can be gotten out of one 4' x 8' sheet of ½" plywood. Starting with the stem, on the right end of the sheet, lay out its shape by measuring 41½" in from the short edge, and square that line across the sheet. Measure 9½" from the underside of the deck squared to the 41½" mark, and run this line out to the short edge of the sheet. Measure 19¼" in from the short edge, and square a line down 7¼" from the underside of the deck; this establishes the junction of the forefoot.

Mark 3" intervals up and down from the deck as shown on the plan, and measure in, from the short edge of the sheet, for the face of the stem and the stem bevel. Drive brads at these points, and spring a light batten around them to establish and mark their outlines.

No dimensions are given for the after face of the stem, but my scale rule (read at 3" = 1') says that it's 3" from

Assembling the deck and deck stringers.

front to back for most of the stem's length, tapering to $2\frac{1}{2}$" at the stem head. (Remember that the plans in this book aren't reproduced at the size of the real plans, so the scale won't work unless you buy the plans.)

The sternpost is laid out the same as the stem, only with different dimensions. Make paper templates for the cheeks to the same shapes as the stem and sternpost, and cut out four of each. Glue the four cheek pieces to the stem; no nails are needed.

With the stem and sternpost marked, it is time to decide whether you are going to use this pea pod for sailing as well as for rowing. If you're just going to row her, there is no need to make the wells for the tongues of the "slipping keel." If you'll be sailing her, look at Sheet 2 of the plans, and mark out the wells on the stem and sternpost.

To mark the stem for beveling, draw a centerline on the stem face, and measure $\frac{3}{16}$" outward from it in both directions, to establish the $\frac{3}{8}$" face width. The stem bevels are figured from these lines and will vary some, but not enough to worry about. The top and bilge panels will fit best if the stem bevels are on the short side. If the bevels are too long, the panels will take a reverse curve, resulting in a "bottleneck" appearance. The sternpost needs no explanation if you successfully got through building the stem.

The well parts of the stem and sternpost are left nearly intact to hold the shape until you're ready to cut. Cut out the rectangular shape first, leaving $\frac{3}{4}$" at the top and bottom to be cut out later with a saber saw after the well framing and well sides are on.

Sawing the stem and sternpost bevels is next. Saw the stem bevel with your band saw set to clear the after-bevel line (bearding line). Work to the line by hand with a block plane and rasp.

Cut the stem bevels with a band saw.

'Midship Frame, Bulkheads, and Bilge Panels

The 'midship frame and bulkheads can be accurately laid out without using a square, by measuring from the edge of the sheet. Don't forget to cut the limber holes—but don't cut them all the way out now, since you will want their corners for help in alignment. Draw vertical centerlines on both faces of the 'midship frame and bulkheads. Glass-butt two more 4' × 8' sheets of $\frac{1}{4}$" plywood together for the

The tongues on the slipping keel fit into wells in the stem and sternpost. Here, cheek pieces are glued to the well framing.

Smooth the stem bevels with a plane, rasp, or belt sander.

The side and bottom panels, the deck assembly, the frames, and the stem and sternpost are all ready to be assembled. You'll cut the bilge panels later.

bilge panels; you don't need them now, but you will later when you are ready to close her in.

Each boat will vary some, so to be on the safe side, cut the bilge-panel ends ½" or more longer than called for on the plans.

Setting Her Up

It is time to set her up. Make sure that the centerline is marked on the underside of the deck, and place the deck on two leveled sawhorses. Glue and fasten the two deck strong-backs (3½" stringers) with ⅞" bronze ring nails. Cut four braces the same height as the sawhorses to support and level the rest of the deck. Place one brace at each end and one brace on each side at the 'midship frame. Glue and fasten the bulkheads to the stem and sternpost.

Temporarily tack the bulkheads to the ends of the deck stringers, using one nail each. (You'll need to remove the deck later in order to tape the long panel seams.) Align the centerlines of the stem and the sternpost webs with the deck centerline, and tack temporary blocks on each side to hold them in alignment. If the tops of the stem or sternpost webs don't lie flat on the deck, you may have to cut the stem notches a bit deeper.

Set the 'midship frame in position on the deck, and temporarily tack it to the strong-backs. When you're satisfied that the deck is level and the stem and sternpost are properly aligned, tack the bottom panel on the sternpost. Then tack the bottom panel to the bulkheads, the 'midship frame, and the stem, making sure that the centerlines are all lined up. Use no glue at this time.

Clamp the forward end of one side panel on the stem at the sheer, and wrap the panel around the hull, letting it lay naturally. Tack the bottom edge of the side panel so that it lies exactly on the chine (corners) of the 'midship frame and bulkheads; continue wrapping it around the hull until it lands on the sternpost's sheer mark.

Step back and take a look: Does the side panel's shape flow smoothly along the hull without twists and humps? If it does, and everything looks right, put on its mate. Pull the nail from the bottom panel at the sternpost, spread glue on

Bulkheads are set up on the underside of the deck. One side panel is clamped in place, and the back end of the bottom panel is tacked down. (The front end is propped up in the photo.) Last chance to make sure everything is properly aligned!

the top of the sternpost and the after bulkhead, and fasten the bottom panel to these pieces for good. Pull the nail holding the bottom panel to the stem, and lift the panel up far enough so that you can glue the 'midship frame, the forward bulkhead, and the top of the stem. Then push the bottom panel down into the glue, and fasten for good.

Force the forward end of one side panel away from the stem just a bit, allowing the nails to hold it in place. (I use #18 smooth-wire, flat-head brads for this because they pull easily.) Spread glue on the stem, whack the side panel nails back in, and fasten with 1" bronze ring nails. This is a lot easier than springing the panel clear of the stem, backing

Bring the front end of the bottom panel down to the stem.

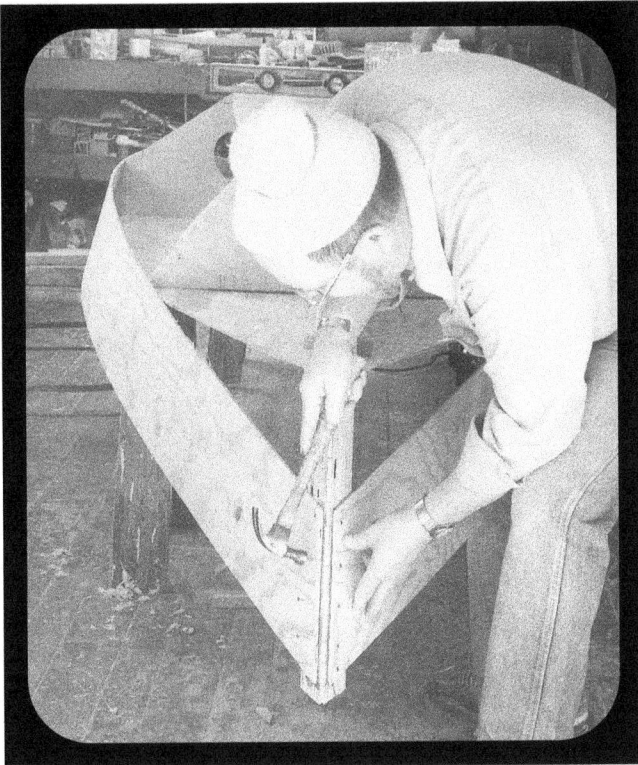

Fastening the side panels at the stem.

the nails out, then trying to reposition the panel again in slippery glue. Make sure that the side panel is in position on the 'midship frame, and repeat the procedure for gluing the side panel to the sternpost. Repeat the process for the opposite side panel.

Fitting Flotation Foam

Now is a good time to fit her ends with flotation foam. The 2" thick, rigid, blue foam sold in 4' x 8' panels for house insulation is best. Don't waste your money on cheap white styrofoam—it won't last and soaks up water like a sponge. With the hull upside down and open, it's easy to fit the foam because you can see exactly how much to shave off. It's not as easy to do this if you wait until the bilge panels are on and then try to fit the foam in from above.

I didn't want the bulk of the flotation sitting directly on the bottom panel, so the last piece is a brick-shaped piece that holds the rest of the foam off of the bottom. This allows me to drain water out in a hurry and hopefully offers some ventilation. For the same reason, I didn't make the sides of the flotation a fussy fit to the hull. After the flotation is fitted, glue it together with epoxy, take it out, and seal the ends. You will put it back in later as a unit.

Installing the Bilge Panels

Now it's time to fit the bilge panels. Before you start, be certain to pull the four nails fastening the bulkheads into the ends of the strong-backs and the two nails driven into the 'midship frame. You are going to pull the deck out later so that you can fiberglass the interior seams, and it's much

easier to do this with the deck out of the way. In addition, it will give you access to the boat's ends—which you won't have if you forget to pull these nails. If you do forget, however, all is not lost, because it's possible to put enough fiberglass on the outside of the hull so that it won't fall apart.

Prepare the bottom panel to edge-fit to the bilge panel by rounding its edge all around. Judging by eye and using a straightedge, plane off enough wood so that the outside edge of the ¼" thick bilge panel lies fair with the outside edge of the ½" thick bottom panel. It is much easier to do this now than after the bilge panel is wired and puttied.

Now, on with the bilge panels. Wire the bilge panel in place after determining its exact forward and aft placement. Start wiring it to the bottom and topside panels at the center, and work toward the bow and stern. The ends of the panel should be tacked with only one small nail—just enough to hold the panel in place while it's being wired. Cut about forty pieces of #18 gauge steel mechanic's wire 4" to 5" long.

Bore ⁵⁄₆₄" holes wherever it looks as though the panel isn't going to willingly line up with the bottom and side panels. Unless you have a small child to scoot under the hull to poke the wires through for you, bore all the holes you think you will need, crawl under the hull yourself, and stick all the wires through at one crawling. You can relieve any tight places with a saber saw, taking off all you want from the bilge panel to make an unfussy fit.

Don't cut into the side panel or the bottom panel; these lines should flow smoothly, keeping the hull fair. Think of the bilge panel as nothing but a conveniently shaped filler.

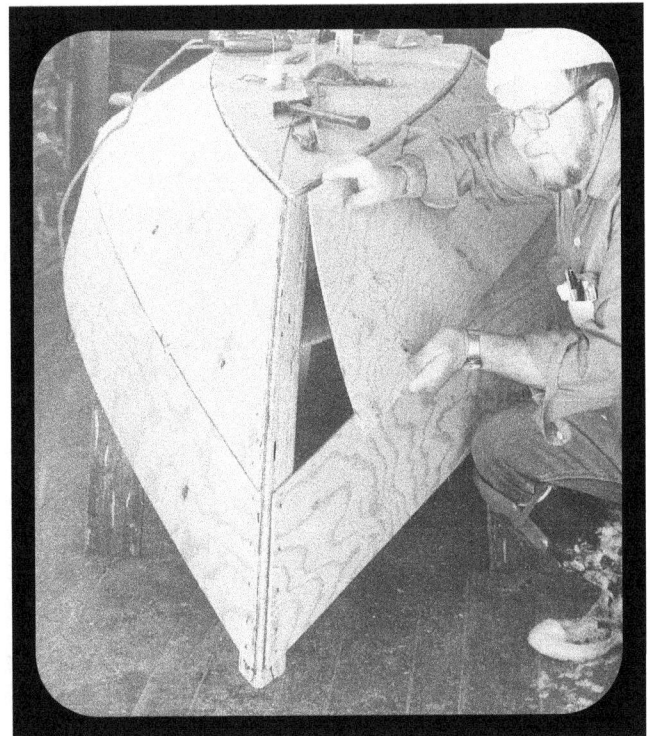

Fitting the bilge panels.

Get it in there, and let the putty and tape fair out any uglies. In fact, there's no need to make perfect joints; the side-, bottom-, and bilge-panel edges are all cut square and left that way. All the joints are intended to be open on the outside of the hull (where they will be filled with putty) and tight on the inside (which keeps the putty from falling through).

Taping the Seams

After the bilge panel is wired in place, release its ends, put glue on the stem and sternpost, and nail it on for good with 1" bronze ring nails.

Now you are ready for the sticky stuff. Glue, putty, and tape the outside seams, using the procedures described in Chapters 4 and 7. In the narrow ends of the hull, where you can't conveniently place fiberglass tape, use a thicker mixture of putty. Also fill the ends of the planking at the stem and sternpost. It is easier to fill the ends by building them out than it is to try to get the end cuts of the panels exactly right. Do the ends last, after the putty starts to thicken (on its last legs, so to speak), and jam it in there in a hurry. No need to be fussy about it; the idea is to get enough on so that when you fair the stem and sternpost, you won't have to go back and fill hollow spots. Before it gets hard as a rock, putty is easily faired with a wood rasp.

It's nice to do all of this resin work with the temperature around 70° and the weather bone dry. This doesn't occur often here in Maine, so I usually let the seams harden overnight before taking out the wires. If you don't feel like getting down under the hull and pulling out the wires, use nippers to cut them off as flush as possible outside the hull, then grind down their ends flush to the hull when you fair the seams for taping. There's no need to go under the hull and pull the other ends of the wires out at this time. You can pull them out easily when the boat is right side up, after the outside seams have been taped.

You can sheathe the boat's exterior with cloth and resin at this time, but I'm always anxious to see what she looks

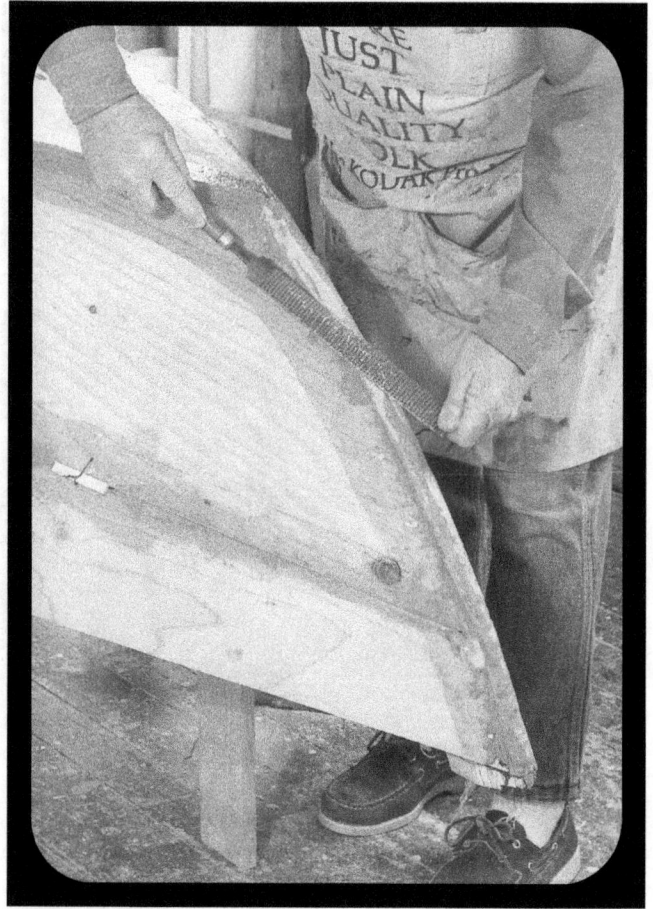

Rounding the puttied stem with a rasp.

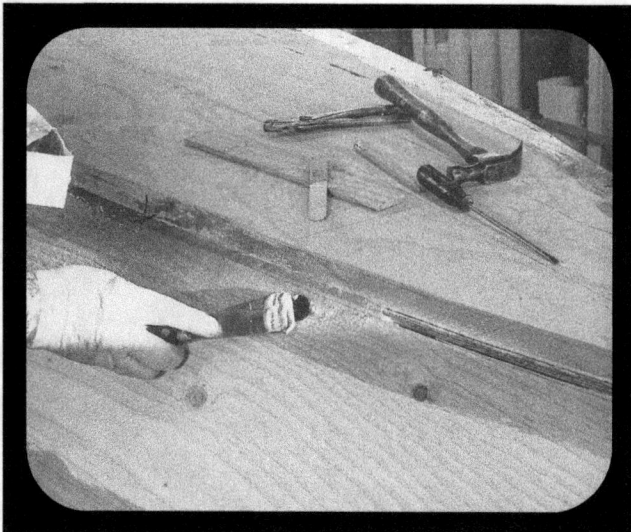

Puttying the outside seams.

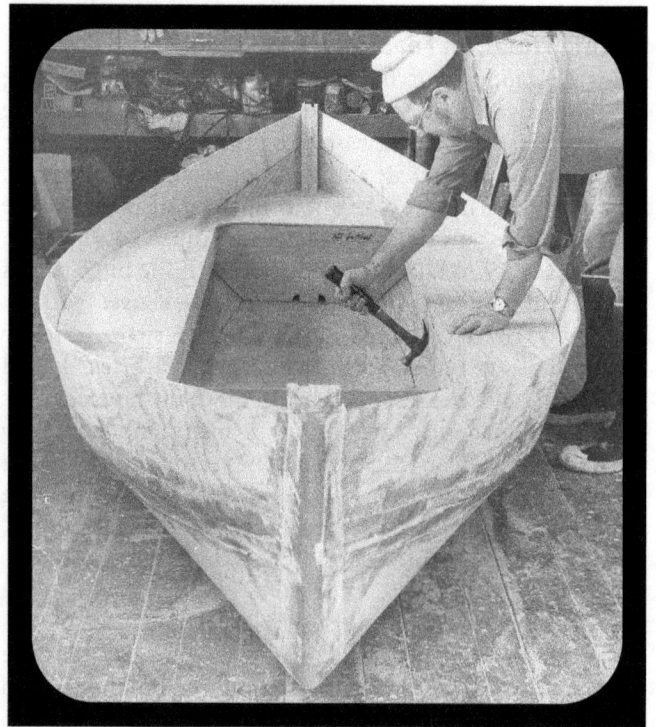

Pull the nails holding the deck stringers to the bulkheads and frames.

Removing the deck.

the extra dollars for waxy finishing resin, use the cheaper laminating resin with a surfacing agent to make it more sandable. You can also cut the waxed resin as much as 30 to 40 percent with acetone. When it is thinned that much, I double the amount of hardener and plan on allowing several days (depending on the weather) for it to set up.

Interior Details and the Slipping Keel

Now it is time for some of the extra woodwork on the inside. Install the breast hooks forward and aft. The foot-brace cleats should be positioned by trial and error. Temporarily clamp an oarlock where designated on the plans, stick an oar in it, sit where you're comfortable on a temporary seat (at the proper height), then position the foot braces to suit. It's better to go to this trouble now than to install them exactly according to the plans and discover later that they are in the wrong place for your size.

The maststep goes in next. The mast partner can go in later, when the deck is fiberglassed in for good.

If you are going to install that clever slipping keel, now is a good time to think about it. Carefully study the drawing, spending plenty of time until you get the whole function and layout in your head. Then, with the boat upside down and starting with the forward well slot, cut its rectangular shape out of the bottom panel. This is easily done by boring four corner-locating holes from inside the boat out through the well slot; or, lacking a drill bit long enough, you can do it by measuring from the bulkhead to the approximate fore-and-aft center of the well slot, and draw 3/4" parallel lines on each side of the centerline to correspond with the inside (1 1/2") dimension of the well. If you are unsure of the exact shape of the well on the outside, start cutting in the center of the well first, and make gradually expanding cuts. A saber saw does the job nicely. The after-well hole is not cut completely out; leave enough of the after portion to act as a bearing for the rudderpost, as indicated on the drawings.

There are a number of ways to make the slipping keel. You can laminate it as shown, which is probably the best approach, or you can cut it out in one piece from a 12' long 2" × 10". Either way, you may find that making a template of the whole layout—tongues and all—is the easiest way to do it. Scrap plywood edges that are 12' long will do the job. Scribe them individually to the bottom panel or make the template in one piece, if your scrap is wide enough.

Make the keel from the template, and tack it in place on the boat right next to the well slots. To determine the shape of the tongues, cut a 2' long board to a width that will fill the slot. Push it up through, and clamp it to the keel. This gives you the angle of the tongue with the keel. Mark across the top of the well from underneath the boat, and you'll have the height to the underside of the deck. Look at the scale drawing of the forward tongue, and you should easily be able to determine its tapered shape. Don't bother to mark the hole for the locking fid

like right-side up and to work on the inside for a change. Another reason for not doing the sheathing now is that the maststep should be fastened from the outside of the hull, and holes need to be cut in the bottom panel for the slipping-keel wells. Because it is easier to do the fastening and cut the wells with no fiberglass on the hull, flip her right-side up and tape her inside seams.

If you remembered to pull those nails that hold the deck stringers to the bulkheads and 'midship frame, the deck will come right out. Therefore, just lift it out and set it aside. Lean the hull over on its bilge, and clamp a brace amidships to the floor to keep her at a comfortable angle for taping and to help keep the joints from sagging and dripping putty. Knock out the limber holes (remember, I asked you to almost saw them out when you made the 'midship frame and bulkheads). Follow the procedure described in Chapters 4 and 7 to make the fillets and apply the fiberglass tape.

Sealing the Hull

Take the top corners off the bulkheads to let her drain when you tip her up to dump out bilgewater. There should also be limber holes amidships for the same purpose. Fiberglass-tape the bulkheads and 'midship frame to the bottom panel with 3" tape and a putty fillet on both sides.

With all the inside taping done, it is time to seal the inside of the hull. Since you have been using polyester resin right along, you will use it as a sealer. (If you've chosen epoxy, be sure to follow the manufacturer's instructions for mixing, sealing, and fiberglassing.) If you don't want to pay

Scribing a pattern for the slipping keel.

Marking the bottom for the rudderpost.

now; that can come later, when the actual keel assembly is fitted to the boat.

The after tongue is done basically the same way as the forward one. If you want, you can hollow the after face of the tongue above the keel to the shape of the rudderpost to form a bearing, instead of using the jaws (Piece No. 24) as shown. The hollowing (or coving) is more work, but it's a nice touch and does away with the jaws.

After locating the after tongue and rudder stock, cut the bottom panel to conform to the rudder stock. Allow perhaps $1/8"$ or less play around the stock, and make and

The assembled slipping keel (and the rudder in the background).

then fasten the forward tongue to the keel so that the keel goes back on the boat exactly where you want it. You don't want the fore-and-aft play of the keel to jam the rudderpost. Although it's not shown on the plans, I recommend that you reinforce the underside of the deck just forward of the rudderpost with a piece of $3/4"$ scrap pine.

The Rudder

With the keel in place, cut the $1\frac{1}{4}"$ closet-pole rudderpost a couple of feet long and shave its bottom end to $5/8"$ for the sides of the rudder cheeks to bear on (No. 27 on the plans). For the rudder, I planed two pieces of pine $5/8" \times 7" \times 17"$ to make the required $1\frac{1}{4}"$ total thickness; this was easier and faster than cutting and gluing the five pieces of $1/4"$ plywood called for in the plans.

With the hull still upside down, lay $1/8"$ spacer sticks on the bottom panel, and position the rudder cheeks on these. Both ends are square to the top of the rudder, so you only need to measure the rudder's width at each end and draw straight lines to determine its shape. Glue and fasten the $1/2"$ end plate as shown. Recess the ends of the cheeks to accept the $5/8"$ end of the rudder stock. There's no need to fuss much here; plenty of glue and a few bronze ring nails driven through the rudder cheeks into the stock while it is sitting aligned on the hull hold it exactly in place.

Installing the Flotation

With the after tongue and rudder in place and the forward tongue bolted to the keel, turn the boat right-side up and fill

Use shims to provide clearance between the rudder and the bottom when marking the shape of the rudder's edge.

her ends with the flotation foam you prefitted. Now is the time to install the foot braces, the mast step, and the support blocks on the bulkheads for the 7½ oars and the spars. With this done, make and fasten the cleat (No. 29) to the deck from underneath before installing the deck itself.

One piece of 2" x 2' x 8' flotation foam will fill both sides under her deck and between the bulkheads, but there are a couple of things to think about first. Bolger points out that flotation under the deck is likely to make her harder to right in case of capsizing. On the other hand, in our cold Maine waters, I would like to be able to get as far out of the water as possible, whether she is right-side up or not, because hypothermia can kill you here. Also, if I'm acrobatic enough to get her right-side up, I'm of the impression that flotation high on her sides under the deck will help keep the open tops of her wells above water for bailing and will help hold her steady while I'm doing it. Unless someone offers me a swimming pool, I'll wait for summer to

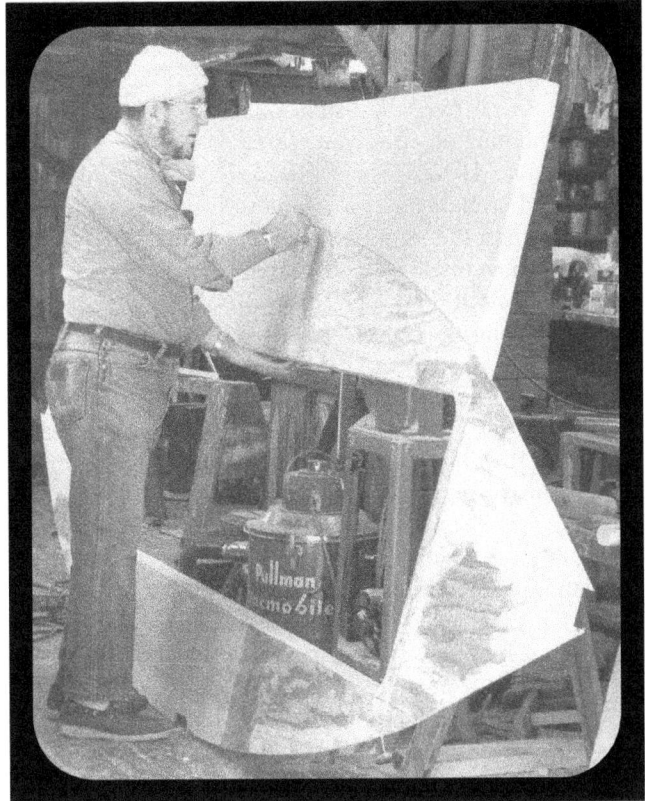

Use the deck edge as a template to cut the side flotation.

find out for sure, but until then, I'd recommend installing flotation under the deck.

Epoxy thickened with Cab-O-Sil makes a good glue for sticking flotation foam to itself and to plywood. Do some testing before using other glues, some of which have a tendency to eat rigid foam. Then, make a final check to see that everything mentioned before has been installed or completed, and put glue on the tops of the bulkheads and the 'midship frame.

Lift the deck back into the boat; you might have to squeeze it down slightly or tap it in place, but it should go in with no difficulty. If the deck wants to lift up in places away from the line, press the deck down and drive #18 wire nails over the top of the deck and out through the sides at the offending places. Cut their heads off, and you can easily pull them after fiberglass-taping the deck. Form the deck seams in the usual way, using a tongue depressor to form a fillet with the putty and reinforcing it with 3" tape.

Sheathing the Exterior

After the deck taping sets up, turn the boat over again and ready her for fiberglassing the outside. Check the hull for any bits of hardened resin sticking out, nail heads, or grain that has run out, causing splintered edges. You don't want any protrusions that will prevent the fiberglass cloth from lying snugly against the hull, or that would entrap air and spoil the bonding. It's easy to miss small specks of resin or

Installing flotation under the foredeck.

nail heads, so when you have done your best to find all of these gremlins, don't confidently start fiberglassing. Instead, put coarse 60- or, even better, 36-grit paper in your orbital sander and go over the whole outside of the hull. Your sander will find any spots you missed.

Cut two 16' lengths of 6-ounce, 38" wide fiberglass cloth, and stretch one piece out the length of the hull, extending past the stem and sternpost. Let the factory edge hang down a couple of inches below the sheer amidships, and let the cloth lie wherever it wants to lie from there to her ends along the bottom panel. With your shop brush, start amidships and brush out all wrinkles, working in both directions. Don't be afraid to bear down while brushing; it is easier to get the wrinkles out of big pieces of dry cloth now than it will be later, when it's saturated with resin.

When you are satisfied that the cloth is lying nicely along the hull, cut off the huge wad of cloth that is draped over her ends, tailoring the cloth so that 4" or 5" of cloth overlap both the stem and sternpost. Trim off the selvedge edge—this will allow the cloth to be pulled and smoothed into place more easily, and it will make for a smoother overlap with the next piece.

Brush the cloth smooth and put the other 16' piece of cloth on the other side of the boat, using the same procedure, and start fiberglassing. You can stick this cloth directly to the bare wood by letting the resin soak through, or you can apply resin to the hull first, then let it dry before putting the cloth on and applying more resin. The cloth sticks to plywood either way. In fact, it is quite difficult to have a failure with a glass-plywood combination.

Fear of the unknown is your worst enemy, so if you haven't done this before and are feeling timid, ask a friend for help, or experiment with pieces of scrap until you gain confidence. Watch the temperature and time, and don't dally! Get the cloth exactly where you want it before pouring the resin on it so that if an area hardens by surprise, the cloth is where it belongs. Pour the resin smack in the middle of the bottom, and work it out in all directions with a roller or squeegee. This way, you keep pushing air out ahead and don't trap bubbles.

You will need a couple of gallons of resin for fiberglassing the outside, along with a 9" sponge roller and a 4" throwaway brush for the last coats. Put the first coat on the cloth with the roller, followed by another coat applied with a brush an hour or so later (or when the first coat shows signs of hardening). This second coat helps fill the weave, but it doesn't do it completely. For the last coat, be sure there is a surfacing agent (wax) in the polyester resin, or you will be faced with an unsandable hull. This last coat cures and hardens the resin for sanding and provides a good base for paint.

Before the resin is thoroughly hardened, trim the overhang of cloth along the sheer with a sharp knife. If you wait too long, you will have to trim it with a saber saw.

Carefully sand the hull. Use a belt sander with a 60-grit belt. Start with the bottom panel, then sand the bilge panels, and finally the sides. Stay away from the chine corners with the belt sander—it's easy to take too much off and flatten corners you want round. Then switch to a ½-sheet orbital sander, again with 60-grit paper, to finish the job.

The gunwales go on now. These are made from spruce, pine, fir, or mahogany. Rip four pieces, ½" × 1½", and put them on doubled, fastening them from inside the hull with 1⅛" bronze ring nails.

Keel, Rudder Stock, Tiller, and Mast Partner

You can measure the locations of holes for the keel tongues and the rudder stock in the deck right off the plans if you are confident enough; I wasn't. One of the characteristics of wood is that it is full of surprises. A slightly twisted keel, or anything that might throw things a bit out of alignment, could end up jamming the rudder. So I elected to fit the tongues in their slots carefully, a little at a time. I did this by tipping the hull on its side and inserting the keel tongues as far as they would go. The forward tongue is no problem, because its home is nothing but a straight-through, rectangular hole. But the after tongue is another story. This tongue bears against the edge of the plywood deck, and the hole for the rudder stock has to be just about perfect.

The first step is to determine the keel's exact fore-and-aft position, which is pretty straightforward because of the

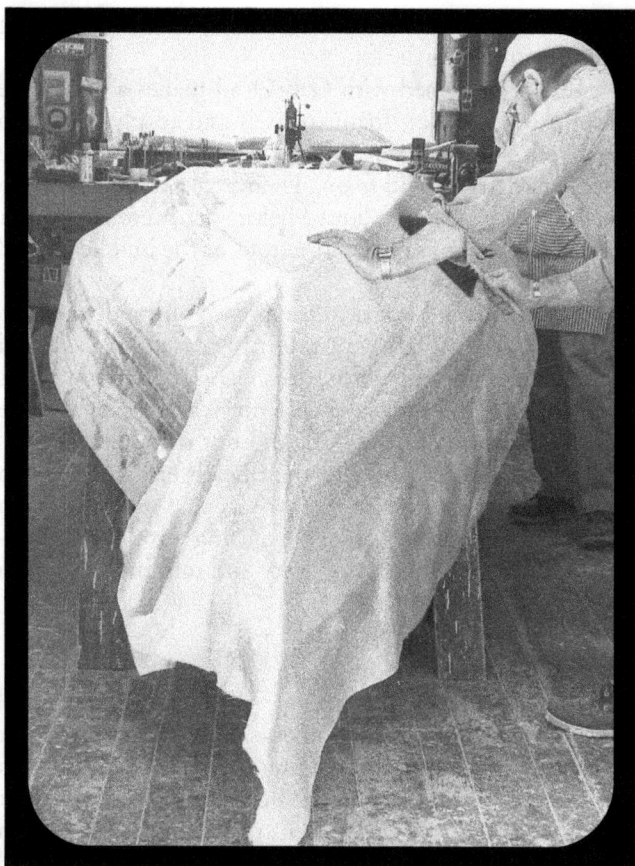

Draping fiberglass cloth over the hull.

A nail has been inserted in the top of the rudder stock. The whole rudder/rudder stock assembly is slid into place, and a sharp rap with a hammer will mark the center of the hole in the deck for the rudder stock.

tongue's location on the keel. When the keel is in place, it shouldn't shift back to jam the rudder stock. This is all figured out on the keel template.

With the hull on her side, drive a nail in the exact center of the rudder stock. Cut the head off, and sharpen the nail to a point. Slide the rudder stock into the well along the after edge of the aft keel tongue until it fetches up at the deck. Then whack the nail through the deck. Stick your compass leg in the nail hole, and swing the $1\frac{1}{4}"$ stock's diameter with your compass. Keep cutting away the deck for the tongue until the keel snugs against the bottom of the hull.

With that done, place the rudder in position with its stock sticking up through the deck, and measure the $\frac{1}{4}"$ hole for the tiller bolt. Take pains to bore this hole square across the stock. When the tiller is folded back with its end in the sternpost slot, the rudder should be in a direct fore-and-aft line with the keel. (Otherwise, you might find yourself going in embarrassing circles or constantly fighting the rudder when rowing.)

With the hole bored for the tiller bolt, recess an area about $\frac{1}{16}" \times 2"$ around the bolt hole, and wrap it with fiberglass tape. The tape should be recessed so that the rudder will slip out easily when you want to ship the rudder. Don't worry about fiberglassing over the tiller bolt hole—just cut through the fiberglass afterwards, before it gets rock hard. And while you're at it, it's worthwhile to make a big fiberglass washer, about 3" in diameter, to slip over the rudder stock so that the cam will rub against it instead of against the deck. The cam is a block of wood screwed to the forward face of the rudder stock; it bears against the deck or the fiberglass washer if you install one.

The tiller is made from $\frac{3}{4}"$ or thicker pine to the dimensions shown. The end of the tiller buries in a notch cut for it in the sternpost and stays in this position to keep

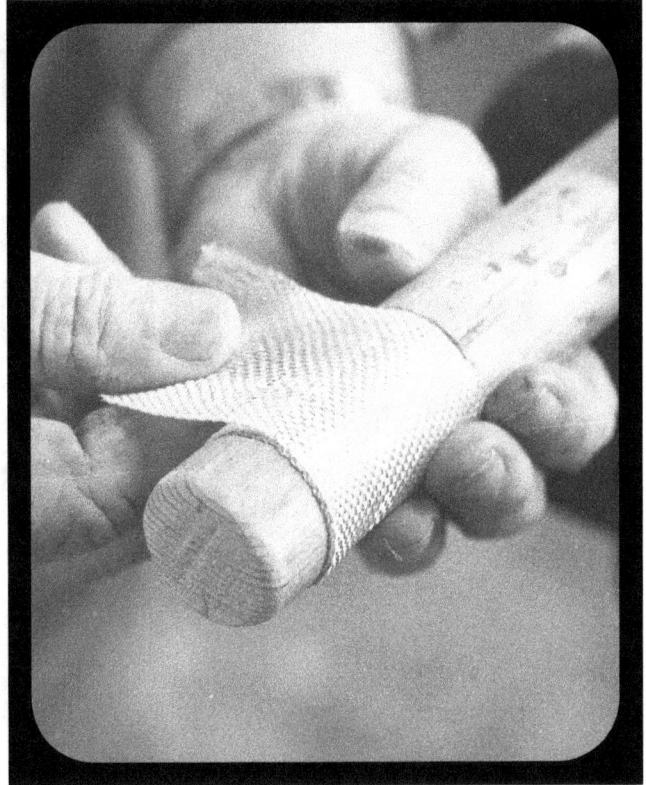

Recess the upper end of the rudder stock and fill the space with a wrapping of fiberglass tape and resin.

the boat going straight while you are rowing. For the straps, I use $\frac{1}{8}"$ brass instead of the stainless steel called for in the plans, because the softer brass cuts easily with my band saw.

Make the mast partner out of two pieces of $\frac{1}{2}"$ plywood, glued together and glued and fastened to the deck.

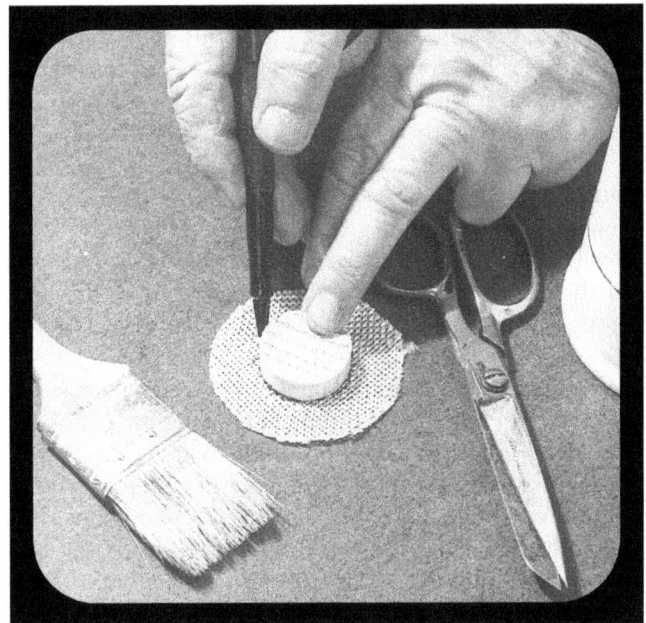

Make a fiberglass washer to serve as a bearing surface for the support cam on the rudderpost.

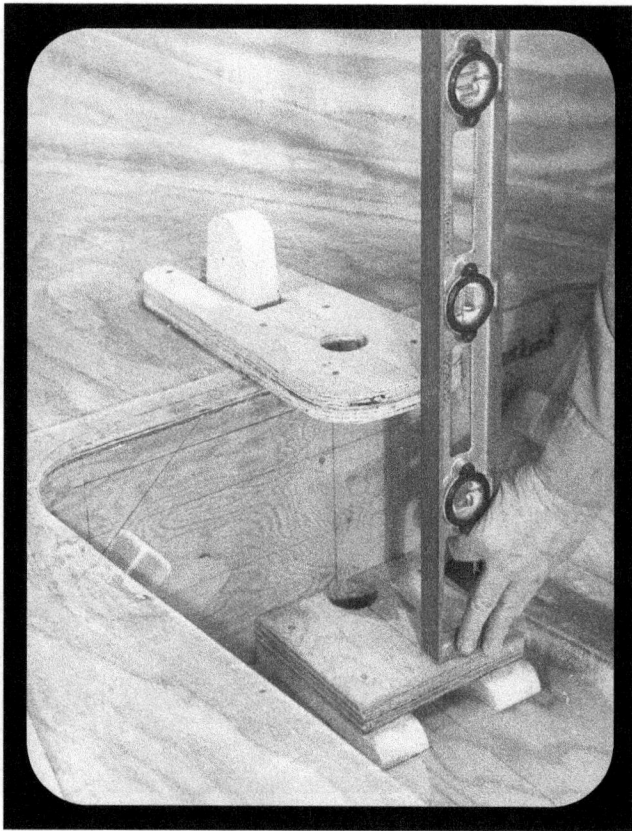

Fitting the mast partner.

I fasten the lower half first, because the nailing is easier, then glue and fasten the upper half to it. The leg-o-mutton rig can be used in the spritsail partner by cutting the opening back ¾" and putting a wedge in front. The partner is put on with the keel in place, then the hole location is determined for the fid to hold the tongue tight to the partner. Make the bottom of the fid hole about ⅛" lower than the top of the partner (same goes for the stern tongue), so that when the tapered fid is driven through the hole, the keel snugs up tightly against the bottom of the boat.

Seats

Rowing seats are going to take a little time, so do these now. But first, rip two sticks that are ¾" x ½" x 7', round off their corners, and glue and fasten them to the deck strong-backs to catch the underside of the seat. The seat rests on these, not on the deck.

Build a jig out of scrap lumber by cutting two pieces of ¾" wood 4" wide by 1'11" long and raking their ends 13° as shown. Add a couple of cross braces to hold the jig's sides apart. Take care to make the jig square and without twist so that it will slide smoothly and evenly along the deck strong-backs. Check the jig for accuracy. Cut the seat bottom to a 1'9" x 1' size. Make it square-edged. Cut the seat sides to a 4⅝" x 1' size, and the top lips to a 3" x 1' size. While you are at it, cut enough for both seats. I know that 3" for the lips seem scant, but it is cut ½" short on purpose

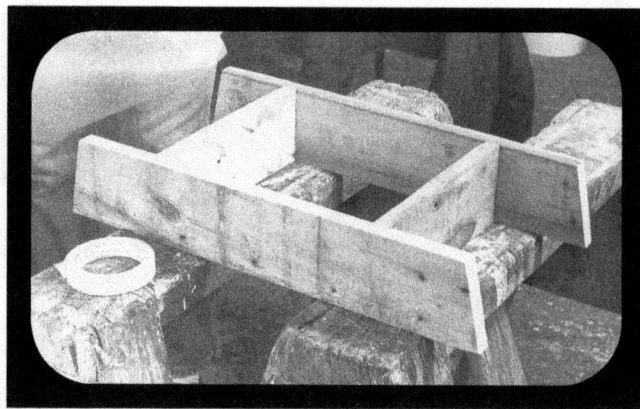

The seat jig.

so that you can form the joint to the sides with putty in a way that will be far stronger than the wood. You are going to fiberglass this seat together—no nails.

Lay the jig upside down on sawhorses and cover its bottom and ends with waxed paper. Tack the seat bottom onto the jig, then the sides. Cut two pieces of wood that are ¾" x 1½" x 1' in size, and temporarily nail one piece at the top of each side to catch the lips. Put waxed paper over the tops of these two pieces, and tack the lips to them. The idea here is to leave a square, open corner between the side and the lip that you'll fill with putty. Fill the seams overly full and then round them off when they're partially cured before applying the 'glass tape. Do the inside joint between the bottom and the sides as well.

Two layers of tape on each side of the joints, plus full sheathing over the seat top and bottom, should provide enough strength, but consider the weight of the passengers and use your own judgment. You might want to use epoxy here, instead of polyester resin, and you can make stronger tape yourself by cutting scrap cloth on the bias instead of using store-bought, 3" tape. You will need to take the seat off the jig to complete the fiberglassing. This is safe to do after the putty has hardened in the joints. If you want, you can fill and tape the outside bottom joint before pulling the seat off of the jig.

Bottom, ends, and lips on the seat jig.

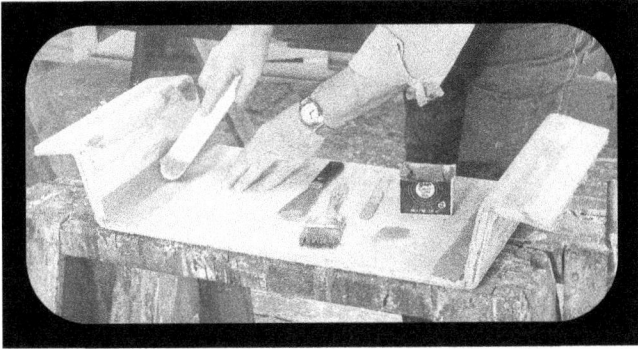
Filleting the seat joints.

After pulling the seat from the jig, try it for size in your boat, and check to see how the sides of the lips bear against the deck. Plane off enough to allow them to just touch or to slightly clear. Look at the drawing of the seat and judge how much to cove under the lips where they ride on the strong-backs. It's no big deal if you don't get the fiberglassing just right the first time; you can always add more or grind some away.

Finishing Her Up

There's not much left now to finish her: just the side cleats, the rowlocks, and the sailing rig if you are going to sail her. You can get lovely Matinicus Island, pea-pod-style, stand-up oarlocks from Ducktrap Woodworking (see Appendix). A hole for her painter can be located from 9" to 12" below the top of her stem. And, of course, there's her paint. I used a cheap, anti-fouling copper for the bottom, white for the boot top, dark blue for the topsides, white or varnished rails, and a very light buff for her interior. These were all water-based paints. In all fairness, I must say that oil-based paints stick readily to a properly sanded, fiberglassed hull (that is, one with a little tooth left to the surface) and stay on nearly forever, without any sign of cracking or peeling. But I've tried oil-based paint over wood on the inside of the hull, even with the sealers and undercoaters, and it won't

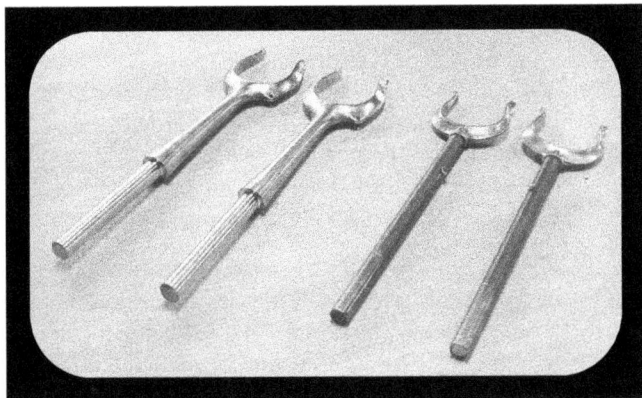
Beautiful cast-bronze, extended oarlocks (left) will make stand-up rowing a touch more aesthetic, but you can fabricate your own, perfectly serviceable, long oarlocks from common horned locks and copper pipe.

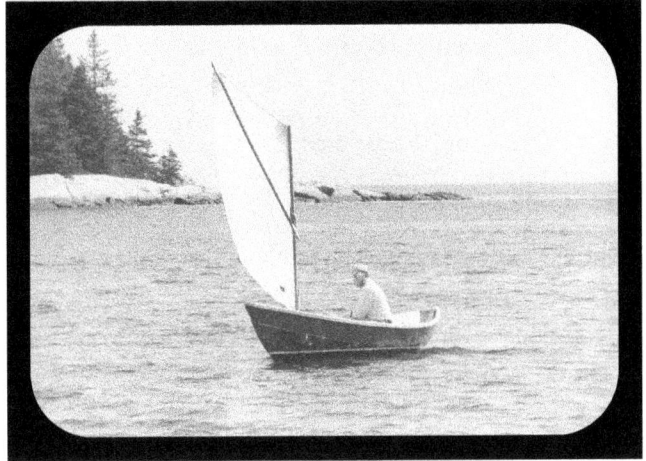
Sweet Pea under sail with the 43-square-foot sprit rig.

stay put. I'm all done with this scraping-and-sanding paint business.

It took me about a month to build Sweet Pea, but I spent some of that time making full-sized patterns. I think that about three weeks of full-time work would be about right for a reasonably skilled builder—more for a first-timer—but who wants to count time when you're having fun?

Under oars, with the sailing keel in, she tracks where pointed, though with some drag from the keel. In close maneuvering, you will want to allow a little extra turning room. With the keel off, there is a noticeable pickup of speed, and you can spin her like a top in her own length.

Sailing with the small spritsail in light airs is less than exciting, but I feel safe with it in heavier weather. If I want more power, I switch to the leg-o-mutton rig.

This boat is light, good looking, and extremely seaworthy. She rows superbly and sails well. Sweet Pea is one sweet package.

BUILDING KEY FOR DESIGN No. 570, SWEET PEA

Materials

4 sheets of $1/4$" x 4' x 8' plywood
2 sheets of $1/2$" x 4' x 8' AC or marine-grade plywood
2 rolls of 3", 6-ounce tape
3 gallons of resin
1 gallon of Fillite powder
1 gallon of acetone
11 yards of 38", 6-ounce cloth

Assembly

1. Sunken deck, $1/4$"; make as shown on Sheet 1 or save on plywood by laying out in sections and taping joints (see diagram).

2. Deck strong-backs from $\frac{3}{4}$" x $3\frac{1}{2}$" x 8', $1\frac{1}{2}$", tapered up to about 3" forward and aft to clear bilge panels. (Make strong-backs $8\frac{3}{4}$" if full-sized templates are used.)

3. 'Midships web frame, $\frac{1}{2}$" with drainage openings at bottom. Don't cut all the way out; leave tab and finish cutting out later before glass taping. Same for forward and aft bulkheads.

4. Forward and aft bulkheads, $\frac{1}{2}$" with drainage openings at bottom. Mark centerline on both faces. The peaks will be full of Styrofoam, so there's no need for other openings.

5. Stern web, $\frac{1}{2}$" (see diagram). Forms sternpost to gunwale and extends forward as a web to the after end of the rudder trunk to support deck.

6. Sternpost cheeks, two courses of $\frac{1}{2}$" on each side to make total thickness $2\frac{1}{2}$". Bevel to $\frac{3}{8}$" face, bevel varying slightly as diagrammed.

7. Block out web with $\frac{1}{2}$" x 1" to make rudder-trunk opening $1\frac{1}{2}$".

8. Head block at bulkhead, 1" x $1\frac{1}{2}$" (see diagram). Sides of trunk, $\frac{1}{2}$" x 10", or could be $\frac{1}{4}$" if there's an economy.

9. Stem, etc., including trunk for tongue of slipping keel, similar to stern (see diagram).

10. Set up deck on tables or horses, bottom up. Attach bow and stern webs, strong-backs, midships frame, and bulkheads. Make sure that deck is supported straight and level and that the midships frame is plumb. Temporarily fasten ends of strong-backs to forward and after frames for now. Deck comes out later for access to inside seams for taping.

11. Sides, $\frac{1}{4}$"; taped butt in the middle. Spring around deck to ends, aligning bulkhead marks, etc., for exact location (see diagram).

12. Gunwales, double $\frac{1}{2}$" x $1\frac{1}{2}$" to finish 1" x $1\frac{1}{2}$".

13. Bottom, $\frac{1}{2}$" (see diagram). Fit Styrofoam in peaks before bilge panels go on.

14. Bilge panels, $\frac{1}{4}$"; fit by trial; fill and tape bottom seams and chine joints. Flip hull right-side up, pull nails from ends of strong-backs. Take out deck. Tape seams, seal peaks, put Styrofoam and deck in, and tape deck for good.

15. Sockets for $\frac{1}{2}$" oarlocks, 4" farther aft than shown. Shim up about vertical over gunwales. Drain through bottom of gunwales. (Location is for rowing with a single oarsman alone or with one or two passengers. To row with two pairs, there should be another set of sockets 16" abaft the after set shown, 2" abaft Sta. 10. The boat is not long enough to row with two pairs and a passenger.)

16. Sockets for extension oarlocks to row standing facing forward. Blocks, $1\frac{1}{2}$" x $2\frac{1}{2}$" x 6", with bearings top and bottom, $\frac{1}{16}$" x 2" x 4" brass or steel for 1" outside diameter pipe shimmed at the top to take $\frac{1}{2}$" oarlocks. Ten-inch length of pipe shown is minimum for adults. The geometry is supposed to work with 8' oars either standing or sitting, but $7\frac{1}{2}$' would be workable.

17. Rowing seats, $\frac{1}{2}$" x 12" with $\frac{3}{4}$" x $1\frac{1}{2}$" stiffeners underneath. Make up with filleted and taped joints. Fit $\frac{1}{2}$" x $\frac{3}{4}$" strips at edge of deck at seat locations; weight should be taken on the strong-backs, not the thin deck.

18. Foot-brace cleats, $\frac{3}{4}$" x $\frac{3}{4}$" x 18"; locate by trial.

19. Slipping keel, double $1\frac{1}{2}$" x $1\frac{1}{2}$", with a triangular filler piece at the after end about $1\frac{1}{2}$" x $2\frac{3}{4}$" x 45". No fastenings to bottom.

20. Slipping-keel forward tongue, $1\frac{1}{4}$" x $3\frac{1}{2}$" x $13\frac{1}{2}$".

21. Fid tapered from $\frac{3}{4}$" x 1" x 5".

22. Carriage bolt, $\frac{1}{4}$" x 6".

23. After tongue/rudderpost, $1\frac{1}{4}$" x $3\frac{1}{2}$" x $16\frac{1}{2}$"; fid as in forward tongue. Plane off $1\frac{1}{2}$" of keel after end to join $1\frac{1}{4}$" tongue. Note locating stop added to forward side of tongue.

24. Rudder-bearing tabs from $\frac{3}{4}$" x $\frac{3}{4}$" x $2\frac{3}{4}$". These match semicircular opening in hull bottom to form a lower bearing for the rudder stock. The upper bearing is the $1\frac{1}{2}$" hole in the deck panel. Some soft, rubberoid pads here and there might reduce rudder chattering without risk of binding.

25. Rudder stock, $1\frac{1}{4}$"-diameter fir closet pole, $19\frac{1}{4}$" long. Bevel flats off sides for $5\frac{1}{4}$" at the bottom to take rudder cheeks. Wrap top $1\frac{1}{2}$" with glass tape to prevent splitting at the tiller bolt. Stop block to prevent dropping out $\frac{3}{4}$" x $\frac{3}{4}$" x $2\frac{1}{8}$" set in forward side at deck level, shown screwed but for frequent unshipping could be clamped to stock.

26. Rudder built up from five courses of $\frac{1}{4}$" with outer courses gripping rudder stock; reinforce around stock with at least 4" tape. Plane off blade to about $\frac{1}{2}$" trailing face; feather edge of outer course should be about $2\frac{1}{2}$" from trailing edge.

27. End plate, $\frac{1}{2}$" x 4" x 17". Cove out internal angles.

28. Tiller from ¾" x 1¼" x 24" with ⅛" x ¾" x 5" stainless plates to ¼" x 2" pivot bolt (see diagram). For rowing, tiller swings over with tip held in a recess in the sternpost.

29. Hook for peak vang from 1½" x 1½" x 6", or could be a stock cleat, but NOT a cam cleat.

30. Sheet cleats from 1½" x 1½" x 6", or stock type.

31. Feet of maststep, ¾" x 2" x 5½".

32. Maststep (or heel collar), double ½" to finish 1" x 6" x 7".

33. Mast partner, double ½" to finish 1" x 6" x 12". See diagram for shape to clear tongue of slipping keel.

34. Mast, 1½" square with ¼" corner radius, 8'0" overall with no taper. See diagram with sail plan.

35. Stop blocks to rack 8' oars and spars clear of bottom, 1½" x 1½" x 3". Seven-and-a-half-foot oars can have one end slung with a lanyard and toggle to the strong-backs.

36. Boom is a 1¼" diameter closet pole, 8'0" overall without the jaws. Slot and pin at outboard end for clew lashing and sheet. Jaws from ½" x 4" x 6"; inside radius, 1½".

37. Sprit same as boom, but with a slot at each end.

38. Snotter, ⅜" x 10'; caught with a knot in the heel slot of the sprit; through a big thimble or a block slung on the mast 3' below masthead; belay on ¾" x 1½" cleat across forward side of mast 13" above the heel.

39. Secure sail to mast and boom with separate ties. Masthead lashing should be numerous tight turns for minimum stretch. Either out or down.

40. Mainsheet fast to end of boom, to hook under (not belay to) leeside cleat; see No. 41 from there.

41. Peak guy and sheet all one length from peak of sprit to end of boom, total about 25' long, ¼" diameter. There should be a mark about 14' from the peak: It can be cleated there most of the time to keep the peak from ever twisting forward of the beam. It may pay to put a strain on it when reaching, to take some twist out of the sail. It should never be close-hauled if the sheet and snotter are set up properly.

PART THREE

MORE
BOATS
TO BUILD

With three boats and a model built with blow-by-blow descriptions, I will move on, looking at twelve more members of the Instant Boat fleet. By now, you know how these boats go together, so giving detailed instructions would be redundant. The descriptions that follow are intended more to help you decide which one might suit your needs and talents. Choosing the right boat can be a tough decision, but as I mentioned before, building a model will give you a good look and feel for what you're getting into before building the real thing. And there's no rule that says you can build only one!

Some of the plans come with Building Keys—that I will use *when they are available*—while others do not. The designer's thinking was probably that certain designs are simple enough so as not to need keyed instructions.

CHAPTER 9
RUBEN'S NYMPH

The original Nymph, which is in my book *Build the New Instant Boats*, and Ruben's Nymph are exactly the same except for their width. With a beam of 4'6", Ruben's Nymph is a full foot wider than her slimmer sister, making her a comfortable load carrier. Six hundred and ninety pounds of weight will put her down to her chine waterline, which means she will carry three ordinary-size people, a big dog, and plenty of provisions—all in one trip and with plenty of freeboard to spare.

Ruben's Nymph is built upside down, similar to other Instant Boats, and no special instructions are required other than those in the building key. I'll just note two little tricks here that might make the work go a bit easier for this boat and for some other boats as well.

When installing a curved bottom, glue and fasten or wire it down at one end and work your way toward the other. As shown in the photo, you can use props against your ceiling rafters to hold the bottom down, and this will prevent the spring of the bottom panel from pulling a reverse curve into the rest of the setup. Wetting the exterior face of the panel will allow it to take the bend more easily.

Sometimes, the best helper is as dumb as a post. To fasten the skeg in place from the inside, you need some way to hold it steady. Clamp it to a piece of 4" x 4", weight it board down with a heavier weight (like a piece of railroad track), then drive the screws from inside the boat.

Ruben's Nymph takes the same fifty-nine-square-foot leg-o-mutton sail that Cartopper and several other Instant Boats use, so if you already have one, you can use it. The rudder and leeboard, too, are the same as for the smaller Nymph.

Her mast calls for lumberyard spruce or similar, $2\frac{1}{2}$" x $2\frac{1}{2}$" x 15'6". There's nothing wrong with making it from wood $2\frac{1}{2}$" thick, although it's unlikely you will find it in stock at your lumberyard. The option is to laminate it from two pieces cut to $1\frac{1}{4}$" x $2\frac{1}{2}$". The glue line will serve as a handy centerline to measure the mast's taper at the intervals shown.

The sprit boom is $1\frac{1}{2}$" square by 9'6", with a hole bored at the forward end to catch the snotter, which runs

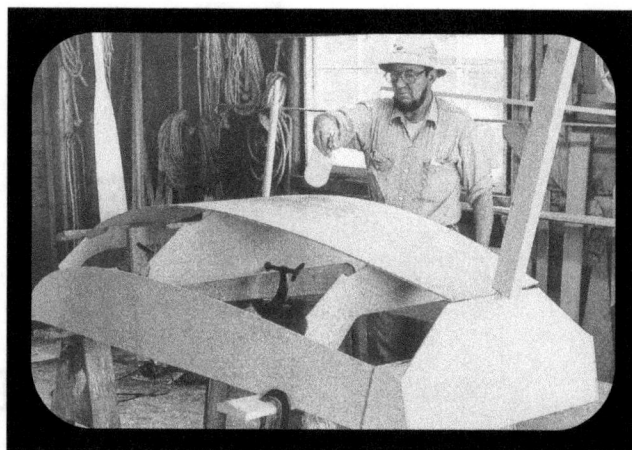

Brace the bottom against the ceiling joists, and wet it down to help it make the bend easier. This photo shows the narrower Nymph design, but the principle is identical.

through a small block (or a thimble, if you prefer) attached to a sling. The sling is held up by cleats on each side of the mast. The snotter runs down and ties off to a cleat on the side of the mast. It's less complicated than it sounds—just look at the rigging details for Cartopper.

Another shot of Ruben's skinnier sister, showing how to stabilize the skeg for fastening from the inside.

A $\frac{3}{8}$" x 1" slot is made at the aft end of the boom. The end of the sheet is tied to the clew grommet, and another knot is tied a couple of inches below this, which serves to hold the boom in place from slipping down when caught by the knot.

The peak grommet is tied through a hole bored at the top of the mast. The sail is attached to the mast by individual ties at each grommet rather than by lacing. If one tie lets go, it's no big deal. But if lacing lets go, your whole sail blows out.

The photos, along with the Building Key, should see you through to the completed boat. You will find Ruben's Nymph one of the most comfortable and easy-to-row boats you could hope for.

BUILDING KEY FOR DESIGN No. 516, RUBEN'S NYMPH

Ultra-simple, tack-and-tape construction technique requires no jig, no bevels, and no major metal fastenings.

Materials (Rowing Version)

3 sheets of $\frac{1}{4}$" x 4' x 8' AC or marine-grade plywood, plus another sheet or $\frac{3}{4}$" scraps for rudder and leeboard.

For fore-aft thwart, 7 board feet of $\frac{3}{4}$" spruce, pine, fir, or mahogany

For gunwales, 1 clear-grained 8'2" x 4"

100' (or about 2 pounds) of 3" fiberglass tape

8 yards of 38" fiberglass cloth (6-ounce) to cover outside of hull

1 gallon of polyester resin, with hardener

1 quart of acetone

3 pounds of Fillite powder

1 box of $1\frac{1}{4}$" #18 wire nails

1 pound of Weldwood dry powder glue (or epoxy or marine glue of your choice)

Layout

Establish the shape of side panels by erecting perpendiculars at one-foot intervals marked along the edge of the plywood sheet, then measuring from edge to sheet and bottom as shown. Drive nails at these points and bend a thin batten around them to define the cut lines. Cut out panels with a saber saw or a small Skilsaw with the planer blade set just deep enough to cut through. Saw out duplicate halves of frame Nos. 1, 2, and 3 and the bow and stern transoms as shown—all square-edged. (Can be made from $\frac{3}{8}$" plywood if you want them heavier.) Be sure to mark centerlines on both sides.

Assembly

Frames, Sides, and Transoms

Butt frame halves together, backing the joint with the butt strap (can be made as one piece if you want). Glue, fasten with smooth wire nails bent over, clamp, and let set. Tack temporary blocks to sides of frames and transoms and bottom panel to catch nails for fastening sides and bottom.

Bore holes at frame locations on sides from inside for small nails if you want to nail into the frames, or just nail to the temporary blocks. Place sides upside down on sawhorses, butt midframe against the sides, making sure the frame top is flush with the sheer, and tack the sides to the frame (no glue). Tack small wood blocks at both ends of the panels for a Spanish windlass (loop of rope, twisted to tighten) to bear on and to draw side panels against frames and transoms.

Bottom

Cut bottom as shown on the plan, marking the centerline on both sides. Align centerlines and tack the bottom in place. If the bottom seems too stiff, give the outside of it a sponge bath with warm water.

Bilge Panels

Cut to shape from the plan, bend around in place, and tie down ends. Mark from underneath final shape from side- and bottom-panel edges; remove, saw to shape, and replace. Gaps up to $\frac{1}{4}$" are acceptable. Make sure that the inside faces of the panels are firm and flat against the frame edge. Tack to the transoms and frames and to the edges of the bottom and sides. Use a "hot-melt" glue gun, or wire if you want—any method of holding the assembly together. Turn right side up and use masking tape on the outside seams to close any seams so that resin will not run out while you are taping the inside of the hull.

Glassing

Starting with the bottom seams, scribe lines parallel to the seams at a distance of $1\frac{1}{2}$" as guides to laying 3" tape. Mix $\frac{1}{4}$ pint of resin with hardener, and give the seam liberal brushing. Add Fillite to the remainder, and stir to a fairly stiff mixture; spread along seam with a rounded stick and remove any excess at the edges with a putty knife. Cut tape to length and lay in mixture; smooth it down with a paintbrush or rounded stick. Immediately coat the whole taped area with resin. Let the resin soak in, then add a second coat. Tape both sides of the frame joints. Turn the boat bottom up. Get the nails out of the way of glassing by drawing them out or burying them. Round off all edges, then tape all seams and glass the whole boat with 6-ounce cloth.

VIEW FROM ASTERN

LIFTING HOLES - SIZE
TO TAKE BLADES OF
STOWED OARS.

VIEW FROM AHEAD

TEMPORARY BRACE

FRAME #3

2' 0 1/8"

1' 2 7/8"

6 1/16"

5 5/8"

1' 3 1/4"

TEMPORARY BRACE

FRAME #1

1' 9 5/8"

6 5/8"

1' 11 1/4"

3 1/4"

1' 3 1/8"

FRAMES & TRANSOMS CAN
BE 3/8" PLYWOOD IF MAT-
ERIAL IS ECONOMICALLY
AVAILABLE; WOULD BE
EASIER TO HANDLE.

TEMPORARY BRACE

FRAME #2

2' 2 9/16"

9 5/8"

1' 4 3/4"

9"

1' 5 1/4"

GUNWALE
FULL SIZE
TO FINISH
3/4" × 1"

W.L. @ 690 LBS.

SKEG FROM
3/4" × 3 1/2"
× ABT. 2' 1"

W.L. @ 330 LBS.

1' 3 1/4"   2' 2 3/4"   2' 8 3/4"   1' 6 1/4"

WIDTH OF MOTOR
BOARD TO SUIT
MOTOR (MAXI-
MUM 4 H.P.).
MAY BE OFF
CENTER TO
CLEAR RUDDER
GUDGEON.

ABT. 10"

MINIMUM OAR LENGTH FOR
EFFICIENT ROWING, 8' 0".

#3   #2   #1

SIDE

TRANSOM   FINISHED

TRANSOM   FULL SIZE

TEMPORARY
STOPS

SIDE   ASSEMBLY

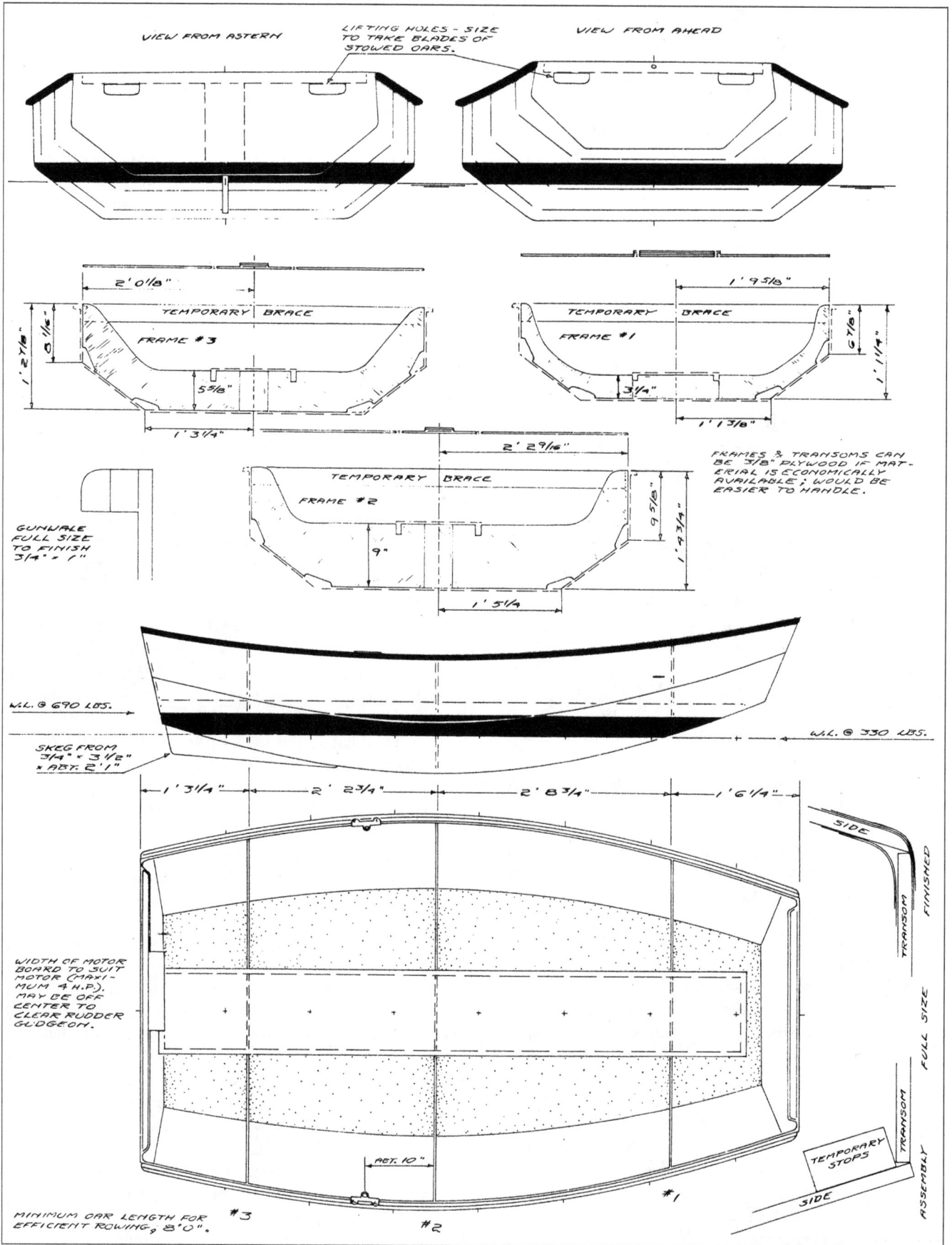

Ruben's Nymph, Sheet 1.

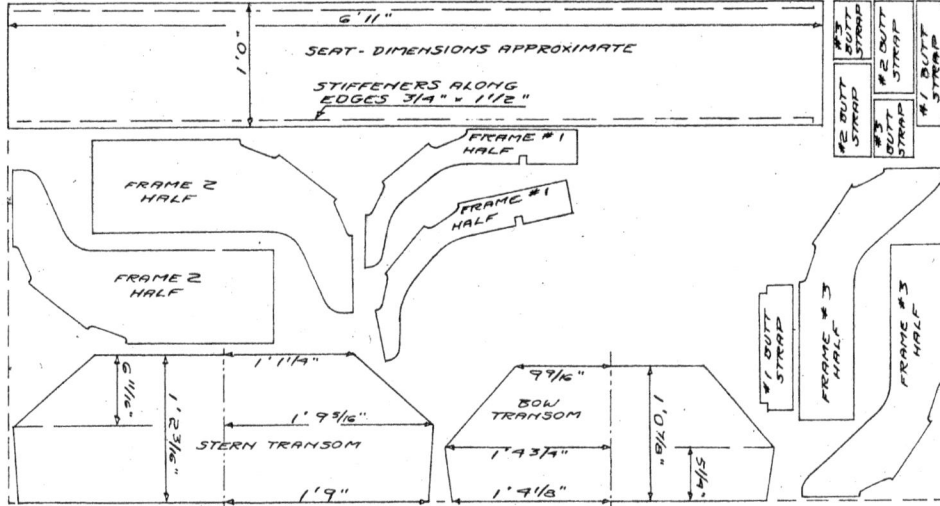

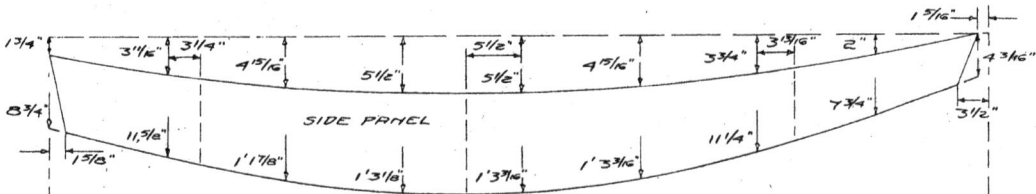

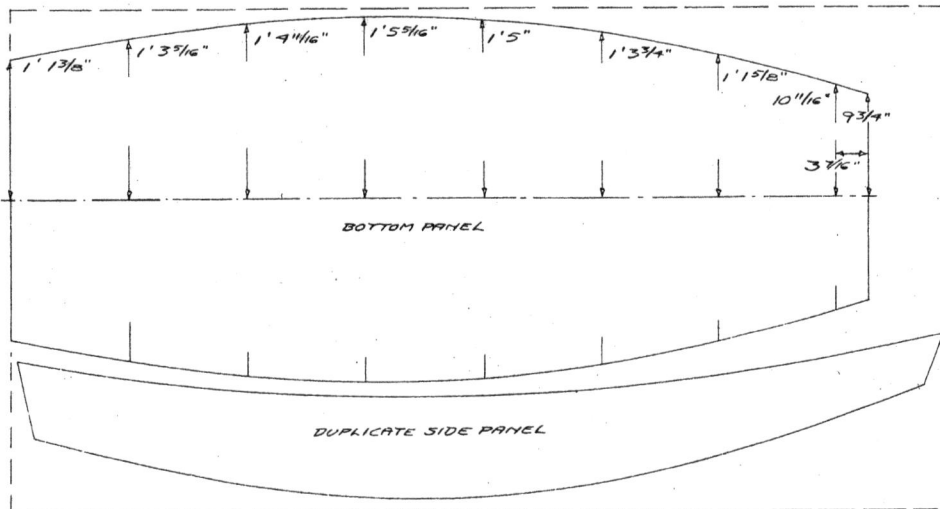

Ruben's Nymph, Sheet 2.

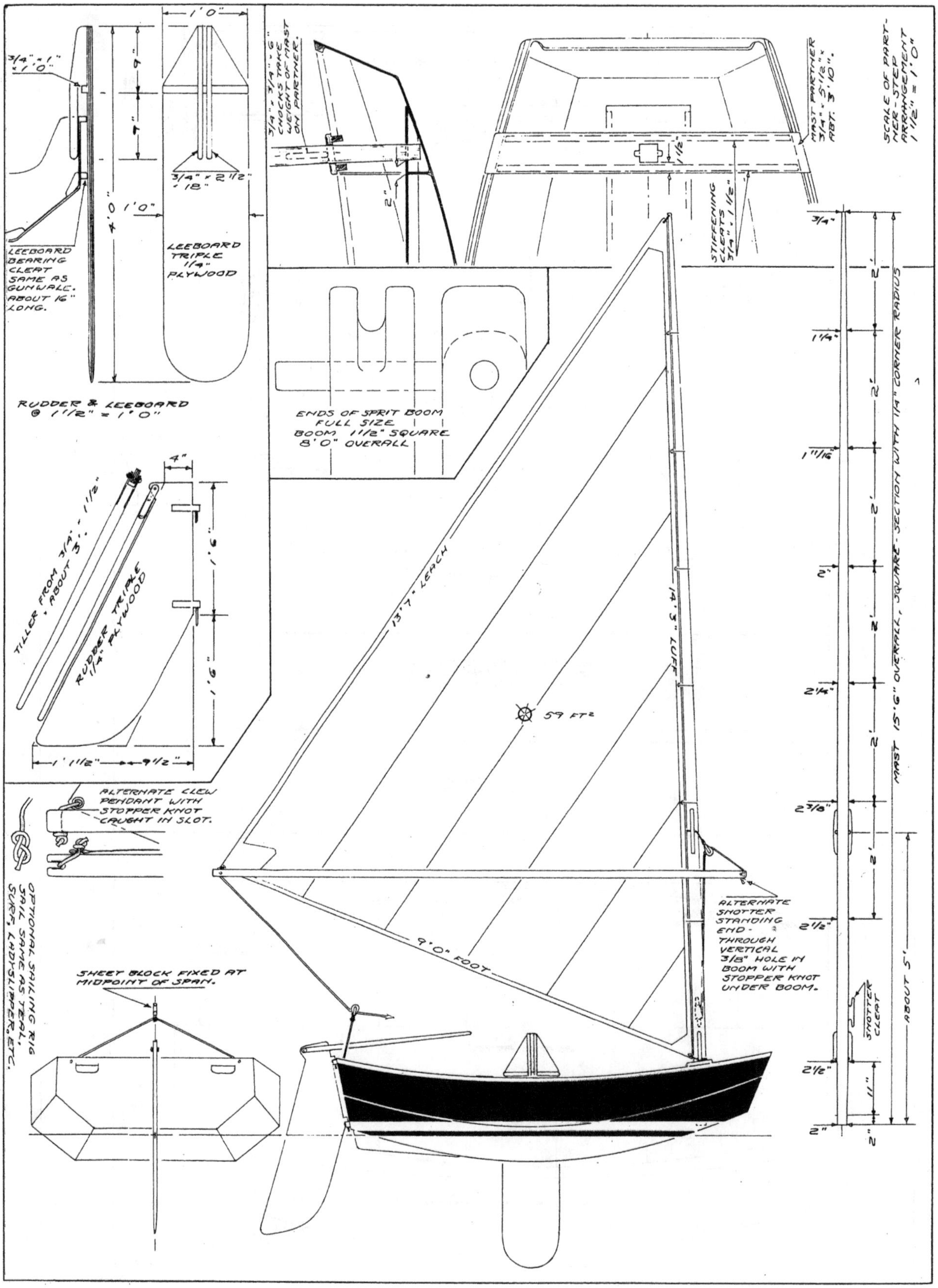

3/4" = 1'-1'0"

1'0"

9"

7"

0'0"

3/4" x 2 1/2" - 18"

LEEBOARD BEARING CLEAT SAME AS GUNWALE. ABOUT 16" LONG.

LEEBOARD TRIPLE 1/4" PLYWOOD

3/4" x 3/4" x 6" CLEATS TAKE WEIGHT OF MAST ON PARTNER.

MAST PARTNER 3/4" x 5 1/2" x ABT. 3'-10".

SCALE OF PARTNER-STEP ARRANGEMENT 1 1/2" = 1'0"

STIFFENING CLEATS 1/4" x 1 1/2"

RUDDER & LEEBOARD @ 1 1/2" = 1'-0"

ENDS OF SPRIT BOOM FULL SIZE BOOM 1 1/2" SQUARE 8'0" OVERALL

TILLER FROM 3/4" - 1 1/2" ABOUT 3'

4"

1'6"

1'6"

RUDDER TRIPLE 1/4" PLYWOOD

1'1 1/2"   9 1/2"

ALTERNATE CLEW PENDANT WITH STOPPER KNOT CAUGHT IN SLOT.

OPTIONAL SAILING RIG SAIL SAME AS TEAL, SURF, LADYSLIPPER, ETC.

SHEET BLOCK FIXED AT MIDPOINT OF SPAN.

13'-7" LEECH

14'-3" LUFF

59 FT²

9'-0" FOOT

ALTERNATE SNOTTER STANDING END - THROUGH VERTICAL 3/8" HOLE IN BOOM WITH STOPPER KNOT UNDER BOOM.

SNOTTER CLEAT

MAST 15'-6" OVERALL - SQUARE - SECTION WITH 1/4" CORNER RADIUS

3/4"

2'

1 1/4"

2'

1 11/16"

2'

2"

2'

2 1/4"

2'

2 3/8"

2'

2 1/2"

ABOUT 5'

2 1/2"

11"

2"

Ruben's Nymph, Sheet 3.

CHAPTER 10
BIG TORTOISE

At 8 feet LOA (length overall), Big Tortoise is 1'7" longer than the original Tortoise, which also appeared in my previous book, *Build the New Instant Boats*. Both boats have the same beam (3'2") but, being longer, Big Tortoise's rocker is less pronounced. Perfectly square ended, this is one stable design, good for carrying heavy loads safely as long as common sense and freeboard are kept in mind.

Big Tortoise requires only two sheets of 4' x 8' plywood and a small amount of lumber for her chines and gunwales. About the only construction difference from "little" Tortoise is the addition of a foredeck. (The shorter boat has only an afterdeck.) You could build a fore-and-aft straddle seat like Tortoise's, which allows you to easily trim the boat fore and aft by shifting your weight, but because of the foredeck, you wouldn't be able to remove it. Thus, a better option may be to install a thwart wherever it is wanted. As for rowing it, pulling or pushing, either way makes little difference in progress, and five-foot oars are ample for the job.

Since it is essentially a box with a rockered bottom, she's simpler to build than Ruben's Nymph and doesn't require taped, filleted seams. She is, however, more of a "pond boat," and Ruben's Nymph will offer a safer, more comfortable ride if there's any chop or swell. And unlike both Ruben's Nymph and the smaller Tortoise, Bolger didn't make provisions for a sailing rig.

Besides service as a load-carrying tender, she has been used for other purposes ashore. Because of her rockered bottom, she or her little brother make a good cradle for kids. Drag her into your living room, put a kid or two in her, and with your foot, press down on one end. She will just keep on rocking. Whoever's in charge of the kids will love that.

And when it is party time, tip her on her side and she makes an Instant Bar. How can you beat that?

Phil Bolger designed Big Tortoise for the Montgomery Boat Yard in Gloucester, Massachusetts. Knowing the competence of this professional yard, he left some of the details up to their discretion, but it's not hard to figure out the construction of the rowing thwart and work out the location of the thwart and oarlocks with a bit of trial and error. I would keep the chine logs and gunwales outside as shown, because this leaves the inside clear for easier painting and cleaning.

The bow and stern transoms are sawn out to the dimensions given and beveled, the framing is sawn separately, then the pieces are glued and fastened together. The top edges of the sides are straight, so use the factory edge of the plywood. Measure down from the edge for the chine and transom edges at the 6" intervals shown. Fair the curve with a batten, cut out the sides, and frame them with ¾" spruce, pine, or fir. Gunwales and chine logs are fastened to the sides before you fasten the sides to the transoms. If you don't want to make the notched joint in between the 2½" wide pieces and the 1½" wide pieces that make up the chine logs, you can just taper the joints. The 1½" wide chine logs are put on without cutting for their bottom curve and are then taken to your band saw and sawn to match the bottom curve of the sides.

To assemble Big Tortoise, lay her on her side on your shop floor, glue and fasten one side to the transom framing, flip her over, and fasten the other side. To fasten the bottom,

(continued on page 103)

Side and transom assemblies. These photos show the smaller Tortoise; Big Tortoise is the same except for the length of the side panels and bottom.

101

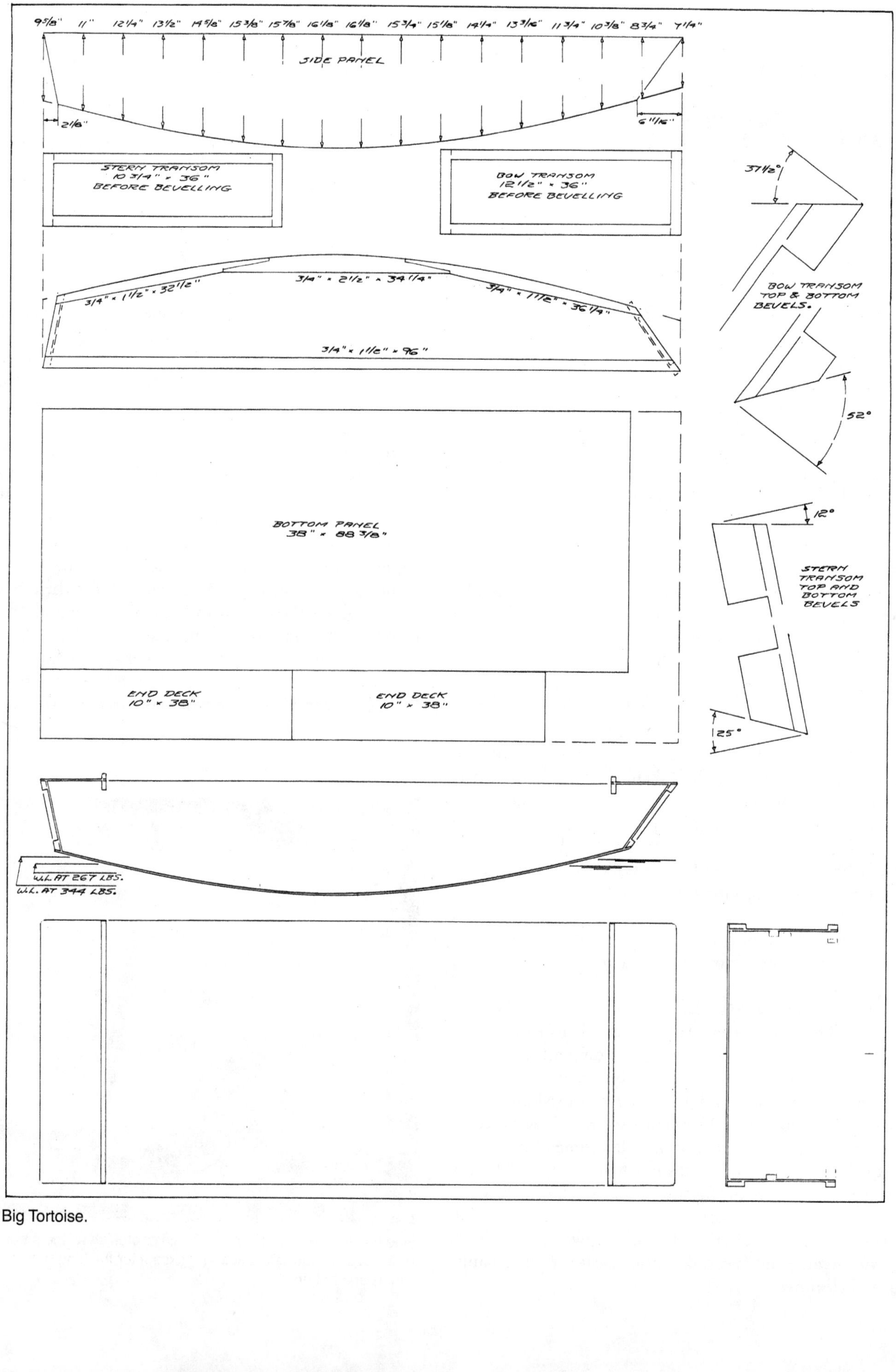
9 5/8" 11" 12 1/4" 13 1/2" 14 5/8" 15 3/8" 15 7/8" 16 1/8" 16 1/8" 15 3/4" 15 1/8" 14 1/4" 13 3/16" 11 3/4" 10 3/8" 8 3/4" 7 1/4"
SIDE PANEL
2 1/8"
6 11/16"
STERN TRANSOM 10 3/4" × 36" BEFORE BEVELLING
BOW TRANSOM 12 1/2" × 36" BEFORE BEVELLING
3/4" × 1 1/2" × 32 1/2"
3/4" × 2 1/2" × 34 1/4"
3/4" × 1 1/2" × 36 1/4"
3/4" × 1 1/2" × 96"
37 1/2°
BOW TRANSOM TOP & BOTTOM BEVELS.
52°
BOTTOM PANEL 38" × 88 3/8"
END DECK 10" × 38"
END DECK 10" × 38"
12°
STERN TRANSOM TOP AND BOTTOM BEVELS
25°
W.L. AT 267 LBS.
W.L. AT 344 LBS.

Big Tortoise.

Assembly couldn't be simpler. If you can nail a box together, you can build this boat.

(continued from page 101)

spread glue on the bottom edges of the side panels and the chine logs, then prop the bottom up at its bow end so that it lays flush with the curve of the sides at the extreme aft end. Fasten the bottom at the transom end first, then work your way forward, bending the bottom to conform to the

No need to brace the whole bottom down at once, as I recommended with Ruben's Nymph. This hull won't budge as you fasten one end and work your way forward.

The nearly complete hull, awaiting gunwale fastenings and decks.

rocker as you nail your way along. I used a piece of railroad track to weight the bottom while I did this, but a friend pushing down on it would work as well. The bottom will take the bend dry, but you can give it a hot-water sponge bath if you think it is needed. My son-in-law Mike Whitman put a 3/8" thick bottom on his smaller Tortoise, and I still wonder how he did it.

Note that the stern deck's forward edges are framed underneath and on top for stiffness. For the location of the thwart and its framing, nothing is shown. I'd locate it roughly on center, with the oarlocks mounted about 1' aft of that, but the sure way to get it right is to set her in the water, get in it, and have someone see how she trims.

Chopping Tray

By way of comparison, look at the little Chopping Tray boat, designed by the late Woodbury Snow. This came into use as a fisherman's and lobsterman's tender on Metinic Island, Maine, in the 1920s or 1930s and was still in use there as recently as the 1990s! It's of a similar style and dimensions to Big Tortoise but is cedar planked and with gradual, turned-up ends rather than sharp-angled transoms. If you would like more of a challenge and need a punt that can take a beating, you might like this one.

The Chopping Tray was built with steam-bent oak drag strips and sides of 15" wide, 3/4" thick pine boards (not 7/8", as indicated on the drawing). Try finding those these days! The bottom planking around the ends has to be hollowed out on the inside to take the curve. The drawing has adequate detail for the rest if you're feeling ambitious. I've included her here mainly as a means of comparing simple and hard ways to build a boat for essentially the same purpose—that is, carrying a load. And carry a load she did!

A fisherman once loaded his Chopping Tray with ten eighty-pound bags of fish salt, plus his own weight—figure about 1,000 pounds in all. There wasn't much freeboard left on his 7' x 3' Chopping Tray, but he made it from his moored boat to shore.

MÉTINIC "CHOPPING TRAY" BEACH BOAT
CR. 1930ˢ TO 1990ˢ DESIGN ATTRIBUTED TO WOODBURY SNOW
LINES AND CONSTRUCTION FROM TWO EXISTING RELICS FROM 1950ˢ
SCALE 1½" = 1'0"   SHEET #1 OF 1   MAY 29 2001
RESEARCH BY H. H. PAYSON   DRAWN BY BOB LANE.

GULL'S EYE VIEW

A BRIEF HISTORY

WOODBURY SNOW DESIGNED AND BUILT THIS LITTLE SQUARE ENDED PUNT IN THE EARLY 1930ˢ, CALLING IT A "CHOPPING TRAY." IT WAS USED AS A BEACH BOAT TO GET OFF ABOARD SMALL POWERED LOBSTER BOATS AT MOORINGS. KNOWN FOR ITS LIGHTNESS, RUGGEDNESS, ABILITY TO GET OFF A CHOPPY SHINGLE BEACH AND ITS GREAT LOAD CARRYING CAPACITY THIS DESIGN WAS USED WELL INTO THE 1990ˢ BY LOBSTER FISHERMEN ON THE SOUTHERN END OF MATINIC ISLAND LYING SIX MILES OFF THE RUGGED COAST OF MAINE.

FRANK POST, WOODBURY'S GRANDSON, SAID HE ONCE SAW THIS PINT SIZED "CHOPPING TRAY" LOADED WITH 10, 80 POUND BAGS OF FISH SALT, PLUS ITS SKIPPER EUGENE STAPLES (ABOUT ONE HALF TON TOTAL LOAD) NOT MUCH FREE-BOARD, FRANK SAID, BUT IT MADE THE TRIP FROM BOAT TO SHORE JUST WHAT IT WAS DESIGNED FOR.

THIS LITTLE PUNT HAS A LOT MORE SOFISTICATION THAN WOULD FIRST APPEAR. EVERY PART AND PIECE CONTRIBUTE TO THE SUCCESS OF THE TOTAL DESIGN.

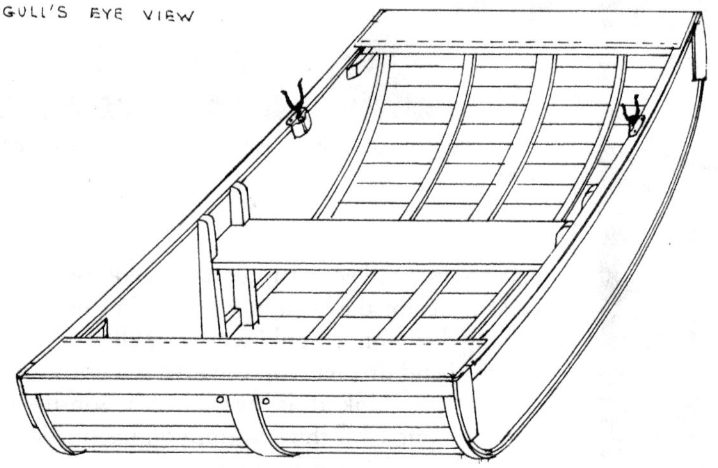

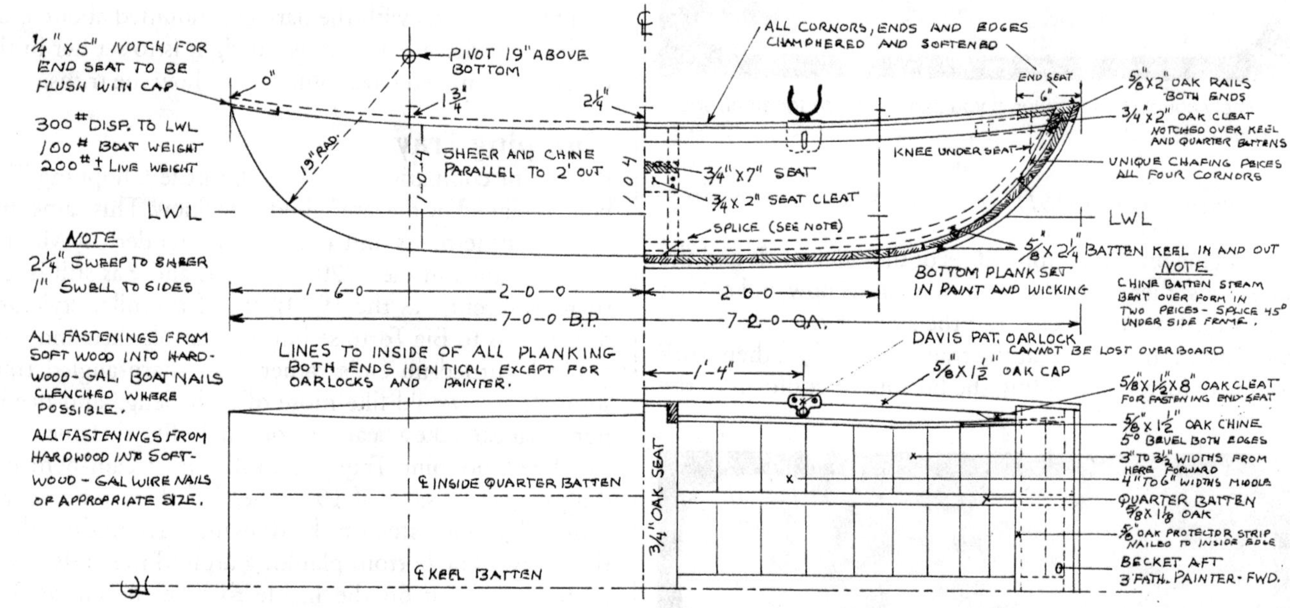

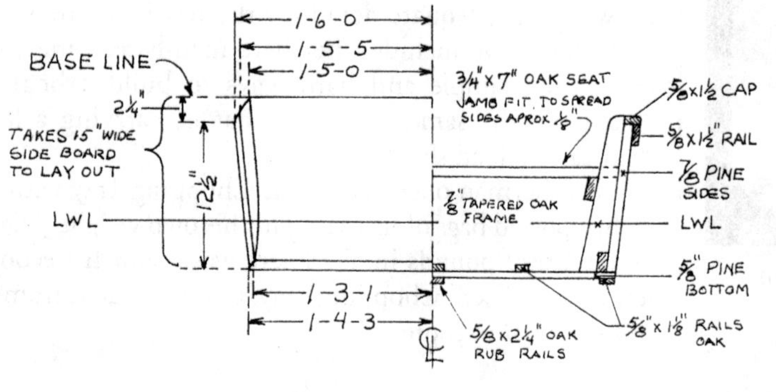

PROBABLE ORDER OF CONSTRUCTION
LAY OUT SIDES BY MEASURE OR FROM PATTERN ATTACH PRE-STEAM BENT CHINES, SEAT FRAME AND END CLEATS. SET UP UPSIDE DOWN ON SAW HORSES USING TEMPORARY CENTER MOLD AND END SPALLS TO CONTROL SHAPE. CROSS PLANK BOTTOM BEGINNING AT ENDS TOWARD MIDDLE. TURN RIGHT SIDE UP. BEND IN BOTTOM BATTENS COLD INSIDE ONLY. CAULK, THEN OUTSIDE RUB RAILS. INSTALL END SEATS, RAILS, CAPS, ETC. JAMB FIT SEAT TO HOLD SPREAD, OARLOCKS, PAINT TWO COATS MILL END GRAY. SPLICE IN PAINTER AND BECKET. DON'T FORGET 6' ASH OARS. ENJOY!

Plans for the Chopping Tray designed by Woodbury Snow. (Courtesy Bob Lane)

CHAPTER 11

AURAY PUNT

Phil Bolger's inspiration for the Auray Punt was the little tenders used in the village of Auray, France. Writing in *Boats with an Open Mind*, Bolger quoted yachtsman Claud Worth, who visited the village and "discovered" the boat, as follows:

The Auray fishermen's dinghies are of practical interest to owners of small yachts. For steadiness, carrying capacity, landing on a beach, or dragging over mud they would be difficult to improve upon. Any amateur carpenter could build one . . . . At sea they are either carried in the lugger or are towed in a fresh breeze; it seemed to be skimming along the top of the water like a hydroplane. The long bow is said to improve their towing qualities and to keep them dry in rowing to windward. Where space is limited there would be no harm in taking 9 inches off it. This dinghy might then be made to fit very nicely, bottom upwards, over the skylights of a small yacht.

Bolger seems to acknowledge the virtues of the punt's long "snout" (as he calls it) but also notes that it adds no buoyancy to the boat, and if you tried to stand up in it, you'd swamp—a fact reflected by Worth's observation that the bow can be cut off "with no harm."

Bolger of course improved upon Worth's drawings, easing the curves to make the boat easier to build. I tested the design by building a model to his drawings, and found that it goes together very well, with no glitches. In one respect, however, I went against the plans, ignoring the directions to deduct plank thicknesses from the dimensions. When building full-size, this will make her ½" wider and ¼" deeper than drawn, and that wouldn't bother me a bit. Just use the dimensions given everywhere and go for it. She can be built with either a chine log or stitch and glue, as drawn.

(continued on page 108)

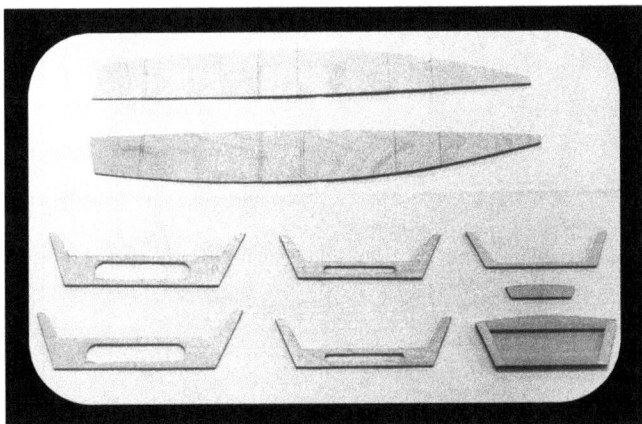

Building a model of an Auray Punt shows how the real thing goes together. Note especially the centerlines on the frames and transoms and the frame-alignment marks on the side panels.

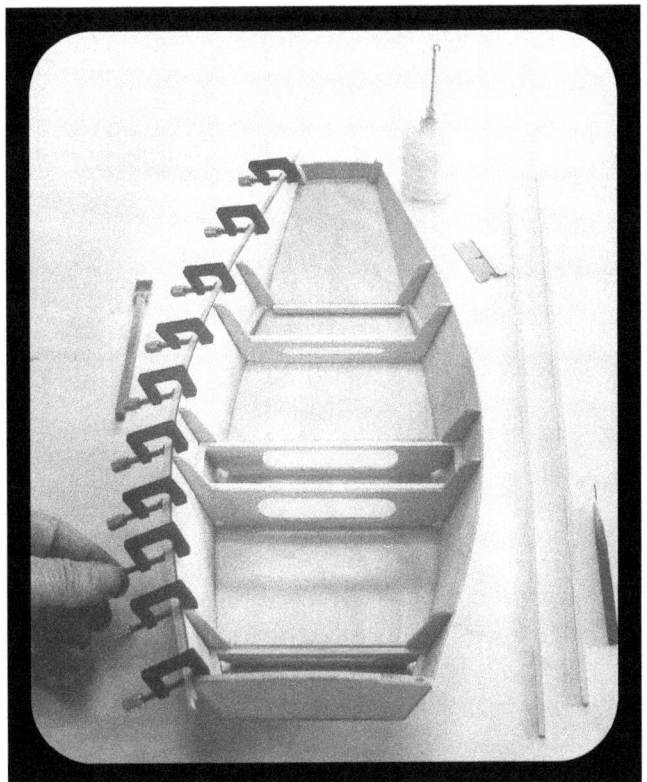

You'll need at least this many clamps to fasten the gunwales on the full-size boat.

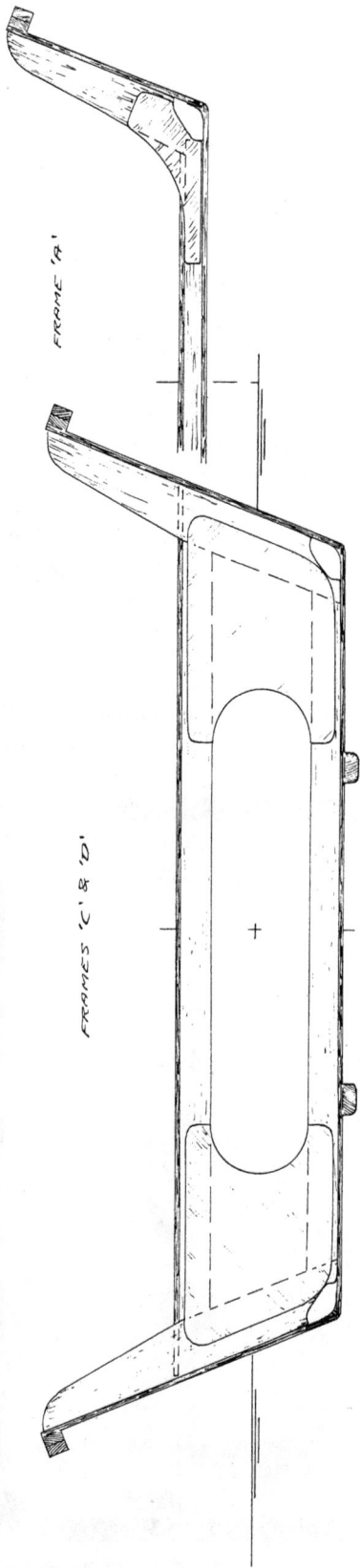

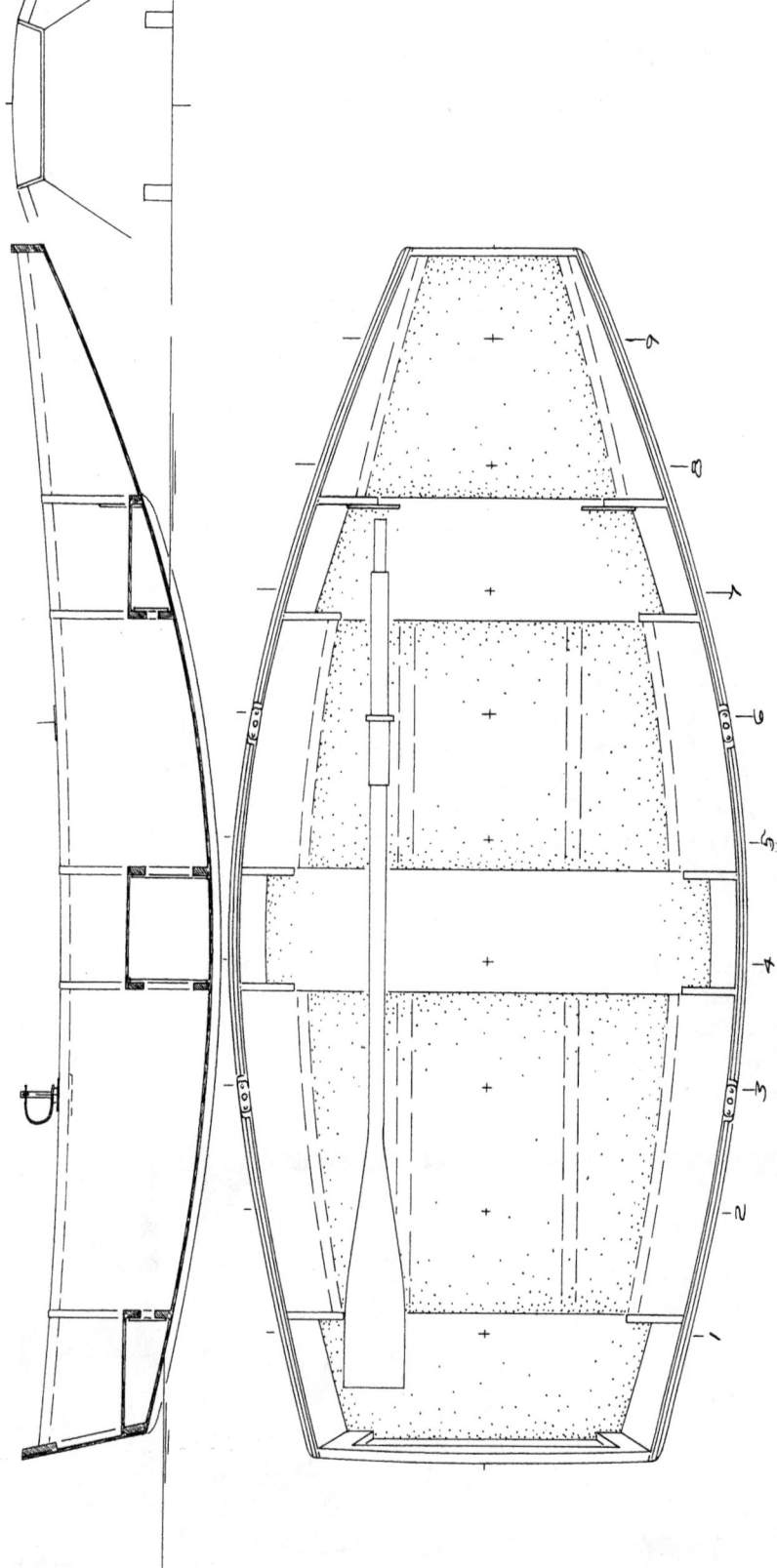

FRAME 'A'

FRAMES 'C' & 'D'

SCALE 3" = 1'0"

Auray Punt, Sheet 1.

Auray Punt, Sheet 2.

The finished punt shows its graceful nose.

(continued from page 105)

BUILDING KEY FOR DESIGN No. 599, AURAY PUNT

Deducting plank thickness is not worth the trouble. Building to the dimensions shown makes her only $\frac{1}{2}$" wider and $\frac{1}{4}$" deeper.

Materials

Plywood

3 sheets $\frac{1}{4}$" x 4' x 8' AC or marine-grade plywood for sides, bottom, frames, and seat tops
1 12-foot long 2" x 4" for gunwales. Thirty feet of ceiling strapping for frame stiffeners. Frames can also be made in one piece from thicker plywood.

Glass Supplies

Roll of 3" glass tape
8 yards of 38" 6-ounce glass cloth. (This amount will glass the entire outside of hull.)
1 gallon of polyester or epoxy resin
$\frac{1}{2}$ gallon of Fillite powder or Cab-O-Sil for making stiff mixture of putty

Fastenings

Bronze anchor nails: $\frac{1}{2}$ pound, $1\frac{1}{4}$" #14; $\frac{1}{2}$ pound, 1" #14; $\frac{1}{2}$ pound, $\frac{7}{8}$" #14

Oarlocks

Phil Bolger–style or brass Wilcox-Crittenden side mount (plates, #4482; horns, #4477)
8 screws for mounting, brass or bronze, $1\frac{1}{4}$" #10 flat heads

Paint and Sealers

Use epoxy or polyester for sealer, whatever you use to glass your boat with. Thin either with acetone or lacquer thinner. If whole outside of hull is glassed, any kind of paint—water-based, oil-based, cheap, or expensive—will last for years. For inside of hull, use water-based paint, since the inside of the boat should not be glassed. Unlike oil-based paint, water-based paint will not crack and peel.

Assembly

Side Panels

Mark across the sheet of plywood in 1' intervals; hook steel tape over the edge of the plywood and measure sheer and bottom rocker. Drive brads at each measurement and spring a light batten around nails. Draw in sheer and bottom rocker, cut bow end tabs; note that forward tab interval is $13\frac{13}{16}$". Stick tabs on with glass or plywood butt joints. Mark locations of frames A, B, C, D, and E and tops of seats.

Transom

$\frac{1}{4}$" plywood to dimensions, framed and beveled as shown. Bow block solid wood, $\frac{3}{4}$" thick to dimensions and beveled as shown.

CHAPTER 12
FISHERMAN'S SKIFF

Back in the late 1940s and early 1950s, on trips in from Maine's Metinic Island where I was lobstering, I would stop by Axel Gronros's boat shop in Rockland for supplies. Axel had immigrated from Finland in the 1920s, and neither time nor lumber was wasted in his shop. In between building new lobster boats and doing repair jobs, the men built this twelve-foot skiff, designed by Axel, in one corner of the shop. They had ¼" plywood sides and cross-planked bottoms, sourced from the ample supply of plank ends left over from lobster-boat construction. These nice skiffs were built upside down on a jig constructed at a comfortable working height so that the builders could work all day long, day after day, without tiring.

The skiff's preshaped sides were cut using a template and plopped down in thumb cleats nailed to the jig. The cleats held the side panels at the right height while the workers bent them around the jig. All pretty clever, I thought. Presto—those flat panels all of a sudden spelled BOAT!

As a young fellow in my late teens, I was impressed with what I saw. And I was even more impressed that a real boatbuilder like Axel would take an interest in me, let alone allow me to borrow his jig, from which I made patterns so that I could build my own skiff.

A while later, when I returned the jig and brought along my finished boat to show Axel, I wondered what his reaction would be. First thing he looked at was the tight end fit of the chines against the stem and transom. Seeing "no half-inch putty" here, his face broke into a big grin. He didn't say much because of his difficulty with the English language, but his grin said it all—that there was some hope for this young "whippersnapper" would-be boatbuilder.

Building her today, I would never take the trouble of cross-planking with ¾" cedar or anything else. It's just too much work, and the more seams you have, the more chances there are for leaks. A plywood bottom to complement her plywood sides is the way to go. And with plywood, you have a choice of buying 8' or 12' lengths. At the price of marine-grade or okume plywood, I'd quite likely go with the three 4' x 8' sheets called for and butt-strap

them or use fiberglass joints. A 12' boat from three sheets of ¼" plywood is not bad at all, and the bottom drag strips give the bottom ample strength.

So aside from the "Chopping Tray" in Chapter 10, this is the only boat in the book not designed by Phil Bolger. Even if you have never built a boat before, you stand a good chance of building this one, as it is about as straightforward as any of Bolger's Instant Boats. You do have to build a simple jig, but if you don't want to cut the chine to make the joint between the bottom and sides, you can build her stitch-and-glue style. In the photos, I've built a model to the scale of the real plans (not the size of the plans as reproduced in this book). The process is so easy that there's virtually no difference in building the full-size boat.

There is no need to build the jig as elaborate as shown on the plans. Here you see the three station molds with their widths and heights on them. They are shown made from 1" x 3" lumber and spaced 3' apart. This is a nice way to make the jig if you have the time and are willing to deal with cutting and aligning that many pieces. As for me, I would make the molds from one piece from ½" plywood each, if I was in a hurry. Notch all their top corners as shown if you are going to use chines.

(continued on page 112)

This model-scale building jig is just like the real thing. Note the notched corners for the chine logs, the diagonal bracing, and the thumb cleats to support the side panels.

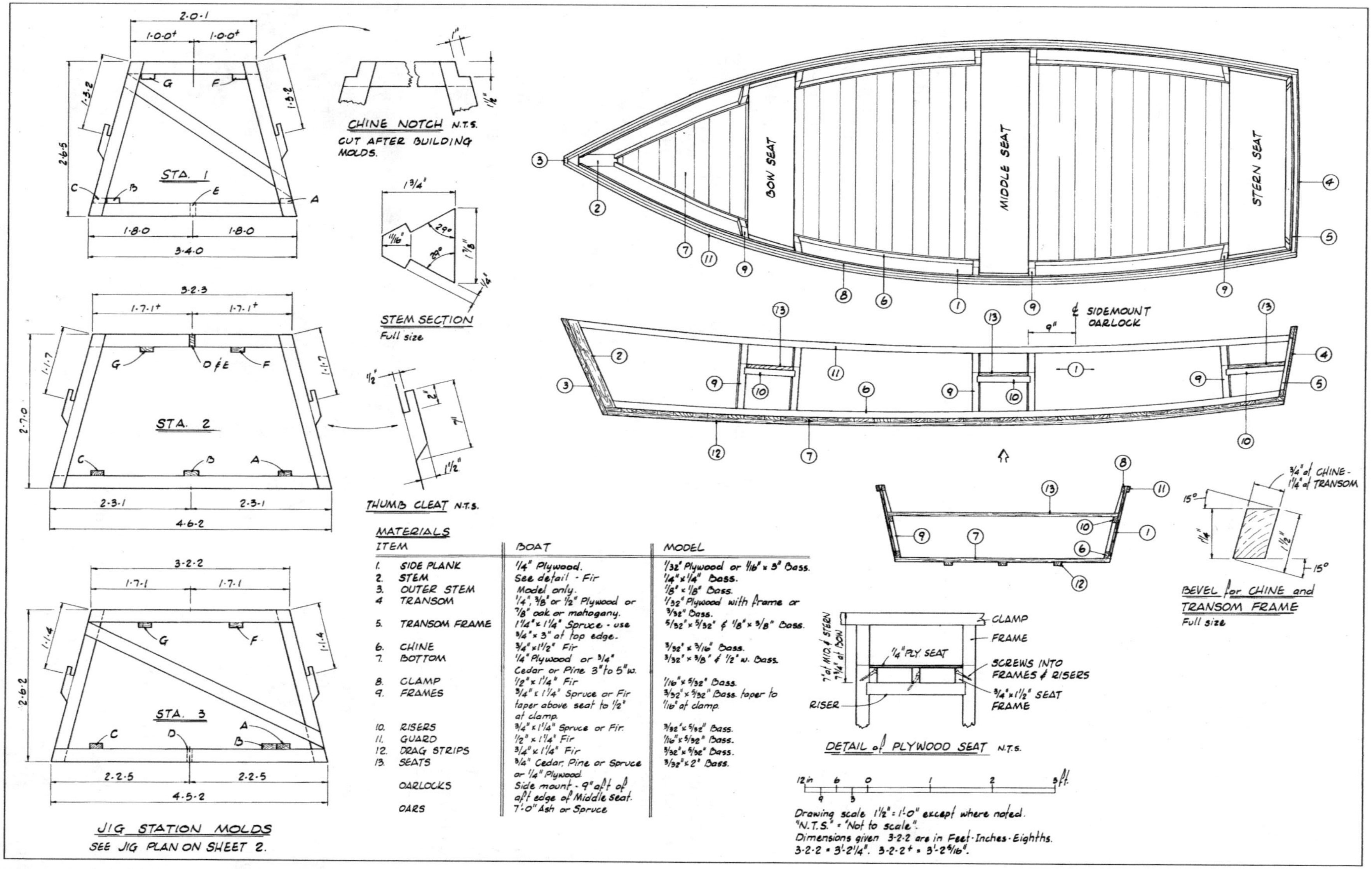
JIG STATION MOLDS
SEE JIG PLAN ON SHEET 2.
STA. 1
STA. 2
STA. 3
CHINE NOTCH N.T.S.
CUT AFTER BUILDING MOLDS.
STEM SECTION
Full size
THUMB CLEAT N.T.S.
BOW SEAT
MIDDLE SEAT
STERN SEAT
SIDEMOUNT OARLOCK
BEVEL for CHINE and TRANSOM FRAME
Full size
3/4" of CHINE - 1 1/4" of TRANSOM
DETAIL of PLYWOOD SEAT N.T.S.
CLAMP
FRAME
1/4" PLY SEAT
SCREWS INTO FRAMES & RISERS
3/4" x 1 1/2" SEAT FRAME
RISER
7" at MID & STERN
7 3/4" at BOW
MATERIALS
ITEM | BOAT | MODEL
1. SIDE PLANK | 1/4" Plywood. | 1/32" Plywood or 1/16" x 3" Bass.
2. STEM | See detail - Fir | 1/4" x 1/4" Bass.
3. OUTER STEM | Model only. | 1/8" x 1/8" Bass.
4. TRANSOM | 1/4", 3/8" or 1/2" Plywood or 7/8" oak or mahogany. | 1/32" Plywood with frame or 3/32" Bass.
5. TRANSOM FRAME | 1 1/4" x 1 1/4" Spruce - use 3/4" x 3" at top edge. | 5/32" x 5/32" & 1/8" x 3/8" Bass.
6. CHINE | 3/4" x 1 1/2" Fir | 3/32" x 3/16" Bass.
7. BOTTOM | 1/4" Plywood or 3/4" Cedar or Pine 3" to 5" w. | 3/32" x 3/8" & 1/2" w. Bass.
8. CLAMP | 1/2" x 1 1/4" Fir | 1/16" x 5/32" Bass.
9. FRAMES | 3/4" x 1 1/4" Spruce or Fir taper above seat to 1/2" at clamp. | 3/32" x 5/32" Bass. taper to 1/16" at clamp.
10. RISERS | 3/4" x 1 1/4" Spruce or Fir. | 3/32" x 5/32" Bass.
11. GUARD | 1/2" x 1 1/4" Fir | 1/16" x 5/32" Bass.
12. DRAG STRIPS | 3/4" x 1 1/4" Fir | 3/32" x 5/32" Bass.
13. SEATS | 3/4" Cedar, Pine or Spruce or 1/4" Plywood. | 3/32" x 2" Bass.
OARLOCKS | Side mount - 9" aft of aft edge of Middle Seat.
OARS | 7'-0" Ash or Spruce
Drawing scale 1 1/2" = 1'-0" except where noted.
"N.T.S." = "Not to scale".
Dimensions given 3-2-2 are in Feet-Inches-Eighths.
3-2-2 = 3'-2 1/4". 3-2-2+ = 3'-2 5/16".

Fisherman's Skiff, Sheet 1. (Courtesy David Dillion)

Fisherman's Skiff, Sheet 2. (Courtesy David Dillion)

(continued from page 109)

The expanded shapes of the side panels, as shown on the plans, are what make building her so easy. Their tops are absolutely straight edged, as you can see, and their bottom shapes are determined by measuring from the edge of the sheet at 1' intervals. Drive brads at these points, spring a batten around them, fair the curves if necessary, and trace along the batten with a pencil, just as you've been doing for the Instant Boats. Then cut out the panels with your circular saw, set for the shallowest cut possible. Before you cut, don't forget to mark the location of the aft face of Station 3, 2'9¾" from the tip of the aft end, as shown.

Far from being an inconvenience, the rabbeted stem can be an advantage when building, because it makes it easy to get the sides and the stem lined up correctly. This stem is easy to make on your table saw, because it's straight, and the bevels are constant. I cut it from a stick 2' long. Start by cutting the 1⅞" "sided" and 1¾" "molded" dimensions on your table saw. Next, set your saw to cut the 29° angles, and cut the angles from the rabbet line to the front face of the stem on both sides. Without changing your blade angle, but setting its height carefully, make the cuts from the bearding line to the back rabbet on both sides. Then bring the saw blade upright to 90°, set its height to ½", and make the cut from the bearding line to the back rabbet, completing the rabbet.

The assembly process is just as easy. Drop the sides in the thumb cleats, align the marks on the panels with the aft face of Station 3 for the proper fore-and-aft placement on the jig, and clamp the panels to the jig. Cut the transom to the dimensions shown, bevel the sides 15° and the bottom 17°. Cut and bevel the transom framing to the same angles, then glue and fasten together.

Glue and fasten the sides to the transom, then glue and fasten the sides to the stem. You can pull the sides in by hand—you don't need a Spanish windlass.

If you're using chines, cut them to 1½" x ¾" x 12' and bevel them 15° top and bottom. Fit them for length, and glue and fasten them in place. Plane all edges flat across for a nicely flushed bottom fit.

With the sides already fastened to the transom, they're next glued and nailed to the rabbeted stem.

I cross-planked the model shown in the photos, in keeping with Axel Gronros's original building method, but I certainly wouldn't build the full-size boat that way today—not when I could do it with plywood to avoid potential leaks.

To lay out the bottom panel, you don't have to measure it as shown in the plans. Just draw a centerline on the underside of the bottom sheet of plywood, plop it on the boat, and mark its shape from underneath, around the hull. Then take it off, set your saw to a 15° bevel to match the flare of the sides, cut out the bottom, and put it back on the boat, gluing and fastening it in place.

Take the boat off of the jig, place it on sawhorses, and install the three drag strips on the bottom, 9" apart. Locate the center drag strip first by drawing a centerline down the length of the bottom, from the center of the stem to the center of the transom. Draw two parallel lines on each side of the centerline to represent the 1¼" width of the drag strip, and bore holes down through the bottom for the fastenings, about 4" apart and staggered on each side of the centerline. Fasten the strip from underneath with ring nails while a helper (in my case, my wife) holds a backing iron on them. Do the outside drag strips the same way.

Terminology

The paragraph on making the stem contains a lot of terms that might be confusing to some. Don't let the terminology confuse you—the procedure is quite simple.

Sided: The side-to-side dimension of a part.

Molded: The front-to-back dimension of a part.

Rabbet line: The curved or straight line where the outside face of the plank meets the stem.

Bearding line: The curved or straight line where the inside face of the plank touches the outer face of the stem.

Back rabbet: The curved or straight line that is the deepest part of the rabbet, at the end of the inside face of the plank.

If you're building with chine logs, plane the bottom edges of the sides so that they're flat across.

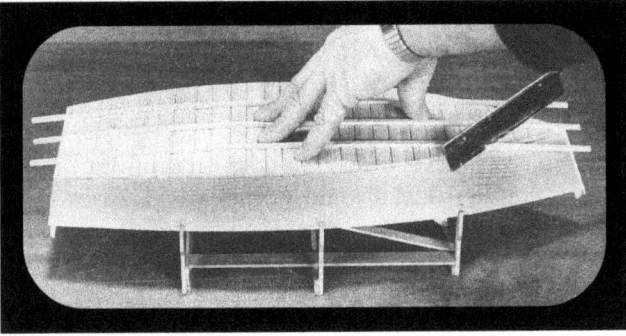

Installing the drag strips. The model was built with a cross-planked bottom, but you can use plywood for a faster job with fewer leaks.

Turn the boat right side up, install the ½" x 1¼" gunwales, the seat risers, and the seats, and she's done.

You will want ribbed oarlocks with edge-mounted sockets for her, and a 2- to 3-horsepower engine if you want to go with power.

This much information, along with the more concise building key, should see you to completion.

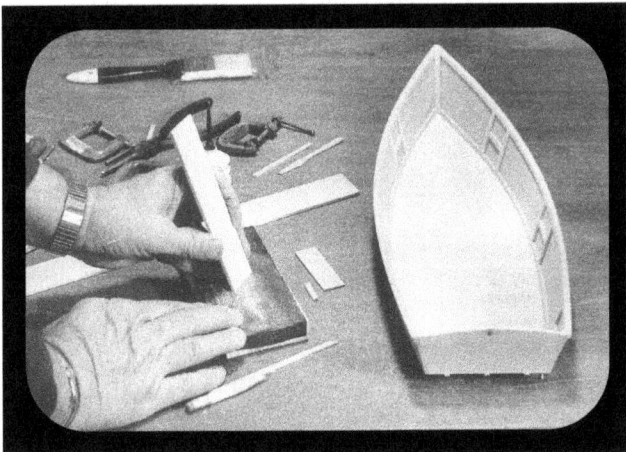

With the seat risers in place, the seats are cut to length and their ends trimmed and sanded to the right angle.

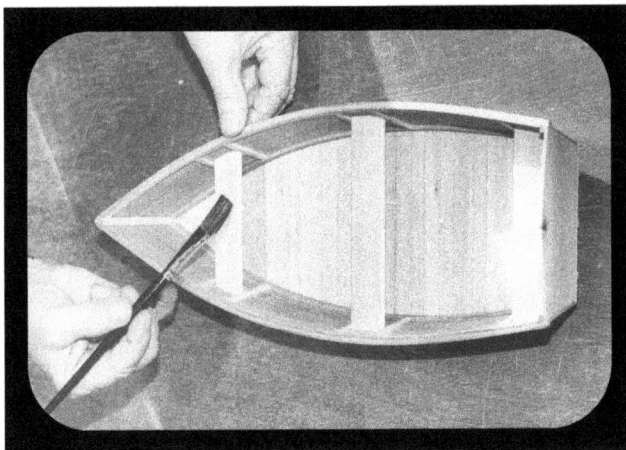

Finishing the interior of the model with thinned varnish. For the real boat, use latex paint.

A graceful little skiff, in a simple, workmanlike way.

BUILDING KEY FOR FISHERMAN'S SKIFF

Jig
Make solid from cheap plywood; is easier and quicker. Or make from 1" x 4" framing. Locate thumb cleats on each mold to height shown; these hold the sides to proper height for assembly. Cut corners of the jig to allow for depth of chine logs.

Hull Materials
Three sheets of ¼" x 4' x 8' AC or marine-grade plywood, or two sheets of 4' x 12' marine-grade if no butt joints are wanted. See Sheet 2 of the plans.

Seats
Can be ¼", ⅜", or ½" plywood framed with ¾" x 1½" stiffeners, or made from ¾" or ⅞" spruce, fir, mahogany, or pine.

Transom
One-fourth-inch plywood or heavier to suit. Shape as shown. Pre-bevel the sides 15° and the bottom 17° before framing. Framings for transom sides and bottom are beveled both edges; finished 1¼" all around for thickness, made 2" longer top and bottom for the sides. Glue and fasten side frames on first, and fit bottom frame in between.

Chines
Cut two ¾" x 1½" x 12' pieces from a board or 2" x 4"; bevel both edges 15°.

Stem
Make from spruce, fir, mahogany, or oak. Length to be 2" longer on top and bottom than depth of sides at bow. Rabbet to catch ends of sides.

Side Panel Layout

Butt 2 sheets of plywood end to end, and mark off 1' intervals as shown across both edges so as to mark both side panels at the same time. Mark seat frames and 2'9¾" line for locating side panels fore and aft on jig. Cut butt blocks ¼" x 4"; keep ends out of way of chines and inwales. Glue and fasten with thin wire copper or brass nails bent over on outside of hull.

Assembly

1. Find level spot for jig and place side panels in the thumb cleats. Position aft ends of sides 2'9¾" from aft face of jig or to suit.

2. Glue and fasten pre-framed transom to side panels. Put in stem. Butt-fit the forward ends of chines to the stem after slipping them into notches previously taken off of jig corners. Clamp chines along the sides back almost to the transom, then spring the end of the chine inboard of (left high) transom framing to hold it while fitting. When you are satisfied with the end fit, take out, glue them, put them back in, and fasten with ⅞" ring nails.

3. Cut chines and edges of sides flat across for bottom-panel placement. If plywood is used, draw a centerline on two end-butted sheets, place on boat, and mark shape from underneath and around sides. Glue and fasten with 1⅛" ring nails.

4. Drag strips are ¾" x 1¼" fir, spruce, or oak placed apart, as shown on Sheet 1. Mark the location on outside of bottom, bore through from outside, then glue and fasten from inside with ⅞" ring nails.

5. Inside and outside gunwales are ½" x 1¼" x 13'. Fit inside gunwales first, glue them, and put them back in. Glue outside gunwales, spring them around the sides, and fasten them from inside with 1⅛" ring nails, passing through the inside gunwale through the side and into the outer gunwale.

CHAPTER 13
STRETCHED DORY

This 19'6" dory is built stitch-and-glue style, and construction is about as simple as it gets for a boat with this much looks.

Her designer, Phil Bolger, must have thought so, too, because he sent no materials list or building key—nothing but the plans. This leaves us to figure out how to build it all by ourselves, so let's do it.

The plans consist of three pages drawn on 17" x 22" paper showing the dory's profile, the plan view (looking down at it), and a body plan (looking at her end views, from stem aft to amidships on the right side of the centerline, and from her tombstone transom forward to amidships on the left).

She is mostly drawn at a 1" = 1' scale with a sectional frame drawing at 4" = 1' and a view of the tombstone construction at 2" = 1'. These different scales are nothing to worry about, because Bolger has given the dimensions for everything.

I'll quickly review how the dimensions are noted. Right below the waterline profile drawing on Sheet 1 is the plan for the seat bearers. (This part is also shown in place in the construction profile drawing immediately below it.) The overall length of the part is given as 9,4,5. The three digits represent feet, inches, and eighths of an inch. Therefore, 9,4,5 means 9'4⅝". (If the third digit is followed by a + sign, add ⅟₁₆". The 3,1,6+ length of the tombstone transom equals 3'1¹³⁄₁₆".) In some places, you'll also see dimensions given in conventional inches and fractions.

On the sectional frame drawing, Bolger shows that the dory's sides are made from ¼" x 4' x 8' plywood, and her bottom from ½" x 4' x 8' plywood. The only information missing here is how much of each. This is easy to figure out by looking at the drawing of the expanded side panel. The location of the butt straps for joining the ends of the 8' plywood clearly indicates that three 4' x 8' sheets are needed. You can easily get two duplicate sides from the three sheets. The sides are cut out square-edged.

The ½" bottom panel is a little more than 2' wide at its midpoint where the butt joint is located, so a 4' x 8' sheet cut down the center and butted wouldn't quite make

it—you'd have to add about 2" to make the proper width. This is too much trouble and a waste of material. What you can do instead is to lay out both ends diagonally on one sheet of plywood, as shown on page 119. Doing it this way gives you the necessary width and even gives you enough space left over for a scarf joint, if you want to do that instead of using plywood or fiberglass butt straps.

Another ½" x 4' x 8' sheet is needed for the three frames. Though a half sheet would do it, many lumberyards won't sell you a half sheet. So there you have it for plywood: three sheets of ¼" x 4' x 8' and two sheets of ½" x 4' x 8' to build her.

Now I'll take a look at how she goes together. It's not my intention here to give you a blow-by-blow instruction for building her right through to the end, but I will help you get started and offer help with some of the harder parts.

The profile shows a 1" x 9,4,5 seat bearer, or stringer, cut from a board or plank that is 8" wide. The part is notched in its center and at both ends to join all three ½" frames together. (Look also at the sectional frame drawing and the plan view to see all the details.) The seat bearer thus determines the heights of the bottoms of the frames, which, in turn, determine the curves of the bottom and the sides. Combined with the shapes and angles of the tombstone and stem, this gives this dory its shape.

The drawing of the tombstone (that's what a dory's characteristically shaped transom is called) shows its overall expanded, finished shape, scull notch and all. To achieve this kind of perfection, with the reverse bevel at its top matching perfectly with the sheer of the sides, isn't likely to happen, not even for very skilled builders. Therefore, my recommendation is that you don't try it, and avoid frustration. Instead, make the transom at least a couple of inches longer than indicated, and cut the top shape and scull notch later, after the dory has been assembled and turned right side up.

Start with a piece of the ¼" plywood called for, and mark off a centerline and all the given widths at the intervals shown. The tombstone sides are not straight lines: They are slightly curved, so you will need to measure, drive

(continued on page 119)

115

RECOMMENDED ROWER/PASSENGER COMBINATIONS @ 1/4" = 1'0"

STRETCHED LIGHT DORY - 19'6" x 4'0"

Tack and Tape construction
3 Movable Seats

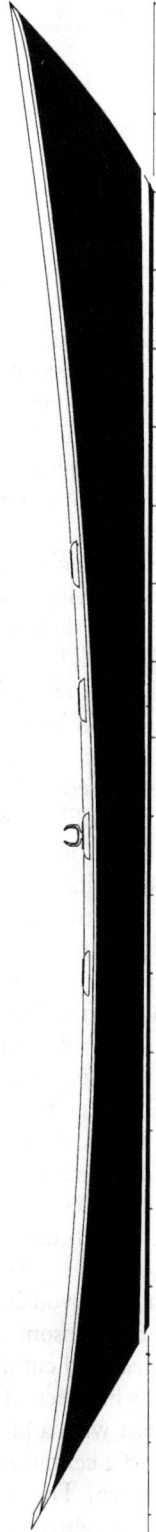

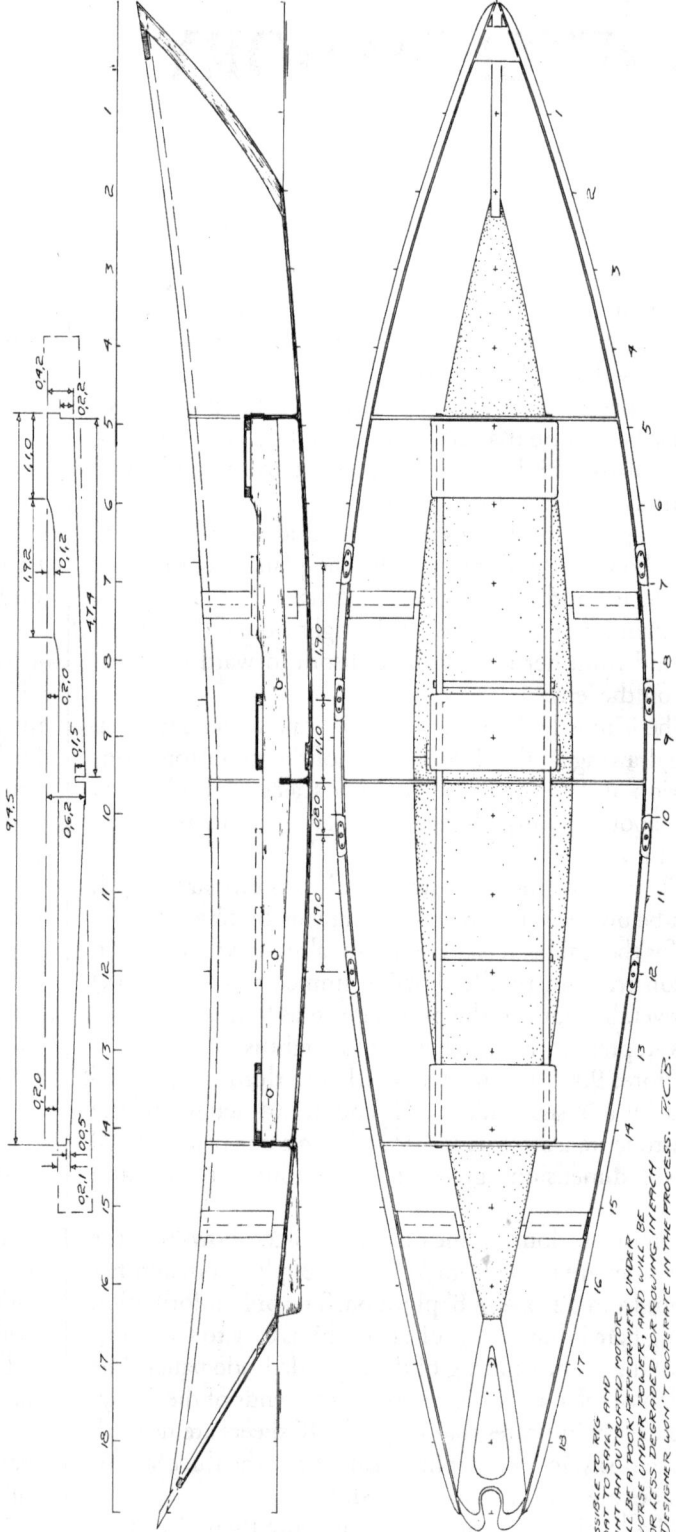

Stretched Dory, Sheet 1.

Stretched Dory, Sheet 2.

SHEER MOLDINGS BENT ON DOUBLE TO FINISH 1 1/2"

SIDE RAILS 3/4" SQ. x 12"

END FRAMES 3/4" x 1 1/2" x 16"

MOVABLE SEATS 1/4" x 12" x 20" MARKE THREE; LOCATE TO LOAD DIAGRAM

SIDE FRAMES 3/4" x 2 1/2" x 12"

FOOT BRACES SHIP INTO HOLES IN BEARERS; LOCATE BY TRIAL.

SEAT BEARERS FROM 1" x 5 1/2" x 9'-4 5/8". SEE DIAGRAM

4" TAPE

2" TAPE

EPOXY FILLING

BOTTOM 1/2" PLYWOOD

SIDES 1/4" PLYWOOD

4" TAPE

HULL SHEATHING CLOTH

BULKHEADS 1/2" PLYWOOD OR CAN BE BUILT UP THICKER

SHIM UP OARLOCK SOCKETS PLUMB

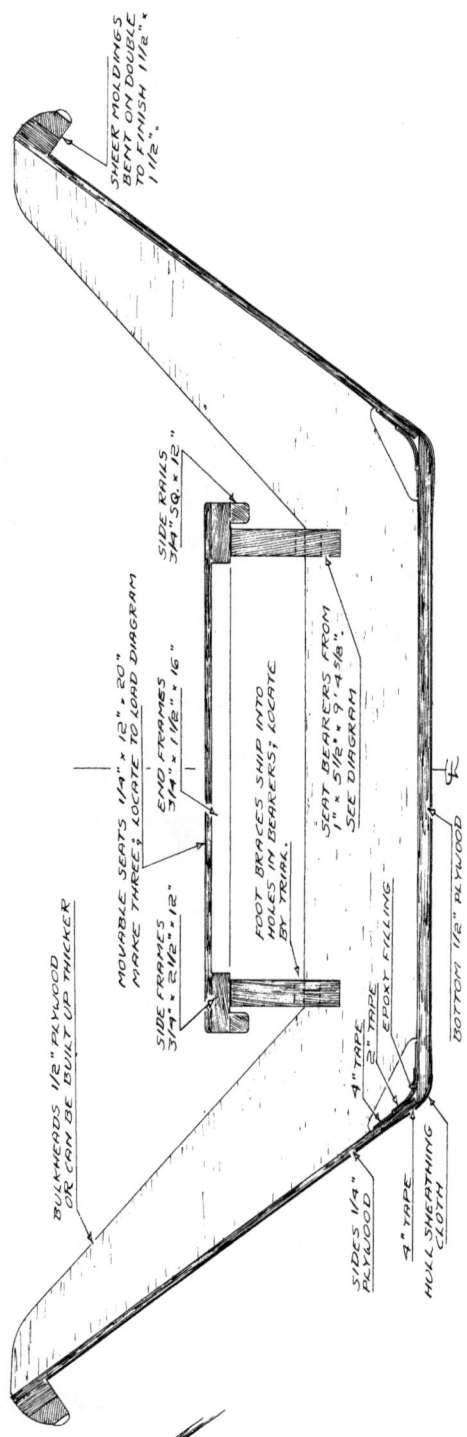

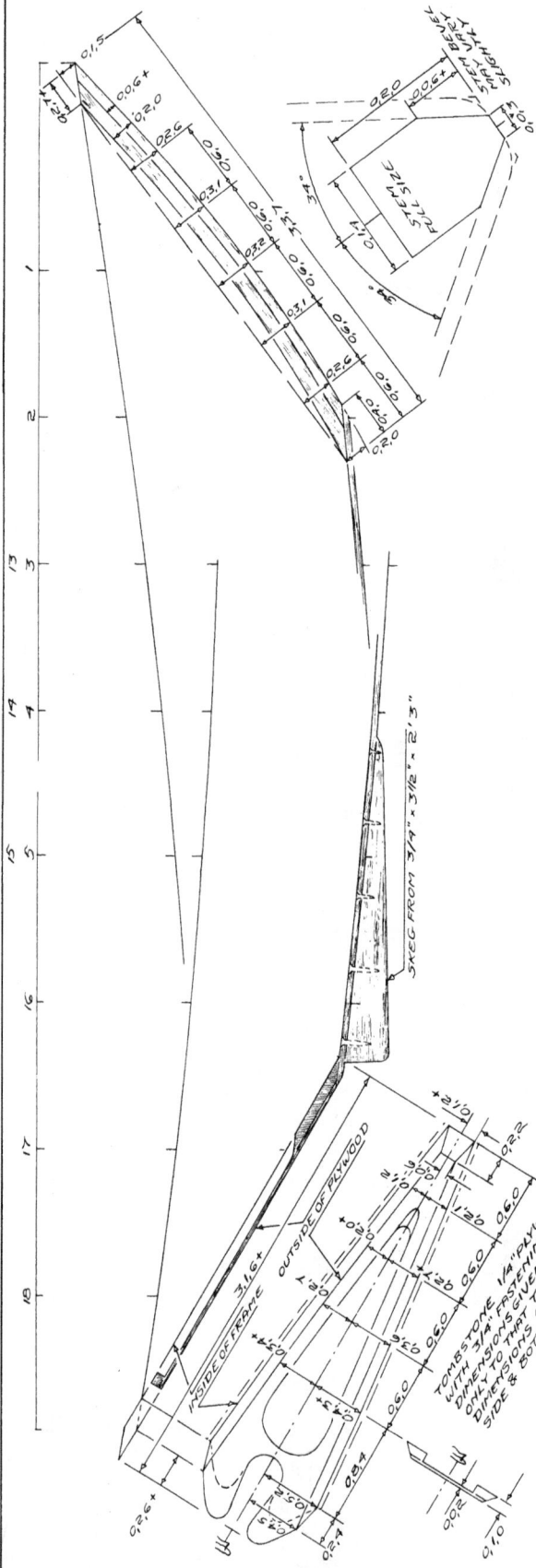

STEM SIZE FULL SIZE

STEM BEVEL

SKEG FROM 3/4" x 3 1/2" x 2'-3"

TOMBSTONE 1/4" PLYWOOD WITH 3/4" FASTENING FRAME DIMENSIONS GIVEN APPLY ONLY TO THAT THICKNESS. DIMENSIONS AT INSIDE OF SIDE & BOTTOM PLANKING.

INSIDE OF FRAME

OUTSIDE OF FRAME

BUILDER SHOULD BE FAMILIAR WITH BOOKS INSTANT BOATS AND BUILD THE NEW INSTANT BOATS BY H.H. PAYSON, PLEASANT BEACH ROAD, SOUTH THOMASTON, MAINE 04858.

Stretched Dory, Sheet 3.

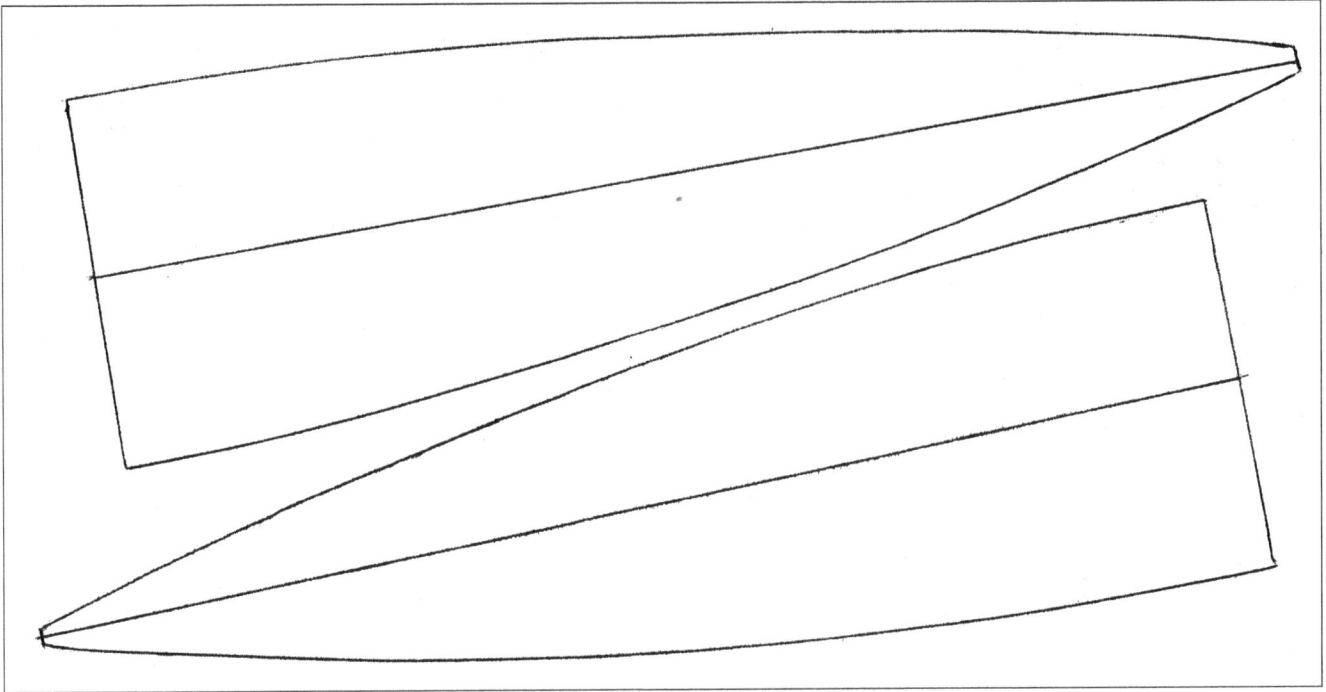

How to get the bottom of a 19'6" boat out of a single sheet of plywood.

(continued from page 115)

brads at the marks, and sweep the lines in with a batten. Cut the panel out square-edged, and frame it with ¾" pine, spruce, fir, or whatever. Glue and fasten the pieces together. Set your table saw or band saw at 41°, and saw the

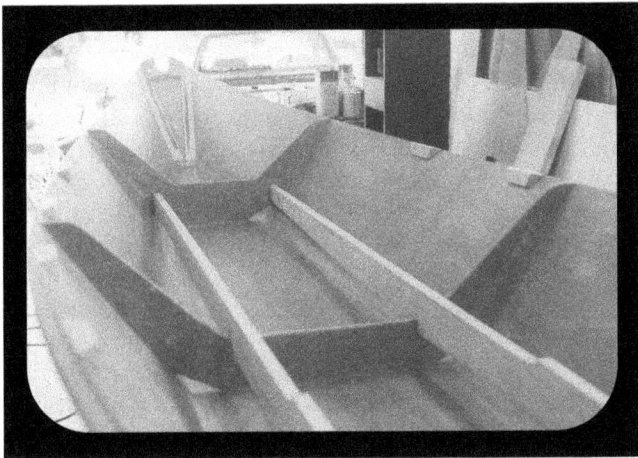

The stringers provide a lot of the Stretched Dory's strength. Note also the transom framing and the rowlock blocks fastened inside the hull, to avoid having to pierce the gunwales, which are under tension.

side bevels. You have to saw the bevel freehand because of the curved sides. As with the side bevels, the angle of the bottom bevel isn't marked on the plans (its length is shown as 0,2,2), but you can pick it up with a bevel gauge or a protractor.

The stem may be made from one piece of spruce, pine, fir, etc., or by laminating plywood to the size shown. It is beveled to a constant 34° for its full length.

Set the seat bearers, or stringers, with the three ½" bulkheads on sawhorses, tack the sides to the frames, then attach the transom and stem. Cut out and butt-join the bottom, pre-beveling it to 36° to match the flare of the sides. This will save time and labor. Do your stitching, gluing, and taping, turn her right side up, and install the gunwales and breast hook. Instead of the laminated gunwales shown, I used one-piece gunwales, 1½" deep x 1", and angle-cut their bottom edge 30° to allow them to bend more easily.

The plans show the oarlocks mounted on the gunwales, which are bored to accept the sockets. I'm not wild about this detail, because gunwales like to break just from the tension of bending them around the hull, and they surely don't need holes through them to help them on their way. Instead, I recommend edge-mount oarlock sockets placed on angled wooden mounts inside the dory.

CHAPTER 14
SEA HAWK

Sea Hawk was designed by Phil Bolger in answer to many requests of Gloucester Light Dory builders who wanted to power their dories. Phil is adamantly against either power or sail in his dory for safety reasons and says he will have no part of either choice.

I can vouch for Bolger's objection to powering the Gloucester Light Dory. Many years ago, a customer asked me to put a motor well in his Light Dory and I said, "NO, the designer says it won't work well, and it's dangerous." The customer said he wouldn't buy the dory unless he could have a well in it. I was in no position financially to turn down the job, so I agreed to do it.

On trials in Camden Harbor with a 2- or 3-horsepower motor on it, we discovered quickly enough what her designer was warning us about. Running straight ahead, she was okay, but the moment you tried to turn, she would snap her gunwale right down to the water. If we hadn't been hanging on to the opposite gunwale, she would have pitched us both overboard. After the trials, the owner didn't say anything, and neither did I—there was no need to.

Moving on to Sea Hawk, Bolger says that he designed her to be "the slimmest boat that would be safe to stand up in, to make a cast from, or to haul up a lobster trap from. Keeping the boat narrow makes for light weight, for easy bends to speed up construction, for a sharp enough bow to punch through the crests of a small chop without being badly stopped, and for a small enough drag to be rowed some distance." He acknowledges that she's no rowboat, per se, but good enough to move under oars when necessary without undue trouble. As a general type, you could call her a "semi-dory." With her narrow beam, her capacity is roughly comparable to many boats that are a lot shorter—in the range of 12' or so—but her greater length and gentler bends allow her to run more easily and faster, make her easier to build, and make her prettier to boot.

Sea Hawk will go 15 knots with a 7½-horsepower engine, and 25 knots or more with 20 horses.

Since it requires a construction jig, Sea Hawk isn't an Instant Boat, strictly speaking. But with the fully developed panel layouts that I've provided, and the one-piece station molds that I recommend (both of which are described below), she comes close, and her bends are so easy that she just about falls together.

BUILDING THE SEA HAWK

Materials
2 sheets of ³⁄₄" 4' x 8' plywood or particle board for the construction jig
1 sheet of ³⁄₈" 4' x 16' plywood, or 2 sheets of 4' x 8' plywood butted together for the sides
2 sheets of ½" 4' x 8' plywood for the bottom, transom, and seats
Pine, spruce, or fir planks 10" x 1½" x 16' for the gunwales, chines and miscellaneous framing

Getting Started

Developing the Side Panel
The first of the features that make for quick, easy building is the fully developed side panel. Developing the shape of the side panel is key to the boat's profile shape, and it isn't given on Bolger's plans. Normally, the builder had to develop it himself, but I've done this for you, so all you have to do is transfer the measurements from the expanded side-panel plans onto two 4' x 8', butt-joined sheets of plywood, cut them out, spring them around the molds with the stem and transom in place, and "presto"—there is your boat.

There are a few ways to develop the side panel. I took the easiest and fastest route. After the jig was built and the transom and stem were in place, I sprung a ½" x 1" batten along the chine line the length of the molds, and another along the sheer. I took a 17' length of red rosin building paper (looks more orange than red) and wrapped it around the battens the length of the boat. It's nice to have two people for this operation, but it can be done alone. Be sure it wraps around smoothly, without edge set or wrinkles, although since it is 3' wide it's not

(continued on page 124)

120

SEA HAWK DORY/SKIFF
L.O.A. 15'-6" X 4'-2"
Maximum Safe Power 20 O.B.C.H.P.
Weight 160 lbs.

FLOTATION @ 830 LBS. DISPL.

SCALE FEET & INCHES

SHOE

QUARTER SKIDS

10"

THWART FLAT-
FOAM BUOY-
ANCY UNDER

SEVEN-FOOT
ASH OAR PORT
& STARB'D

THWART FLAT
FOAM BUOY-
ANCY UNDER

SECTION @ STATION #6

SCALE INCHES & EIGHTHS

THWART FLATS 3/8"

QUARTER BRACES 3/8"

MAXIMUM SAFE
POWER 20 O.B.C. H.P.
MINIMUM FREE-
BOARD WEIGHT
90 POUNDS.

RECOMMENDED
POWER 5 H.P. TO
15 H.P.

MAXIMUM SAFE
HORSEPOWER
LOAD 500 LBS.

N.B. AS SHOWN,
BOAT IS UNSTABLE
WHEN SWAMPED;
FOR FULL RANGE OF
STABILITY, ENCLOSE
BOW/BACK TO MOLD
#2, AND QUARTER
AREAS AFT UP TO
BUOYANCE & FILL
VOIDS WITH FOAM.

BULKHEADS 3/4" THICK
FIR, PINE, OR CEDAR

BUOYANCY UNDER THWARTS EXPANDED OR
BLOCK FOAM; IF BLOCKS, SUPPORT CEDAR
OF BOTTOM ON TRANSVERSE CLEATS AND
ENCLOSE IN PLASTIC BAG FOR PROTECTION.
THIS BOAT WILL POSITIVELY FLOAT BUOY-
ANCY OF FOAM ABOUT 400 POUNDS.

FASTENING CLEATS
3/4" x 1-1/2" FIR
OR MAHOGANY

STANDARD SCUPPER
(FOR SKI-PLANKING
OVER CHINES)

CHINE LOGS BEVELLED
SAME AS SHEER MOLDINGS,
FROM 3/4" x 1-1/2" FIR

OPTIONAL SPRAY RAILS
SAME AS SHEER MOLDING;
(RECOMMENDED WITH
10 H.P. OR MORE)

BOTTOM 1/2" PLYWOOD

SHOE FROM 1/1/2" SQ/PINE
OAK OR MAHOGANY

DAVIDSON SCUPPER
(CHINES INSERTED
AFTER SIDES ARE IN PLACE)

QUARTER SKIDS 3/4"
SQUARE OAK OR MAHOGANY
ABOUT FOUR FEET LONG,
(MAY BE OMITTED IN
LOW-POWERED BOATS)

SHEER MOLD-
INGS FROM
1" SQUARE OAK,
MAHOGANY, OR,
FIR.

SIDES 3/8" PLY-
WOOD

FASTENINGS 1" #8
BRONZE OR EVERDUR
FLAT HEAD WOOD SCREWS
OR MONEL BARBED NAILS.

Sea Hawk, Sheet 1.

Sea Hawk, Sheet 2.

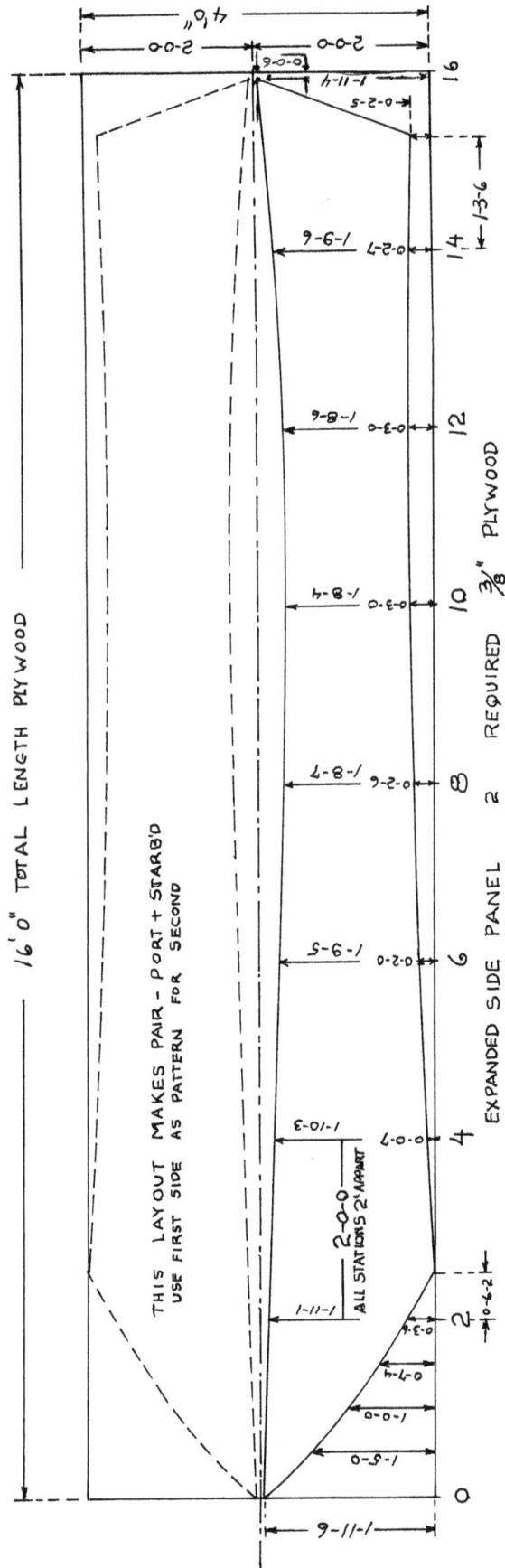

Side panel expansion. (Courtesy Dennis Hansen)

This photo shows the first Sea Hawk under construction. To build the jig, the forms were set up on a simple ladder frame of 2" x 4"s. Battens were sprung around the chine and sheer, and stiff, red rosin paper was hung on the battens to create templates for the developed shapes of the side panels.

(continued from page 120)

likely to bend edgeways. Staple or tape the paper in place, mark along the sheer and chine and along the stem and transom, and you've done it.

The two sheets of plywood for the side panels, which are end-butted, are cut right down the center with virtually no waste. Cut the paper pattern and trace it on your plywood, leaving extra wood 1" or so all around. Then cut out the plywood panels and spring them around the molds, making sure that they lie flat against the molds everywhere. Then mark its final shape against the chine and sheer battens and cut it out. Nothing to it.

With two people, you could just bend a 2' x 16' panel around the molds and skip the paper method, but that's because Sea Hawk's bends are so easy. Paper is easier to bend around the molds than plywood, and for a boat with more twist to the panels, paper works great.

Another method of developing (also called expanding) the shape is spiling. This takes time but is a very accurate method. Make up a spiled side pattern by tacking lengths of thin plywood together. Using any available scraps, even short pieces, works fine, as long as they're the same thickness and long enough to span each mold to which they are tacked. These should lay naturally along the molds and be end-butted to each other, then fastened securely with butt straps so that there's no play between them. You might have to cut some of the butts on a slight angle to allow the batten to spring around the station molds roughly parallel to the chine batten.

Tack the spiling batten to the molds near the chine batten, and set your dividers a little wider than the widest gap between them. Holding the dividers plumb and without changing their setting, scribe the line of the chine onto the spiling batten. Take the spiling batten off the boat, saw it to shape, remove the chine batten, and spring the template you've just shaped in its place. Repeat the procedure for the sheer template.

Then, with both the sheer and chine templates on the boat, lock them together by tacking short scraps of plywood between them every few feet. This doesn't require any fussy carpentry—just make sure the joints are solid. Mark the locations for frames 2, 3, 5, and 6, which will be the seat supports. Take the template off the jig, lay it down on the plywood, and trace the shapes to cut.

Both of these methods work well. I used the red paper method for Sea Hawk and the spiled plywood template for most of the Instant Boats to get their shape so that you wouldn't have to do it. And sure, there are more ways to do it, but this a fast, easy, and accurate way.

Before I get off this subject, suppose you want to make a simple, flat-bottom skiff of your own design with flared sides, and you want to see what size plank you need to get the shape of your boat. Make a scale half model first ($1\frac{1}{2}$" to 1' is good), with the length, beam, and depth desired, then just bend a piece of paper or light cardboard around the side of your model and stick it in place while you trace around the sheer, the bottom, the edge of the transom, and the stem. Take the paper off, and there's the precise shape for your side panel. It doesn't look a thing like your model looks in profile, but believe me, when it is bent around your molds, there's your boat—just like your model. Then use your architect's scale rule to determine the rest of the dimensions. It's just that simple. This is the same method that is used on the full-size boat. Now that you are all inspired for making your own templates, you likely won't bother to use mine.

Making the Molds

Making the molds according to the plans is quite time consuming. Each mold has to be built up from four pieces of wood that all have to be joined carefully, then bolted to the long 2" x 4" stringers of an elaborate, ladder-frame jig. We'll look at that method in more detail down below, but a faster way to build a single boat is to make each mold in one piece from cheap plywood.

The measurements for Sea Hawk's molds are presented differently than for all the other Instant Boats. Take a look at Cartopper, for example, and you'll see that all the dimensions are shown right on the drawings of the frames. Here, however, the heights and widths are given right on the boat's profile and plan drawings. Heights are measured from a baseline, and widths (half breadths, really) are given from the boat's centerline. Let's see how that works, using Mold No. 4 as an example.

Say you have a 4' x 8' sheet of plywood laying on horses in front of you. Look on the boat's profile at Mold No. 4, and you will see the measurement 1.7.1. The first digit represents feet; the second one is inches; and the third is eighths of an inch. So 1.7.1 represents 1'7⅛". (If the measurement were 1.7.2, the third digit would represent two eighths, or ¼".) This is the height from the baseline to the sheer. (You're building the boat upside down.) Conveniently, the edge of the plywood sheet is your baseline. At each end of the sheet, mark this height and draw a line straight across.

Now look at the other dimension for Mold No. 4: 2.11.5. Go back to the ends of the plywood and make marks 2'11⅝" up from the baseline on both ends, and draw another line across. This gives you the total height of the mold in profile from the baseline, which is the edge of the plywood at the bottom of the boat.

Now you'll get the shape of the sides for Mold No. 4. Look at the plan view (looking at the boat bottom up), and you will see that the bottom width is 1.4.4 and the sheer width is 2.0.1. Draw a centerline on the plywood at right angles to the mold heights. This centerline doesn't really have to be in the center of the plywood sheet, but it has to be far enough from either end to take in the angle of the sides. This angle is automatically established when you draw the lines right across the sheet for the bottom widths at 1'4½" and 2'⅛" on both sides of the centerline. Where the width lines cross the height lines are the corners of the mold. Remember that since you're building the boat upside down, the wider pair of marks, which represents the sheer, is closer to the baseline, and the narrower pair, which represents the chines, is above them.

Note that Mold No. 6 heights are 1.6.7, 2.0.0, 2.6.0, and 3.0.0 from the baseline. The reason for the extra heights is to give "close reference" points for establishing the widths for the slightly rounded sides back near the transom. When the widths are established at each of these points (1.6.0, 1.8.5, 1.11.1, and 2.1.0) and a small batten is sprung through them from chine to sheer, this slight curve will appear. That's easy enough, isn't it? All you have to do is know where you are headed and measure accurately. There's a note on the plans that says the offsets are given to the outside of the plank, but you can ignore this—just build to the dimensions shown.

If you want to assemble the molds from smaller pieces of lumber, as the drawings and photos show, draw a centerline on a piece of plywood, and draw all six frames to that centerline using the same method described above. Then build your molds right on the plywood, one at a time. I would start with Mold Nos. 6 and 5, since they're the same height from the baseline, then work my way forward for Mold Nos. 4, 3, 2, and 1.

When the molds are set up, they are placed 2'3" apart except for Mold No. 1, which is 1'10¼" from

Mold No. 2. Note that thwart flats (seats) are supported by the bulkheads that form the bottoms of Mold Nos. 2 and 3, and 5 and 6 (if you build the molds up from pieces).

Mark the locations for the thwart flat side supports (labeled "fastening cleats" on the Station No. 6 cross section) on the inside face of the side panels. You'll install them later, when the boat is turned right side up. If you're cutting the molds from single pieces of plywood, mark the bulkhead locations, too.

Transom and Stem
With the molds made, the transom and stem are next. The transom is made from ¾" plywood, with height and width measurements clearly shown. If you don't trust your measurements to be exactly precise, you can leave the top outer corners a bit high to compensate, if you happen to make deeper side panels than planned. Phil Bolger's measurements are very accurate, and when I was building the prototype, the side panels matched the transom sides precisely. I mention the higher transom corners as a safety precaution, because it is much easier to take off height than to put it on later.

The transom sides are beveled 6°, the bottom 19°, and the transom's top reverse bevel 26°. The ¾" framing is sawn separately and beveled, then glued and fastened to the transom. Temporary legs hold the transom in place for fastening to the sides, or the transom can be held freehand while you are fastening it.

The measurements of the stem's forward profile are given at 3" intervals, starting right at its upper tip. Lay out the stem from the end of a sheet of plywood, and sweep its curve in with a small batten. Its *molded* shape (the thickness seen in the profile view) is 2½", and it is *sided* (i.e., its width from port to starboard) 2¼". It is made by laminating two pieces of 1⅛" spruce, fir, or pine, or three layers of ¾" plywood. The stem is beveled at a constant 32° from the centerline. Leave it long so that you can fasten it to the strong-back during setup.

To assemble the jig, set up two long 2" x 4" stringers and fasten the molds to them at the intervals shown on the plans with nails or bolts. If you've cut the molds out of plywood, tack cleats to the top edges to give yourself something to fasten through. Fasten the extension legs on the transom to the stringers, and fasten the top of the extra-long stem to a cross piece that you nail across the stringers at the bow. Check the molds for squareness across the stringers, and brace them perfectly plumb. You're now ready to set her up.

Assembling Sea Hawk
With the molds braced and lined on a centerline, and the stem, transom, and sides cut, she is ready to go together. To make assembly easier, fasten thumb cleats—little wooden hooks—on Mold Nos. 5 and 3 at the sheer line to catch the

sides. Measure 2.3.0 from the bottom aft end of each side panel, drop the sides in the thumb cleats, check that the location marks you put on the panels are aligned with Mold No. 6, tack the sides to the molds—just one nail in each side of the mold is enough—and away you go. Fasten the transom and stem to the sides, and you are almost ready for the bottom.

Stitch-and-Glue, or Chines?

At this stage, you must decide if you are going to build this boat stitch-and-glue style or with a chine. The difference is in how the bottom will be fitted and fastened to the sides.

The bottom is made from two sheets of 4' x 8' x ½" plywood, butt-strapped or scarfed to length. If you are building stitch and glue, don't bother to plane the side panels' edges flat across, since the glass and goop will fill the gap.

If you are building with chines, they go in before the bottom goes on. They can be made of pine, spruce, or fir, ¾" x 1½". Cut them with 24° bevels, top and bottom. Glue and fasten these flush to the inside edges of the sides, then plane down the edges of the sides for a flat surface straight across.

Fitting the Bottom

And, of course, the bottom fit is done with the same method you have used before. Draw a centerline on the

The sides are on. I installed the chine logs later, after the hull was off the jig, and modified the scuppers in the bulkheads accordingly, as shown in the plans. If you'd notched the molds, you could install the chine logs before the sides go on.

bottom, lay it on the boat and align it carefully, then mark its fit to the sides from underneath. Take the bottom off, and cut it out with your circular saw at 24° for the cut (to save beveling after it is installed). Put it back on the boat, and glue and fasten it down with bronze ring nails.

Putting on Center Shoe and Quarter Skids

With the bottom on, she is closed in. Pull the nails you put in the molds to hold her sides in place, and lift her off the molds. Clean up any excess glue, place her upside down on sawhorses, and put on her center shoe and quarter skids. I omitted the quarter skids and the spray guards on my boat without experiencing any troubles in calm conditions, but you would probably want to install them if you plan to use the boat in rougher waters.

Bulkheads and Thwart Flats

Turn her right side up and put in the bulkheads for the thwart flats. You already have their sides fit, since they are the same as the molds, and their heights are shown on the boat's profile. Don't forget to put in the limber holes for water drainage, and fill under the flats with foam buoyancy.

Gunwales

I made the gunwales ("sheer moldings" on the plans) ⅞" x 1½" deep, with their bottoms beveled 30°, because I like them this way and they are less vulnerable for getting knocked off the boat's side if you are coming down on a float or someone else's boat.

Quarter Knees, Breast Hook, and Oarlocks

The quarter knees and breast hook go in next. Quarter knees need no explaining, as they are clearly shown, but some builders have trouble fitting breast hooks. An easy way to do it is to lay a thin piece of cardboard against the

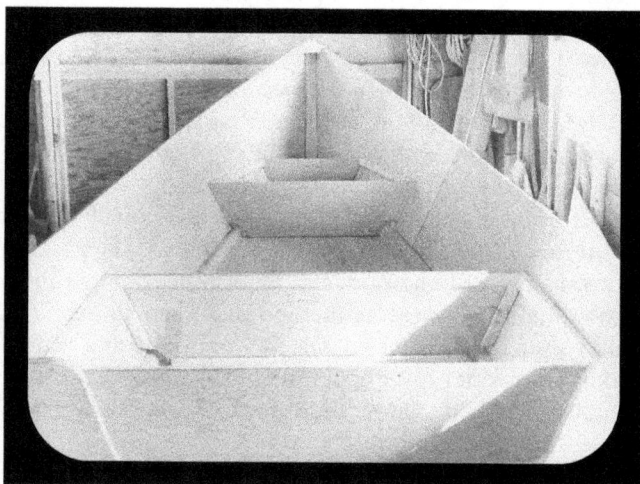

A view of the chine logs and bulkheads. Note how the scuppers fit around the logs.

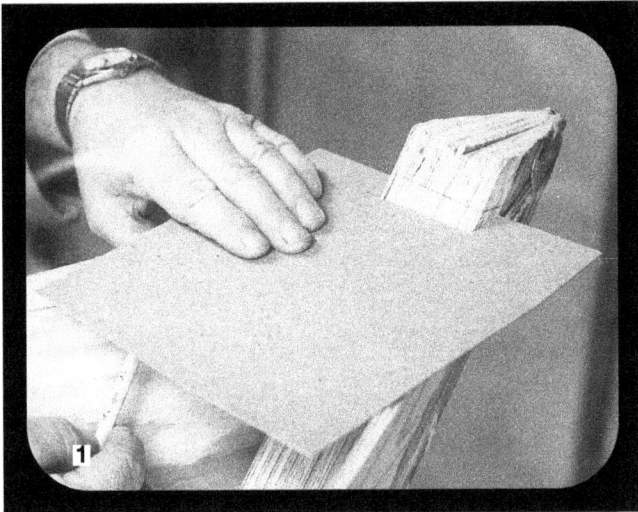

After cutting a tight fit around the stem, scribe the underside of the breast hook pattern where it touches the sheer.

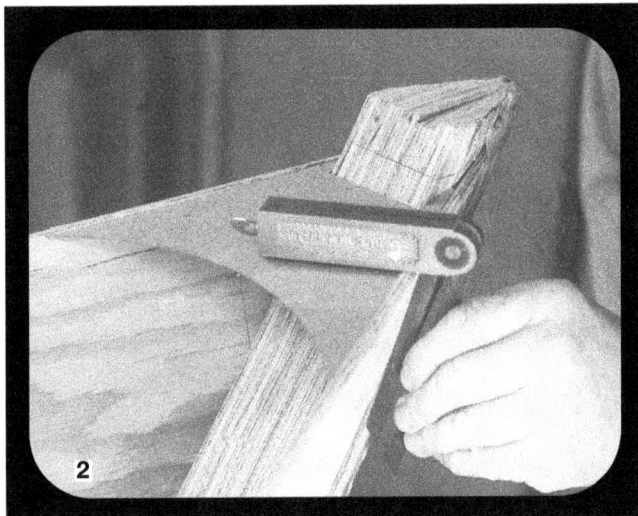

Take off the angle of the sides with a bevel gauge, and bevel the sides of the breast hook accordingly.

Making a pattern for the breast hook.

stem and across the planking, mark its shape from inside, underneath, take it off, and cut it to fit.

To find the bevel fit of the breast hook to the sides, place your adjustable bevel gauge with the body lightly on the cardboard and the arm following the flare of the side panel for a cross-sectional fit, or vice versa. Fitting to the stem is done with the body against the stem and the arm flat across the fit of the top of the cardboard breast hook. This is a simple, flat breast hook. If you want it crowned, then it has to be thicker to allow for crowning. A block plane and spokeshave will do the crowning job nicely.

The only thing left is the oarlocks, which would be the ribbed kind mounted with edge-mount sockets.

Sea Hawk's building technique is a little different from that of the Instant Boats and is perhaps slightly more of a challenge. But she's by no means difficult, and your reward is a fast, light boat. If it had wings, it would almost fly.

This fine, fast semi-dory has none of the vices of a conventional dory under power.

CHAPTER 15
DIABLO GRANDE

Diablo Grande is a larger version of Bolger's Diablo: The beam has gone from 5'0" to 6'3", and the length overall has stretched from 15' to 18'. Both are tough and fast, highly capable workboats and exhilarating play boats. If you have built the smaller Diablo, you will have no trouble building Diablo Grande from the building key: She is built the same way. She can be built open or with a watertight deck with which she is self-bailing, so that she can be left on a mooring exposed to weather.

The description of the smaller boat, which appeared in *Build the New Instant Boats*, applies equally well to Diablo Grande:

The source of [the boat's] versatility comes clear when you study her plans. With her relatively narrow bottom and her deadrise extending well above her waterline, she presents a minimum of wetted surface when lightly loaded, and it takes a really substantial increase in weight to pull that deadrise down even a few more inches into the water. [She] will not wallow under any reasonable burden of passengers or cargo, and with her [ample] beam, there's plenty of room for both.

If built open, she needs quarter seats, a strong mid seat, a bow seat, and flotation. There are enough frames in her so that she will be strong enough either way she is built.

If you like the Diablo hull shape but want a different size, consider Phil Bolger's Texas Dory Boat designs. These are available in 17', 19', 22', 26', and 30' lengths. Not Instant Boats, the Texas Dory Boats require some lofting, but not much, and the plans are available from the author (H.H. Payson and Co.; see Appendix for contact information).

(continued on page 132)

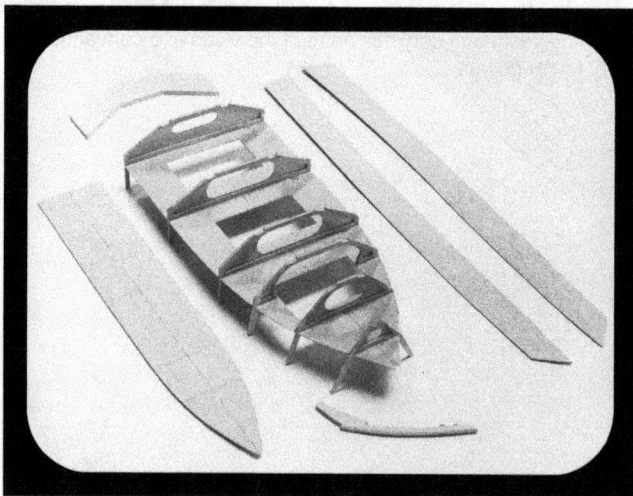

The model demonstrates the construction method for the full-size Diablo Grande. The frames and deck comprise the building jig for the hull panels.

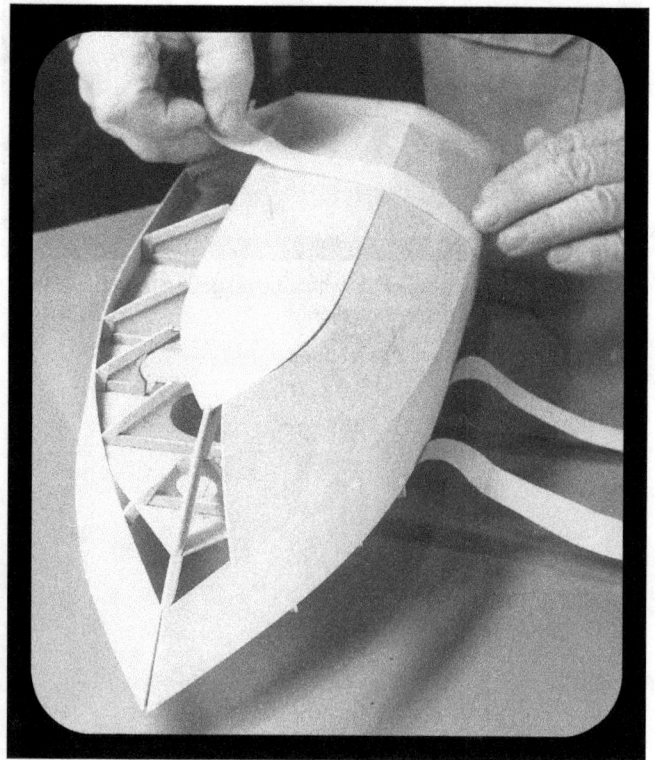

Masking tape holds the bilge panel in place while the glue hardens. Full size, you might get away with masking tape, but your other options during setup are wire stitches, duct tape, or hot-melt glue.

Diablo Grande, Sheet 1.

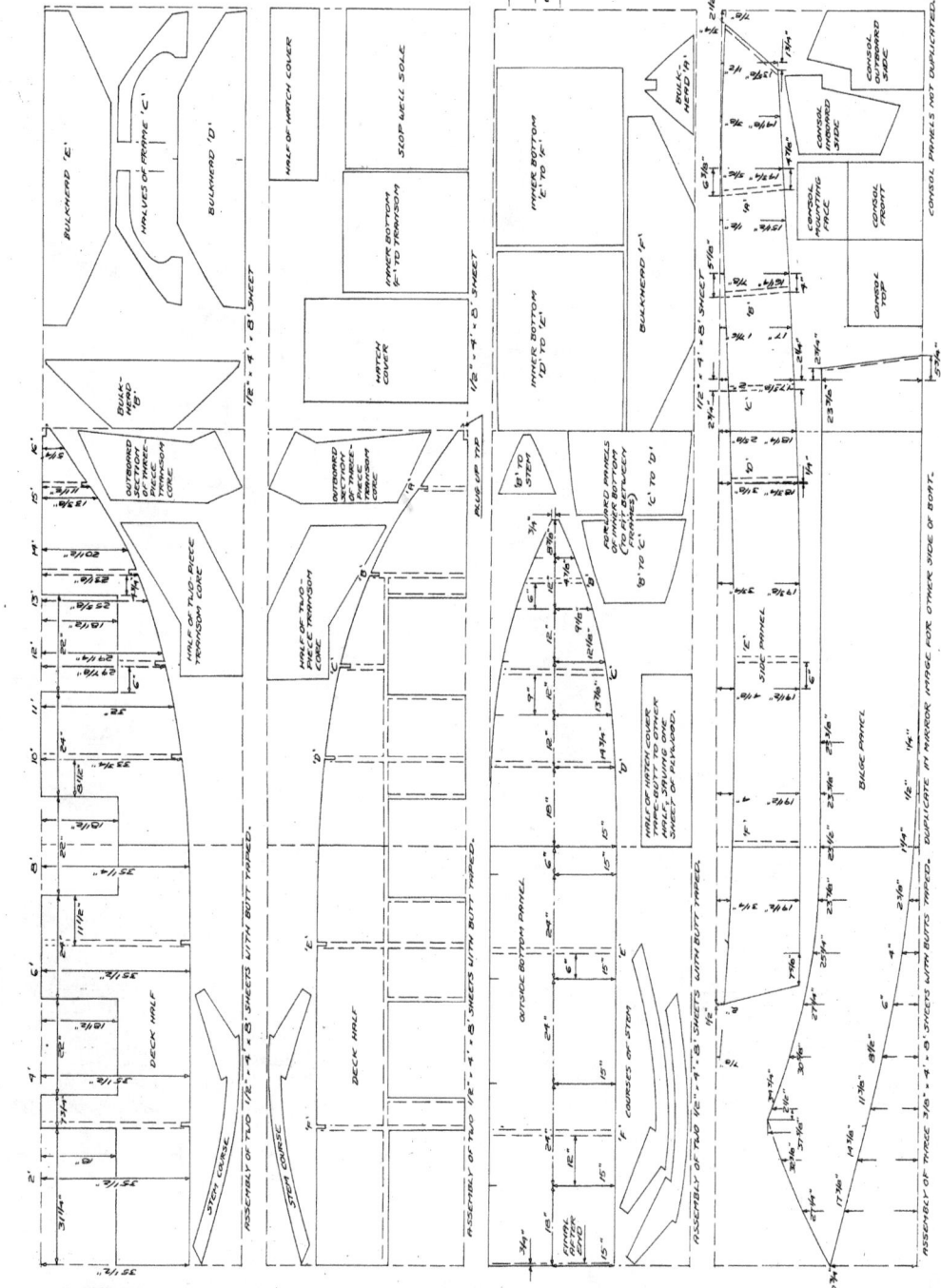

Diablo Grande, Sheet 2.

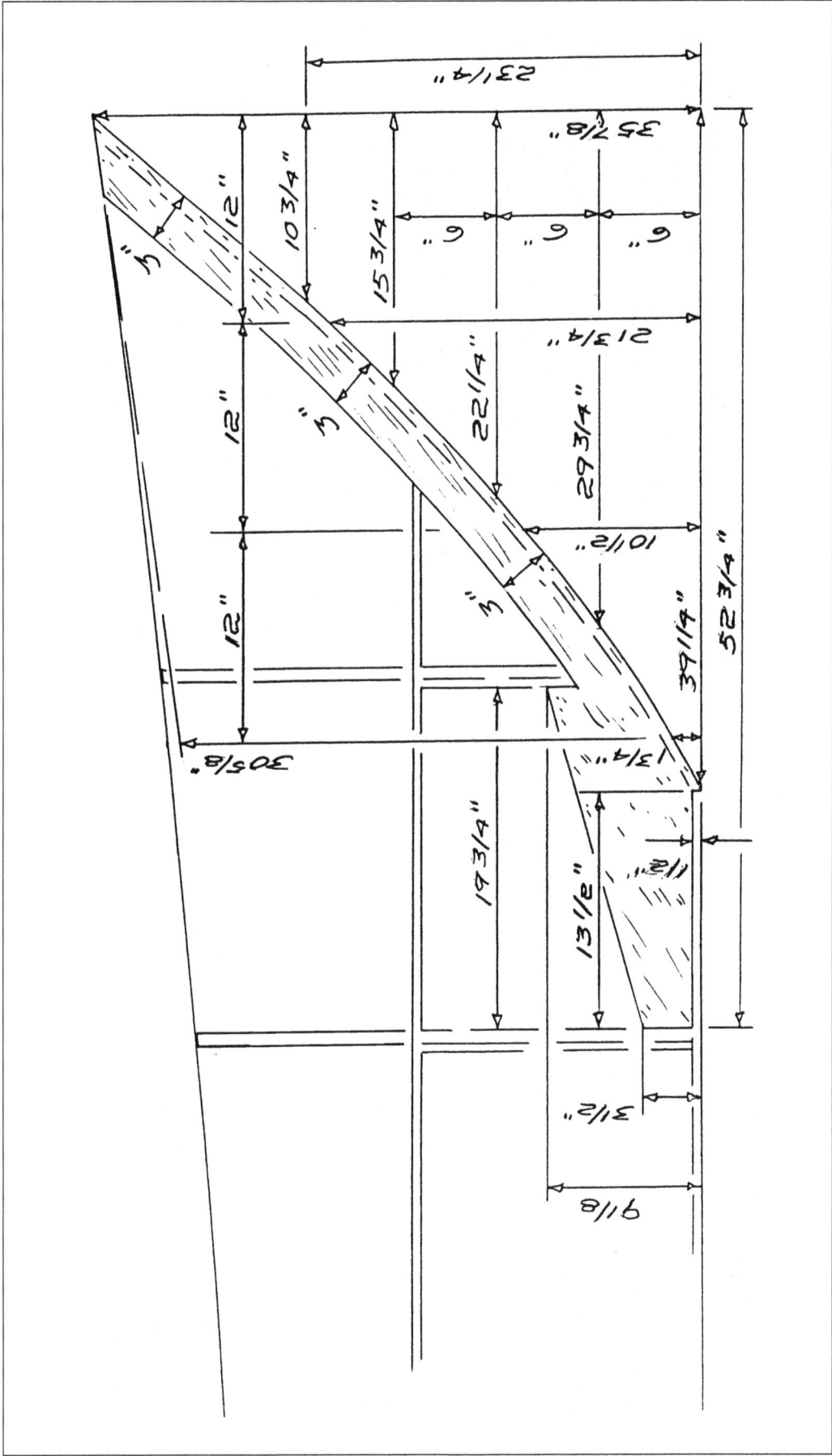

Phil Bolger didn't have enough room to include the stem details on the plans, so he made this separate drawing.

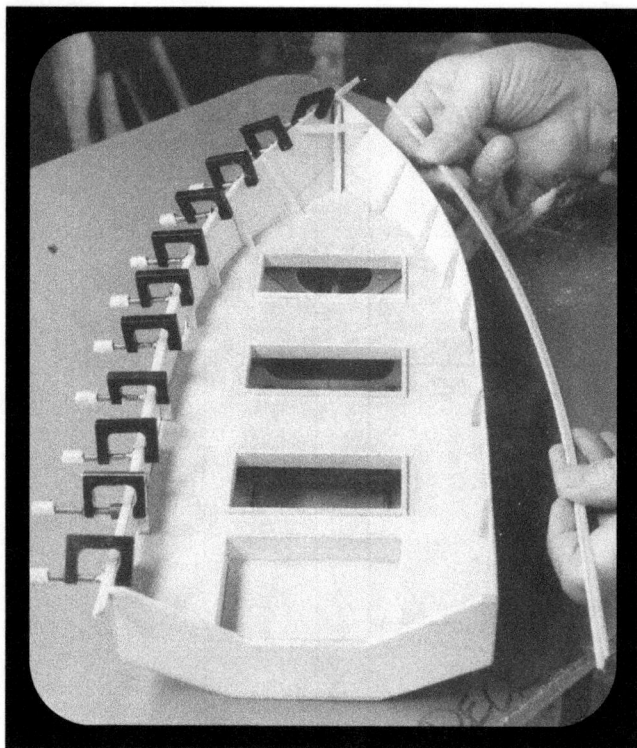

Springing the gunwales in place.

(continued from page 128)

BUILDING KEY FOR DESIGN No. 603, DIABLO GRANDE

Diablo Grande may be built open like Diablo, but with the stern well deck and the forward deck left in, or with a watertight deck, as shown. She also may be built right side up or upside down according to the builder's choice. This building key is for an upside-down orientation.

Materials

6 sheets, $3/8$" x 4' x 8' plywood.
10 sheets, $1/2$" x 4' x 8' plywood
20 yards of 38", 6-ounce glass cloth
2 rolls of 3" glass tape
3 gallons of epoxy or polyester resin
1 gallon of Fillite powder
1 2" x 6" x 20' house framing for gunwales and spray rails.

Side Panels

Lay out as shown; butt-tape 3 sheets of $3/8$" plywood together; make mirror image.

Bilge Panels

Make 2 from $3/8$" plywood; mirror image, as shown.

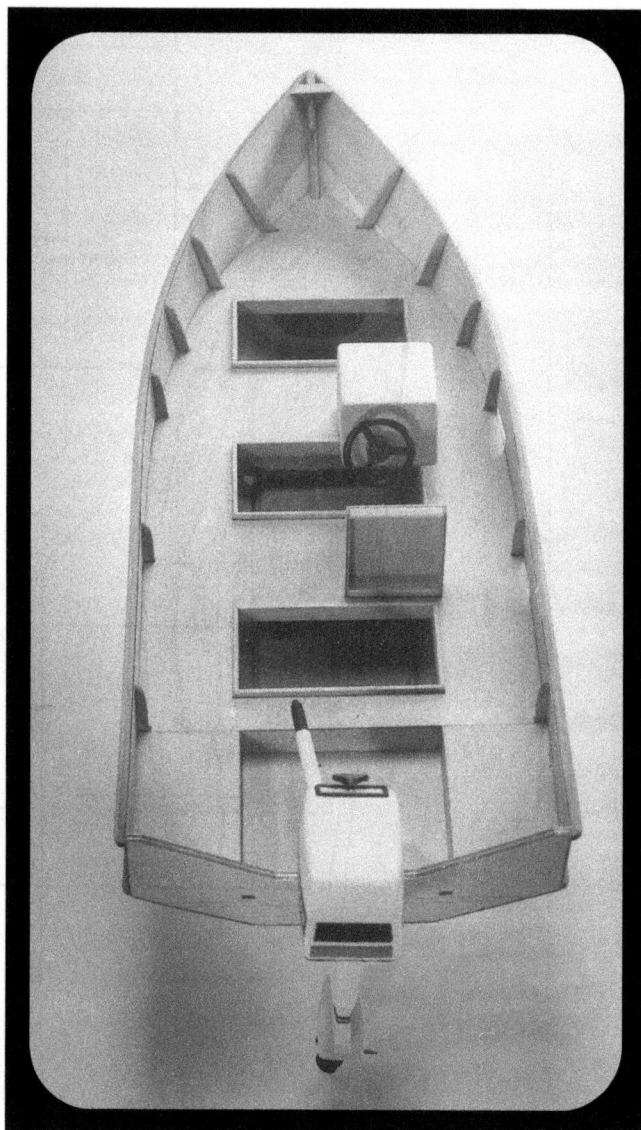

The finished mini Diablo Grande.

Bottom Panel

From 2 sheets butted together with matting and tape. Mark station locations.

Transom

4 from $1/2$" plywood; 2 solid inner and outer, 2 core fillers. Bottom bevel, 14°; top bevel, 19°.

Stem

From 4 layers of $1/2$" plywood, draw profile view (see separate sheet at $1 1/2$" = 1'). For stem bevels, see full-size stem layout. For locations, see profile lines drawing on other sheet (Section A from top of stem to Section B, and from Section B to bottom of stem).

Bulkheads

$\frac{1}{2}$" plywood framed with $\frac{3}{4}$" x $2\frac{1}{2}$" spruce or fir.

Assembly

1. Build the deck first. Cut notches for the bulkhead frames, place deck on level stringers sitting on sawhorses. Place bulkheads on deck, stick frames in precut notches, and align centerlines with centerline of deck. Temporarily nail or screw to deck.

2. Bottom panel, side panels, bilge panels, all sawn square-edge. Outer layer of bottom panel goes on next. Glue and fasten to frames with $1\frac{1}{4}$" bronze ring nails.

3. Stem laminate goes on now but not fastened yet.

4. Glue and fasten transom to bottom panel.

5. Glue and fasten side panels to transom, bring sides around bulkheads, and align their bottom edges with chine corners of bulkheads.

6. Check stem alignment to bottom panels' centerline, and temporarily drive in a couple of nails. Bring sides in to stem, glue and fasten, and drive nails home. Check stem alignment again to bottom panel; glue and fasten for good.

7. Fit bilge panels tightly inside; open outside to hold stiff mixture of fiberglass putty.

8. Wire joints together as needed with 20-gauge mechanic's wire.

9. Brush seams with resin, let soak in, and fill with stiff mixture of glass putty made from resin mixed with Fillite powder, Cab-O-Sil, or microballoons. Let seams harden overnight.

10. Next day, pull out wires, round seams, and glass with 3" tape. Glass outside of hull (transom first, then stem); put big sections of cloth in between.

11. Turn hull right side up and remove temporary fastenings from bulkheads; pull deck out.

12. Saw out inner bottoms and taper their sides on a table saw, as shown; glue and fasten to outer bottom with $\frac{7}{8}$" bronze ring nails or screws; remove $\frac{1}{2}$" scrap from bottom of stem and slip in (inner bottom B).

13. Cut out spray rails, mark location on hull, and bore holes through hull from outside. Glue rails and place on hull, and fasten from inside with 1" bronze ring nails.

14. Give inside seams a coat of resin. Mix up a fairly stiff putty of resin and filler, place in seam with rounded stick, place tape in fresh putty, and allow 20 minutes or according to temperature or when first coat soaks in and starts to harden. Long seams should be done early in the day, shorter seams when temperature rises.

15. Tape both sides of bulkheads to bilge panels and bottom panels.

16. Frame afterdeck and well area.

17. Seal hull with thinned resin.

18. Put deck back in hull, and glass-tape (same glass procedure) to side panels; fasten to tops of bulkheads.

19. Put on laminated gunwales, fit deck covers, and build console.

CHAPTER 16

18' CLAMSKIFF

She won't win any prizes for beauty. But whether she's lobstering, clamming, musseling, doing harbor work, or just fishing, here's one big, tough skiff that does it all and asks for more.

Phil Bolger designed Clamskiff for me to replace an old Novi boat my son, Neil, lobster-fished out of for many a year. Neil finally said, "She's worn out," and mentioned that he was a little afraid of her. "Standing in her the last fishing season," he said, "on her worn-out frames and worn-out undulating bottom, was like riding on an old carpet." Neil didn't dare fish out of her for another year, fearing she'd leave him out there.

In my twenty-five years of association with Phil Bolger, encompassing thirty-five boat designs up to that point, this was the first time I'd ever asked for a boat with a flat bottom, plumb sides, and a plumb stem. But I wanted these features for good reason: They contribute to a boat that's easy to build, even for the unskilled.

But even more important is the comfort of standing on the perfectly flat, steady-as-a-rock surface of the boat's

With Neil Payson, lobster fisherman, math teacher, and author's son aboard, Clamskiff shows that she's steady as a rock, even with an uneven load.

bottom and hauling lobster pots straight up over the side without bending your back. I had spent thirty years lobstering—some of it in small open boats with varying degrees of deadrise and side flare.

I had even designed and built my own outboard-powered, round-bottom, carvel-planked boat many years previously. Not knowing that much about building at the time, I over-bent my steamed frame tops inward at the suggestion of an old-timer who insisted they'd straighten out some later, giving me all the side flare I'd want. It never happened—the frame tops kept their tumbled-in position, giving her topsides tumblehome over nearly her entire length, with the result that she looked like a cigar.

This was back in the early 1950s, when there were plenty of homebuilt workboats afloat, and mine looked no worse than some of the others. I used her day after day and found—unexpectedly, and much to my delight—that hand-hauling pots over her tumbled-in sides without bending my back was a pleasure—at least in comparison to hauling them over the flared sides of my old dory. *That* called for both bending my back and reaching out over her sides, always off balance, and always with the result of an aching back at the end of the day.

It's hard to come by designs for big, boxy skiffs that are easy to work out of and easy and economical to build, and that will get up and go. Perhaps it's prejudice against their looks. Although you see them occasionally in harbors, going about their business of lugging heavy loads and doing what they're supposed to do, no one seems to know or care who designed or built them. Today, with prices sky-high on anything that floats, perhaps these work skiffs' time has come.

Two of my sons, my wife, and I built ours outdoors over a few weekends, Instant-Boat style, from fourteen sheets of 4' x 8' x ½" 4-ply underlayment plywood, using house-framing lumber for chines, gunwales, and miscellaneous framing. We didn't ask for 4-ply underlayment plywood; we asked for 5-ply AC, but the southern hard pine, 4-ply variety, was delivered instead and it worked fine. And at the price of $18.49 per sheet, the price was right.

(continued on page 138)

W.L. AT 1100 LBS.
DISPLACEMENT.

CONSOL CAN GO
OFF-CENTER.

SECTION AT 8'
LOOKING FORWARD

MOLD AND FRAMES AT 51 5/8"

TEMPORARY
BRACES

29 1/2"

21"

16"

18 1/2"

ABOUT
3.25
CU.FT.
FOAM

STEM FULL SIZE
2 1/2" SQUARE

26 1/2°

18'

FOAM BUOYANCY
IN FOREPEAK
ABOUT 140 LBS.

17'

16'

15'

14'

13'

12'

11'

OPTIONAL
CONSOL

10'

9'

8'

7'

6'

5'

PANEL OVER
FUEL TANK

PANEL OVER
FUEL TANK

4'

BUOYANCY
BLOCK
ABOUT THREE
CUBIC FEET
EACH SIDE

3'

2'

TOTAL FOAM BUOY-
ANCY AFT ABOUT
400 LBS.

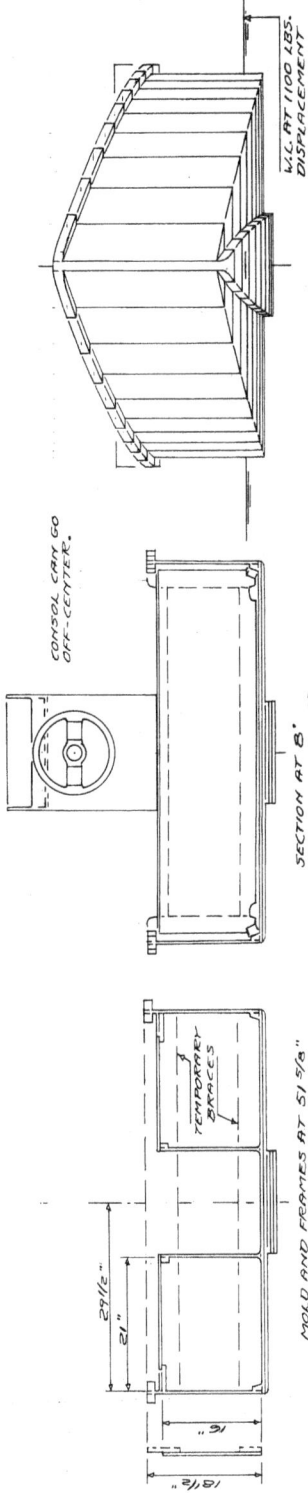

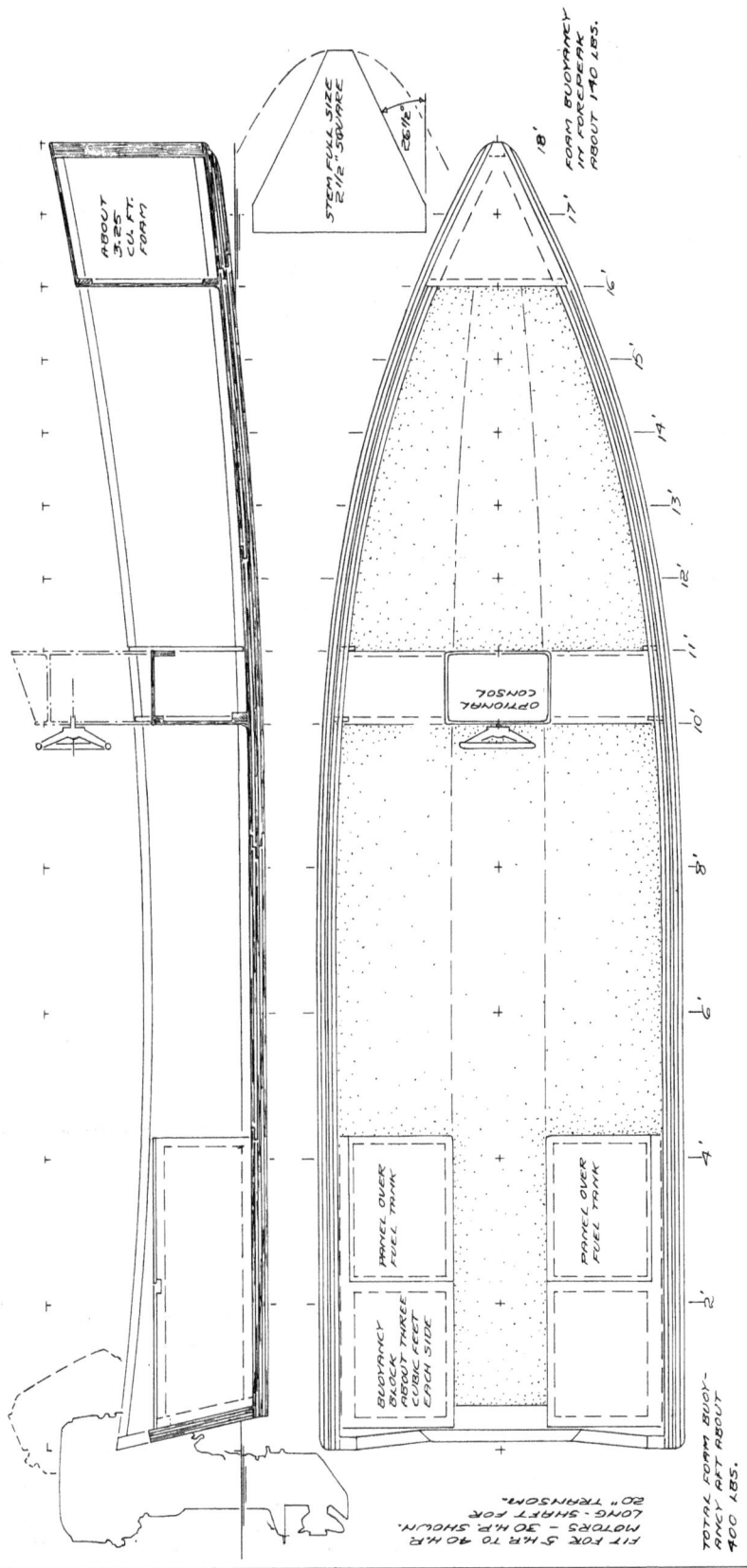

FIT FOR 5 H.P. TO 40 H.P.
MOTORS – 30 H.P. SHOWN,
LONG-SHAFT FOR
20" TRANSOM.

18' Clamskiff, Sheet 1.

18' Clamskiff, Sheet 2.

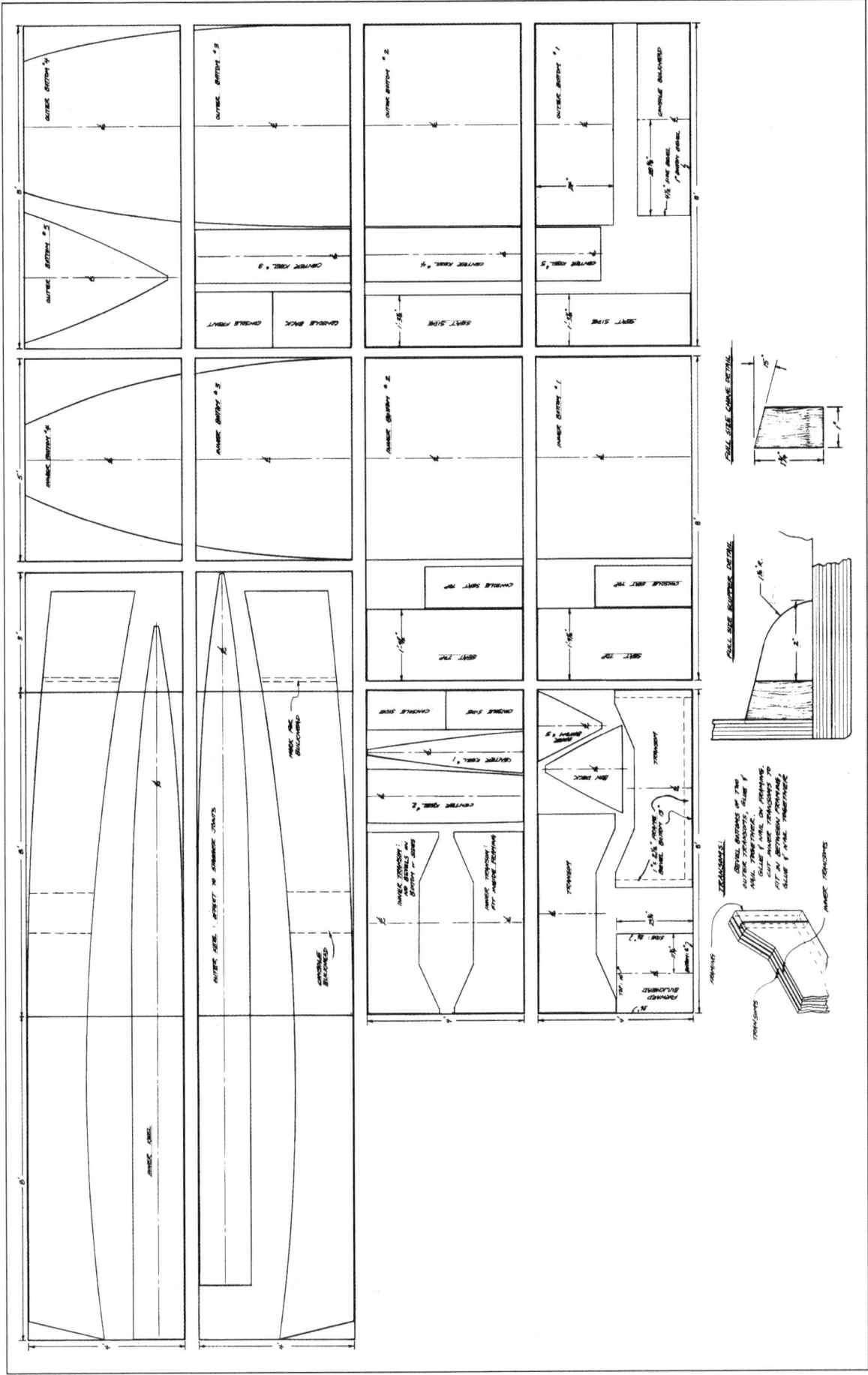

18' Clamskiff, Sheet 3.

Even though Clamskiff is heavily built, her flat bottom means that she planes easily with moderate horsepower.

(continued from page 134)

The fourteen sheets totaled $258.86. Three 1" x 6" x 20' pieces of porch flooring for framing, five gallons of polyester resin, and 41" of 50", 10-ounce cloth all brought her together, ready for launching, for a bit less than $500. (The other Instant Boats use 6-ounce cloth, but we use the heavier cloth here because Clamskiff will be used hard.) We did shop around some for fiberglass and resin prices. For instance, you can expect to pay eighteen dollars or less per gallon if it comes shipped in a can (for epoxy, add another fifty bucks). It does make a difference how and where you shop.

Building her outdoors and covering her at night worked fine. Outdoors wasn't by choice: My shop was full of models—too many to pack away and dig out again. One benefit of working outdoors included no problems with resin smell, dust, or noise (we're out in the "boonies"). The sun also helped at times in hurrying the resin to cure. This was the first boat I'd built outdoors, and I'd do it again. The photo sequence shows how easily she went together. You could build her by the stitch-and-glue method, if you wish, but building with chines and ring nails is quicker and cheaper.

Sea trials proved her worth. With a long-shaft, 25-horsepower Yamaha outboard, she reached somewhere between twenty and thirty miles per hour, getting up on plane on the 1½" x 16" wide plywood shoe, which also

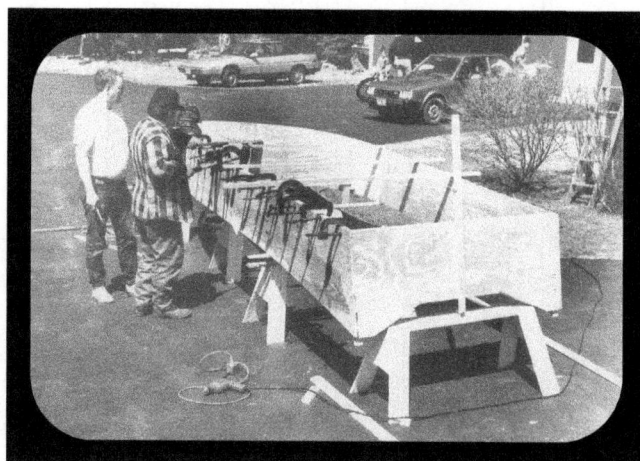

The author's sons, Neil Payson (left) and David Payson (right), use cross spalls to hold the sides at the proper width when springing in the chine logs.

The chines are in place and the first bottom panel is going on. The upright tacked to the transom holds a chalk line, which is stretched to the stem to check alignment.

The 16" x 1" shoe gets Clamskiff up on plane quickly and slows sideways drift when the boat is stopped to haul lobster pots.

helped slow her downwind drift when she was stopped in a crosswind. Her strong, ample sheer kept her from dipping her ends under. She's rated to take up to a 40-horsepower engine, but even 25-horses will move her along.

Clamskiff turned a profit for her owner in her first year of use. Considering her price, you might put her in the class of "disposable boats," but she's still going strong after thirteen years. You can build her from these plans drawn at a 1" = 1' scale on 22" x 34" sheets, including layout and these instructions.

Using battens to strike the waterline.

The first layer of the bottom is nearly complete.

Builder Bill Robelen IV backs up the work with a sledghammer while author's son, Neil Payson, drives nails to fasten the inner gunwale.

Midship bulkhead, showing limber hole cut in the frame.

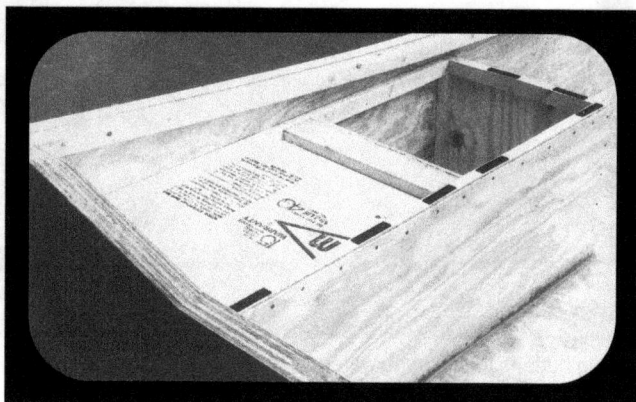

The quarter seats and bow triangle are filled with flotation foam.

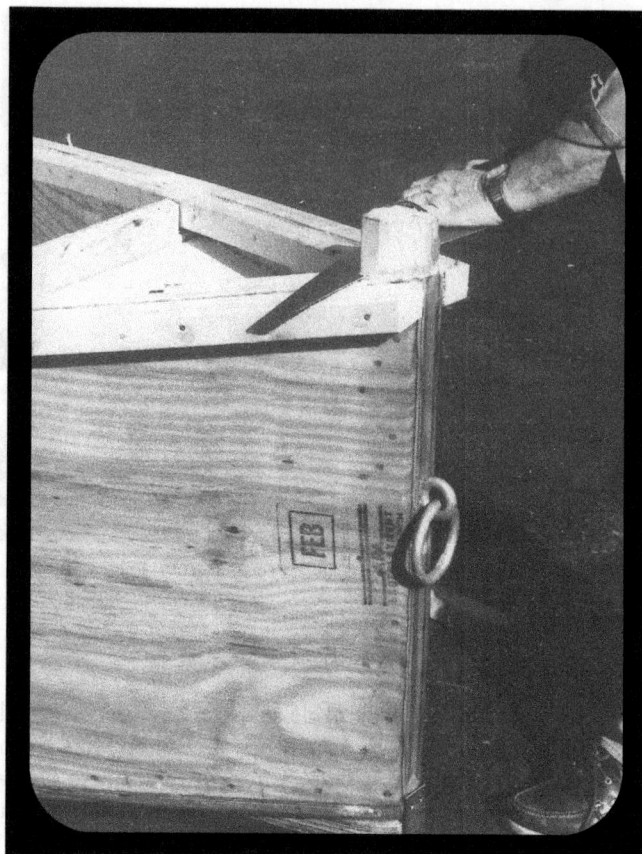

Install a big (½" x 4") ring bolt, and trim the stem flush with the sheer before installing the foredeck.

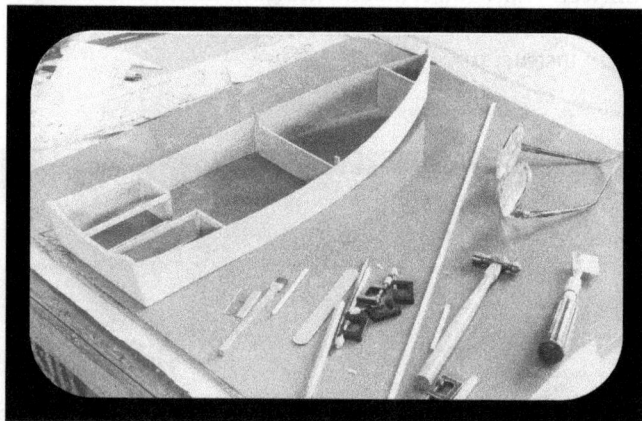

There's plenty of room to modify Clamskiff's interior arrangements, and doing it at a model scale is quick, cheap, and easy.

BUILDING KEY FOR DESIGN No. 606, 18' CLAMSKIFF

Materials

Exterior
14 sheets 4' x 8' x ½" AC or marine-grade plywood. Layout is for glass butt joints. Plywood is hollowed out for layer of 3" wide matting with 4" tape.

Porch Flooring
1" for chines, transom framing, and miscellaneous (about 36 square feet) or from 3 2" x 6" pieces of house-framing lumber, which is often available in 18' or 20' lengths, eliminating scarfing.

Stem
From 2½" square x 2'6" spruce, fir, or mahogany, with ½" x 4" bow eye.

Glass Materials
1 roll of 4" glass tape
18 yards of 10-ounce cloth

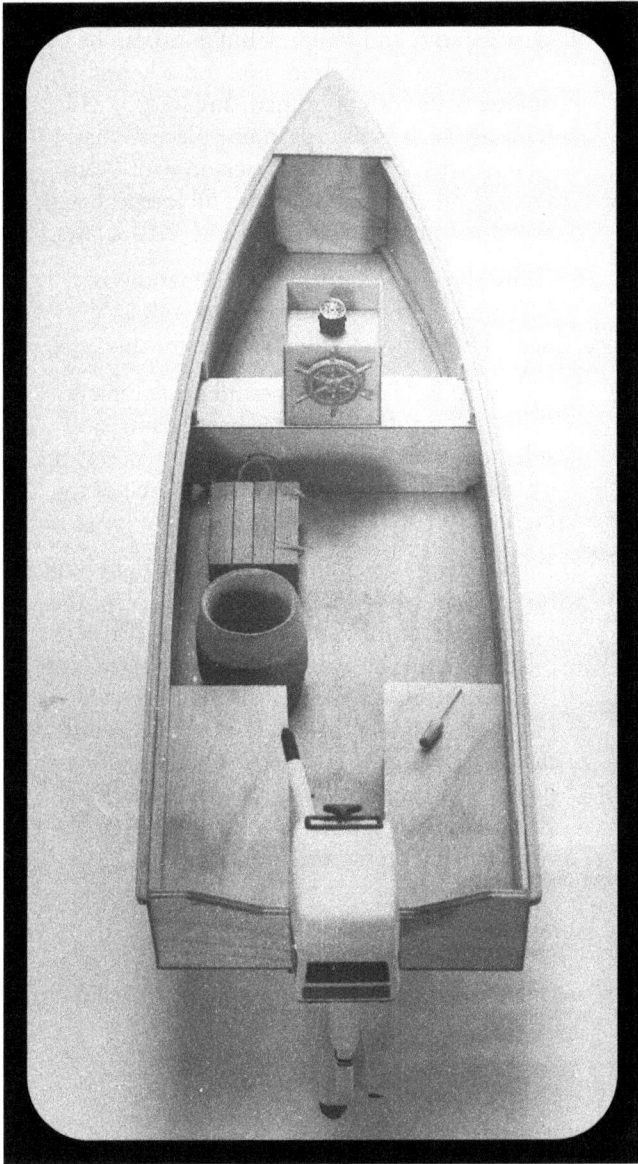

Rigged for lobstering.

5 gallons of resin (epoxy or polyester—epoxy is best but is much more expensive)
1 gallon of Fillite powder
1 gallon of acetone or equivalent
1 quart of epoxy to mix with Fillite powder.
Microballoons, or Cab-o-Sil, for gluing chines, gunwales, etc., if you are not going with epoxy all the way.

Nails
2 pounds of $7/8$" bronze ring nails
3 pounds of $1\frac{1}{4}$" bronze ring nails

Flotation
About 9 cubic feet Styrofoam house insulation—about 3 sheets of 4' x 8' x 2".

Temporary Supports
3 2" x 4"s

Assembly

1. Cut two outer transoms; bevel bottoms 13° as shown. Glue and fasten full-size transoms together and frame with 1" x $2\frac{1}{2}$" porch flooring. Cut two inner transoms (same size as the outer transoms but minus the frame width), no bevels; glue and fasten between framing.

2. Lay out sides (mirror image) on 3 sheets, end-butted together. Support pieces on board spacers every 2' or so; use wider boards under joints and cover with waxed paper. Mark sides for console and forward bulkhead placement. Glass-butt the joints, let them harden, and saw sides to shape. Carefully turn sides over so that they don't jackknife, and glass the joints on the other side.

3. Frame and bevel stem, console bulkhead, and forward bulkhead, as shown. Fasten sides to transom with $1\frac{1}{4}$" nails and epoxy thickened with Fillite powder, Cab-O-Sil, or micro balloons. Glue and insert console bulkhead (remember to cut the limber holes first); fasten cleats at the rear ends of the sides and pull sides in together with a Spanish windlass. Glue forward bulkhead; slip it in place, and fasten both bulkheads with bronze ring nails. Glue and fasten stem.

4. Check hull for squareness at the stern. (Sides and bottom are straight for the first 8' forward of the transom.) Before installing chine logs, fasten spacers the same length as the transom across the sides at the top and bottom, to ensure that the sides don't bow out. Stretch chalk line from center of stem to center of transom; check that centerlines of stem, console bulkhead, and forward bulkhead are in alignment before installing chines.

5. Cut chine logs 1" x $1\frac{3}{4}$"; bevel tops 15° (these are bigger than called for, but will go in okay). Glue with thickened epoxy and fasten with $1\frac{1}{4}$" nails or screws. If installing either chine pulls the hull slightly out of alignment, clamp a piece of 2" x 6" flat to the outside of the hull on the opposite side to pull the hull back into alignment before fastening bottom planking.

6. Temporarily fasten cleat across inside transom $3\frac{1}{2}$" from bottom to catch ends of three 2" x 4"s laid on edge 15" apart to support bottom from

sagging while nailing. Nail a short piece of 2" x 4" across the forward ends of the long 2" x 4"s, and install braces to the ground or floor. Spread thickened epoxy on chines and transom for first layer of 4' bottom, put on with toothed spreader, and fasten with $1\frac{1}{4}$" bronze ring nails to chine logs and transom. Fasten the inner and outer layers of the bottom to each other with $\frac{7}{8}$" nails or screws spaced in 6" squares. Set nails along joints about $\frac{1}{8}$" deep; hollow joints with disc sander with 20-grit paper. Saturate joints with resin. Lay strip of matting and a layer of tape. Saturate well, cover with waxed paper, draw joint with wide putty knife, and let cure.

7. Give outside of hull a coat of resin, let harden, sand lightly, and apply cloth. (This is the cautious way. If you are experienced, let temperature and how fast you can work large areas be your guide.) Glass transom first, then rest of hull. Trim overhang along sheer after resin has begun to set but while it's still soft. Seal interior of hull with thinned polyester or epoxy.

8. Bed the first layer of the keel in slurried resin; fasten with $1\frac{1}{4}$" nails, slightly toenailed. The middle and outer layers of the keel, made from short pieces, are nailed down one at a time. Keel can be glassed or sacrificial (i.e., without protection).

9. Quarter seats and forepeak bulkhead can be made tight to keep clean (no limber holes). Fill quarter seats with Styrofoam and lock in with framing. Make seat tops in one piece so that whole cavity is accessible; stick on with Velcro. Put $\frac{1}{2}$" x 4" bow eye in stem;, fill forepeak with Styrofoam. Put deck on with $1\frac{1}{4}$" #10 screws.

10. Gunwales—from two glued laminations of $\frac{3}{4}$"(inside and out) and fastened with $1\frac{1}{4}$" nails. Hull is turned right side up for this.

11. Waterline is 3" at 1,100-pound displacement. Paint hull inside with water-based paint; outside, too, if desired. Most any paint will stay on a glassed hull. Trials show 5" waterline not too high. A $\frac{3}{4}$" boot top looks good.

12. Paint scheme: green for outside hull, light buff for interior, white for gunwales, copper for the bottom, white for the boot top. Either latex or oil-based paint outside will stay on glassed area because the glass stabilizes the wild plywood grain. On unglassed areas, latex will wear off instead of cracking and peeling, as will oil-based paint. Repaint only when absolutely necessary. (Let paint wear off.) Layers of paint trap moisture, causing premature rot rather than longevity.

CHAPTER 17

15'6" CLAMSKIFF

This smaller version of the 18' Clamskiff needs little elaboration, since she's a carbon copy of the larger one.

She's rated for up to 35 maximum horsepower, but 15 to 25 horsepower would be plenty to drive her at a respectable speed. She uses a long-shaft motor.

The building procedure is nearly the same as for the larger version and calls for the same $\frac{1}{2}$" thick sides and 1" thick bottom, all from 4' × 8' sheets of plywood. Only the bottom plywood layout is different, since a 4' × 8' sheet laid lengthwise will do for her width. The next sheet is cut 9" shorter to stagger the joints between the two layers of the 1" thick bottom. The building key has the materials list and assembly procedures, so we will let it take over from here.

BUILDING KEY FOR DESIGN No. 618, 15'6" CLAMSKIFF

Materials

11 sheets of 4' × 8' × $\frac{1}{2}$" AC or marine-grade plywood. Layout is for glass butt joints—plywood hollowed out for layer of 3" wide matting with 4" glass tape on each side of joint.

1" Porch Flooring

16' lengths, about 32 square feet for chines, gunwales, transom, and bulkhead framing, or from standard house framing (wider planks usually have the best grain and are freer from knots)

Stem

$\frac{1}{2}$" × $1\frac{3}{4}$" × 2', spruce, fir, or mahogany. Cut excess length off later.

Ring bolt, $\frac{1}{2}$" × $3\frac{1}{2}$"

Glass Materials

12 yards of 38", 10-ounce cloth

Roll of 4" glass tape

4 gallons of resin (epoxy or polyester)

1 gallon of Fillite powder (micro balloons or Cab-O-Sil)

1 gallon of acetone or equivalent

1 quart of epoxy to mix with Fillite powder, micro balloons, or Cab-O-Sil, for gluing chines, gunwales, etc.—any job calling for gluing

Nails

2 pounds of $\frac{7}{8}$" bronze ring nails (all nailing called for is with bronze ring nails)

3 pounds of $1\frac{1}{4}$" bronze ring nails

Flotation

About 11 cubic feet of Styrofoam house insulation: about 4 4' × 8' × 2" sheets

Assembly

1. Cut 2 transoms from $\frac{1}{2}$" plywood to dimensions shown; bevel bottoms $12\frac{1}{2}°$ and tops (reverse bevel) 17°. Glue and nail together.

2. Pre-bevel bottom ends of side frames $12\frac{1}{2}°$ and bottom frame same. Glue and nail side frames to transoms, then bottom frame between. No notches needed for chines or gunwales shown.

3. Cut two inner transoms; no bevels, sides, or bottom to slip in between framing; glue and fasten.

Layout of Sides

1. (Mirror image) On 2 8' sheets, end-butted together, laid on spacers every 2' or so to keep plywood off floor or driveway to allow for sawing. Use wider board under joint and cover with waxed paper.

2. Mark sides for all bulkheads.

(continued on page 147)

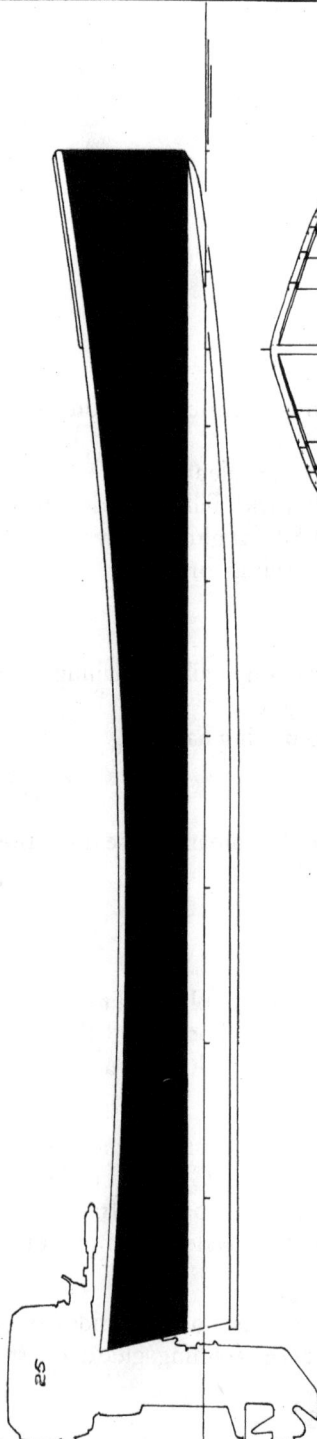
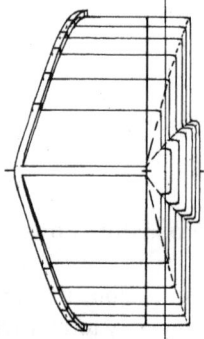
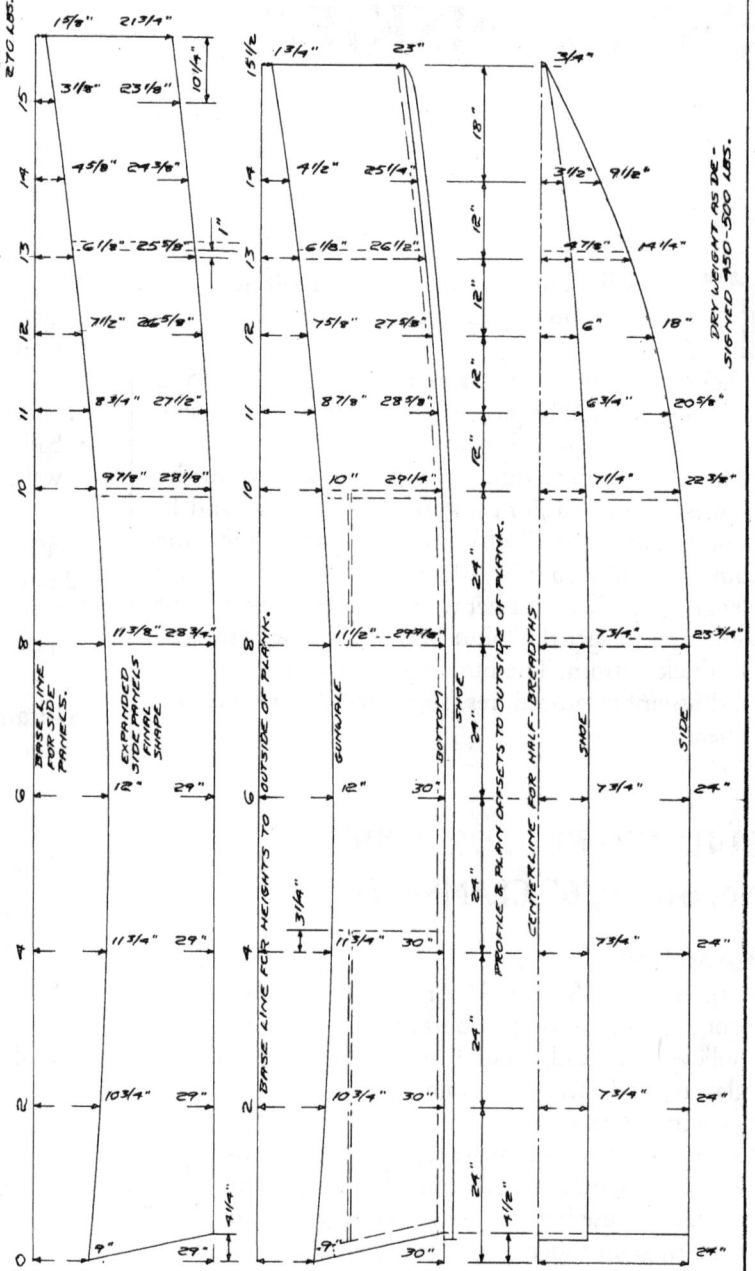
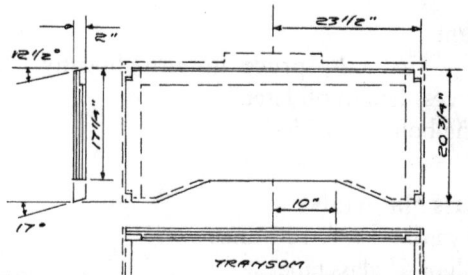

15'6" Clamskiff, Sheet 1.

15'6" Clamskiff, Sheet 2.

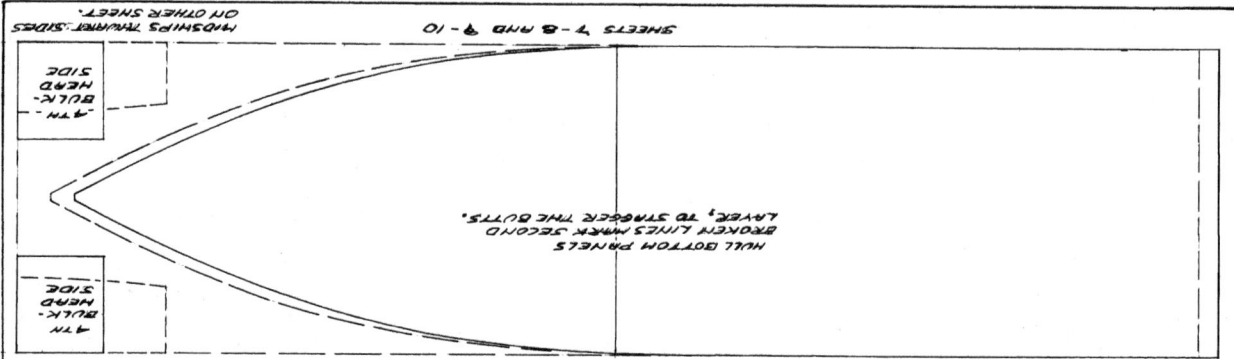

MIDSHIPS THWART SIDES
ON OTHER SHEET.

SHEETS 7-8 AND 9-10

4TH
BULK-
HEAD
SIDE

4TH
BULK-
HEAD
SIDE

HULL BOTTOM PANELS
BROKEN LINES MARK SECOND
LAYER, TO STAGGER THE BUTTS.

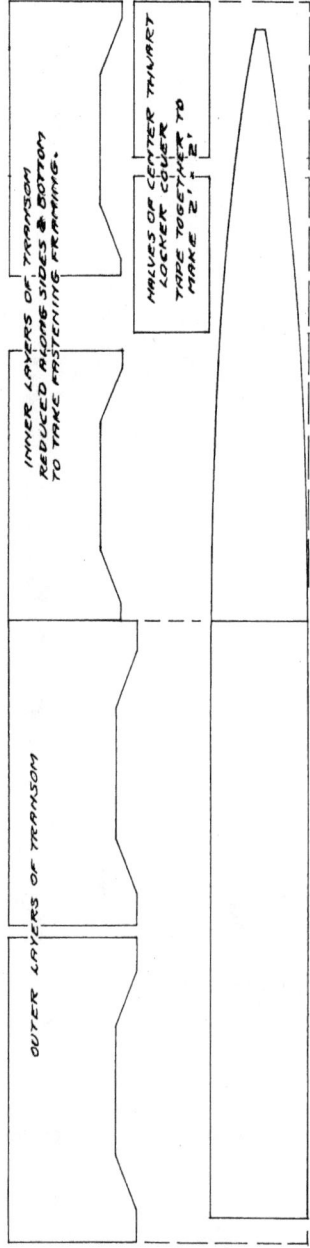

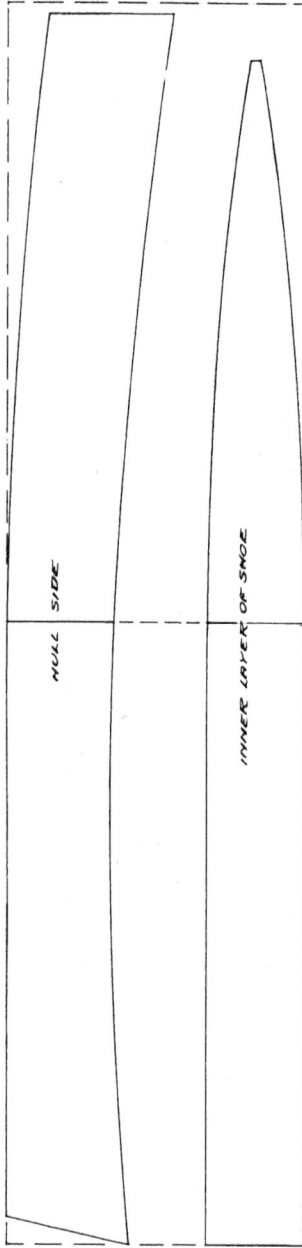

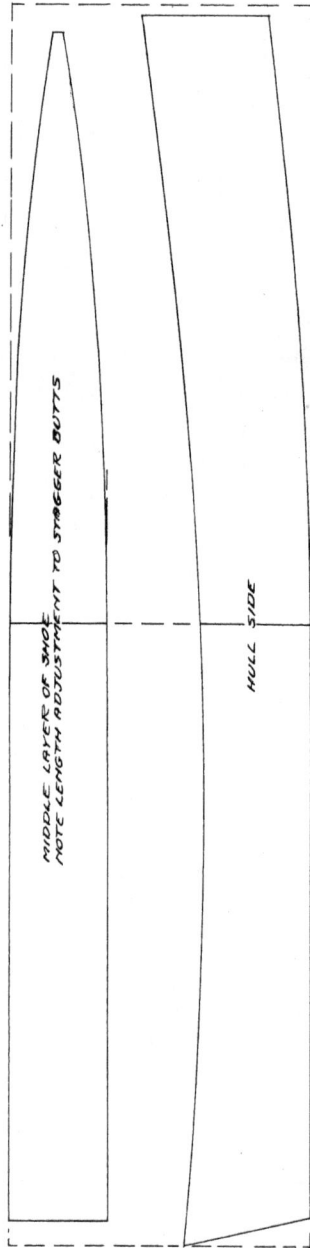

INNER LAYERS OF TRANSOM
REDUCED ALONG SIDES & BOTTOM
TO TAKE FASTENING FRAMING.

HALVES OF CENTER THWART
LOCKER COVER
TAPE TOGETHER TO
MAKE 2'. 2'.

OUTER LAYERS OF TRANSOM

HULL SIDE

INNER LAYER OF SHOE

MIDDLE LAYER OF SHOE
NOTE LENGTH ADJUSTMENT TO STAGGER BUTTS

HULL SIDE

SHEET 5-6

SHEET 3-4

SHEET 1-2

15'6" Clamskiff, Sheet 3.

(continued from page 143)

3. Glass-butt joint and let harden; saw sides to shape. Carefully turn sides over and glass joints on other side.

Stem and Bulkheads

1. Frame and bevel bulkheads as shown; be sure to mark centerlines and cut out waterways for chines.

2. With sides upside down, glue and fasten to transom with $1\frac{1}{4}$" nails.

3. Temporarily fasten 3 4' sticks across her sides, 2' apart from the stern.

4. Put in Frame No. 8; glue and fasten.

5. Nail stick on outside of bow ends of sides.

6. With Spanish windlass, bring sides in together and put in Frame No. 10. Then put in the forward bulkhead and the stem.

7. Stretch the chalk line from center of transom to center of stem.

8. Check centerlines of frames before installing chines. Cut chine logs 1" x $1\frac{3}{4}$"; bevel tops 15°.

9. Glue with thickened epoxy and fasten with $1\frac{1}{4}$" nails. If the installed chines pull the hull slightly out of alignment, clamp a piece of 2" x 6" flat to the opposite side to pull it back in alignment before fastening bottom planking.

Bottom Planking

1. Take 4' sticks off. Mark centerline on both sides of an 8' sheet of plywood. Mark off 8' along chines from the transom.

2. Temporarily fasten cleat across inside face of transom at the centerline, $3\frac{1}{2}$" below edge of the framing. This is to rest the end of an 8' 2" x 4" (actually 2" x $3\frac{1}{2}$") on edge, to support plywood bottom panel and keep it from sagging; brace its forward end to the floor.

3. Spread glue lavishly on transom, chines, and Bulkhead No. 8, and fasten bottom panel to the chines with $1\frac{1}{4}$" nails. Note that the 4' x 8' bottom panel is used to square the assembly. She is a box section for 6', so pull or push the sides out flush with the plywood edges, and nail them for 6'. Make sure that the bottom-panel centerline lines with Bulkhead No. 8, and finish nailing the bottom to the chines and the bulkhead.

4. Cut 9" off the end of another 8' sheet. Spread glue on it and on the bottom panel. Place it with its end at the stern, and fasten it to the bottom panel along the chine, transom, and No. 8 framing with $1\frac{1}{4}$" nails.

5. Fasten the sheets together with $\frac{7}{8}$" nails or screws in a 6" square grid pattern.

6. Lay forward sheet on hull and mark shape from underneath.

7. Remove, cut to shape, and repeat gluing and nailing process.

Glassing Hull

1. Round all chine corners and areas to be glassed $\frac{3}{8}$" or more. Give outside of hull a coat of resin, let harden, and sand lightly with 60-grit or heavier sandpaper, and proceed with cloth—this is the cautious approach. If experienced, let the temperature and how fast you can work large areas be your guide.

2. Glass transom first, then rest of hull. Trim overhang along sheer while soft. Seal interior of hull with thinned polyester or epoxy.

Keel

1. Put on inner keel bedded in slurried resin (note that it sticks out past the transom an inch).

2. Fasten with $1\frac{1}{4}$" nails slightly toenailed, and to other keels the same.

3. Round off edges and glass or leave sacrificial.

Quarter Seats—Forepeak Bulkhead

1. Can be made tight to keep clean (no limber holes). Fill quarter seats with Styrofoam, and lock in with framing that's glued and screwed to bottom.

2. Make seat tops in one piece so that whole cavity is accessible; stick on with Velcro.

3. Put $\frac{1}{2}$" x $3\frac{1}{4}$" ring bolt in stem; fill forepeak with Styrofoam.

4. Put foredeck on with $1\frac{1}{4}$" #10 screws.

Gunwales

1. Are finished double inside and out, 1" x $1\frac{1}{4}$". Put two freshly glued gunwales together and put them immediately on the outside.

2. Clamp to hull and fasten from inside with 1¼"
nails. Put one on the inside, fasten, then put on
the other with the same nails.

Waterline

1. Mark with string or batten.

2. Paint inside hull with water-based paint; outside, too, if wanted. Most any paint will stay on
a glassed hull.

Paint Scheme

Green for outside hull, light buff or gray for interior.
White gunwales, copper bottom. Either latex or oil-
based paint will stay on glassed area because the glass
stabilizes the wild plywood grain. On unglassed
areas (inside), latex will wear off instead of cracking
and peeling, as does oil-based paint. Repaint only
when necessary (let paint wear off). Layers of paint
trap moisture, causing premature rot rather than
longevity.

CHAPTER 18

SNEAKEASY

Writing about Sneakeasy in *Boats with an Open Mind,* Phil Bolger explained that the boat was designed for an owner who:

. . . wanted a fast launch to use in the canals of a Florida coastal development and nearby bays and bayous. Aside from some style and character, he wanted a boat that wouldn't have much wake to disturb a neighborhood in which everybody keeps a boat tied up at the back fence.

Reminiscent of the classy mahogany speedboats of the 1920s, Sneakeasy has a flat bottom and shallow draft that make her easily driven and allow a speed of about twelve miles per hour with the 7.5-horsepower motor noted on the plans. As Phil wrote, "The light motor and minimum fuel demand are elements of the light weight that's basic to no-wake running."

Sneakeasy isn't limited to slow, quiet running, however. With a 35-horsepower engine, she'll go thirty-two miles per hour, and you could go a lot faster with more horses. But you might not want to. Go too fast, and in a sharp turn, she'll likely trip over her square chine and tip you out. As Phil said:

The long shoe down the middle of Sneakeasy's bottom is intended to stop her from skidding, but at a high enough speed it will lose effectiveness. She's quite capable of making 50 or 60 mph, but nobody should take children for a ride in a high-powered boat like this.

Okay, so this is a boat that can go slow, very quietly, or go very fast, but should do so only with a great deal of care and eyes wide open to her limitations. She's not made for rough water. But she goes together very quickly and easily, considering her size and looks.

But without any instructions given, where do you start?

Start by finding a good, comfortable spot, and with plans in hand, spend a few hours, or whatever time it takes, to understand where to begin and how fancy you want to build her.

The hull is simple enough to build, since it is basically a box section, but the turtleback deck, planked with ³⁄₈"

thick individual planks all nibbed into a covering board, isn't. To get around this difficulty, you could build the deck from ¼" or thinner plywood.

BUILDING THE SNEAKEASY

Materials

Before you can get into any of the building procedures, you have to figure out the basic materials. Biggest items first: Using the scale rule at ¾" = 1', you see that both sides of the boat can be cut from four sheets of ¼" × 4' × 8' plywood, end-butted, if you lay out the panels facing opposite directions. Another three or four ¼" × 4' × 8' sheets are needed for the frames, etc. Four sheets of ½" × 4' × 8' are needed for the bottom, plus another for the transom and the bottom butt straps. You will need 33 lineal feet of 3½" × ¾" pine, spruce, or fir for her floorboards, and about 40 lineal feet for the framing on the frames. For chines, clamps, and gunwales, I'd buy a couple of the clearest 2" × 8" × 14' boards I could find, and plan on scarfing the gunwales and chines. The transom sheathing is made from 2" × 4"s.

Of course, there is more stuff you might want to buy (which is apparent on the plans), so I'm not going into how many nails, screws, fiberglass, and paint you will need. Sneakeasy, with her lightness of building and tendency to pound at high speeds, is a good case for using epoxy throughout her building. What is given here is enough to get you started.

Assembly

Be sure the transom location and all the frame locations are precisely marked on the sides, which are cut out square edged. Build the frames for Frames Nos. 2, 4, 6, 8, and 10. Bevel the ones for which bevels are indicated, and notch them for the chines and sheer clamps. (Clamps are what the coamings and deck are nailed to.) I recommend that the clamps be molded deeper than the 1½" shown; therefore, cut the notches deeper accordingly. And be sure that the centerline is marked on all the frames.

(continued on page 152)

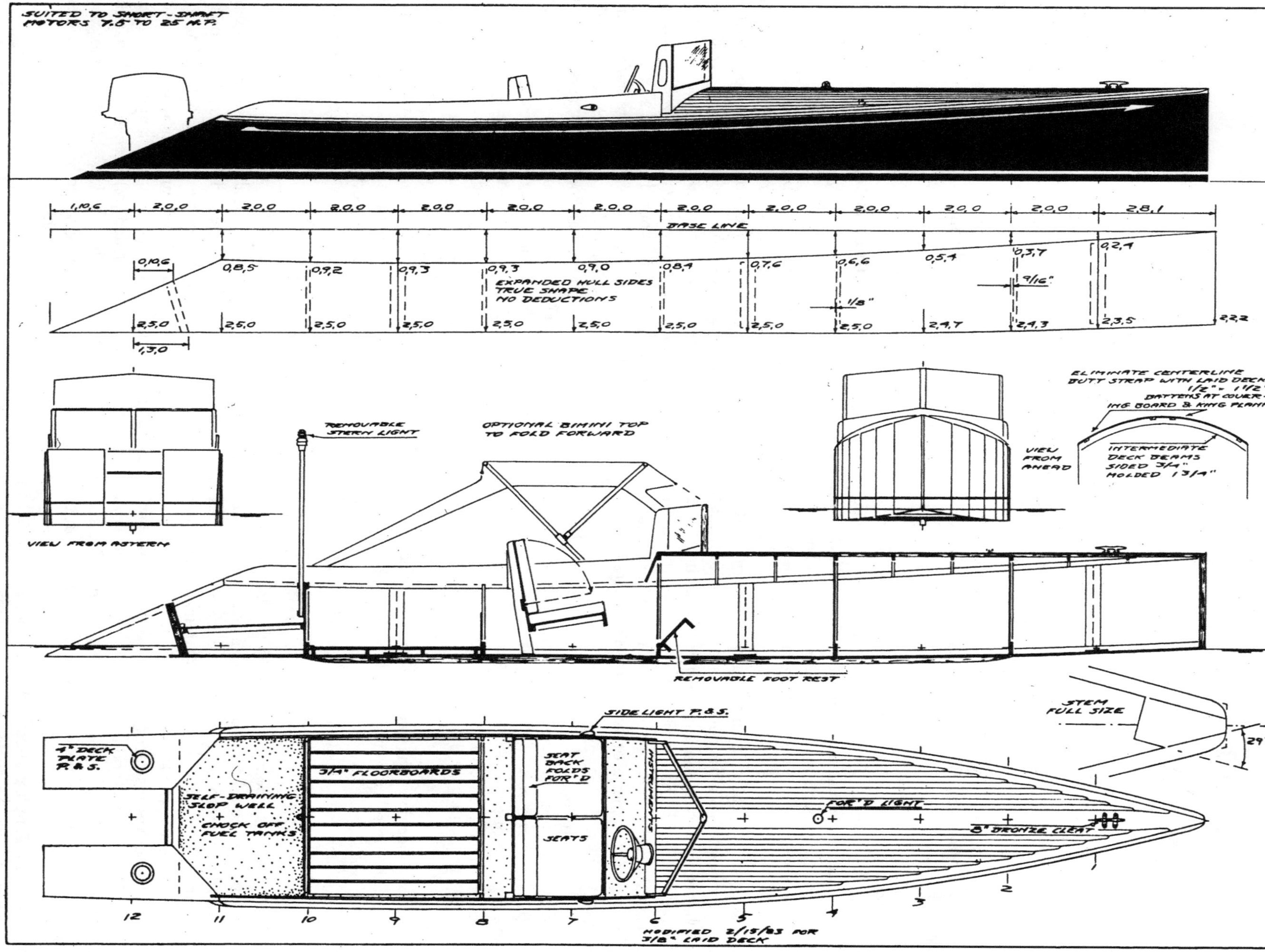

SUITED TO SHORT-SHAFT
MOTORS 7.5 TO 25 H.P.

BASE LINE

EXPANDED HULL SIDES
TRUE SHAPE
NO DEDUCTIONS

ELIMINATE CENTERLINE
BUTT STRAP WITH LAID DECK.
1/2" - 1/2"
BATTENS AT COVER-
ING BOARD & KING PLANK

INTERMEDIATE
DECK BEAMS
SIDED 3/4"
MOLDED 1 3/4"

VIEW FROM AHEAD

OPTIONAL BIMINI TOP
TO FOLD FORWARD

REMOVABLE FOOT REST

REMOVABLE STERN LIGHT

VIEW FROM ASTERN

STEM
FULL SIZE

24°

PORT LIGHT

SIDE LIGHT P. & S.

6" BRONZE CLEAT

INSTRUMENTS

SEAT
BACK
FOLDS
FWD

SEATS

3/4" FLOORBOARDS

SELF-DRAINING
STEP WELL

CHOCK OFF
FUEL TANKS

4" DECK
PLATE
P. & S.

MODIFIED 2/15/83 FOR
3/8" LAID DECK

28.1
92.1
2.3.5
0.5.7
2.1.3
0.5.4
2.4.7
0.6.6
2.5.0
0.7.6
2.5.0
0.8.4
2.5.0
0.9.0
2.5.0
0.9.3
2.5.0
0.9.3
2.5.0
0.9.2
2.5.0
0.8.5
2.5.0
0.9.6
2.5.0
1.7.0

9/16"
1/8"

20.0 20.0 20.0 20.0 20.0 20.0 20.0 20.0 20.0 20.0 20.0 20.0

1.9.6

12 11 10 9 8 7 6 5 4 3 2

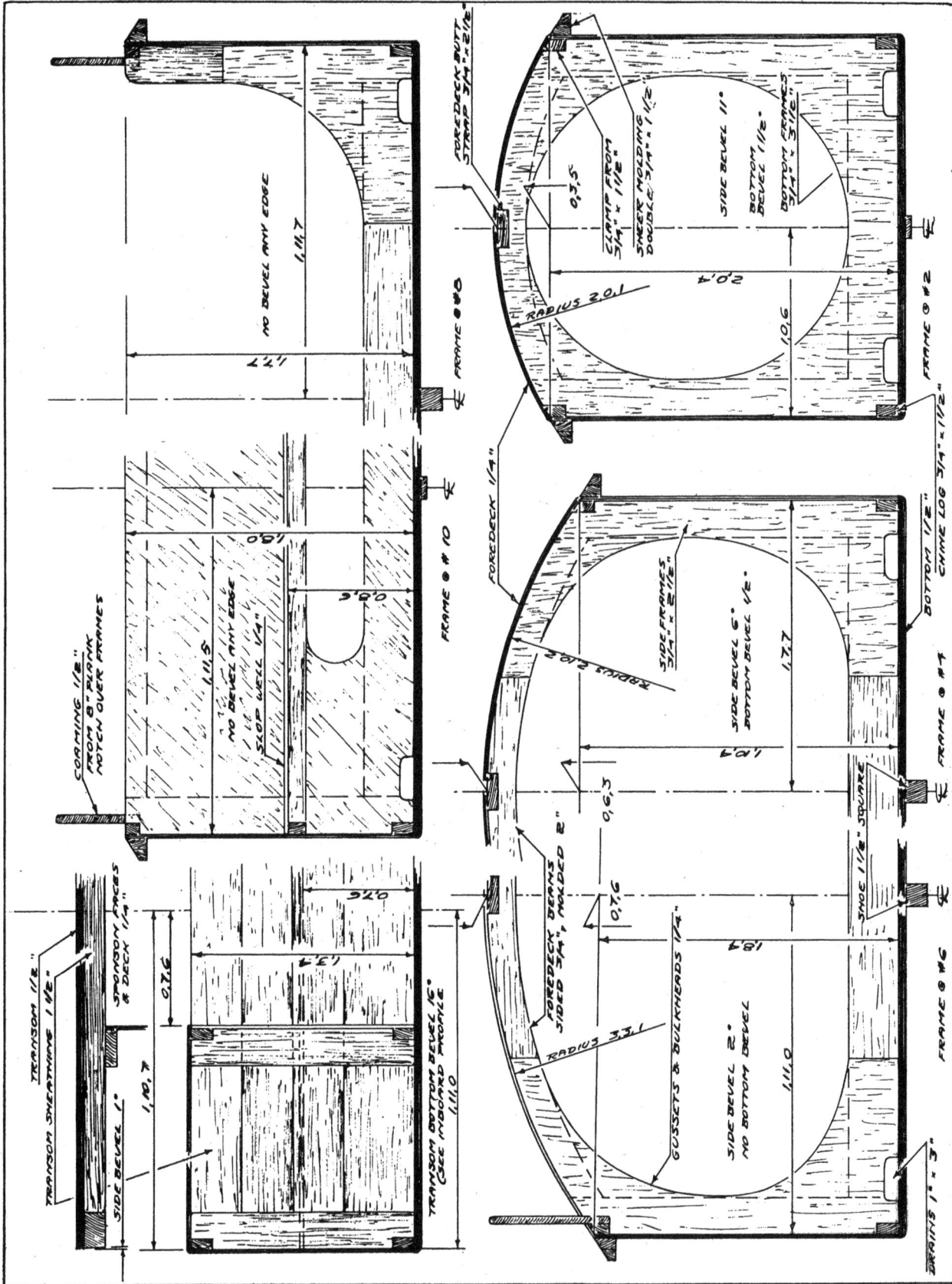

Sneakeasy, Sheet 2.

(continued from page 149)

You will build her upside down on three or more saw-horses. You can get by with three by fastening the sides to Bulkhead Nos. 10, 6, and 2, then slipping in Nos. 8 and 4. Cut the stem 29° as shown, then glue and fasten it to one side. Bring the other side in. Make sure that both edges of the sides are same height; then glue and fasten.

The transom is sheathed with planking that is fastened to ½" plywood, beveled, then glued and fastened in place. Now, if you have remembered to notch the frames, you can glue and fasten the chines in place. Make a final check to see that all the centerlines are marked everywhere and that the limber holes are cut (they are hard to put in later if you forget them) before the bottom goes on. Also, be sure that there are no dried clumps of glue in the way to hold the bottom from being flat-fit to the chines. Work cleanly.

The bottom-panel butt joints can be made with straps, as shown, or with fiberglass. Regardless of how it is done, draw centerlines on both sides of the 4' x 8' sheets. The one underneath is for aligning with the centerlines of the frames, and the one on the other side is to align the 1½" square shoe so that the boat will track straight. The shoe tapers at its ends and is glued and fastened to the bottom before the bottom is put on the boat. This is a whole lot easier to do now than when the boat is upside down and you have to fasten the shoe from underneath. Fitting the bottom to the shape of the sides is easy: Just match the centerlines of the bottom with the frames, tack the bottom in place, and mark its shape from underneath around the sides. Then take it off and cut it out. If you butt-strap the bottom sections together, you'll need help to put it back on. If you're working alone, you can put it on in sections, Clamskiff-style.

Note the triangular "sponsons" that extend out beyond the bottom aft and form a tunnel on both sides of the engine. I'd let the bottom extend out to support them, and box them in as shown, leaving a 15½" wide tunnel. Framing for the sponsons is external. Note that the bottom extends beyond the transom by 3". The chines butt against the inside of the transom; they do not pass through.

With her bottom on, she can be turned right-side up and finished topside. The sponsons' sides and tops are closed in, and clamps for the coaming and the deck go in.

I'd put the gunwales on before the coamings or the deck go on, because you can reach inside for good clamping. As for the deck, I'd take the easiest way and put it on with ¼" plywood. If you find it a bit stiff to bend, put some hot, wet towels on it and let it set awhile. A few remaining things, such as the slop well, the floorboards, the seats, and the windshield, complete her. If you've gotten this far, you can do the rest.

CHAPTER 19
CATFISH

For extended, comfortable cruising, this little 15' 1½" stitch-and-glue boat has a lot going for it. Ballast is in the form of a free-flooding keel, which means you don't have to lug extra weight around with you. When you put her on her trailer, it all runs out.

Catfish has a spacious, open-topped, walk-through cabin, with room for a portable toilet up forward. Should she suffer a knockdown, she can lay flat on her side without shipping water. The big cockpit allows room for overnighting with a shelter from a canvas spray hood, which can be made with a choice of the two styles shown, both of which are easy to put up and take down. Her rudder is inboard, and it has an end plate to ensure a good bite in the water when the boat is heeled.

A 3- to 5-horsepower motor is ample to drive her when the wind goes down. I haven't built her full-size, but I found no hard spots when I built a model of her. Like the other Instant Boats, she is built upside down. The sides go on first, then the bottom panel, and finally the bilge panels to close her in.

Catfish has quite a few parts and pieces, but the building key with a numbered building sequence provides adequate guidance. The only thing missing is a bill of materials. She takes ten sheets of ¼" x 4' x 8' plywood, a small amount of spruce, fir, or pine plank for the keel and stem, and a small amount of ¾" thick lumber for the framing

(continued on page 158)

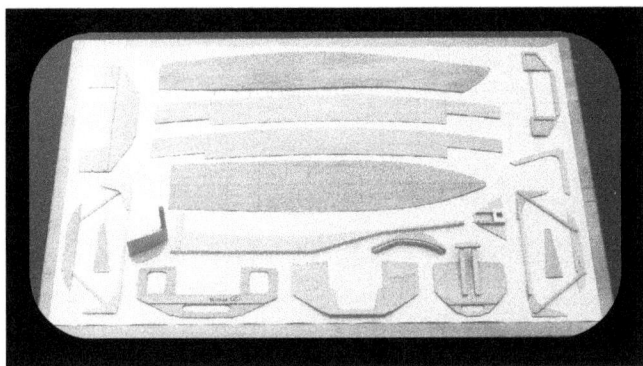

A temporary batten along the bottom centerline holds everything in alignment while waiting for the stem and forward bulkhead to go in.

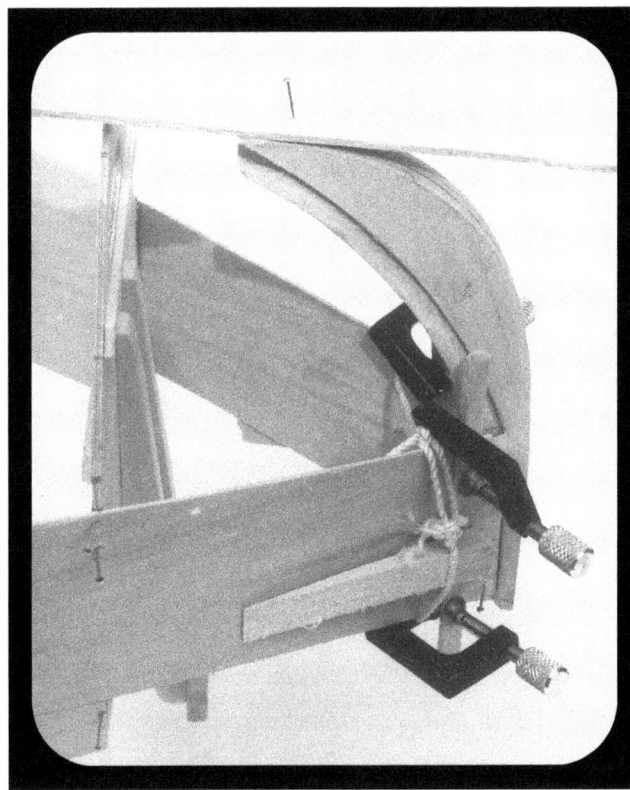

Building the model Catfish revealed no difficulties in her construction. Here are all of the main components.

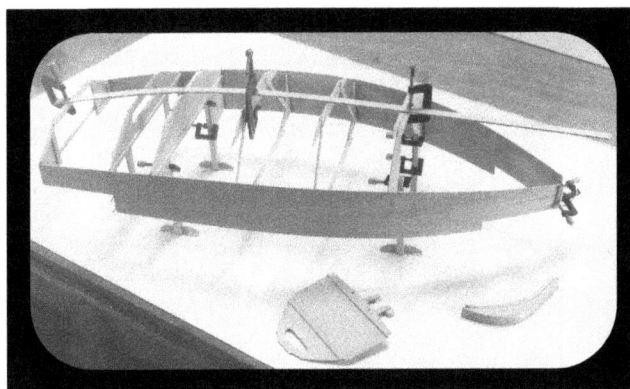

Use a Spanish windlass to hold both side panels into the stem rabbet for fastening.

Catfish, Sheet 1.

Catfish, Sheet 2.

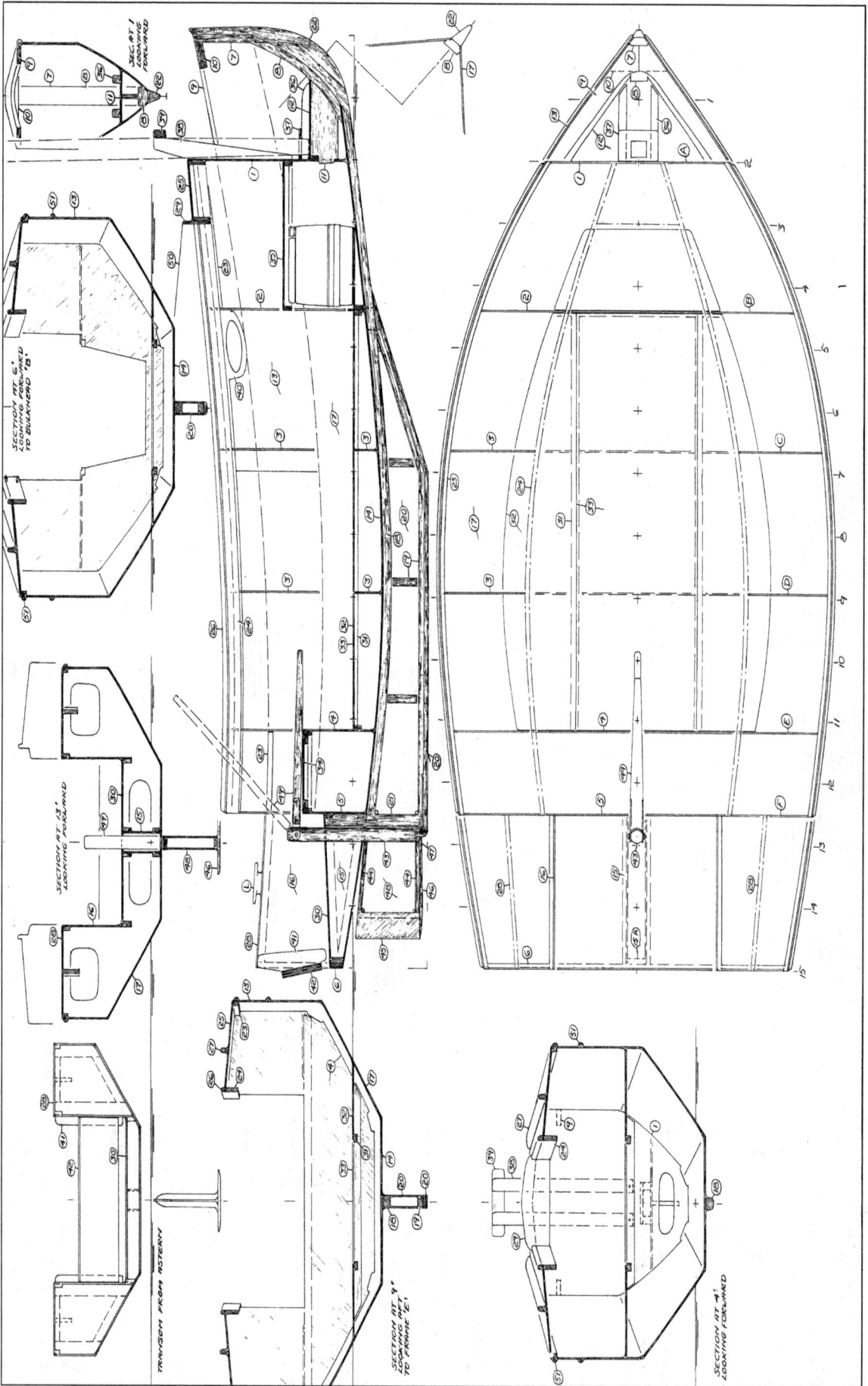

Catfish, Sheet 3.

Catfish, Sheet 4.

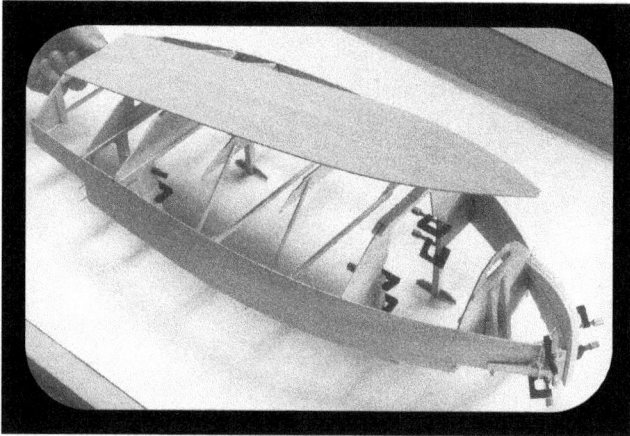

Before fastening down the bottom, make sure its centerline is aligned with the centerlines on the bulkheads and frames.

(continued from page 153)

called for here and there. These are all common lumber-yard materials, so make a good ballpark estimate, and if you don't buy enough, you can always go back and buy more. But with lumberyard materials so inexpensive, compared to more exotic boatbuilding lumber and plywood, I always buy more than I think I need. I'm sure to use it eventually, and if I break or mismeasure a piece, it saves me a trip to the lumberyard.

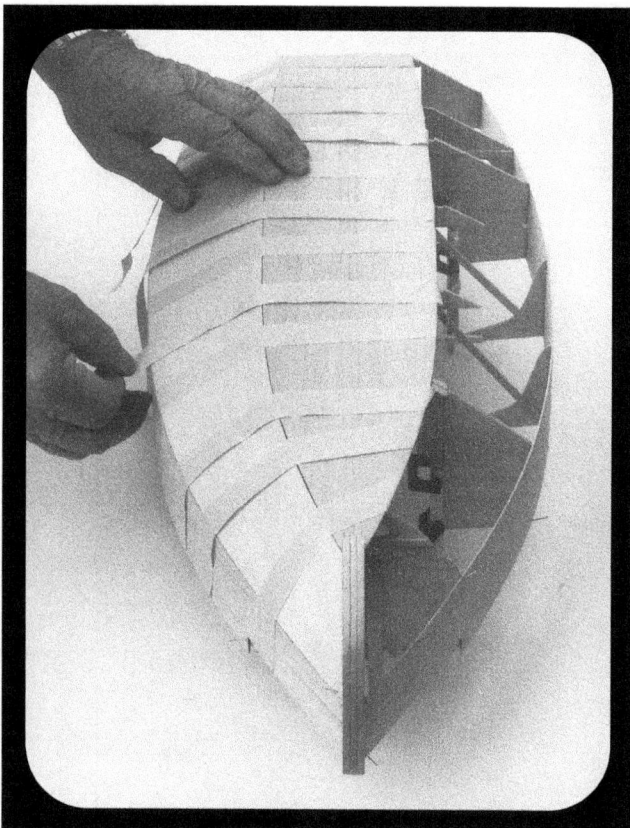

With one bilge panel fitted, begin closing in the hull.

The interior structure and hull panels are complete. The clamped-on legs that supported the structure at a comfortable working height before she was flipped right side up will be removed before installing the decks and cabin structure.

BUILDING KEY FOR DESIGN No. 589, CATFISH

Materials

All plywood is ¼" marine-grade, epoxy-sealed, for minimum trailer weight. It can be thicker for durability up to ½" for any or all panels, except that the bilge panels should be double ¼" in that case, as plywood thicker than ¼" will take the twist in the forebody hard, if at all. Added weight to this extent will have very little effect on the sailing performance of the boat.

Assembly

1. Bulkhead A is watertight above the well flat No. 12. It is stiffened for assembly by

"Closed in," except for the quarter decks. Catfish has an unusual, walk-through cabin with an open top that can be enclosed with a canvas cover.

The inboard rudderpost is in its own watertight compartment. Although there is a lot of framing, you can see that it's all pretty straightforward.

A handsome profile.

$3/4$" x $1\frac{1}{2}$" cleats taking the well flat and the foresheets, and a $3/4$" x 3" beam across the top to take the deck fastenings.

2. Bulkhead B can be installed without the central cutout, with temporary bracing that will also stiffen it until the hull is assembled. Floor timber across the bottom forward face, $3/4$" x 2" with a 7° bevel.

3. Deck knees and floor webs are braced together for assembly to form molds.

4. Frame E similar to Frame B.

5. Bulkhead F watertight in way of motor well, with openings as shown to the spaces under and at the sides of the well. (All these bulkheads, etc., will need stiff temporary bracing, more than is shown, to hold their shape during assembly. Note the drain openings at the corners except in the watertight areas; these will simplify taping the panel joints later, but they should not be completely cut out until the side and bottom panels have been located and installed.)

6. Transom has all-around $3/4$" x $2\frac{1}{2}$" fastening frame; the dimensions are of this framing before beveling. Bevel on the bottom, bilges, and sides is slightly greater than 10°; the deck has a 5° reverse bevel.

7. Upper stem, $1\frac{1}{2}$" x $3\frac{1}{2}$" x about $15\frac{1}{2}$". Bevel $37\frac{1}{2}$° from 2" forward face.

8. Lower stem laminated or sawn to finish $1\frac{1}{2}$" x $3\frac{1}{2}$"; forward face about $1\frac{5}{8}$" with bevel varying from 44° to 45°; finish the bevel by trial.

9. Breast hook built up of plywood to diagram $3/4$"thick.

10. Breast hook doubler, $3/4$" x 5" x $11\frac{3}{4}$".

11. Girder under maststep, $\frac{3}{4}$" x $5\frac{1}{2}$" x about 16".

12. Watertight well flat to diagram.

13. Side panels to diagram, with glass-taped butts.

14. Bottom panel to diagram.

15. Rudder well to diagram with walls spaced $3\frac{1}{2}$"; $\frac{3}{4}$" x $1\frac{1}{2}$" framing on the outside. Block on inside of transom frame, 1" x $2\frac{1}{2}$" x $3\frac{1}{2}$". Pad out rudderpost No. 21 to $3\frac{1}{2}$", with a $\frac{3}{4}$" x $2\frac{1}{4}$" doubler each side, in way of rudder well.

16. Sides of motor well to diagram, with $\frac{3}{4}$" x $1\frac{1}{2}$" framing. (Assemble side and bottom panels around bulkheads, etc., transom, and stem, bottom up. True up guidelines and brace to eliminate twist.)

17. Bilge panels fitted in place, *not trusting the given diagram,* to loosely join the bottom and sides, and taped in place on the outside; note that the more filler putty is used between the plywood edges, the stronger the joint will be; a tight fit of the plywood panels is not desirable.

18. Bottom shoe, $1\frac{1}{2}$" x $2\frac{1}{2}$", reduced to 2" in way of the plywood keel walls.

19. Framing of box keel, 2" thick by 1" along the bottom and forward edges, $1\frac{1}{2}$" for the 3 vertical spacers; the spacers should have clearance on top and bottom to ventilate and drain.

20. Sides of keel to diagram, drained and vented at each corner. Shoe at bottom and forward edges, 1" x $2\frac{1}{2}$"; left square along the bottom, rounded off up the forward edge.

21. Rudderpost, 2" x $2\frac{1}{4}$", bolted through Bulkhead F.

22. Stem cap sawn out as shown or as convenient. (The hull can now be turned right side up, as gently as possible since it will be quite flexible at this point. The insides of the bottom and bilge joints can now be filled and taped.)

23. Sheer clamps, $\frac{3}{4}$" x 1". Check the fairness of the curve against the precut deck panels before securing the clamps permanently.

24. Deck carlins, $\frac{3}{4}$" x $2\frac{1}{2}$"; these can be canted outboard if they take the profile curve hard.

25. Decking to diagram.

26. Standing room coamings, $\frac{3}{4}$" square.

27. Outer coamings form deck stiffening, from 1" x $1\frac{1}{2}$"; screw from the underside at 4" intervals, with generous fillets to the top of the deck.

28. Afterdeck flat on each side of motor well; $\frac{3}{4}$" x $3\frac{1}{2}$" fore-and-aft beams sawn on the top edge to the sheer profile.

29. Forward coaming of standing room from $\frac{1}{2}$" x $5\frac{1}{2}$".

30. Motor well flat, watertight, coved up at sides and bulkhead edges.

31. Floorboard stringers, $\frac{3}{4}$" x $1\frac{1}{2}$".

32. Fixed floorboards with fillets to bilge panels.

33. Removable center section of floorboards.

34. Locker top; 48" removable top can be in two or three sections; sides fixed and filleted to hull side panels.

35. Step is flat with removable section over portable toilet.

36. Feet of mast heel collar, $1\frac{1}{2}$" square.

37. Heel collar double to finish, $\frac{1}{2}$" x 6" x 8".

38. Partner posts from $2\frac{1}{2}$" x $3\frac{1}{2}$" x 28"; bolt through top beam of bulkhead, screw from bulkhead elsewhere, glue, and fillet.

39. Cavil, $1\frac{1}{2}$" x $2\frac{1}{2}$" x 13", bolted to posts.

40. Deadlights, $\frac{1}{4}$" clear plastic screwed to $\frac{3}{4}$" blocking inside.

41. Posts of motor mounting board from $1\frac{1}{2}$" x $3\frac{1}{2}$" x 14", glued and bolted to sides of motor well.

42. Motor-mounting board built up of plywood to finish $1\frac{1}{4}$" x 8" x $31\frac{3}{4}$", bolted to posts top and bottom.

43. Rudder stock, $2\frac{1}{2}$" diameter x $26\frac{1}{2}$"; wrap top and bottom with glass tape to prevent splitting.

44. Top and bottom webs of rudder blade from $\frac{3}{4}$" x 2" x $28\frac{1}{4}$".

45. Trailing edge of rudder, $\frac{1}{4}$" x 5" x 13"; see large-scale section.

46. Rudder end plate plywood built up to $\frac{1}{2}$" x 12" x $21\frac{1}{4}$"; fillet to sides of rudder blade.

47. Rudder pintle plate, $\frac{1}{16}$" x $1\frac{1}{2}$" x 4" metal. Pintle, $\frac{1}{2}$" diameter x $1\frac{1}{2}$" welded to the end of $\frac{1}{4}$" x $2\frac{1}{2}$" x 12" heel plate on the keel.

48. Rudder walls plywood; drain and vent at each corner of the free-flooding, open center.

49. Tiller from $1\frac{1}{2}$" x $2\frac{1}{2}$" x 34"; straps to rudder stock, $\frac{1}{8}$" x $1\frac{1}{2}$" with $\frac{3}{8}$" x $3\frac{1}{2}$" bolt.

50. Spray hood; see sail plan for approximate shape. It's supported by two jawed struts shipping into ears in the fabric and jammed on the coamings. The sides are stretched with lanyards to the outer coamings. The forward lanyards are supposed to be brought back under the edges of the hood so that it can be released from inside at the forward end to handle the halyards or anchor without going on deck. For camp cruising, a tent can be slung from the raised boom and gaff at any height; also stretched to the outer coamings. It should overlap the after end of the spray hood a foot or more.

51. Trim moldings, 1" half-round or to taste.

52. Rigging: All $\frac{1}{4}$" braided Dacron with options noted.

   A. Sheet: 45', standing end on swivel shackle block with becket-like Schaefer 02-17; lead through swivel block on traveler horse like Schaefer 02-05; back through boom block and in to hand or to a leeside cleat placed to taste.

   B. Throat halyard block pendant about 4'; caught with a stopper knot through a hole about 6" below masthead.

   C. Throat halyard, 25'; standing end on gaff jaws; through swivel block like Schaefer 02-05. Hook the fall under the cavil No. 39 and cleat on deck.

   D. Peak halyard, 33'; from gaff, through dumb sheave (i.e., a faired hole) in the masthead; fall same as throat halyard.

   E. Topping lifts: lazyjacks (two), each 26'; standing ends, 2' below masthead; down through dumb sheaves on the boom and in to pins in the boom jaws for adjustment.

   F. Hoist ties, $\frac{1}{8}$" in separate loops around the mast; see diagram.

   G. Reef clew earrings (upper and lower), 21' and 19'; standing ends on port side of boom; up through grommets on the leech of the sail, down through dumb sheaves on the starboard side of the boom, and in to cleats, not shown, on the boom near the jaws.

   H. Reef points to sailmaker's preference; the number shown is adequate.

   I. Separate ties, not a lacing, through grommets on the head and foot around the boom and gaff. (Note that by selectively slacking and tightening these ties, and the hoist ties, the draft of the sail can be adjusted somewhat; e.g., slacking those in the middle of the gaff will throw more fullness into the top of the sail.)

   J. Clew and peak lashed out to holes through the ends of the boom and gaff. No adjustment needed for Dacron sails.

   K. Tack and throat lashings through holes in boom and gaff jaws, with lashings cinched next to the sail.

   L. Traveler horse about 6', belayed to an 8" cleat on each end to be readily removable when sail is not set.

CHAPTER 20
CHEBACCO

Phil Bolger conceived the cat-yawl Chebacco with Essex, Massachusetts, boatbuilder Brad Story to fit the niche market for trailerable day sailers. The first few were built cold-molded, but this proved too labor-intensive. Switching to sheet-plywood construction made more sense.

This design has a lot of nice features. The use of water ballast, which can be drained out when you're done sailing, makes Chebacco much easier to transport and handle on the trailer. The long, shallow keel/skeg partially houses the centerboard, which consequently doesn't intrude so high into the cabin as it would otherwise. There's a great big cockpit and enough room below to store gear or duck out of the weather.

The rudder design is a particularly nice touch. It's well-protected by the skeg. Being inboard (in other words, not hanging off the transom), it allows the use of simple tiller steering without any tricks like a curved tiller or steering ropes to get around the mizzenmast. Although extremely shallow, the rudder is effective nonetheless because of the end plate, and that contributes to the boat's virtues as a skinny-water explorer. According to the designer:

The Chebacco's flat bottom, or wide keel, allows the shallow draft. The high and wide chines give reserve stability and buoyancy. These boats have no ballast, but they can't be capsized by less-than-hurricane winds or any sea that is not breaking heavily. With their low freeboard and big cockpits, they're meant to be fair-weather boats, but they can deal with rough water given prudent handling.

Chebacco is built much like Cartopper, and chances are that if you can build any of the other multi-chined boats, you can build Chebacco, too. Brad Story gave us the detailed material list, and Chebacco enthusiast Bill Samson, of Dundee, Scotland, developed the "how-to" instructions. The instructions, step-by-step building photos, and other Chebacco information appear on www.chebacco.com, a useful site for anyone interested in this boat. Founded by Samson, the site is now run by Richard Spelling, who also granted me permission to use this material.

BUILDING KEY FOR DESIGN No. 589, SHEET-PLY CHEBACCO

Materials

Plywood
15 sheets of ½" marine-grade fir
3 sheets of ¼" marine-grade fir for house top and centerboard filler

Epoxy
10 gallons of resin (1 gallon fast hardener for construction, 1 gallon of slow hardener for cloth)
Centerboard Case Cheeks: Oak, 6/4" x 8" x 10', 2 pieces
3 stainless-steel or bronze through-bolts at each end

Floors
1½" fir (2" construction lumber, or 4" ripped)

Cloth
6-ounce, 40 yards for hull, deck, house top
1 roll (400 yards) of 4" tape for seams and joints

Sole
1" x 4" fir, square edge porch flooring: 10 pieces of 14' and 5 pieces of 10'

Cleats
1" x 4" fir, ripped in half, used all over the boat, including the "clamp"

Spars
Mast, 6" x 6" construction fir, or 3 pieces 2' x 6"
Mizzen, 4" x 4" fir
Boom, gaff, mizzen sprit: 1 piece 4" x 6" x 10' construction fir

(continued on page 169)

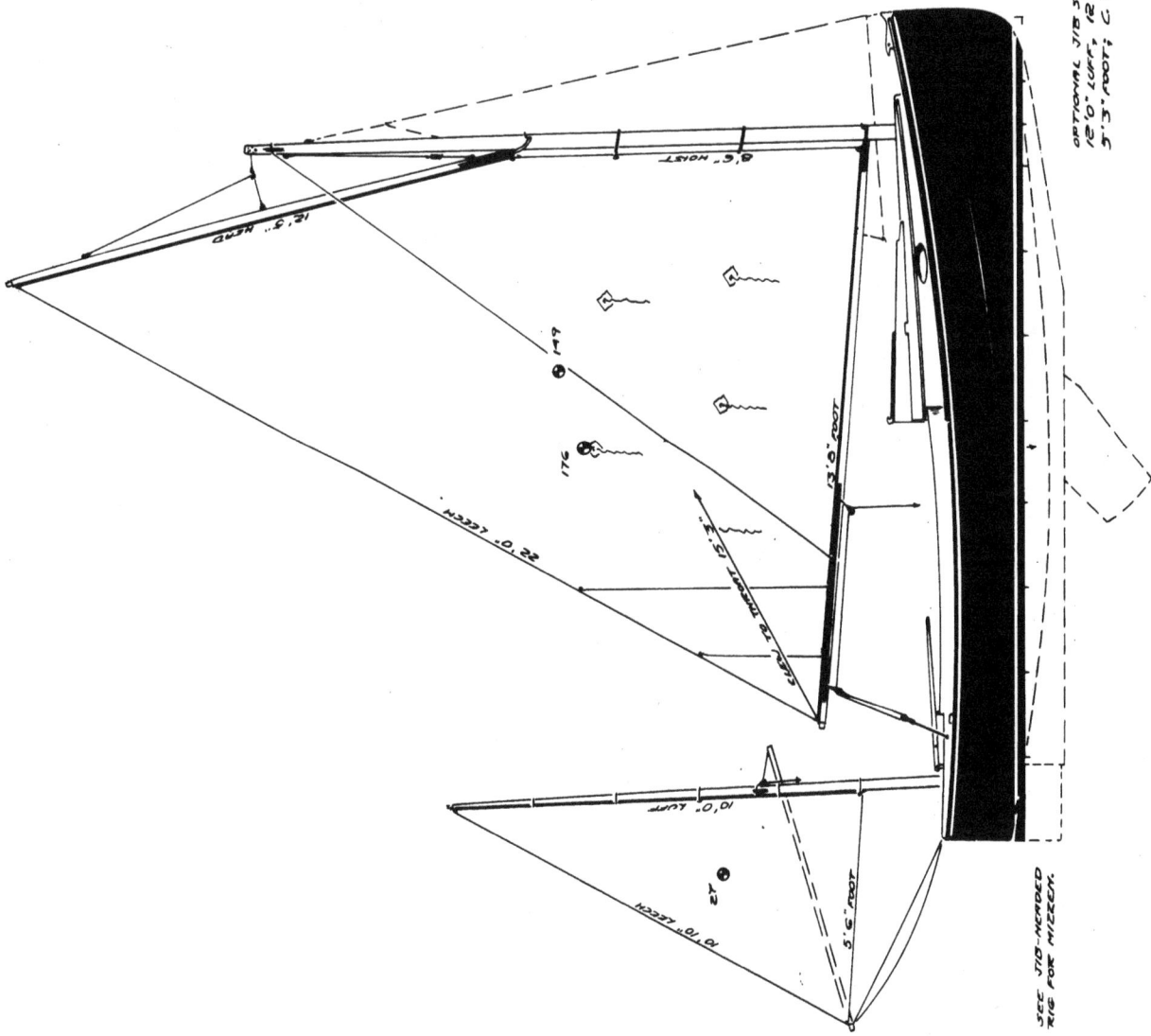

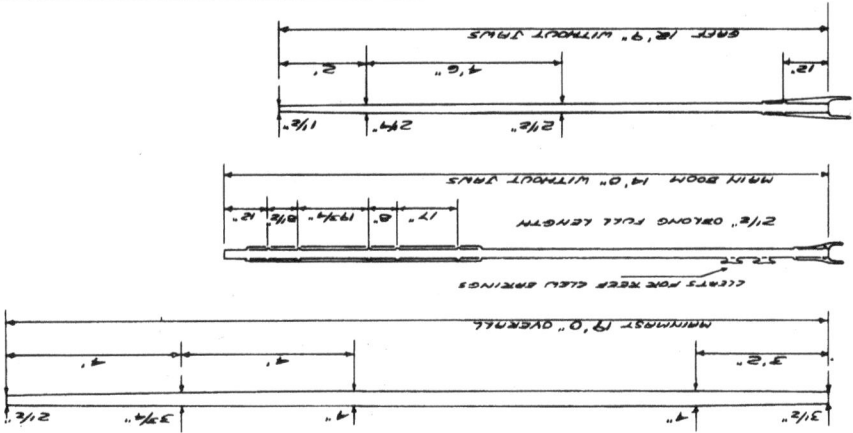

Chebacco, Sheet 1.

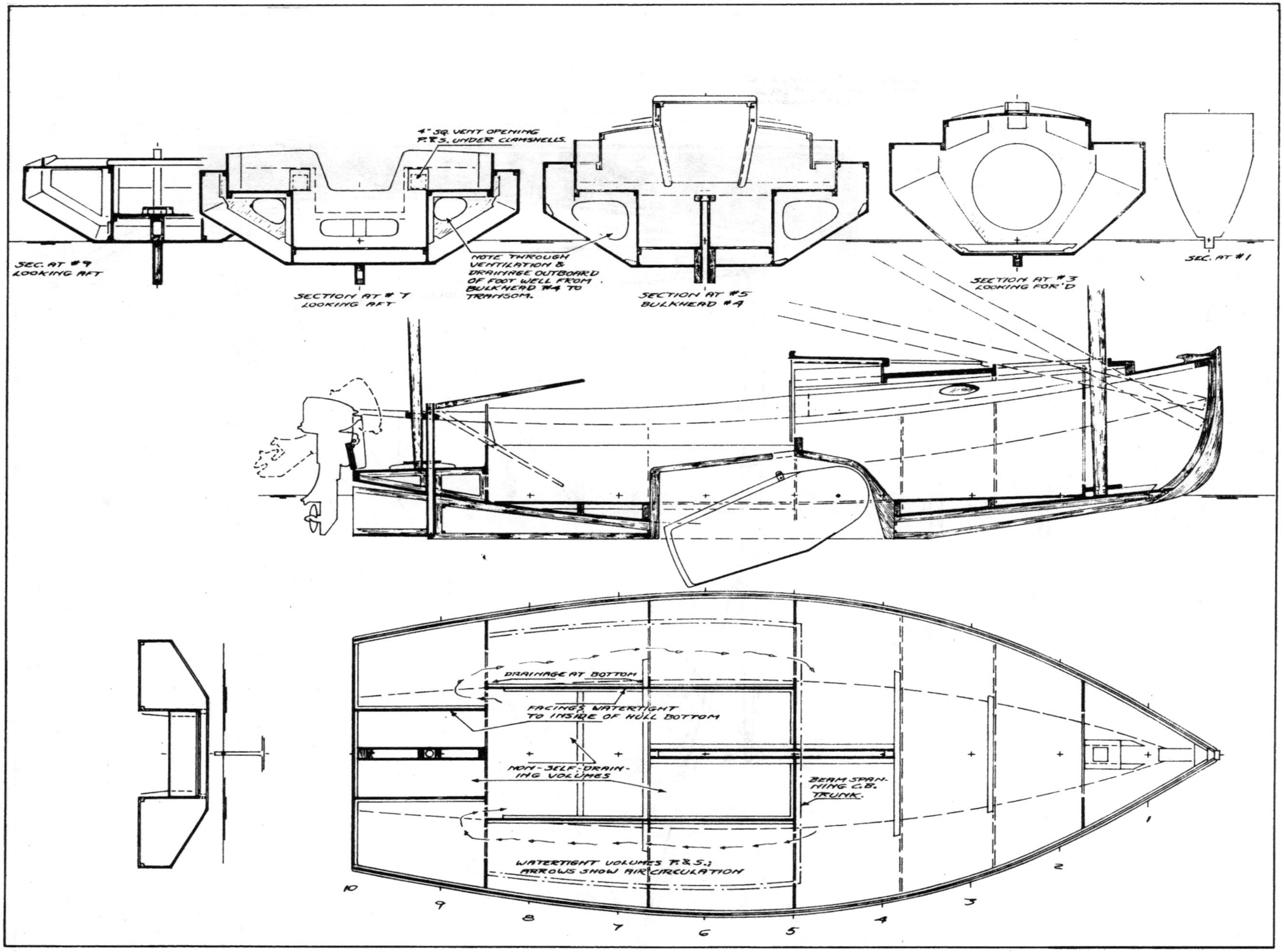

SEC. AT #1

SECTION AT #3
LOOKING FOR'D

SECTION AT #5
BULKHEAD #4

NOTE: THROUGH
VENTILATION &
DRAINAGE OUTBOARD
OF FOOT WELL FROM
BULKHEAD #4 TO
TRANSOM.

4" SQ. VENT OPENING
PT. & S. UNDER COAMINGS

SECTION AT #7
LOOKING AFT

SEC. AT #9
LOOKING AFT

BERTH SPAN-
NING C.B.
TRUNK.

DRAINAGE AT BOTTOM

FACING AFT. FREIGHT
TO INSIDE OF HULL BOTTOM

NON-SELF-DRAIN-
ING VOLUMES

WATERTIGHT VOLUMES P. & S.;
ARROWS SHOW AIR CIRCULATION

Chebacco, Sheet 2.

Chebacco, Sheet 3.

Chebacco, Sheet 4.

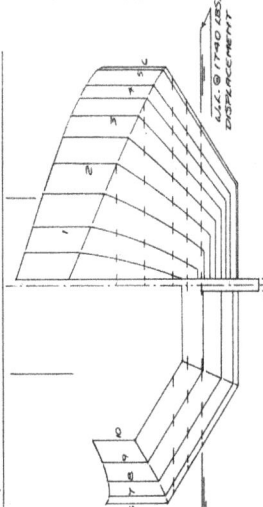
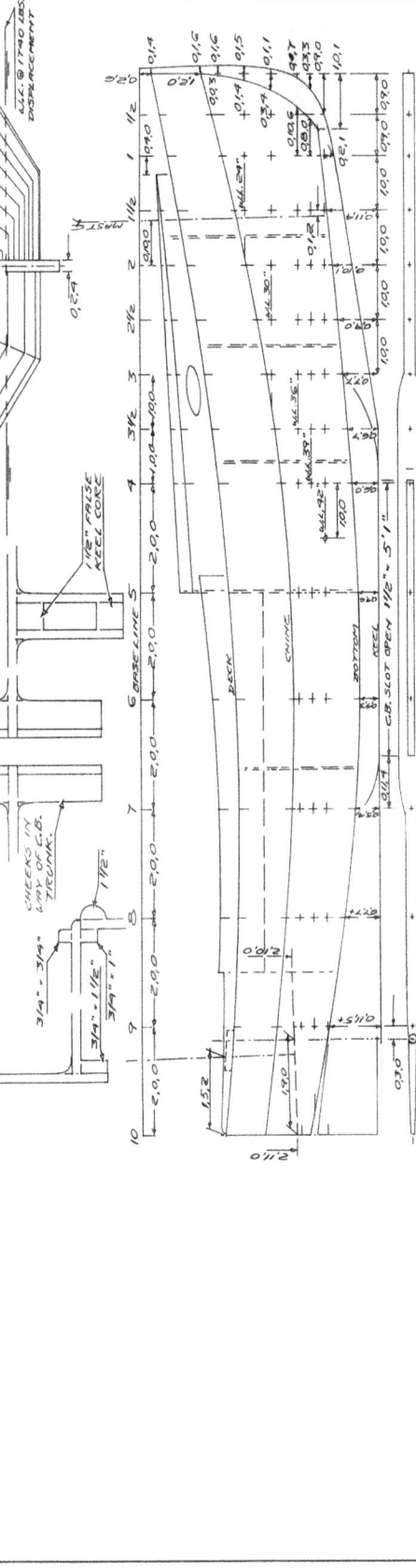
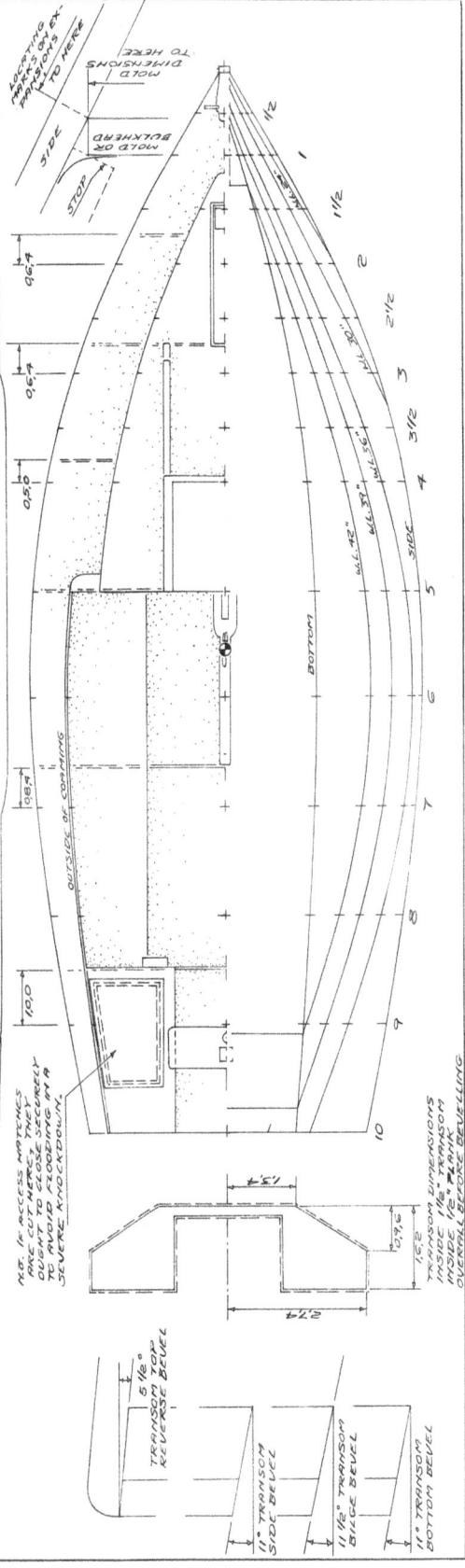
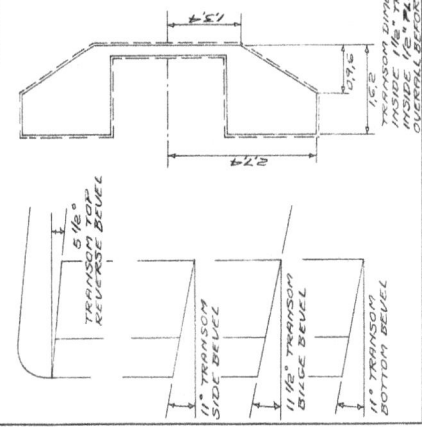

Chebacco, Sheet 5.

Chebacco, Sheet 6.

(continued from page 162)

Blocks (All Harken numbers shown; or equivalent)

Mainsheet block: 1222 single upright big bullet block; 1144 swivel base for main sheet cam swivel, cam cleat—mounts on centerboard trunk

Halyard, main: 3001 $2\frac{1}{4}$" single block; 1002 $2\frac{1}{4}$" single block with becket

Topping lift: 1132 big bullet cheek block

Turns topping lift: 1222 single upright bullet block

Turns both halyards: 1223 double upright bullet block

Mizzen sheet, turns halyards around companionway slides, etc.: 8237 nylon bull's-eye fairleads

Keep bridle on gaff, grommets on boom, etc.: 6137 stainless eye straps

Snotter on mizzen: $11\frac{3}{4}$" single block

Ends of mizzen sheet: 2 small cam cleats

Cleats

1 4-hole 8" mooring cleat
2 4-hole 6" quarter cleats
2 2-hole 6" cleats
3 topping lift and halyards
1 centerboard pennant
1 mizzen snotter

Rigging

Topping lift: $\frac{5}{16}$" braid, 35' with 5" diameter loop

Peak halyard, throat halyard: $\frac{3}{8}$" braid, 42' with small eye

Mizzen snotter: $\frac{3}{8}$" braid, 10' with 3" diameter loop

Mizzen sheet: $\frac{3}{8}$" braid or 3-strand nylon, 20', eye seized in middle

Main sheet: $\frac{3}{8}$" nylon (or larger), 3-strand, 50', block with becket

Centerboard pennant: 6' with 1" diameter loop

Mizzen grommet (holds block and snotter): $\frac{3}{8}$" line, sized for one 1" and one 4" diameter loop

2 grommets (hold sheet blocks to boom): $\frac{3}{8}$" × 4"

Assembly

1. Get your plywood. I used 22 sheets of $\frac{1}{2}$" plywood. If you intend to laminate the forward end of the bilge panels rather than twist the $\frac{1}{2}$" plywood, then make that 20 sheets of $\frac{1}{2}$" and 4 of $\frac{1}{4}$". There's something to be said, too, for laminating the cabin roof. If you do that, you'll need 18 sheets of $\frac{1}{2}$" and 8 sheets of $\frac{1}{4}$" plywood.

2. Choose your building site. It is undoubtedly best to build in a shed if one is available. I, and

a couple of other guys, have used a temporary polyethylene tunnel like the one whose plans can be had from Stimson Marine (see Appendix for contact information), although it might get a bit hot in warm climates. If the climate is warm, then you can build outdoors and throw a tarp over the boat when you aren't working on it. You'll need at least 3 feet all around the hull for comfort when you are working on it.

3. Set up your backbone. The style of backbone is up to you. I used a "ladder" made of 2" × 6"s, with the "rungs" spaced to match the bulkheads/molds. I set this up on legs about a foot off the ground with packing under the feet to keep everything level. This is crucially important if you want to avoid building a twisted hull. Gil Fitzhugh of New Jersey is using a plywood box section backbone that is working very well.

4. Mark out the bulkheads and transom on the sheets of ply, following the dimensions given in the plans. It isn't necessary to loft the lines, as the dimensions on the plans are accurate enough. Marking out actually takes longer than cutting them out! I found that this was very hard on the knees and would recommend getting knee pads before you start. Incidentally, it's a good idea to plan the layout of components on the ply sheets before you start, in order to minimize wastage.

5. Cut out the bulkheads and transom. The molds (Nos. 2 and 3) can be made from what we in the United Kingdom call "chipboard"—could this be the same as U.S. particle board? Most of the cutting out can be done with a handheld circular saw—the curves are pretty gentle. A saber saw (U.K. "jigsaw") can also be used but gives wobbly edges that need planing up. I used (masochist that I am) a hand saw—crosscut with hardened teeth—that got through the wood surprisingly quickly and without the nervous tension that always seems to go with handling power tools. Try it!

6. (Optional). You can pre-coat all of your plywood components with epoxy after cutting them out. It's much easier to get a drip-free coat on a horizontal surface than a vertical one. The downside is that all the gluing surfaces need to be roughened up, and you'll need to protect the epoxy from UV degradation before you paint it.

It's also a pain having to wait for this to dry before you get to the next stage.

7. Make the stem. I laminated mine from off-cuts of ½" ply (seven layers) glued side by side and liberally coated with epoxy. I cut the bevels on a band saw, making sure not to cut too deeply. The final bevels will be determined once the stem is set up with the bulkheads and molds.

8. Before you set up the bulkheads it's a good idea to glue on the 1½" x 4" "floors" on Bulkhead Nos. 4 and 5 and the framing around the transom. I used a mixture of yellow (pitch) pine and construction-grade fir for these. The plans give accurate instructions for beveling the transom and its framing—do this now.

9. Following the measurements given in the lines plan, fix the bulkheads, molds, transom, and stem to the backbone using simple battens and nails that will be removed later. Be *very* careful to line everything up accurately using a spirit level, and double-check the heights of the gluing surfaces for the bottom. I found a *lot* of fiddling was necessary at this stage. Once you've fixed on the topsides, you are committed, and there's no going back!

10. Mark out the topsides and bottom on the ply, using a bendy batten to mark fair curves for their edges. This is vitally important for the finished look of the craft. Cut them out and join up the parts with butt straps, as shown in the plans. Pre-coat with epoxy if desired, then roughen up the gluing surfaces.

11. Mark the positions of stem, molds, bulkheads, and transom on the topsides and bottom.

12. Temporarily fit topsides to bulkheads using screws and cleats as necessary. An extra pair of hands helps here, although it can be done single-handed by suspending the topsides with string from the shed roof. Some fine adjustments to the bulkheads will probably be needed at this stage.

13. Once you are satisfied with the positioning of the topsides, glue them on and apply epoxy fillets. Notice that there is no need to bevel the bulkhead edges. The epoxy fills the gaps and, indeed, a stronger joint results.

14. Fit the bottom and glue it in much the same way as the topsides.

15. Next, make the bilge panels. No dimensions are given for these on the plans because the fine adjustments of the previous stages could result in significant variation in the bilge-panel shapes. The panels are made a section at a time and then fitted, with butt straps being applied on the boat.

16. The shape of the bilge panel can be determined by laying a long sheet of wrapping paper (as stiff as possible) along the gap between topsides and bottom that the bilge panel will fill. The shape of this gap is transferred to the paper by rubbing colored chalk along the edges. It is best to do this on each side of the boat separately, as there could be small differences. Notice that because the bottom and topsides are not beveled, the shape traced will be too large by about ½". This can be trimmed away later as fitting of each panel progresses.

17. Mark out the shape of the *front* section of the bilge panel on a sheet of ply and cut it out. Fit this section starting at the stem and screwing on cleats inside to make it lay against the topsides and bottom, working aft, trimming it to size as you go. There is tremendous twist in this panel, and I used a Spanish windlass (twisted rope) attached to a clamp at the aft end of the panel to pull it into position. There is a colossal amount of potential energy in this twisted panel, so take care that it doesn't accidentally come loose and decapitate you! I found that, with the plywood I was using, if I left it clamped in position for a day or so, the plywood took up its shape and had less tendency to spring back when further work was done. (Alternatively, laminate this section in situ using two layers of ¼" plywood.)

18. Glue front section of bilge panel into position, both sides, and apply epoxy fillets as necessary.

19. Fix butt straps to front sections of bilge panels. (This may involve trimming one of the molds.)

20. Fit and glue the other two sections of the bilge panels. They are easy-peasy compared to the front section.

21. Tape all the joints, inside and out, with 4" glass tape.

22. Fair the outside of the hull using a power sander (I like the dual-action type) and a long

sanding board with 60-grade paper on it. Fill all hollows and sand out all humps at this stage. It sounds straightforward but takes *ages* to do right. Any unfairness at this stage will stick out like a sore thumb on a glossy hull. BE SURE TO USE A BREATHING MASK AND GOGGLES WHEN YOU DO THIS—EPOXY DUST CAN BE VERY BAD FOR YOU!

23. You can now glass the outside of the hull, or wait until the centerboard case and keel are fitted before you do so. I did it at this stage because it is less fiddly.

24. Apply a layer of 6-ounce glass cloth (I used plain weave) to the outside of the hull, using about three coats of epoxy to fill the weave. *Beware of drips, sags, and runs!*

25. This is a good time to make the centerboard case (and the centerboard). This is a straightforward bit of joinery and needs no special explanation. Note, however, that the case protrudes through the bottom of the boat to the level of the outside of the keel.

26. Fit the centerboard case to the hull. This is an awful job, as it involves cutting the slot in the bottom and making sure it lines up accurately with the slot in Bulkhead No. 4 and its associated floor. I used a combination of saber saw, hand saw, abrasive disk, and files, along with a liberal sprinkling of four-letter words as I was working inside the hull and sawdust, epoxy dust, and glass dust rained down on me. Goggles are a good idea—I didn't wear any and had to go to the hospital to get a sliver of epoxy removed from my cornea at this stage.

27. The keel pieces, cheeks, and outer stem can now be made and fitted. I stuck to the plans with a built-up hollow keel (remembering the drainage holes). Brad Story and other builders have gone for solid wooden keel pieces—fir or oak. With my small-scale woodworking equipment, the built-up option was easier. I made the stem from two thicknesses of 1¼" thick fir.

28. Glass the stem and keel.

29. Back to sanding and fairing. This shouldn't be too bad if the last lot was done well. Again, take precautions against inhaling the dust.

30. Once the hull has been sanded and faired, it is a good idea to paint it so that there will be no worries about UV degradation of the epoxy. I used a white epoxy paint undercoat (Veneziani Plastolite) that was sanded, with fairing done where the paint (inevitably) showed up irregularities that had been hiding until now. I used a Veneziani polyester filler (rather like car-body filler) that was applied easily and sanded well. This was topped with a two-part linear polyurethane gloss (Veneziani Gel Gloss) applied using a paint pad. The finish is unbelievably hard. I used the same stuff on a skiff five years ago and it hasn't needed repainting, so I claim the extra expense of these fancy paints is worthwhile. Having said that, most builders use conventional marine enamel on top of the epoxy. So it's up to you. The waterline needs to be struck at this stage. The area under the waterline should be painted with anti-fouling. I put this straight on the epoxy. It *could* be better to paint the epoxy first with conventional paint and then the anti-fouling paint—I don't really know what is best. I used a long-handled roller to apply the paint to the inside of the centerboard case.

31. Turn the hull over.

32. Fillet inside joints and glass tape them. (Lapstrake builders are on their own up to this point; from here on in, it's the same process.)

33. Add remaining floors.

34. Fit and glue inwales.

35. Fit and glue framing for seats, carlins for decks.

36. Finish inside of hull with three coats of epoxy. Foam-roller application is easiest. Watch out for runs!

37. Make decks, seats, outboard well panels, etc., to fit framing; pre-coat with epoxy and then glue/nail in place.

38. Make cabin sides and glue into position.

39. Add framing to tops of cabin sides and fair in preparation for cabin roof.

40. Cut out cabin roof and glue/screw in position.

41. Make hatch slides (I used fir) and glue/screw in position.

42. Add trim pieces to hatch opening and mast opening.

43. Make slides for washboard and fix.

44. Make hatch and washboard.

45. Cut ventilator holes in rear compartments and fix on clamshell covers.

46. Fix on "shelves" to support floorboards in cockpit.

47. Make and fix maststep.

48. Make floorboards—loose fit.

49. Glass decks and fair surface.

50. Paint.

51. Make spars; get (or make) sails.

52. Add fittings, cleats, etc.

53. Rig her up and go sailing!

CHAPTER 21
BUILDING OARS

With the price of a pair of 7' spruce oars now well over a hundred dollars, you might want to consider making your own. Why spruce? Because spruce oars are light and springy compared to ash oars, which feel like clubs in comparison. Pine and fir are okay, too. All can be bought from your local lumberyard. Alaskan Sitka spruce is the best, but it costs so much that you're looking at the price of a pair of good ready-made oars.

Spruce, of course, is a softwood. It isn't as strong as ash, a hardwood that also makes good oars, but it's plenty strong enough for the lightweight plywood boats in this book, and it's lower in weight and in cost than ash.

I'm talking about plain-ol' oars here, not spoon blades, and not weighted near the grips, although they do have a slight rib down both faces of the blade for reinforcement. I've tried a variety of classier oars, but the plain, straight-blade oars I've used all my life still suit me fine—as long as they are made of lightweight spruce.

What length oars do you need? Bolger's plans sometimes list their length, and sometimes they don't. But for a rough estimate one and one-half times the beam of the boat works. This would be a bit short for the 4' beam of the Stretched Light Dory, which has deeper sides and lower seats than most boats of the same beam. This dory wants at least 7' oars, and 7½' are okay, too. My own choice is for slightly shorter oars when rowing in choppy water. They don't catch a wave as quickly and give you a shower of water, and are not as likely to get knocked out of the oarlocks.

Most oars you buy today are 1⅝" in diameter near the grip and taper to about 1¼" near the neck of the blade. When you buy a 2" x 8" plank from your local lumberyard, what you get is a 1½" x 7½" plank. This means that your oar loom near the grip can only be 1½", but that is okay for these light boats, especially if the oars aren't especially long.

I wanted to see for myself how to make a pair of homemade oars, and how they would work. I picked the clearest 2" x 8" (so-called) spruce I could find, stretched it out on a couple of sawhorses, and laid out a pair of 7½' oars for stand-up rowing in my Sweet Pea.

First I copied the shape of the blade from another oar I liked and made a pattern from scrap ¼" plywood. I traced the pattern onto the stock, then drew a centerline down the entire length, from the end of the grip to the end of the blade. I sawed it to shape on a band saw, then turned it on edge and drew a centerline on the other axis, again from the grip to the end of the blade. Then I drew in lines on both sides of the centerline to represent the thickness of the blade at its edges. These lines are absolutely necessary on both of the narrow faces of the board if you want an accurate pair of oars. Don't try to do this by eyeball! The blade is then sawn on edge to the centerline of the blade, leaving the blade ribbed to about the neck of the blade.

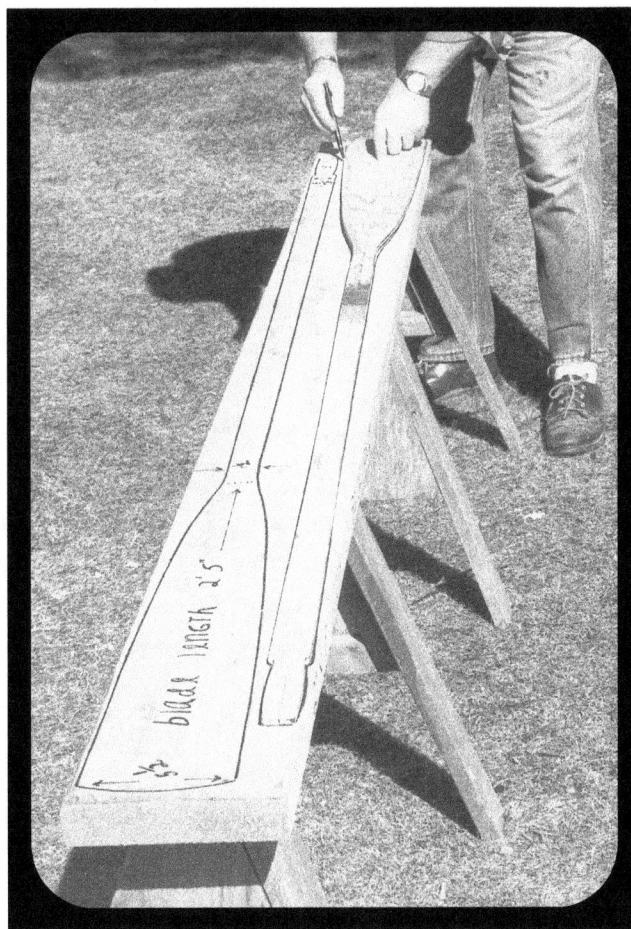

Marking out a pair of 7' oars. The blade length is 2'5", and the maximum width is 5½". Don't forget to draw in the centerlines.

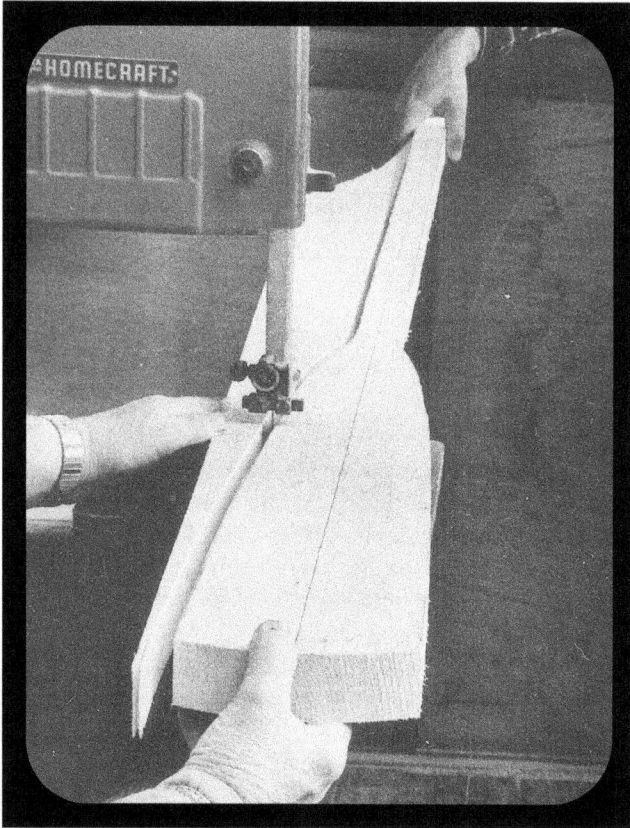

Saw the oar on the flat with a band saw.

You can take off much of the blade's excess thickness with a band saw, but don't cut it too close. Leave the fine work for hand tools.

The blade is then gradually tapered with an electric block plane, leaving the center of the blade slightly ribbed. It is thickest near the neck and flatter as it nears the end of the blade. This part of the operation is pretty much done by eyeball, but still use the lines drawn on the oars as a guide.

Mark the centerline on the other axis, then draw in the blade's thickness and taper.

Finish tapering the blade with an electric or manual block plane.

The loom is the shaft of the oar. In order to get from the square-sectioned shaft to its finished, round shape, you will "eight-side" it. Make up a spar gauge, as shown in the accompanying figures, and draw it down the loom. As the loom tapers, cock the spar gauge so that both bearing surfaces remain firm against the wood. You can get rid of some of the extra wood along the loom for eight-siding with your table saw as long as you freehand it, keeping in mind that the amount to take off is less as you approach the neck of the blade. For sure, don't saw the loom with it against the fence or you will remove too much wood. If you are in doubt of your skill, the safest way is to eight-side the oar with a hand plane. Then sixteen-side it with a hand plane, working by eye.

You'll make another simple tool to sand the loom round. Take a short piece of closet pole, drill it straight down the axis, and fasten a piece of $1/4$" rod through it, with one end sticking out enough to chuck into an electric drill. Cover the closet pole with a nonslip surface, like a piece of tire inner tube. Turn a 60-grit sanding belt inside out, and slide it over the loom, with the oar supported at both ends. Now place your closet-pole mandrel into the loop of the sanding belt, pull down on the loop, and turn on the drill. Keep it moving

Using a spar gauge to mark the loom for eight-siding.

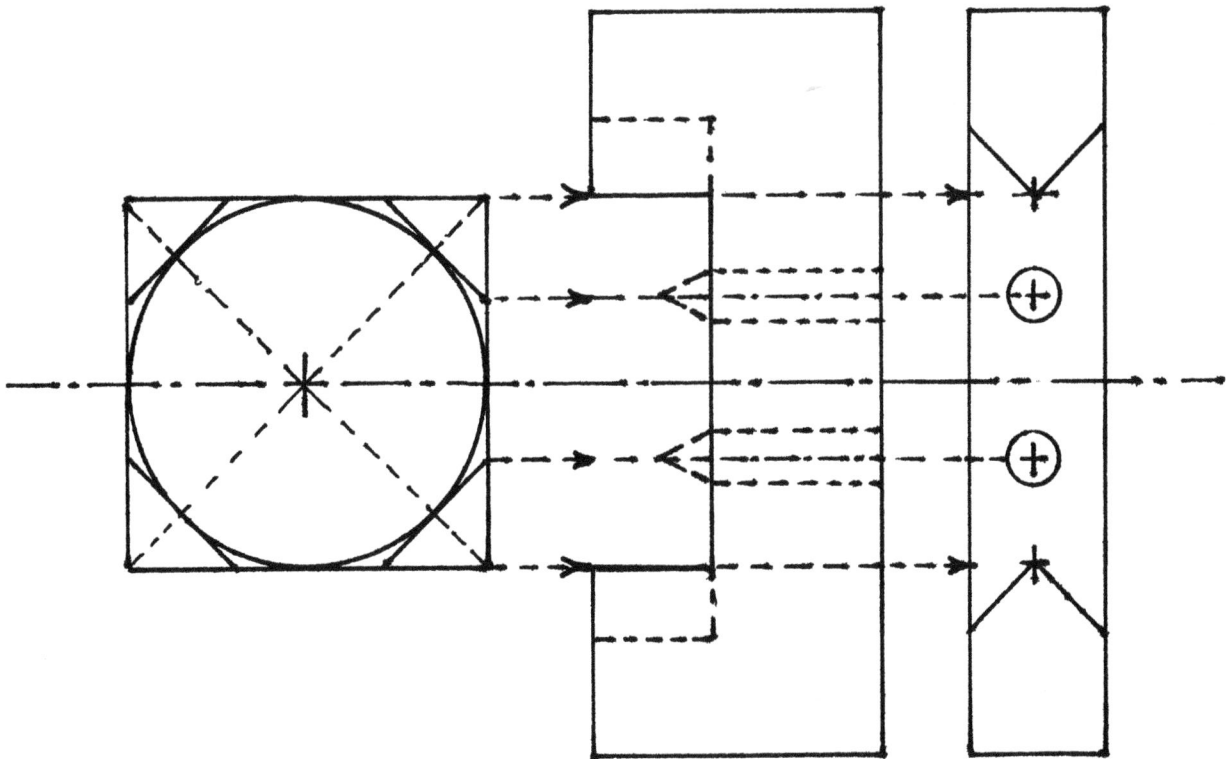

Spar gauge. (Illustration by Robert Lane)

Eight-side-tapering the loom by freehanding it (carefully) on a tilting-bed table saw.

up and down the length of the oar, and pretty soon, the 16-sided shaft will be round. It sure beats hand sanding! This simple, fast, and effective sanding method of sanding spars, etc. was given to us by the late boatbuilder, Bud McIntosh. It is just about a toss-up whether to take this much trouble to make it for one pair of oars, but it certainly is if you plan on making more spars, oars, etc.

Cut the oars' grips to their square shape on a band saw. Mark the round shape at the end with a compass or a circle gauge, and use a spokeshave or coarse sandpaper to take off the corners and bring it down to round.

Finish the oars however you wish, with sealer and paint or varnish. Leave the grips unfinished, as this will give you a more comfortable, nonslippery grip that won't raise blisters.

After you have your oars varnished or painted, you will want to cover the area of the looms that rests in the oarlocks to protect them from wear. First, you have to determine exactly where that protection is needed. Since this depends on the beam of the boat, the height of the gunwales, and the way you row, the easiest and most accurate way is to get in your boat, sit down on the seat, stick your oars out as if you were rowing in a comfortable position, and mark where the oars bear on the oarlocks. Figure on 8" or more for leathers or twine covering, centered on that mark.

I used a heavy, braided nylon line. I cut a clean end on the line with a rope-cutting gun that had a red-hot blade (a match will do) and fastened it to the loom with an escutcheon pin. Then I wrapped the nylon tightly around the loom and fastened the end with another pin.

The "button" keeps the oar positioned on the oarlock, keeping it from slipping overboard if you let go for a moment. It also helps shed water so that drips from the blades end up back where they belong, not in the boat. I used ⅜", three-strand Dacron line for the button. Cut the line "with the lay," or diagonally, between two strands, instead of straight across. This will make such a neat joint that you might not even see where the ends are. Epoxy the button against the end of the braided nylon protection, not around it.

I first saw this kind of rope oar protection made by a fisherman, and I marveled that it lasted so long and was easily replaced. I think the fancy button was my addition, although I'd guess that few fishermen would likely take the trouble with either the protection or the button.

If you have no talent, need a pair of oars quickly, or you're broke, go to a lumberyard, buy a closet pole, cut a ¼" slot in it, nail and glue in a piece of scrounged ¼" plywood, and wait for better times. On a brighter note, you probably could leave these oars in your boat without fear of anyone taking the trouble to steal them.

Once you have your oars, you'll have to choose a set of oarlocks and sockets. There is quite a variety available, with different horns, metals, and openings. There is the open

Finished oars, minus wear protection.

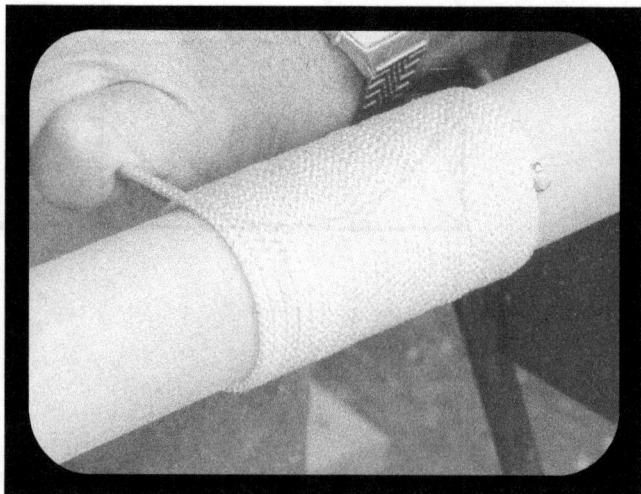

Wrapping braided nylon line for wear protection.

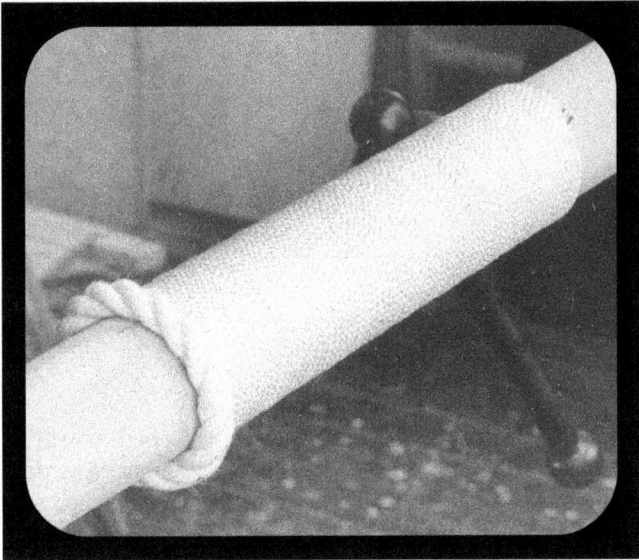

Finished wear protection, with "button" in place.

kind with a 2" opening, a ribbed variety, a round kind that totally encloses the oar, and the Davis kind that is called "barn-door oarlocks." I'm not sure why they are called that, but perhaps because they are hinged, and you can drop them down when not in use. Since they are all one unit,

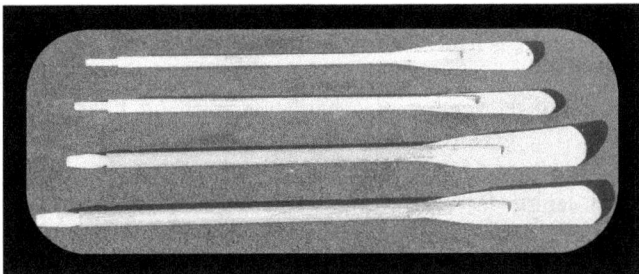

El-cheapo closet-pole oars. They ain't pretty, but they're quick to make and they work just fine.

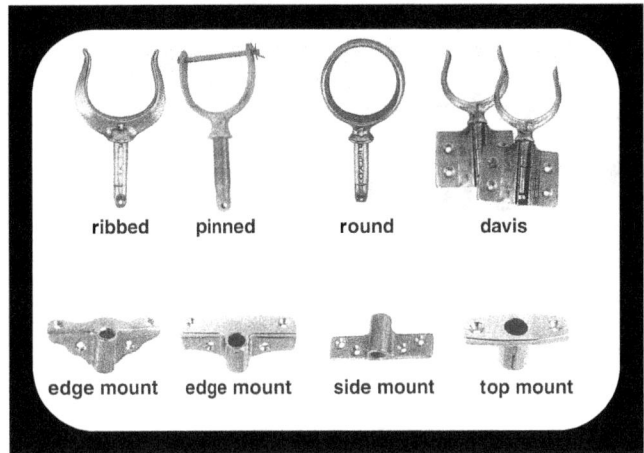

Oarlocks and sockets. (Courtesy Hamilton Marine)

there is no way you can drop them overboard. They are fastened from the top of the rub rail and to the side of the boat.

My favorite is the common brass oarlock with a straight shank, used with an edge-mount socket that requires no hole to be bored through the rub rail, thus weakening it. The socket is fastened with $1\frac{1}{4}$" #10 screws fastened from the top and the sides, holding on like a bulldog from two directions.

Another kind of oarlock has a pin across its top that passes through a hole in the oar's loom. This arrangement calls for the oar to be in a fixed position—the oar can neither be slid in nor out, nor can it be rotated for feathering. I can't advise you on where to bore that hole, because I can't imagine using oars that are locked in a fixed position—and especially not being able to feather. I suppose these fixed-position oarlocks must work for someone, and they must be happy with them. As for me, I'd be interested in watching them being used in choppy water.

CHAPTER 22
MOORINGS

Now that you have your boat and your oars, you have to consider how to transport it and where to keep it. Smaller boats like Cartopper, with its light weight, narrow beam, and short length, can either be cartopped or slid in the back of a pickup. Heavier boats like Diablo Grande, the Clamskiffs, and Sneakeasy need a trailer, if they're not going to live on a mooring. The more rollers the trailer has, the easier it is to launch and retrieve the boat, so make it easy for yourself and buy one with plenty of rollers.

Instant Boats are built and used everywhere—some in freshwater, others in saltwater with a moderate tidal range, and some in areas where the tide leaves your boat completely dry until the next flow. Different locations call for different mooring systems.

Here in Maine, if we have enough depth of water, we use a float system rigged with an endless haul-out line wrapped around a tree or stake and running to a ring in a Styrofoam float at least 18" in diameter—bigger, if the chain that attaches the float to the staple in the mooring block is really heavy. A 1/4" chain is plenty strong to hold a boat up to the size of Diablo Grande. Whether the chain is galvanized or black iron makes little or no difference in saltwater. Having used both kinds over the years when lobster fishing, the extra cost of galvanized chain was absolutely not worth it when it came to longevity.

Should you want to use rope from the rock to the float ball, I would use 3/4", three-strand nylon spliced around thimbles so as to keep the rope from chafing. These thimbles can be opened up slightly to allow the thimble to squeeze over the ring in the float ball, then squeezed together again for eye splicing.

You can't splice? Then find someone who can. Most fishermen know how to splice, because in some cases only a splice will do. Boy Scouts and Sea Scouts usually know how to splice, or you could certainly look it up in a book—it's not hard at all. I would avoid using shackles, because they have a tendency to fail. But if you do use them, be sure to safety-wire the screw to keep it from backing off.

Use a lap link to fasten the chain to the eye in the float ball. A lap link is a special link that can be spread apart and linked to the chain and around the eye in the ball and squeezed together again. You can also use one between the chain and the staple in the mooring block. A better method, though, is to place a ring in the end of the chain, pass the chain through the staple, then pass the tail of the chain through the ring and up to the float. This allows you to replace the chain without having to take the mooring ashore.

Instead of a ball float, you can use a wooden float made in the shape of a cross, as shown in the accompanying illustration. You have to use rope between this float and the mooring block, because chain would sink it. Note that the haul-out line renders over a bolt or pin (the larger the better) instead of running through a pulley. Pulleys don't last long in saltwater, and they clog up with seaweed. In freshwater, though, a pulley is fine.

Where I live, the tidal range is pretty large, and low tide leaves my boat high and dry. For her mooring, I use the simplest version of a haul-out, with no float of any kind. The granite block weighs about 100 pounds, and it has a 1/2" staple in it with a short piece of 1/4" chain about 2' in length fastened to the staple with a lap link. On the other end is a metal ring with about a 4" diameter and a 1/2" thickness. This is lap-linked to the upper end of the chain through which the haul-out line renders.

The haul-out line is made of 1/2", three-strand nylon. It is cut long enough to reach from a stake with a notch in it driven in the beach above the high-water mark, to the mooring, and back to the stake, plus enough scope to leave a little slack so that the boat won't snub up when the tide comes in. A tail runs from the endless line up to the boat. You could rig this as a bowline, with a huge loop as the endless loop, and the tail as the bowline's standing part. On the end of the tail is a heavy-duty stainless-steel or bronze snap hook that clips into the eye mounted in the boat's stem.

When using this haul-out, I pull her in from her mooring, and she follows like a dog on a leash until she hits the beach. I unhook her, drop the line, and away we go for a day's sail. Returning, I beach the boat, pick up the tail, and snap the hook in the eye and pull her out until I feel the knot of where the tail is tied on the haul-out hit against the ring. I then drop the haul-out line in the notch of the stake and

(continued on page 181)

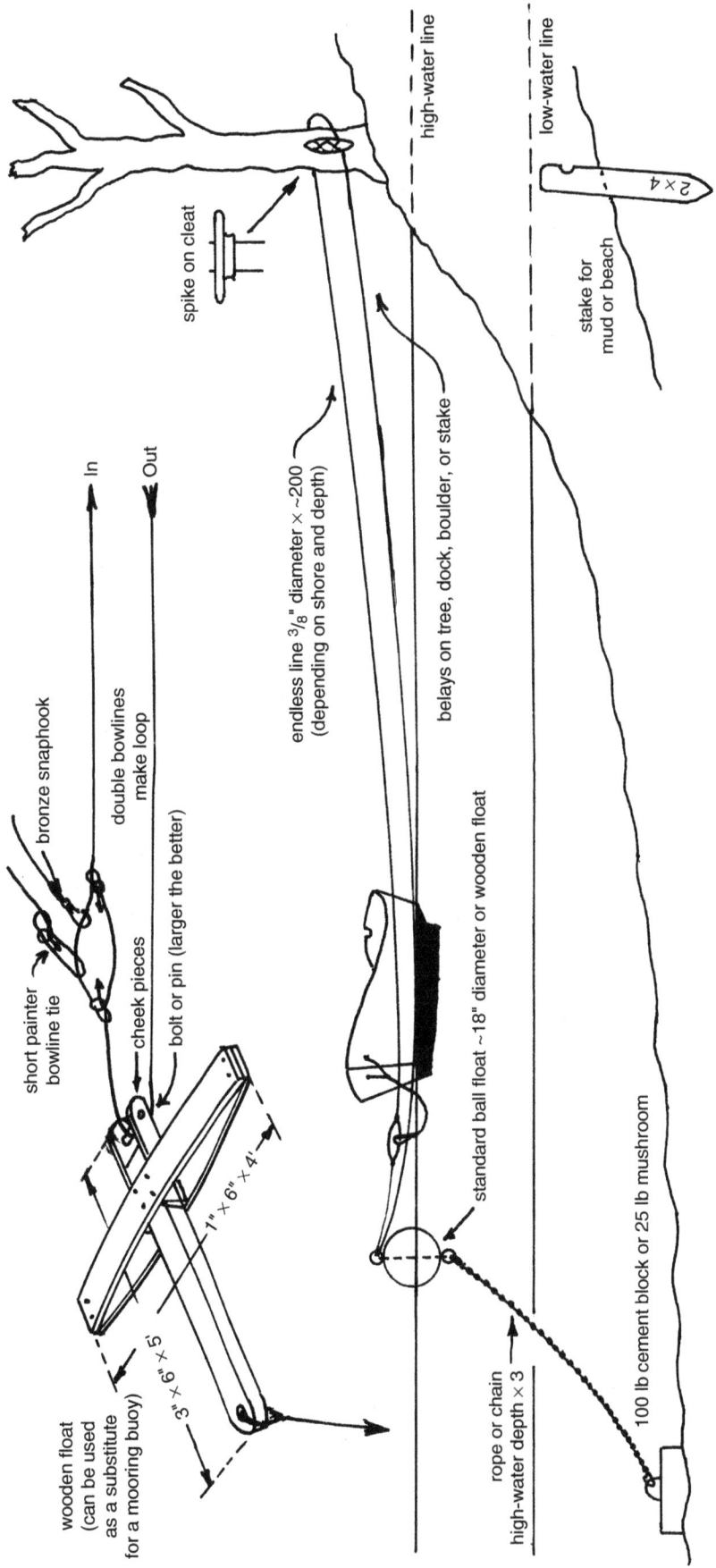

In

Out

short painter
bowline tie

bronze snaphook

double bowlines
make loop

cheek pieces

bolt or pin (larger the better)

wooden float
(can be used
as a substitute
for a mooring buoy)

3" × 6" × 5'

1" × 6" × 4'

spike on cleat

endless line ³/₈" diameter × ~200
(depending on shore and depth)

belays on tree, dock, boulder, or stake

high-water line

low-water line

2 × 4

stake for
mud or beach

standard ball float ~18" diameter or wooden float

rope or chain
high-water depth × 3

100 lb cement block or 25 lb mushroom

Small-boat mooring system. (Illustration by Robert Lane)

notch to secure line
with extra hitch

high tide

endless 3/8" line

slope of beach or flats

2" × 4" × 3' stake to drive in to mud

bronze snaphook or tie

In →

← Out

short tail of line

100 lb cement block or 25 lb mushroom

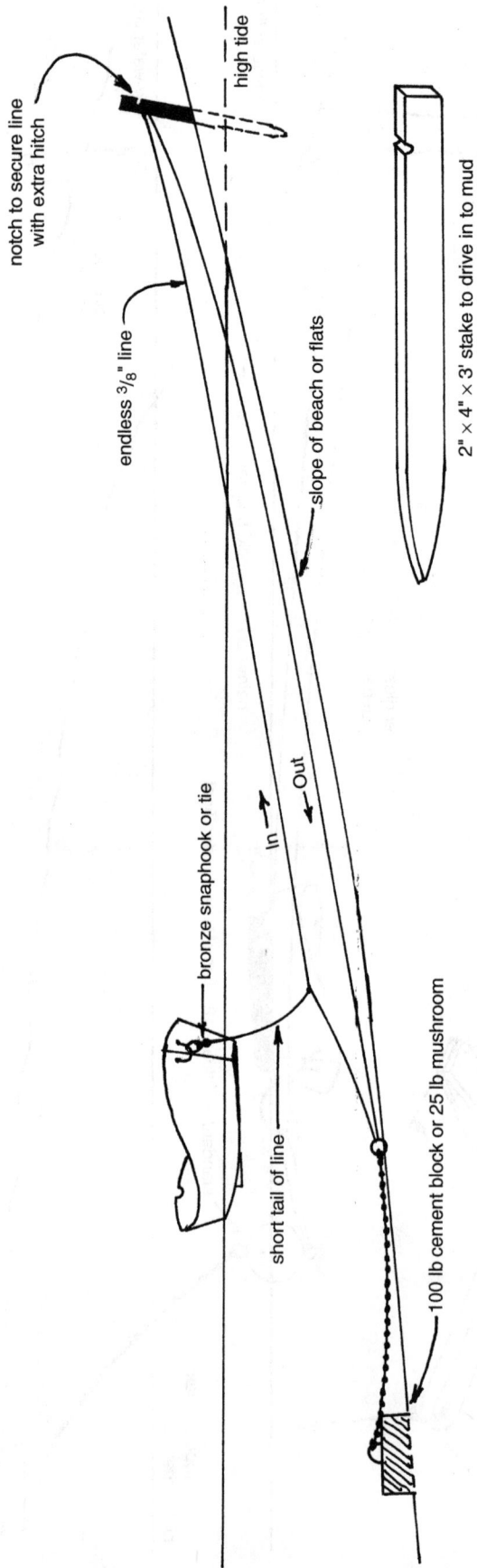

Small-boat tidal mooring. (Illustration by Robert Lane)

take a hitch with it around the stake to keep it in place—and that's it. She's always there when tide and time serve.

In these two methods described, you pull the boats in with a haul-out line. If you don't want to use one and you have a skiff instead to reach your boat, then you would use basically the rig with a ball float and a length of float rope, with a float near the end and a snap hook at its end.

These light haul-outs are great for small, lightweight skiffs up to 150 or 200 pounds, in protected waters, as long as you use common sense. Inspect the lines frequently and repair or replace them the moment you detect any wear, and keep the boat bailed out to keep its weight down. Heavier boats like the 18' Clamskiff belong on a heavy-duty mooring, with a mushroom anchor or a suitably sized concrete or stone block, and you'll need a skiff to reach it.

Temporary Mooring

If you like to explore islands and beachcomb like I do, here is a simple easy way of temporarily mooring your boat in a tidal area without being stranded. I always keep extra line aboard my boat—a 3/8" nylon line of about 30' or so for a painter to tie onto a stock anchor (which I carry if there is no tree handy where I'm landing to tie her to). I carry another shorter, 3/8" line tied to a 15-pound mushroom anchor for when I want to stay awhile and for anchoring her off the beach. The end of this line is tied to the transom for whatever depth of water there is; the mushroom anchor is balanced on top of the afterdeck near the transom, and the boat is given a push out to where I judge the tide isn't going to leave me. A quick tug on the painter led ashore topples the mushroom overboard, and there she sits until I'm ready to leave, at which time I just haul her in, mushroom anchor and all. Lacking a mushroom anchor, a stone serves the purpose nicely.

For larger boats, you'll need heavier gear for a permanent mooring. Note the well-made, thimbled splices at all connections and the snap hook at the end of the pendant.

Speaking of anchors and anchoring reminds me of a time I took a greenhorn kid lobstering with me. Come noontime, I said, "We will run over to that island and eat our lunch. When we get over there, I'll stop her and back her down and you throw the anchor over, will ya?" "Sure," he said, and threw the anchor over WITH NO LINE ON IT! So with that parting shot, there must be hope for us all.

Build lots of boats and have fun—it's what boats are all about.

APPENDIX

RESOURCES

Plans, Patterns, and Sails for Boats in this Book

H. H. Payson and Co. (plans and sails)
31 Pleasant Beach Rd.
South Thomaston, ME 04858
207-594-7587
www.instantboats.com

Peter Spectre
Compass Rose (full-size patterns)
P.O. Box 201
Spruce Head, ME 04859
207-594-2457

Stimson Marine, Inc. (shed plans)
261 River Road
Boothbay, ME 04537
207-380-2842
www.by-the-sea.com/stimsonmarine/

Plywood and Lumber

Boulter Plywood Corp.
24 Broadway Dept WB
Somerville, MA 02145
617-666-1340
617-666-8956 (fax)
www.boulterplywood.com

Harbor Sales
1000 Harbor Court
Sudlersville, MD 21668-1818
800-345-1712
800-868-9257 (fax)
www.harborsales.net

Edensaw Woods Ltd.
21 Seton Road
Port Townsend, WA 98368
800-745-3336 or 360-385-7878
360-385-5215 (fax)
www.edensaw.com

M. L. Condon Lumber
248 Ferris Ave
White Plains, NY 10603
914-946-4111
914-946-3779 (fax)

Maine Coast Lumber
17 White Birch Lane
York, ME 03909
207-363-7426
207-363-8650 (fax)
www.mainecoastlumber.com

Hardware and Fiberglass Suppliers

Ducktrap Woodworking
Walter Simmons
P.O. Box 88
Lincolnville Beach, ME 04849
207-789-5363
207-789-5124 (fax)
www.duck-trap.com

Hamilton Marine, Inc.
P.O. Box 227
Searsport, ME 04974
207-548-6302
207-548-0481 (fax)
www.hamiltonmarine.com

Spruce Head Marine
P.O. Box 190
Spruce Head, ME 04859
207-594-7545
207-594-0749 (fax)
www.merchantcircle.com/business/Spruce.
  Head.Marine

Jamestown Distributors
17 Peckham Drive
Bristol, RI 02809
800-497-0010 or 401-253-3840
www.jamestowndistributors.com

Surfacing Agents

Advance Coatings Company
42 Depot Road
Westminster, MA 01473
508-874-5921
www.advancecoatings.com

Model Supplies

BlueJacket Ship Crafters
160 East Main St.
Searsport, ME 04974
800-448-5567
207-548-9974 (fax)
www.bluejacketinc.com

Micro-Mark
340 Snyder Ave
Berkeley Heights, NJ 07922
800-225-1066
908-665-9383 (fax)
www.micromark.com

GLOSSARY

Abaft. Aft of, as in, "A schooner's mainmast is abaft the foremast."

Aft. Toward the stern.

After. Closer to the stern.

Amidships. In the middle portion of a boat. As an adjective, *midships.*

Athwartships. Running across the hull. As an adjective, *thwartship.*

Baseline. A line, usually parallel to the waterline, drawn on boat plans and used as a reference for all vertical measurements when lofting the lines of a hull.

Batten. A thin, flat length of wood that can be sprung through a series of reference points and thereby used to determine and draw a fair curve through the points.

Bearding Line. The point where the inside face of the planking touches the outside face of the stem as it enters the rabbet.

Becket. A piece of rope used to confine a spar.

Bedding Compound. A nonhardening, elastic putty that is used like a gasket between wood and mounted hardware to exclude water.

Bevel. An angle cut along the edge of a timber or across its end to produce an exact fit between parts of a hull.

Bilge. The lower internal region of a hull, or (often as "turn of the bilge") the region of maximum curvature between the bottom and sides in a cross-sectional view of a round-bottomed boat.

Breast Hook. A thwartship structural member near the stem.

Bulkhead. A thwartship panel dividing a hull into sections. Equivalent to a frame mold in an Instant Boat.

Butt. To join end-to-end or edge-to-edge. As a noun, a butt strap or butt block fastened across such a joint to hold the two elements together. Also, the lower end of a mast.

Carlin. A piece of deck framing that runs fore and aft and forms the inboard edge of the side decks and is connected to and supports the stud beams.

Carvel Planking. A method of planking in which the strakes or planks are fastened to the frames of a hull edge to edge.

Centerboard. A short, hinged retractable keel used to reduce leeway in a sailboat. It is raised and lowered through a watertight case, or trunk.

Centerline. On boat plans, a line dividing a hull into two identical fore-and-aft sections, and used as a base for establishing thwartship measurements when lofting. Also, a vertical line on thwartship members used to align them during assembly.

Chine. A longitudinal joint where panel edges meet in a hull constructed of a sheet material such as plywood. Most commonly, the joint between sides and bottom in a flat- or V-bottomed boat.

Chine Log. A reinforcing strip of wood along the inside or outside of a chine, to which the joining panels are fastened.

Cleat. A fitting to which a line can be made fast. A protruding wooden or metal fitting on a spar, functioning to limit the movement of the spar through an aperture, such as a cleat on a mast that stops its downward movement through a mast partner. Finally, any short length of small dimensional lumber used for miscellaneous framing needs.

Coaming. A raised vertical wooden guard around a cockpit or hatch to keep water on deck from running in.

Deadrise. The upward slant of the bottom of a hull to the chine in a V-bottomed hull, or from the keel to the turn of the bilge in a round-bottomed hull.

Dory. A flat-bottomed craft that has flaring sides and a narrow stern. It is capable of carrying heavy loads but is very tender when light.

Double-ended. Having a sharp end at both bow and stern (e.g., a canoe or a peapod).

Downhaul. A line by which a sail is adjusted.

Dumb Sheave. A faired hole through which a line may pass.

Edge-set. To drive one panel down forcibly to meet the panel below despite irregularities in the panels.

Fair. Said of a graceful curve that changes gradually and has no bumps, hollows, or flat places. Used also as a verb.

Fall. The entire length of line in a tackle.

Fid Pin. A tapered, pointed tool, usually wooden.

Fillet. A thick bead of resin filler applied to an inside seam then finished with fiberglass tape.

Flare. The outward angle of a boat's sides between waterline and sheer when viewed in cross section.

Flush. Even or level with, not protruding.

Foot. The bottom edge of a sail. Also, the butt of a mast.

Frame or Frame Mold. A thwartship member to which planking is fastened.

Freeboard. At any given point along a hull, the height of the sheer above the waterline.

Gaff. The spar to which the head of a gaff sail is lashed. It has a set of jaws that run up or down the mast when the sail is hoisted or lowered.

Garboard. In a carvel-planked boat, the plank next to the keel, either port or starboard.

Grommet. A round, metal eyelet or a ring of rope sewn into a sail or other piece of cloth.

Gunwale. The longitudinal strengthening strip that runs along the sheer of a hull from bow to stern. (Pronounced gunn'l)

Halyard. The line, reeved through a block or similar device, with which the sail is raised.

Head. The top corner of a jibheaded sail or the top edge of a quadrilateral sail. In a gaff rig, the head of the sail is attached to the gaff; in a lug rig it is attached to the upper yard.

Heel. As a verb, the tendency of a sailboat to lean from the vertical in response to the pressure of the wind on the sails. Also used as a noun in that sense, as in "the angle of heel." Also as a noun, the foot or butt of the mast or the end of a frame at the keel (in a carvel-planked hull).

Horse. A transverse metal rod, metal loop, or loop of line that the inboard portion of a sheet can travel along, allowing the boom or the jib club to swing across the hull without being tended when making short tacks: traveler.

Inboard. Within the limits of the hull area.

Inwale. A long piece of wood fastened at the top edge of the inside face of the ribs in an open boat. It generally serves the same purpose as a clamp in a decked boat.

Jaws. A U-shaped fitting on the inboard end of a boom or gaff that allows the spar to swing around the mast.

Jib. A triangular sail set forward of the mast.

Jig. A wooden structure on a fixed base on which the parts of a boat can be assembled. A jig determines the shape of the part.

Keel. The main structural member and longitudinal backbone of a hull; it usually extends below the hull to help keep the boat on a heading and reduce leeway.

Knee. A strengthening timber that is fastened to two angled members and distributes stress to both.

Knot. A measure of speed equal to 1 nautical mile (2,000 yards) per hour. It is incorrect to say "knots per hour."

Lapstrake. A method of planking in which each strake slightly overlaps the one below it, giving the appearance of clapboards.

Lazyjacks. System of lines and pulleys that keeps the lowered mainsail on top of the boom.

Leech. The after edge of a fore-and-aft sail.

Limber Holes. Apertures in bulkheads that allow water in the bilge to move from one section of the hull to another.

Lofting. The process of laying out the patterns of the parts of a hull full size, working from plans drawn to scale.

Luff. As a verb, to head up into the wind so much that the forward edge of the sail begins to shake. As a noun, the forward edge of a fore-and-aft sail.

Lugger. A small fishing or coasting vessel that carries one or more lugsails.

Mast. The vertical spar that is the main support column of the sailing rig.

Mast Partner. A transverse member located at a height just below the sheerline of a boat, through which the mast passes to acquire steadiness and bearing.

Mast Step. Piece used to anchor the heel (bottom) of the mast.

Mold. A pattern of a transverse section of a hull, set up in construction but removed when the hull nears completion. A frame mold acts as a mold but remains in the finished hull.

Mooring. A method of anchoring in which a boat is made fast to a heavy weight that is more or less permanently fixed to the bottom.

Nail Set. A steel rod that has a small, blunt end and is used to drive a nailhead flush with the wood or to countersink it slightly below the surface. It is placed on the nailhead and struck with a hammer.

Offsets. A table of measurements from the baseline and centerline that establish points defining the shape of a hull. Offsets are used to loft and lay down the lines of a boat full size.

Outboard. Outside the limits of the hull, or in a direction away from the centerline.

Painter. A line made fast to the bow of a boat and used for temporary tie-ups and for towing.

Peak. In a gaff sail, the after upper corner of the quadrilateral.

Pintle. A vertical pin or rod used to hang or hinge a rudder. Pintles are attached to the forward or leading edge of the rudder and slide into gudgeons fixed to the stern of a boat.

Prebore. To bore a hole in wood that a nail or other fastening will be driven into. Preboring reduces the danger of breaking out or splitting. The holes should be slightly smaller than the wire diameter of the shank of the fastening.

Quarter. One of the two outboard quadrants of a boat's stern. May also be used as a verb: A boat is said to be *quartering into the seas* when its bow is directed slightly to port or starboard of a steep head sea.

Rabbet. A beveled recess cut into the stem to receive the forward, or hood, ends of the planking and into the keel to receive the lower edge of the garboard strake.

Rake. A departure from the vertical of any member of a boat, such as the stem, transom, or mast.

Reach. A point of sailing. A boat is on a broad reach when the wind is coming from abaft the beam, and on a close reach when the wind is coming from forward of the beam but abaft the close-hauled position.

Reef Cringle. A hook-shaped device that snares the grommets on the luff of the sail.

Reef Earing. A short line used to haul down and secure the reef cringle.

Rig. The arrangement of a sailboat's mast and sails.

Rocker. The fore and aft curvature in the keel.

Rub R. A strip added to the outer side of a vessel's topsides to absorb friction from docks and pilings.

Rudderpost. The shaft of the rudder.

Scantlings. The dimensions and sizes of all structural parts used in building a vessel.

Scarf. As a verb, to glue two beveled pieces of wood end to end or edge to edge; beveling allows the pieces to overlap without an increase in thickness. As a noun, describes a joint so made.

Scull or Sculling Notch. A half-round notch cut out in the top of the transom of a boat to support a sculling or steering oar.

Scuppers. Holes or open pipes above a boat's waterline that drain water overboard.

Seam. The joint between two planks or strakes.

Seize. To bind together; or, to put a stopper on a line. Line for seizing is always smaller and lighter than the line to which it is applied.

Sheer. The uppermost line of a hull viewed in profile, also called the sheerline. The top plank, or strake, on a hull is the sheerstrake.

Sheet. A line used to control the positioning of a sail in relation to the wind. On a sail attached to a boom, the sheet is made fast to the boom near its outboard end; on a loose-footed sail, it is attached to the clew.

Shim. To wedge up or fill out with thin sheets of metal or wood.

Skeg. A small keel-like projection under the stern that keeps a flat-bottomed boat to track in a straight line.

Slipping Keel. A removable keel.

Snotter. A line that bears on or near the butt of a sprit to maintain its thrust against either the clew of a jib-headed sail or the peak of a quadrilateral sail.

Spanish Windlass. A length of line looped around the planks or side panels of a hull to pull them into place, usually by means of a lever that twists the line and constricts the loop. In action it resembles a tourniquet.

Spar. Any timber (mast, boom, gaff, or sprit) used to support a sailing rig.

Spile. To determine and scribe a line that defines the shape of any element in a hull so that it will exactly fit an adjoining element as required. Most frequently, to transfer the shape of the upper edge of a plank or strake onto the bottom edge of the plank to be fastened immediately above it.

Sponsons. Projections from the hull that increase flotation or add lift when underway.

Sprit. A spar used to set a spritsail by extending the clew of a triangular sail or the peak of a quadrilateral sail.

Spritsail. Any sail set by means of a sprit.

Station mold. The temporary transverse frames around which a boat is built.

Stem. The foremost vertical or nearly vertical structural member of a boat's hull; sometimes called a cutwater.

Step. As a verb, to erect and secure a mast in place on a boat. As a noun, any construction or device in the bottom of a hull that the butt end of a mast is set into.

Sternpost. The vertical (or near vertical) backbone member that supports the transom.

Stringers. Longitudinal planking on the inside of the hull panels adding to the hull's strength; also provide a base for seats.

Tender. As a noun, a small boat used for general service to a larger boat. As an adjective, said of a boat that is quick to heel because of a shift in the load or pressure from the wind.

Throat. The forward upper corner of a quadrilateral fore-and-aft sail.

Thwart. A transverse member, often a seat for crew or passengers.

Thwart Flats. Seats.

Tombstone Transom. The characteristic shape of a dory transom.

Topping Lift. In a fore-and-aft rig, a line reeved through a mast block to the end of the boom, used to support the weight of the boom to keep it clear of the cockpit or to facilitate lowering sail. The Light Schooner has topping lifts.

Transom. The after face of the stern of a boat; often, the entire stern.

Traveler. A crosspiece, athwartships on a sailboat's cabin top, cockpit or transom to which the mainsail's boom is fastened. Used to control the angle of the mainsail.

Trim. As a noun, the fore-and-aft positioning of a hull in the water. As a verb, to alter that positioning, as in "trim her down by the bow." Also, to haul in on a sheet, bringing the clew of a fore-and-aft sail nearer the boat's centerline.

Trunk. A narrow boxlike structure, open to the sea at the bottom of the boat, through which a centerboard or daggerboard can be lowered to extend below the bottom; also called a case.

Tumblehome. The inward curve of the upper sides of a hull toward the centerline.

V-bottomed Boat. A chine boat whose deadrise is flat, rather than curved, between the keel and the chine; sometimes called a deadrise boat.

Vang. A line leading from the peak of the gaff of a fore-and-aft sail to the rail on each side; used to steady the gaff.

Waterline. Any horizontal line on a boat's profile generated by a plane parallel to the surface of the water. The LWL, load waterline, is the upper limit of a boat's draft under normal conditions with the designed load.

INDEX

Numbers in **bold** refer to pages with illustrations or tables.